The Mormon Rebellion

James Ferguson, Adjutant General, Nauvoo Legion, 26 December 1856.
Courtesy John Sharp Ferguson.

THE MORMON REBELLION
America's First Civil War,
1857–1858

David L. Bigler
and
Will Bagley

University of Oklahoma : Norman

Library of Congress Cataloging-in-Publication Data

Bigler, David L., 1927–
    The Mormon Rebellion : America's first civil war, 1857–1858 /
David L. Bigler and Will Bagley.
          p. cm.
    Includes bibliographical references and index.
    ISBN 978-0-8061-4315-6 (paper) 1. Utah Expedition (1857–
1858). 2. Mountain Meadows Massacre, Utah, 1857. 3. Mormon
pioneers—Utah—History—19th century. 4. Mormons—Utah—
History—19th century. 5. Utah—History—19th century. I. Bagley,
Will, 1950– II. Title.
    F826.B54 2010
    979.2'02—dc22
                                                    2010032845

The paper in this book meets the guidelines for permanence and
durability of the Committee on Production Guidelines for Book
Longevity of the Council on Library Resources, Inc. ∞

Contents

Illustrations

Preface

Thus was peace made—thus was ended the "Mormon War,"
which, miracle dictu, was much less sanguinary and direful
than the "Kansas War," and may thus be summarily historized:
killed, none; wounded, none; fooled, everybody.

—Special Correspondent Lemuel Fillmore, "How Peace Was Made,"
New York Herald, 19 July 1858, in Gove, *The Utah Expedition*, 351

Those who were lucky enough to grow up in Utah in the middle of the twentieth century heard about the state's glorious history from the time they could understand English. This storied mix of legend and fact celebrated their pioneer ancestors who built the bridges, killed snakes, and fought the Indians, who they learned were the descendants of an ancient branch of the Children of Israel called the Lamanites. A key element of this tale was how the United States in 1857 sent an army to persecute their long-suffering Mormon progenitors, based on nothing more than the malicious reports of corrupt carpetbaggers. Valiant forebears rallied under their inspired leader, Brigham Young, to defeat an invading army using guerrilla tactics that shed not a drop of blood. This brought America to its senses, and the president sent commissioners to negotiate an end to what will be forever remembered as "Buchanan's blunder."

This hero tale is part of a much larger mythology calculated to educate and inspire with an appreciation of a noble heritage. It was a great story, but even as young boys who developed an early love of history, we found our religious education so improbable and told with such a sanctimonious gloss that we turned to other subjects, such as the Homeric cycle and the history of Rome. It was only much later, after learning of our ancestors' roles in burning an army supply train and murdering a band of passing gamblers, that we began to study our state's history with a new appreciation. Over the years, we learned that the story of the conflict known variously as the Utah Expedition, the Mormon War, or, in Daniel J. Boorstin's well-chosen words, "the unsung and inglorious Civil War of 1857–58," reflects how the events of 1857 and 1858 are still taught not only in Utah textbooks but in sober national histories. This history has one serious problem: except for the episode's acquisition of its unfortunate nickname, none of it ever happened.

After witnessing the conference that ended the Utah War, a forgotten young newspaper reporter wrote that the only casualty of the conflict was the truth.[1] The clash came to a temporary resolution in June 1858, when the leaders of the Church of Jesus Christ of Latter-day Saints—the Mormons—accepted President Buchanan's "full and free pardon to all who will submit themselves to the authority of the federal government." Seldom have two hostile forces faced each other for so long under such tense conditions as did the U.S. Army and the Nauvoo Legion, Utah's territorial militia, without provoking fatal violence, and seldom has such a significant conflict been so misrepresented in the historical record.

After decades of silence, in the 1880s Mormon historians claimed this episode as their own and transformed the story of a contentious struggle between an American republic and a homegrown frontier theocracy into a mythical hero tale. In this carefully constructed legend, a patriotic but misunderstood and abused religious minority defied the imperial ambitions of an unjust and unrighteous government and bloodlessly defended their religion and their families against unprovoked persecution and tyranny.

American historians ignored the incident or essentially accepted the Utah version of the story until Howard R. Lamar's *The Far Southwest* and Norman F. Furniss's *The Mormon Conflict, 1850–1859* appeared in the 1960s. Since Furniss's untimely death, only one other book-length study of the war, Gene A. Sessions's edition of Donald R. Moorman's unfortunate *Camp Floyd and the Mormons: The Utah War*, has been published, and essentially it is a homage to the mythic history. Other works, such as our friend Harold Schindler's classic *Orrin Porter Rockwell: Man of God, Son of Thunder*, helped popularize the heroic view of Mormon resistance.

1. Boorstin, *Americans: National Experience*, 64. Our thanks to historian William P. MacKinnon for alerting us to Lemuel Fillmore, the actual author of the "fooled, everybody" quote, which has long been attributed to Captain Jesse Gove.

All this work was done without open access to the critical sources that lay buried in Utah's archives, especially in the territorial militia records and the papers of Brigham Young. Not until William P. MacKinnon, a former General Motors executive and an independent historian, recognized the importance of the conflict and began his studies, culminating in his groundbreaking work *At Sword's Point: A Documentary History of the Utah War*, of which the first of two volumes appeared in 2008, has more equal access to such sources been allowed—although experience has taught us that some historians are more equal than others.

While we have spent decades seeking out new sources to better understand this conflict, not until the events of 11 September 2001 did we fully realize the present need for a balanced and accurate reinterpretation of this forgotten struggle. The United States finds itself engaged in a battle with theocrats, engaging fanatics who are much more dangerous and perhaps even more committed than the religious rulers who had imposed what President James Buchanan called "a strange system of terrorism" on the people of Utah Territory.[2] The evidence that anyone ever learns anything from history is scant indeed, but we hope that some good will come from an honest look at the Utah rebellion of 1857–58, and at the problems the American republic faced and the mistakes it made when it first wrestled with theocracy.

---

2. James Buchanan, "Proclamation," 6 April 1858, in Hafen and Hafen, *Utah Expedition*, 333. As far as we can determine, this is the first use of the word "terrorism" in a federal document.

Acknowledgments

Over the five decades we have been researching the history of the American West, we have accumulated more debts than we can properly recognize. For brevity's sake, we will refer readers to the many pages of acknowledgments in our previous works on the Mormon frontier, notably *A Winter with the Mormons*, *Blood of the Prophets*, *Fort Limhi*, and *Innocent Blood*.

The opening of the Brigham Young Collection at the Church History Library and Archives, The Church of Jesus Christ of Latter-day Saints, and the release of selected collections of many LDS Church records on DVD in 2002 now permits historians to reassess many events in Mormon history. This new openness helped motivate us to take another look at the Utah War. We have also been greatly assisted by the generosity of historians Polly Aird, John Bond, Robert Briggs, John Eldredge, Jared Farmer, William P. MacKinnon, Ardis E. Parshall, and Kris Wray, who shared with us much of the material they have transcribed over the years. As always, Walter Jones and Gregory C. Thompson at the University of Utah have been invaluable allies. We must also express our gratitude to Yale University's Beinecke Rare Book and Manuscript Library, the Utah Humanities Council, and the Tanner Humanities and Wallace Steger centers at the University of Utah, whose sponsorship of grants and fellowships has made this work possible.

Abbreviations

The following abbreviations are used in the footnotes:

Beinecke Library — Yale Collection of Western Americana, Beinecke Rare Book and Manuscript Library, Yale University, New Haven, Conn.

BYC — Brigham Young Collection, MS 1234, LDS Archives

BYU Library — Special Collections, Harold B. Lee Library, Brigham Young University, Provo, Utah

Journal History — Journal History of the Church of Jesus Christ of Latter-day Saints, LDS Archives

LDS Archives — Church History Library and Archives, Church of Jesus Christ of Latter-day Saints, Salt Lake City, Utah

Marriott Library — Special Collections, J. Willard Marriott Library, University of Utah, Salt Lake City

Millennial Star — *The Latter-day Saints' Millennial Star*, British Mission, 1840–1970, LDS Archives

National Archives — National Archives and Records Administration, Washington, D.C.

USHS — Utah State Historical Society, Salt Lake City

UTMR — Utah Territorial Militia Records, Series 2210, Division of Archives and Record Service, Utah State Archives and Records Service, Salt Lake City

The Mormon Rebellion

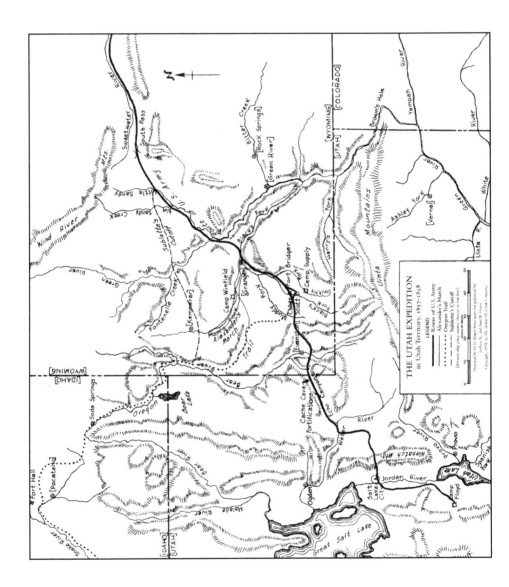

Introduction

This is the first rebellion which has existed in our Territories
and humanity itself requires that we should put it down in such
a manner that it shall be our last. To trifle with it would be to
encourage it and render it formidable. We ought to go there with
such an imposing force as to convince these deluded people that
resistance would be in vain and thus spare the effusion of blood.

—President James Buchanan, 8 December 1857

When James Buchanan unseated Brigham Young as governor of Utah in 1857 and ordered U.S. troops to escort Young's successor to Great Salt Lake City, he intended to assert U.S. sovereignty in the insubordinate western territory, not provoke a conflict. The consequence was not only the nation's first civil war, but also one it has forgotten. Overshadowed by the Civil War four years later, the confrontation between U.S. and Mormon soldiers on the empty reaches of the Rocky Mountains and the Great Basin produced no pitched battles. Over the long run, the benefits it brought for both sides would affirm the wisdom of Buchanan's action. His decision would also offer good reason to remember the military showdown and to ponder whatever insights it might offer a democratic republic engaged in a long struggle with Zealots who claim that their authority comes directly from God.

This would suit, if not fulfill, the motives of America's fifteenth president, who took office in March 1857 with the best of intentions. At a time of rising sectional strife, the Pennsylvania Democrat said that his only desire was "to live in the grateful memory of my countrymen," and he vowed to serve only one term.[1] To achieve this selfless ambition, he applied to the growing chasm between the North and South the skills

---

1. James Buchanan, Inaugural Address.

in conciliation and diplomacy he had acquired as a senator, secretary of state, and ambassador to Great Britain. To appease the South, Buchanan defended the 1854 Kansas-Nebraska Act, which repealed the 1820 Missouri Compromise's ban on slavery in the lands of the Louisiana Purchase north of the southern Missouri line, opened new territories to the spread of slavery by popular ballot, and ignited the border war known today as "bleeding Kansas," a prelude to the Civil War. If well-intended, such efforts to keep Southern states in the Union did little to pacify militant secessionists and outraged abolitionists.

Buchanan believed that slavery was morally wrong, but he also agreed with the U.S. Supreme Court's infamous Dred Scott decision, which held, among other things, that slaves were property, not citizens. And in opposition to Lincoln and his new political party, he supported Illinois senator Stephen A. Douglas's somewhat tortured "popular sovereignty" doctrine, which held that territories should address such troublesome "domestic institutions" as slavery at the ballot box. The president tried to restrict the definition of "institutions" to slavery, but the Mormon leaders who ruled Utah Territory could see that their polygamous marriages fit the president's idea of "domestic institutions" if anything did.

To the degree that Buchanan's view of polygamy was at all clear, it seemed to respect the Mormon position. With the religious doctrines of the faith, "however deplorable in themselves and revolting to the moral and religious sentiments of all Christendom," he would not interfere, he said. At the same time, he drew the line at theocratic rule. "There no longer remains any government in Utah but the despotism of Brigham Young," the president told Congress in December 1857 after the Mormon leader took popular sovereignty to its logical conclusion and seized unbridled power. "This being the condition of affairs in the Territory, I could not mistake the path of duty. As Chief Executive Magistrate I was bound to restore the supremacy of the Constitution and laws within its limits," he said.[2] The path of duty set opposing American armies in motion four years before Confederate guns opened fire on Fort Sumter.

In dispatching U.S. troops to Utah, Buchanan followed the approach taken by two governors before him to put down alleged rebellions in

---

2. James Buchanan, "Message of the President," 8 December 1857, 5, 6.

their states. As he attempted to prevent secession by appeasing the South, his actions showed that he saw no room for such compromise when it came to Young's rejection of federal authority in the defiant territory. The president failed to take seriously the revolutionary aim of the fast-growing millennial movement, if he knew very much about it at all, which was doubtful. For Young and his followers professed to be the true heirs of the U.S. Constitution and challenged the very legitimacy of the federal government. Their destiny was to prevail over the United States and all other manmade systems of government and establish God's Kingdom as a literal political entity to rule the world upon the return of Jesus Christ, which was imminent. They meant to supersede Buchanan and the government he stood for, not to make peace with it, a stance inherently hostile.

All of this is in line with the observation of distinguished American historian James C. Cobb, who said, "The past is not static or finite, but dynamic and fluid. It is subject neither to closure nor containment, but flows unchecked through the present and into the future."[3] It has little bearing, however, when it comes to the early history of Utah and the distinctive American faith known as Mormonism. In this peculiar realm, what has flowed from the last half of the nineteenth century more often than not resembles the manufactured past that George Orwell described in *1984,* his visionary novel about a utopian society: "The past is whatever the records and the memories agree upon. And since the Party is in full control of all records, and in equally full control of the minds of its members, it follows that the past is whatever the Party chooses to make it."[4]

Yet a different Mormon past clearly did exist—a past at odds with the one with which most interested readers are familiar. In that better-known narrative, mobs of bigots drive innocent victims from place to place, endlessly persecuting them for their religious beliefs. In the Mormons' eyes, they were the minority others loved to hate, and they relished the role, wearing it as a badge of honor and using it to damn anyone who opposed them. Since Americans have always shrunk from accusations of religious intolerance, their view was often accepted as mainstream. Still

3. James C. Cobb, "For the South, There Is No Closure," *Wall Street Journal,* 8 May 2001, A26.

4. George Orwell, *Nineteen Eighty-four: A Novel* (New York: Harcourt, Brace, 1949), 221.

today, historians who dare to question faith-promoting versions of the Mormon past are immediately branded "anti-Mormon," which pigeonholes their work and stifles open debate.

At the same time, a cursory look at the pattern of conflict at the faith's consecutive locations during the twenty years from 1838 to 1858 reveals a story strikingly different from the commonly accepted version. In this revealing sequence, one finds history repeating itself in the 1838 Mormon War in Missouri, in 1845–46 in neighboring Illinois, and in the Utah War of 1857–58. In this series of recurring conflicts, fighting spread from town to county to state and finally to national levels in keeping with the millennial faith's rapid growth: it continued after 1858 at a low boil for another forty years. Today the same body of faith is rightfully respected as a model of civil order and a pillar of traditional American values. As one religion editor observed, today's Mormonism "produces some of the most productive, law-abiding, patriotic and community-minded citizens the country has ever seen."[5]

One might wonder how such radical change came about. Could it be that Americans in those days were more bigoted and belligerent than they are today toward faiths unlike their own? Were they merely slow to see the peaceful intentions of their Mormon neighbors and the benign nature of their beliefs, as historians of the faith often profess? Or does this change suggest that some believers are merely slow to learn from experience and persist in doing what leads to conflict again and again until they at last tailor their beliefs to the accepted norms of society? And why should anyone care about all this in the first place?

Answers to these questions are relevant today as the nation faces the relentless element of a worldwide religion determined to spread a theocratic form of government over the earth. The actions and motivations of such fanatics are hard for free people, including Mormons today, to understand. They find it difficult to comprehend the mindset of believers who bear the banner of truth—final, absolute, and eternal—and cannot tolerate peaceful coexistence with any beliefs but their own. To compromise would be to deny the superiority of their own convictions.

History matters. It is why we should know and understand the past, however painful, and never allow it to be re-created in whatever shape

5. Naomi Schaefer Riley, "Chronicle of Darkness," *Wall Street Journal*, 11 July 2003.

is needed at the moment, as Orwell said. And much might be learned from the history of a distinctively millennial movement on American soil during the nineteenth century.

America's only armed conflict between church and state had its origins in upstate New York in about 1824, when the heavens opened after millennia of silence and God spoke once more to mankind as He had in the time of Moses. In reopening direct communication, He reintroduced the form of government known as theocracy, defined as "Government of a state by the immediate direction or administration of God; government or political rule by priests as representing the Deity."[6] God took the reins of government through an inspired spokesman on earth. After seeming to stand afar off for ages, the Divine King, in the eyes of believers, became *de facto* ruler of the world. In 1854, Jedediah M. Grant, about to become Brigham Young's second counselor in the church's First Presidency, explained: "If you maintain the fact that the Priesthood of God is upon the earth, and that God's representatives are upon the earth, the mouth-piece of Jehovah, the head of the kingdom of God upon earth, and the will of God is done upon earth as it is in heaven, it follows that the government of God is upon the earth."[7]

When the Almighty intervenes in history and restores His government upon the earth, nothing can be as it was. The voice of final truth, absolute and eternal, makes human wisdom foolishness, empties mortal institutions of meaning, and grants to the one through whom He speaks unlimited power. It makes archaic the covenants, such as the rule of law, on which social order has depended. It radicalizes language, the foundation of common interest and cooperative endeavor, and gives words meanings not commonly understood or accepted, words that distort and mislead. Since human institutions are no longer authentic, for example, the word "mob" can apply to all forms of earthly authority, sheriffs' posses, state militias, even the U.S. Army, which Young in 1857 called "an armed mercenary mob."[8] Common law and the ordinances of human

---

6. W. T. Harris, ed., *Webster's New International Dictionary of the English Language* (Springfield, Mass.: G. & C. Merriam Co., 1919), 2140.

7. Jedediah M. Grant, "Discourse," 19 February 1854, in *Journal of Discourses*, 2:13.

8. Brigham Young, "Proclamation," in Buchanan, *Utah Expedition*, 34–35.

legislatures no longer apply. Where God in person governs, history itself becomes a record without meaning or purpose.

To the truth seeker, this new reality offers many rewards. No longer need he bear the anguish of uncertainty and an endless search to discover who he is and how he can be sure of self-awareness hereafter. Moreover, he can know for sure why he came into being at this point in history. To an early Mormon believer, the signs of his time all pointed to the reason. After two thousand years of waiting, Jesus Christ's return was imminent, even at the door, and could be expected within a few years, or certainly within one's lifetime. The believer had been placed on earth in its last days to establish the Kingdom of God and help create the sanctified people whose righteousness would prepare the way for Christ to come and open His millennial rule.

Shortly before Joseph Smith's untimely death in 1844, the self-professed Mormon prophet pronounced: "I calculate to be one of the instruments of setting up the Kingdom of Daniel by the word of the Lord, and I intend to lay a foundation that will revolutionize the whole world."[9] Amid the tumultuous cultural storms that roared through the 1830s and the economic riptides that swept over the early 1840s, the certainty with which Mormonism resolved backwoods America's most contentious religious controversies and answered all of life's most difficult questions attracted a diverse and able band of brothers, along with an equally remarkable corps of women. The movement's constant trials and troubles either quickly cast them aside or forged them into true believers.

Seekers no more, those who believed now belonged to God's Kingdom. They knew who they were and what they had come for. They were here to fulfill God's divine purpose and follow His revealed word and His inspired prophet in all things. Released from the burden of uncertainty that life's choices impose, they now knew the true meaning of free will. They were free to choose: either to obey Him and gain the promise or defy Him and suffer His judgment.

If the rewards are great, the blessed assurance that a theocracy gives includes an unwanted corollary. Prior to the millennium, a theocracy, ruled by God from the heavens above, cannot live within a democratic republic, governed by its people from earth below, without civil warfare.

---

9. Smith, *History of the Church*, 6:365.

By nature, the two governing systems are incompatible and cannot exist side by side, or one within the other, without conflict. As long as both live under the same roof, there will be a struggle for supremacy that can end only when one compels the other to either bend or be gone. Mormon leaders understood this. Among their flock they stoked a sense of persecuted innocence and viral hostility not only to the American government, but against its people as well. "It is a stern fact that the people of the United States have shed the blood of the Prophets, driven out the Saints of God," said Jedediah Grant, one of the three most powerful men in Deseret, the Mormons' Great Basin home, and "consequently I look for the Lord to use His whip on the refractory son called 'Uncle Sam.'"[10]

James Buchanan may have failed to win the honorable remembrance he craved for his mishandling of the crises leading to the Civil War, for which he is generally reviled by historians. But his forthright response to Brigham Young's challenge to federal authority, at least at the outset, deserves credit as measured by the eventual outcome of America's longest struggle between church and state. Yet not even on this front does he receive any praise. Instead, the historical record has been written, as Orwell described, to project his actions to defend the government of the people he represented as Buchanan's blunder.

This volume seeks to correct that record and provide a new factual basis for considering the causes and consequences of this largely unknown confrontation. We believe facts matter: every historian is entitled to an opinion, but not to his or her own facts. Readers will draw conclusions about the meaning of this story as dramatically different as we have, but we hope our work will shed new light on an important, colorful, and largely forgotten episode in America's past.

10. Jedediah M. Grant, "Discourse," 2 April 1854, in *Journal of Discourses*, 2:148.

CHAPTER 1

To Sow the Wind
Beginnings

These people had violated the laws of the land by open and avowed
resistance to them—they had undertaken without the aid of the
civil authority to redress their real or fancied grievances—they
had instituted among themselves a government of their own,
independent of and in opposition to the government of this state.

—Missouri governor Lilburn W. Boggs, 1838

The Mormons openly denounced the government of the United States
as utterly corrupt, and as being about to pass away and to be replaced
by the government of God, to be administered by his servant Joseph.

—Illinois governor Thomas Ford, 1854

I am at defiance of all Earth and hell to point out the first thing
that this people have ever committed where in righteousness
it could be called an infringement upon our government. I am
at the defiance of all hell [and] Governments, but especially
ours. . . . We have observed good, wholesome rules and laws, but
now they can pass over every Mobocratic spirit and institution,
every violation of the Constitution, they pass over it as nothing,
and raise a force to come and slay all the Latterdaysaints, men,
women and children. . . . We will keep revolutionising the world,
until we bring peace to mankind, and all hell cannot help it.

—Utah territorial governor Brigham Young, 1857

During the winter of 1857–58, the military arm of a defiant theocracy confronted an American army on the high plains of today's southwestern Wyoming. To the east, some eighteen hundred solders, regulars and volunteers, of the U.S. Army's Utah Expedition were camped around the burned ruins of Jim Bridger's trading post. Between them and the winding Echo Canyon entry to Salt Lake Valley stood the hosts of latter-day Israel, also known as the Nauvoo Legion or the Utah Territorial Militia, some four thousand strong. As each side waited for spring to open the way to shed the other's blood, Congress asked President James Buchanan why he had taken the action that touched off the nation's first civil war, a teapot version of the one that would open in Charleston Harbor four years later.

In reply, the president handed national lawmakers the letters and reports compiled over six years that had compelled him in May 1857 to order the U.S. Army to escort a new governor to Utah to replace Brigham Young, whose term in that office had expired in 1854. More importantly, the troops were also to serve as a *posse comitatus* in imposing federal authority over the vast Mormon-controlled western territory.[1] Buchanan's action to bring a rebellious territory to heel had led to an armed revolt.

The president's response, titled "The Utah Expedition," took in some six dozen reports, mainly written by U.S. officials from 1851 to 1857, alleging treason, duplicity, disloyalty, and other serious offenses. Forty-six of the documents came from the Office of Indian Affairs. In conveying them to the president, Charles E. Mix, acting commissioner, said that they illustrated the "policy pursued by the Mormons, which aimed at the establishment of an independent Mormon empire."[2] Congress found it hard to take such an allegation seriously and delayed Buchanan's request for four new regiments to put down the rebellion.

---

1. Young's four-year term had expired in 1854, but he stayed on under a provision of the territorial organic act that allowed a governor to serve "until his successor shall be appointed and qualified." No replacement had been named prior to Buchanan's appointment of Alfred Cumming in 1857. A *posse comitatus* is a force representative of all citizens called under the authority of a political jurisdiction to enforce the law.

2. Charles Mix to Jacob Thompson, 22 February 1858, in Buchanan, *Utah Expedition*, 124, 125.

People in the western states, however, had learned to take Mormon aspirations *very* seriously. In Missouri, they had seen little peace after 1831, when the Almighty through a professed prophet identified Jackson County as the location of the Garden of Eden and proclaimed the Santa Fe Trail jumping-off town of Independence as the site of New Jerusalem, the City of Zion. As ardent believers poured in from such exotic places as New England, New York, and Canada, many harboring abolitionist sentiments, fighting spread over five western Missouri counties. The state's Mormon War came to an abrupt end in 1838, when Governor Lilburn W. Boggs ordered the militia to exterminate the troublesome religionists altogether or drive them from the state "if necessary for the public peace."[3] As his words indicate, the search for causes of the 1857–58 Mormon rebellion must begin with sources of conflict between the millennial-minded religionists and their Missouri neighbors twenty years before.

Among the most volatile of these was the issue of landownership. In Zion, the Lord owned the land. To gain a safe harbor against the storms of the Last Days, converts sold their former property and submitted the proceeds to the church as described in the Book of Acts.[4] In a perpetual land-acquisition scheme, the bishop in Zion then applied the money to purchase land in Jackson County and lease a tract back to the consecrator to keep as an inheritance, "unless he transgresses."[5] To implement this system, Joseph Smith announced the revealed plan of New Jerusalem.

The City of Zion was a picture of millennial order and communistic economic purpose. Drawn to a square mile, the plot featured ten-acre blocks, each with twenty half-acre lots and streets 132 feet wide that ran by the compass. Each lot was to hold one house, and all dwellings were to stand twenty-five feet from the street. On the outskirts enough land was projected for "the agriculturist" to supply the city. Farmers were to live in the city and harvest food from land inheritances on the outside to serve all alike. "When this square is thus laid off and supplied," Smith instructed, "lay off another in the same way, and so fill up the world in these last days, and let every man live in the city, for this is the city of Zion."[6]

3. Smith, *History of the Church*, 3:426.
4. See Acts 5:1–11.
5. Smith, *History of the Church*, 1:365–66.
6. Ibid., 1:357–58.

A reflection of the beehive symbol, the City of Zion on paper appears harmless enough, but a closer look shows its confrontational nature. The projected urban center is exclusive, even hostile toward outsiders, for whom it holds no room. A sign on the outskirts might read "New Jerusalem, Outsiders Keep Out." It also violates both the intent and the provisions of federal land laws, created to promote private landownership.

As its plot shows, the City of Zion was a millennial ideal. It was a place of refuge prior to the Lord's imminent arrival and a place of peace and divine rule afterward. In the meantime, however, the concept was coercive and hostile toward neighboring landowners, who depended on their property to survive. New Jerusalem was never built in Missouri, but its plot, with minor alterations for topography, became the model for all future Mormon cities. The consequences were predictable. It would be difficult to imagine an urban concept more at odds with the values of self-governing citizens of a republic.

If the Mormons' early beliefs about landownership made nearby residents uneasy and nervous, their doctrines regarding American Indians made their frontier neighbors' hair stand on end. A revered scripture of the faith, the Book of Mormon is the purported history of Hebrews from the tribe of Manasseh who migrated to the New World in about 600 B.C., before the first destruction of Jerusalem. Their offspring, known as Lamanites, became today's Indians, a "remnant of Israel" in the Americas. Most white Mormons believed then and continue to believe today that they also descend from Joseph through his younger son, Ephraim, so Mormons and Indians share a vital bond. They are both of the lineage of Abraham through Isaac, Jacob, and Joseph, and are first cousins some six hundred or so generations removed.

Young believed in this lineage intently and quite literally: "We are of the House of Israel, of the royal seed, of the royal blood," he told his followers in 1855. Their missionaries purposely sought the Indians, but not the Gentiles, as did the Apostle Paul, "because they are disobedient and rebellious," he said. "We want the blood of Jacob, and that of his father Isaac and Abraham." In a family with ten children, one might be "purely of the Blood of Ephraim," he explained, while the other nine were Gentiles, a disparaging term. But if the latter strongly desired to join the royal seed of Israel, there was a transfusion ritual by which non-Israelite blood could be flushed from their veins: "Joseph said that the

Gentile blood was actually cleansed out of their veins, and the blood of Israel made to circulate in them," Young said.[7]

The Book of Mormon prophesied that the Lamanite remnant of Israel would return to the faith of their forefathers, help build New Jerusalem in America, and become again "a white and delightsome people."[8] To fulfill this necessary condition of Christ's return, Mormon missionaries had gone out to the frontier to carry the good news to their Native kinsmen soon after the church's founding. Like the City of Zion, this may strike some as peculiar, but innocent on its face. Yet below the surface lies an explosive corollary long since defused by time. For in the days of Zion's redemption, said the prophet Micah, "the remnant of Jacob shall be among the Gentiles . . . as a young lion among the flocks of sheep; who if he go through, both treadeth down and teareth in pieces." Moreover, the Book of Mormon prophet Nephi repeated Micah's forecast, but made it conditional, "if the Gentiles do not repent."[9]

The escape clause held little comfort for families who lived in isolated cabins on the Indian frontier, especially when Mormon missionaries visited nearby tribes. From the earliest days of the millennial movement, the doctrine had stirred opposition from its neighbors. Nor did it steady the nerves of overland emigrants when Indians scornfully called them "Mericats," meaning Americans, to distinguish them from Mormons. Irrelevant today, the belief was a potent source of rumor, misunderstanding, and conflict across the frontier that did not end in 1857 with President Buchanan's ordering troops to Utah.

As the army marched west, Young instructed a trusted lieutenant to tell the Indians in their path "that if they permit our enemies to kill us they will kill them also." Ominously he said, "the prospect is *that all Israel* will be needed to *carry on the work of the last days*."[10] Less alarming but equally

---

7. Brigham Young, "The Blood of Israel and the Gentiles," 8 April 1855, in *Journal of Discourses*, 2:269. Joseph Smith based this doctrine on British Israelism, an ideology that claims that northern Europeans are direct descendants of the Ten Lost Tribes of Israel.

8. In recent years, the phrase "white and delightsome" has been changed to "pure and delightsome." See the Book of Mormon, 2 Ne. 30:6.

9. Ibid., Mic. 5:8 and 3 Ne. 20:15–16.

10. Young to Andrew Cunningham, 4 August 1857, BYC. Italics in the original. The term "All Israel" expresses the ancestral ties between Mormons (Ephraim) and Indians (Manasseh).

change-resistant was Mormons' trust in revealed justice as opposed to what their prophets denigrated as "man's law." In Missouri, Justice of the Peace Adam Black swore that some one hundred armed Mormons had surrounded his house and forced him "to subscribe to an article which I refused to do, until instant death was threatened me." He alleged that Joseph Smith himself led the party. The paper Black signed under duress certified that he was not connected to any mob and would not be. As soon as the intruders left, he ordered the commander of the county militia "to disperse said body, and maintain the supremacy of the law."[11]

A criminal court of inquiry into "high treason, and other crimes in the state" in Richmond, Missouri, in November 1838 heard witnesses describe other clashes between revealed rule and manmade laws. John Whitmer testified that when he had supported "the supremacy of the laws of the land," he was told that "when God spoke he must be obeyed, whether his word came in contact with the laws of the land or not." Afterward, when the disaffected follower told the Mormon prophet that he wished to control his own property and "be governed by the laws of the land," Smith shot back, "Now, you wish to pin me down to the law."[12] One does not pin the Almighty or His prophet down to man's laws.

Meanwhile, if the Mormons' beliefs about Indians, landownership, and law made outsiders uneasy, the millennial religion's military aspirations made their neighbors sleep with one eye open. Only four years after the church was formed, the first manifestation of a Mormon military tradition appeared. In 1834, Joseph Smith led a ragtag force of about two hundred men, known as Zion's Camp, in an ill-fated attempt to recover consecrated lands in Jackson County, Missouri. After the collapse of various financial schemes, Smith fled the Mormon settlement in Kirtland, Ohio, in the dead of night.[13] He arrived in Missouri at the Mormon settlement of Far West in March 1838, and by fall the state

---

11. *Document Showing the Testimony Given before the Judge of the Fifth Judicial Circuit of the State of Missouri, on the Trial of Joseph Smith, Jr., and Others, for High Treason, and Other Crimes against That State*, 26th Cong., 2nd sess., 1841, S. Doc. 189, serial 378, 2.

12. Ibid., 33.

13. The assertion that religious persecution forced the Mormons to leave New York and Ohio does not stand up to analysis. Smith directed his followers to move from New York, and Mormon congregations survived in Kirtland, Ohio, until long after the young prophet's death.

was embroiled in a civil war. The "Mormon War" was largely fought between ragtag state militia companies, with the Mormon forces including many members of a secret organization known as the Sons of Dan, or the Danites, a name inspired by Jacob's blessing on one of his twelve sons: "Dan will be a serpent by the roadside, a viper along the path, that bites the horse's heels and causes the rider to fall backwards."[14] Initially the brotherhood was intended to suppress internal dissent, but its focus soon shifted outward.

One of the covert group's earliest fights occurred over a phenomenon that historians usually refer to as a "tendency" of the faith to vote as a bloc, as if moved by a kind of herd instinct. When thirty or so Mormons came to cast their ballots in Gallatin, Missouri, in 1838, the old settlers tried to stop them. "When I called out for the Danites," an arriving voter said, "a power rested upon me such as one as I never felt before."[15] In the ensuing melee, many on both sides were hurt by knives, clubs, and rocks, but the outnumbered Danites at last prevailed. The fight was notable as the first confrontation over Mormon voting practices, which chalked up majorities over the next forty years that no secret ballot could ever inspire.

After the Gallatin fight, Joseph Smith disavowed the Danites, who vanished, at least on the surface, as an organized body, and gave his support to the new Army of Israel, the first of the larger, more visible military outfits presented to non-Mormons as legitimate militias. A legacy from the Missouri period, however, was a dread of the Danites among their neighbors that Mormons did little to discourage.

The Sons of Dan won the fight in Gallatin, but not the first Mormon War, which escalated into a skirmish with Missourians at Crooked River, in which the Mormons won the fight and their first martyr, Apostle David Patten. The victory and the fear it inspired prompted Governor Boggs to mobilize the state militia and issue his notorious extermination order. Even before it reached western Missouri, a local mob massacred seventeen of Smith's followers at Haun's Mill.

Driven from their homes during the brutal winter of 1838–39, the Mormons left Missouri with bitter memories and enduring grudges:

14. Gen. 49:16–17.
15. Account of John L. Butler, Journal History, 6 August 1838, LDS Archives.

they quickly forgot the farms the Danites had burned and the cattle they had rustled, but the maltreated Saints meticulously cataloged their grievances in 678 individual affidavits and on a petition signed by 3,419 citizens, which told "the story of a people wrongfully deprived of their rights as free men and women," as LDS scholar Clark V. Johnson put it. They itemized losses in land and personal property totaling more than $395,000, while Joseph and Hyrum Smith each claimed $100,000 in damages, in part to cover more than $50,000 in fees paid to Missouri lawyers.[16]

The prophet's followers pooled their resources and struggled eastward across the Mississippi River into western Illinois, where the sympathetic inhabitants received them with kindness. Locked in a cell, Smith exhibited a genius for martyrdom and survival. After his jailors conspired in his escape, President Smith demonstrated how to turn disaster into triumph: his dedicated missionary apostles cast the conflict as the persecution of an unpopular religion and the driving of the Latter-day Saints from their prosperous Missouri farms as a national disgrace. The story of their suffering garnered oceans of benevolent ink and won an immense amount of sympathy for the Mormons.

Although the number of members who abandoned the faith in the wake of the Missouri ordeal is impossible to know, it created another example of the "very curious accumulation and loss of members constantly going on in the Mormon community."[17] Whatever the number, those who emerged from the refiner's fire and stayed loyal found themselves even more deeply committed to the new religion. Remarkably, when Joseph Smith created the Mormons, he accomplished something few others have ever done: he invented a people. He convinced his followers that they were literally the Children of Israel, God's new chosen people, a "peculiar people" exceptional and distinct from their fellow Americans. But neither Smith nor his followers had learned from their hard knocks: in their new gathering place, they marched in lockstep down the same road to another Mormon war between theocratic and republican systems of rule, but this time on a larger scale. The predict-

16. Johnson, *Mormon Redress Petitions*, xxii–xxviii, xxxiv.

17. Special Correspondent, "Dissensions and Quarrels among the Mormonites," *New-York Daily Times*, 15 July 1853, 8.

able conflict in Illinois seemed to show that the more fervent the believers, the more slowly they learned from experience.

On a scenic bend of the Mississippi River, some fifty miles north of Quincy, they established an exotic metropolis named Nauvoo, "the beautiful," and designated it as the Corner Stake of Zion. Wooed by the hope of revelation-cast votes, state lawmakers gave the city a charter that empowered Smith to establish "a government within a government, a legislature with the power to pass ordinances at war with the laws of the state, courts to execute them with but little dependence upon the constitutional judiciary, and a military force at their own command," Illinois governor Thomas Ford said.[18] The sovereign city-state was a working model for the theocratic institutions later created in the Great Basin of the American West. At Nauvoo, Smith also revealed the doctrine of plural marriage, or polygamy, denied in public but practiced in secret by a select circle of Mormon leaders.

Meanwhile, the new lodestone of Zion by 1842 made the city one of the largest urban centers in Illinois as believers heeded the call to come out of Babylon from North America and Europe. Its booming population and voting practices spelled temptation for those who hungered for political power. In Nauvoo, candidates favored by Mayor Smith normally won unanimously, except for an occasional voter or two who failed to get the word.[19] Such elections gave Smith growing control over county government and even threatened to hand him the reins of power in Illinois and unwarranted influence over the state's role in national politics.

But the editor of the *Quincy Whig* said that bloc voting was a sword that would cut both ways in Illinois, as it had in Missouri. The "clannish" practice of casting ballots "at the direction of one man, and this a man who has acquired influence over the minds of his people through a peculiar religious creed," Sylvester Hewlett said, was "repugnant to the principles of our Republican form of Government." He added that its "future effects would be disagreeable to think of—bitter hatred and unrelenting hostility will spring up, where before peace and good will had an abiding place."[20]

18. Ford, *History of Illinois*, 2:66.
19. Quinn, *Mormon Hierarchy: Origins*, 107–108.
20. *Quincy Whig*, 22 January 1842, in Hallwas and Launius, *Cultures in Conflict*, 83–85.

Nor was voting the only familiar source of conflict at Nauvoo. Governor Ford's description of the theocratic kingdom on the Mississippi was validated in 1843 when the municipal court on a writ of *habeas corpus* freed Smith from arrest by a Missouri sheriff for attempted murder. Smith told his followers that "the municipal court had more power" than higher jurisdictions, and he "restrained them no more" from using violence in self-defense.[21] The city council promptly passed an ordinance that no arrest warrant from another jurisdiction could be served in Nauvoo without the mayor's consent. The penalty for violating the city ordinance was prison for life.

Nauvoo became a sanctuary for counterfeiters and organized bands that preyed on the city's neighbors with little fear of arrest.[22] When robbery victims from other places pursued culprits into the Mormon metropolis, said Governor Ford, Nauvoo courts fined them for daring to look for their stolen property. "Many people began to believe in good earnest that the Mormons were about to set up a separate government for themselves in defiance of the laws of the State," the governor said.[23]

Given this fear, it was hardly surprising that neighbors took alarm as the Nauvoo Legion paraded publicly in its three arms, infantry, cavalry, and artillery, before admiring throngs of Smith's followers. Ostensibly part of the state militia, the semi-private army grew under compulsory military training to about four thousand men, nearly a third the size of the U.S. Army at the time, far beyond any legitimate need for defense. At the head of this finely uniformed and intimidating force was the nation's highest-ranking military officer, the gaudily costumed Lieutenant General Joseph Smith. The Nauvoo Legion succeeded Zion's Camp, the Sons of Dan, and the Army of Israel as the latest, but not the last, manifestation that a theocracy's compulsion to prevail to universal dominion included a military dimension. The Legion's cohorts stood at the disposal of Mayor Joseph Smith "in executing the laws and ordinances of the city," approved by Councilman Joseph Smith, and interpreted by the Nauvoo Court under Chief Justice Joseph Smith.[24]

21. Smith, *Intimate Chronicle*, 109.
22. For the extent of lawlessness, see, Godfrey, "Crime and Punishment," 195–222.
23. Ford, *History of Illinois*, 2:155–56.
24. Smith, *History of the Church*, 4:239–49.

The people of western Illinois had held out an open hand of friendship and relief to a flood of suffering refugees who streamed across the Mississippi River in 1839. But within four years, the region's formerly peaceful and law-abiding residents had all but forsaken the rule of law and become ready to wage war against their new neighbors. Increasingly hemmed in, the Mormon prophet typically did not try to pacify his enemies. He raised his sights instead to a vision of a world empire ruled by God through revelation to a prophet of the Last Days, himself. And he prepared to move his followers to a new, higher plane.

In April 1842, Smith received by revelation the name of an organization by which the God of heaven would "set up a kingdom, which shall never be destroyed," as foretold by the prophets: "Verily thus saith the Lord," said the Almighty King. "This is the name by which you shall be called—The Kingdom of God and His Laws, with Keys and power thereof, and judgment in the hands of his servants, Ahman Christ." The secret body's mission was to set up God's kingdom, which Daniel foretold would "brake in pieces" the world's kingdoms.[25] The Lord's revealed title was so awkward that its members called it the Living Constitution, the Council of the Kingdom, or simply the Council of Fifty. But the vaulting task they took on to establish God's Kingdom as an earthly government was not subject to change.

Three months later, the prophet began to prepare his followers for a radical new way of life. Writing in the Nauvoo paper *Times and Seasons*, which he edited, Smith said that "monarchical, aristocratic, and republican forms of government" had risen to power in the past, only to fall "prostrated in the dust." All had spoken "with a voice of thunder," he said, "that man is not able to govern himself." It was now Jehovah's purpose, he went on, "to stand at the head of the universe and take the reins of government in his own hand," as he had done in the time of Moses.[26] "Their government was a theocracy," he said. "They had God to make their laws, and men chosen by him to administer them," a possible reference to the secret council he had just formed. Spoke the prophet of the Last Days: "So will it be when the purposes of God shall be accomplished."[27]

25. Dan. 2:44; and Smith, *Intimate Chronicle*, 153.
26. "The Government of God," *Times and Seasons*, 15 July 1842, 855–59.
27. Ibid.

As pressure grew on Springfield to repeal Nauvoo's charter, Smith's actions took on the look of desperation. In December 1843, Nauvoo leaders asked Congress to put the city beyond the reach of Illinois law-makers by making it an independent federal territory with Smith as gov-ernor. But it was unlikely that Congress would create a territory out of a city within an existing state and endow it with independent status. This may foretell why the Mormon prophet made his next move. In February 1844, Smith announced his candidacy to become the next president of the United States and sent missionaries across the nation to work for his election. At the same time, he was making even more ambitious plans behind closed doors. Less than four weeks later, he formally organized the Council of Fifty.

Smith himself soon coined a name for the form of government he advocated, later repeated by Lieutenant John W. Gunnison in his percep-tive description of Mormon society in Utah. In the Nauvoo church paper, Smith said in 1844, "I go emphatically, virtuously, and humanely, for a THEODEMOCRACY, where God and the people hold the power to conduct the affairs of men in righteousness."[28] Eight years later, Gunnison said, "they call their system of government, a 'Theo-Democracy;' and that, in a civil capacity, they stand as the Israelites of old under Moses."[29]

Noted historian David McCullough has observed that nothing had to happen the way it happened: history could have gone in any number of different directions in any number of ways at any point along the way.[30] One might wonder how the story of a unique American millennial reli-gion might have gone if its dynamic founder, who claimed to hold two-way communication with Jehovah, had personally led his followers to the place God had chosen to establish His Kingdom in the vast northern lands of the Republic of Mexico.

But he did not survive. Ironically, his downfall was caused by dis-sension within the ranks of obedient believers who seemed to outsiders always to march as one. On 7 June 1844, dissenters published the first and last issue of an opposition newspaper, the *Nauvoo Expositor*. Among other things, the new sheet flatly opposed "every attempt to unite church and

28. Joseph Smith, "The Globe," *Times and Seasons*, 15 April 1844, 5:508–10.
29. Gunnison, *The Mormons*, 23.
30. McCullough, "Knowing History."

state." Pointedly, it also reprinted an editorial from the latest issue of the *Quincy Whig* that spelled out the reason for the growing unrest and hostility among Mormon neighbors: "It is not so much the particular doctrines, which Smith upholds and practices, however abominable they may be in themselves, that our citizens care about—as it is the anti-republican nature of the organization, over which he has almost supreme control. . . . The spectacle presented in Smith's case of a civil, ecclesiastical and military leader, united in one and the same person, with power over life and liberty, can never find favor in the minds of sound and thinking Republicans. The day has gone by when the precepts of Divine Truth, could be propagated at the point of a sword."[31]

In a fatal move, Smith instructed the city council to brand the offending sheet a civic nuisance and order it destroyed. The action set off the well-known series of events that culminated on 27 June 1844 when rogue militiamen broke into the jail at Carthage, Illinois, which held the thirty-eight-year-old prophet and his older brother, Hyrum, and murdered them both. Governor Ford proved unable to prevent the crime or the subsequent drift into lawlessness and civil warfare. The rest of the Nauvoo story was a replay of Missouri—and for the same reasons. The opposition and fear that the Latter-day Saints raised wherever they concentrated during their hard sojourn did nothing to change their habits, but it did leave the thousands of adherents who stayed with the church after Smith's murder with a legacy of bitterness and resentment.

The "mantle of Joseph" now fell on the strong shoulders of a man ready to lead. Brigham Young had spent only eleven days of his forty-three years in a classroom, but he was a shrewd judge of men and had been a dedicated student of the Mormon prophet from the moment he first fixed his gray eyes on the younger man. From that day on, he had taken lessons in leadership from Smith, closely observing his mannerisms, expressions, body language, and self-confidence as a prophet. Knowingly or not, Young had gone to school on the man he admired to prepare for his own time to lead God's people.

Young knew that the prophet of latter days had sealed his calling with his blood: it was now up to him to fulfill the God-given task of rebuilding His Kingdom in the American West. No one was more ready,

31. "Resolutions," *Nauvoo Expositor*, 7 June 1844, 2.

none more devoted. As the senior member of the Quorum of the Twelve Apostles, he moved in sure steps to consolidate his power and become president of the church, then its prophet, seer, and revelator, positions of authority that had been held by his predecessor. But Young never considered himself to be the equal of the man he replaced. He always saw himself as a faithful servant and an apostle of Joseph Smith.

Before leading the first company west, Young joined fellow apostles of the ruling quorum to which he belonged in issuing a proclamation that displayed how little they had learned from the Mormon wars in Missouri and Illinois. Boldly they reaffirmed the doctrines that had led to their expulsion from Missouri and the fall of Nauvoo and made future conflict in Utah predictable. This remarkable document sets forth the revolutionary beliefs that compelled an expansionist millennial movement to establish divine rule prior to Christ's return and to do so within their own lifetimes. With the possible exception of Buchanan's 1858 report to Congress, it stands alone as the most important source on the causes of the Mormon rebellion. Yet it is also the most ignored.[32]

The missive proclaimed that the Second Coming was not a distant prospect: it had already begun. Addressed "To all the Kings of the World; To the President of the United States of America; To the Governors of the several states; And to the Rulers and People of all Nations," this uncompromising declaration is an ultimatum to the nations of the world to surrender to God's rule or suffer the consequences. "Know Ye:—That the kingdom of God has come as has been predicted by ancient prophets, and prayed for in all ages: even that kingdom which shall fill the whole earth, and shall stand for ever."[33] The eloquent if bellicose tone of this important epistle reveals the authorship of Apostle Parley P. Pratt, early Mormonism's most gifted theologian, writer, and propagandist. "The great Elohim Jehovah has been pleased once more to speak from the heavens; and also to commune with man upon the earth, by means of open visions, and by the ministration of HOLY MESSENGERS," it announced.

Especially confrontational was the aim "to reduce all nations and creeds to one political and religious *standard*" and put an end to "strife

32. Pratt, *Proclamation of the Twelve Apostles*. The quotations in the next several paragraphs are drawn from this document.

33. A reference to the prophecies of Daniel referred to above.

and war." This revolutionary purpose rested on the belief that God had inspired the framers of the U.S. Constitution to create a land of religious freedom where His Kingdom could be restored and supersede, as it prevailed to universal dominion, all earthly realms, including the American republic. Accordingly, the nation's charter was a necessary step toward millennial government, not an end in itself. Believers viewed this as a higher form of patriotism. They revered the American constitution as the founding document of God's Kingdom and saw themselves as its true heirs. But their enemies called it treason.

The proclamation also revealed why U.S. Indian agents generated so many of the documents Buchanan sent to Congress to defend his actions. The apostles testified that the Indians of North and South America" were a "remnant of the tribes of Israel, as is now made manifest by the discovery and revelation of their ancient oracles and records," referring to an essential scripture of the faith, the Book of Mormon.[34] They were "about to be fathered, civilized, and made *one nation* in this glorious land," the declaration continued. The Almighty would gather "the natives, the remnants of Joseph in America, and make of them a great, and strong, and powerful nation." He would "establish a holy city, and temples, and seat of government among them, which shall be called Zion."

The rulers and Gentile people of the world could not be "idle and disinterested spectators" as the Kingdom rolled forth to establish Jerusalem as the capital of the old world and the city of Zion in the new as the center of universal rule. They would either stand with the "covenant people of the Lord" or oppose them to their eventual sorrow and destruction. To escape the consequences of ignoring this warning, the Gentiles were first required to repent and become citizens of the Kingdom of God. After that, they were told "to put your silver and your gold, your ships and steam-vessels, your railroad trains and your horses, chariots, camels, mules and litters, into active use, for the fulfillment of these purposes." All people must "come to the same standard; for there shall be one Lord, and his name one, and He shall be king over all the earth."

If the Gentiles did not repent, said the author of the proclamation, the Native kinsmen of the Mormons, the Lamanites, would go among

---

34. The original italicized the word *Indians*: the proper name for the tribes, Lamanites, was given in the Book of Mormon.

them and "tear them in pieces, like a lion among the flocks of sheep." Their destruction would be total, "an utter overthrow, and desolation of all our Cities, Forts, and Strong Holds—an entire annihilation of our race," Apostle Pratt said, "except such as embrace the Covenant, and are numbered with Israel."[35] The thought of a Mormon-Indian alliance in a region athwart the overland trails would hardly add joy to the travel of American families going west to Oregon and California.

Now Brigham Young would take his followers into the heart of lands controlled by Indian peoples, whose prophesied alliance with the Mormons had already struck fear and created hostility on the frontier. Early in 1846 he led the exodus from Nauvoo west to the Missouri River, where he located an emigration base named Winter Quarters at present-day Omaha, Nebraska. The following year, he captained the first Mormon party that left the United States to establish God's Kingdom as a sovereign dominion, free and independent, in the unsettled wilds of the great American West.

The location that God and Young chose for the gathering place of His people offered isolation and abundant room in which to grow—both necessary conditions to establish God's Kingdom in the Last Days. There none would come to hurt or make afraid as they grew in number and gathered strength for the inevitable march to world dominion. "If the people of the United States will let us alone for ten years, we will ask no odds of them," Young recalled saying in 1847.[36]

The divinely favored land was the Great Basin of western America, a vast arid and empty region of high-altitude desert and mountain ranges running north to south from which no water flowed to any ocean. At its widest point, the landlocked province extended from present-day western Wyoming to the crest of the Sierra Nevada in California. It reached from southern Oregon in the north to Baja California in the south. Today the basin's rim encloses most or part of six western states.

On crude maps of the period, the Republic of Mexico claimed the immense region. In the year the Mormons possessed it, however, it was inhabited only by several Shoshonean peoples, each a distinctive tribe who made war on all others not of their kind. After gaining independence

35. Parley P. Pratt, *Mormonism Unveiled*, in Crawley, *Essential Parley P. Pratt*, 23–24.
36. Brigham Young, "Discourse," 13 September 1857, in *Journal of Discourses*, 5:226.

from Spain in 1821, Mexico had failed to protect its northern provinces from the hostile Indians who stopped and then reversed Hispanic civilization's northward thrust. By 1847, its northernmost outpost was Tucson, which was virtually under siege by Apache tribes, while its true northern border had shrunk hundreds of miles south of the boundary it claimed. No Mexican official would ever venture as far north as the valley of Great Salt Lake.

There the vanguard of Brigham Young's pioneer company of 143 men, three women, and two children landed in July 1847. Slowed by mountain fever, Young himself arrived on the twenty-fourth to behold the expansive valley and officially pronounce it the place for God's Saints to gather. Shining in the distance were the salt-laden waters of Great Salt Lake, the largest remnant of the Great Basin's prehistoric freshwater bodies, which once covered a surface area almost equal to Lake Michigan.

The stalwarts who made up what they called "The Camp of Israel" were almost all as remarkable as their formidable leader. They were mostly farmers, but the band included architects, blacksmiths, carpenters and cabinetmakers, doctors, gunsmiths, hatters, lawmen and lawyers, mathematicians, musicians, former Indian agents, politicians, potters, printers, slaves, and wagonwrights. They came from England, Scotland, Ireland, Germany, Denmark, Norway, and virtually every state in the Union. Men of such caliber were responsible for the success of the Latter-day Saints in settling the Great Basin, where they founded and built more than three hundred villages, towns, and cities. As far as possible in a harsh and arid region where only 4 percent of the land was arable, they made "the desert blossom as a rose." Brigham Young was one of the greatest leaders in American history, but such men and women formed the bedrock of his astonishing success: without them, he could have accomplished nothing.

Close behind Young and the Pioneer Camp came 275 veterans and dependents of the U.S. Army's Mormon Battalion. At the request of Mormon leaders for government help in moving to California, President James K. Polk had approved the enlistment of 500 Mormons in 1846 to serve in the Mexican War and keep the faith loyal to the United States. Young himself had recruited "volunteers" as old as sixty-seven and as young as fourteen to fill out the battalion roster. Afterward, he thanked

Polk for his "friendly offer of transferring 500 of our brethren, to the land of their destination."[37]

Young later told a different story to foster "a bitter vindictiveness against the Government." In that alternate account, the battalion was recruited at the behest of the federal government; it was a ploy to deplete the Saints and further the destruction of the church. A former Mormon spokesman, T. B. H. Stenhouse, told President U. S. Grant that no other story had done so much to shape "the sentiments of the Mormon people against the Government."[38] The revisionist account reveals a resentful, if not hostile, attitude toward the U.S. government that affected Young's leadership over his thirty-year career in the West and influenced his decision to throw off the federal yoke in 1857.

On the journey west, Young had reprimanded members of the Pioneer Camp for laughing out loud, using profanity, and playing checkers. Foolish conduct did not suit those chosen to find the place "where the Standard of the Kingdom of God could be reared," he said.[39] The day after his arrival at Great Salt Lake was Sunday, respected as a day of rest, but on Monday he attended to an important task. While others plowed and irrigated, Young and seven others climbed a steep knoll to the north of today's city and dedicated the hill, seemingly shaped and located for that very purpose, as the place "where the Standard of the Kingdom of God could be reared." Isaiah's prophecy that "he shall set up an ensign for the nations" would then be fulfilled.[40]

The 1847 arrivals next laid out a new urban center in accordance with a blueprint whose features revealed the mind of its designer. Young faithfully saw to it that his plan was followed exactly, and he made sure that surveyor Henry Sherwood understood "how many degrees of variation of compass there is at this spot, so that the City may be laid out perfectly Square North & South, East & West."[41] The plan of the new Mormon

37. Young to Polk, 9 August 1846, in Bigler and Bagley, *Army of Israel*, 69–71.

38. Stenhouse, *Rocky Mountain Saints*, 237, 241, 249.

39. Kenney, *Wilford Woodruff's Journal*, 3:187–89.

40. Isa. 11:11–12. The party included apostles Heber C. Kimball, Wilford Woodruff, George A. Smith, Ezra T. Benson, and Willard Richards, fellow Council of Fifty members William Clayton and Albert Carrington, and possibly others.

41. Bagley, *Pioneer Camp of the Saints*, 241.

city was almost an exact copy of the one Joseph Smith had envisioned in 1833—the millennial metropolis of New Jerusalem, the City of Zion, where the Lord would come in Missouri. Still unbuilt in that state, the city was designed to implement the Lord's will regarding consecration and stewardship. Two years before, believers had been told by revelation to consecrate their property to the church "with a covenant and a deed which cannot be broken." Every man would then be made "a steward over his own property," or as much as was "sufficient for himself and family. But those who sinneth and repenteth not," the Lord warned, would be "cast out" and "not receive again that which he has consecrated unto the poor and needy of my church, or in other words unto me."[42]

As created in the Great Basin, the city modeled after New Jerusalem included a six-square-mile enclosure, called the Big Field, which was divided into ten-, twenty-, forty-, and eighty-acre parcels. These were assigned to farmers in addition to their lots in the city. Closer in were five-acre lots marked off for allocation to "the mechanics and artisans."[43]

At the outset, Young made clear that God owned the land, not Mexico or he himself. Unlike his predecessor, he had no land to market. Every man would have enough for his city lot and farm plot, but not more than he needed, he said. Moreover, stewards must "be industrious & take care of it" and "keep his lot whole for the Lord has given it to us without price."[44] Since the Lord owned it, the land could not be sold or privately held. "No man will be suffered to cut up his lot and sell a part to speculate out of his brethren," he ordered.[45]

The delighted clerk of the Camp of Israel related the good news to a friend in England. "One thing wonderful for all you Englishmen to know, is, you have no land to buy nor sell; no lawyers waiting to make out titles, conveyances, stamps, or parchments," Thomas Bullock wrote. "We have found a place where the land is acknowledged to belong unto the Lord, and the Saints being his people, are entitled to as much as they can plant, take care of, and will sustain their families with food."[46] But there was more to Bullock's glad tidings than the promise of free land.

42. Smith, *History of the Church*, 1:357–59.
43. Ibid., 1:60.
44. Kenney, *Wilford Woodruff's Journal*, 3:236.
45. Smith, *Intimate Chronicle*, 369.
46. Bullock to Griffith William, 4 January 1848, *Millennial Star* 8:10, LDS Archives.

For the Englishmen who accepted his invitation would become worker bees in the communal design symbolized by the beehive on today's state flag and seal. Under this scheme, the food gatherers, or farmer bees, would reside in the city, or central hive, and harvest food from the plots assigned to them on the outside. The produce would go into tithing houses for storage and distribution to all according to their needs.

But the concept failed to square with the resources that God provided in the place He had chosen. Instead, it transferred a former revelation suitable for the fertile Midwest to a desert region that offered only limited soil and water resources, but a storehouse of minerals. To rest the fledgling theocracy's growth potential on farming and rule out mineral development was self-defeating.

In the meantime, the Great Basin valley rang with preaching unrestrained by the fear that outsiders might be listening or concern that what was said might be written down for historians one day to ponder. Young underscored the Indians' part in rolling forth God's Kingdom: "the Elders would marry Wives of every tribe of Indians and showed how the Lamanites would become a White & delightsome people" to fulfill a Book of Mormon prophecy.[47] His followers would take "their squaws wash & dress them up teach them our language & learn them to labor & learn them the gospel of their forefathers," he predicted.[48]

As for the United States, Young said he knew that many in its government had "a hand in the death of Joseph & Hyram [*sic*] [Smith] & they should be damned for these things & if they ever sent any men to interfere with us here they shall have there throats cut & sent to hell." With "uplifted hand to Heaven," Apostle Wilford Woodruff said, he swore "while he lived to make every preperation [*sic*] & avenge the blood of the Prophets & Saints."[49]

The clerk of Young's pioneer camp heard even stronger language that pointed directly to the Mormon leader's defiance of the United States ten years later. "He hoped to live to lead forth the armies of Israel to execute the judgments & justice on the persecuting Gentiles & that no officer of the United States would ever dictate him in this valley, or he would

47. Bagley, *Pioneer Camp of the Saints*, 243.
48. Kenney, *Wilford Woodruff's Journal*, 3:241.
49. Ibid.

hang them on a gibbet as a warning to others," wrote Bullock. Young "showed the spot where the Ensign would be hoisted & never have any commerce with any nation, but be Independent of all." The 28 July discourse was "most powerful and impressive," he said. [50]

In six months, Brigham Young had led his people to the place that God had chosen for them to build His Kingdom in the Last Days, and he had made himself the undisputed leader of the fervent millennial movement. In so doing, his attitude was defiant. He neither accepted defeats in Missouri and Illinois nor did he learn from them. Instead he would prepare to renew the struggle when he was ready and wage it over the same ground. Give us ten years and we will stand up to anyone, he said.

He had sown the wind with the seeds of conflict to come.

50. Journal of Thomas Bullock, 28 July 1847, in Bagley, *Pioneer Camp of the Saints*, 244.

CHAPTER 2

This Land Is My Land—
or Yours?

You have settled upon territory which lies geographically in
the heart of the Union. The land you live upon was purchased
by the United States and paid for out of their treasury. The
proprietary right and title to it is in them, and not in you.

—President James Buchanan, 6 April 1858

Twenty-nine days after Brigham Young "assumed the mantle" and took
control of Joseph Smith's millennial religion at Winter Quarters on
the Missouri River in December 1847, two members of his flock fifteen hundred miles to the west recorded an event that would forever
change Young's vision to establish God's Kingdom as an earthly state.
The discharged Mormon Battalion veterans were the only eyewitnesses
to report it on the day it happened.

"This day some kind of mettle was found in the tailrace that looks
like goald," wrote Henry W. Bigler on 24 January 1848 at Sutter's Mill,
east of what is now Sacramento, after workmen turned the American
River's South Fork into the millrace to test the water flow on the wheel.[1]
Soon after, fellow Mormon Battalion veteran Azariah Smith affirmed
the historic discovery in northern California. "This week Mr. Marshall
found some pieces of (we all suppose) Gold, and he has gone to [Sutter's]
Fort, for the Purpose of finding out," he said, and inserted the date: "the
24th."[2] The two Mexican War veterans, recorders of news that would

1. Paul, *California Gold Discovery*, 62.
2. Bigler, *Gold Discovery Journal*, 108.

electrify the world, were among the six Mormons James Marshall had hired to help build the mill.

So it was that the Great Basin, chosen by the Saints in large part for its isolation, was suddenly and squarely put in the path of a great population shift west. The sovereignty of the Kingdom depended on a buildup of obedient believers. Now its ramparts would be breached by a human tsunami of bickering, nosy fortune hunters, hell-bent to seek the root of all evil in California. Before the Mormon theocracy was ready to stand on its own, the outside world would come booming across its lands.

Between the start of the Gold Rush in 1849 and 1860, nearly two hundred thousand people traveled overland to the new El Dorado. Most followed trails that kept to the north or south of the Mormon settlements, especially if they hailed from Missouri or Illinois. But the number of California-bound emigrants passing through Utah during this time was roughly double the count of settlers who came to "Deseret" to build the Kingdom. And the shining temptation in the Sierra Nevada proved irresistible to many stewards of Zion, yoked to an unrewarding communistic agricultural design: as even they dreamed of gold, forever gone was the new Zion's separation from the world.

Less than two weeks following the discovery of gold, an even more hurtful blow fell on the newly born theocracy. In the nation's second-largest land acquisition, Mexico on 2 February sold to the United States virtually the entire present U.S. Southwest, including all of today's states of Utah, California, and Nevada, most of Arizona and New Mexico, and parts of Colorado and Wyoming. The Treaty of Guadalupe Hidalgo gave President James K. Polk everything he wanted for less than $20 million. It ended the Mexican War, but opened the issue of slavery in the new territories and introduced a new conflict—a fifty-year struggle for supremacy between God's Kingdom in Utah and its parent republic.

Together, the discovery of gold and the creation of a continental nation with the acquisition of the American Southwest were the most decisive yet underrated events in the history of the expansionist religious movement in the West. Over time they would impose lasting changes on its vision to establish God's Kingdom as an earthly state and shape the destiny of the nation itself.

In the meantime, the sudden impact of the land switch was shocking. At a stroke, the Latter-day Saints were squatters on federal land. Their cities were based on a premillennial concept that held no room for out-siders and failed to suit the land policies of a dynamic nation. In Zion the land was reserved for the true or adopted blood of Israel, the descendants of Ephraim (white settlers) or Manasseh (American Indians). Suddenly land owned by God became vulnerable to the values of a nation that sold some two-thirds of its domain to private owners at bargain basement prices during the nineteenth century. The Mormon Kingdom was sup-posed to swallow up the United States and all the nations of the world, not the other way around.

Mounting an unintended but direct threat to divine land ownership was the 1841 Preemption Act. This liberal measure allowed any citizen, or an intended one, twenty-one years of age or older, to build a cabin on public land and obtain the preferred right to buy 160 acres for $1.25 per acre.[3] All it took to sell the Lord's land to any and all comers, including so-called Gentiles, was settlement of the Indian claim and an official sur-vey to establish a base line and meridian and divide the land into thirty-six-square-mile townships of thirty-six sections, each a square mile of 640 acres, further divided into four 160-acre homesteads.

The upshot was that U.S. land laws would make life in Mormon country exciting, if not downright hazardous, to anyone sent by Wash-ington to survey the land. The first to encounter this potential danger was Captain Howard Stansbury of the U.S. Topographical Engineers, who led an 1849 expedition to carry out a survey of Great Salt Lake and freshwater Utah Lake. Congress wanted an investigation of the largest body of water between the Great Lakes and the Pacific Ocean, as well as a report on the ability of new settlements to supply the overland emigra-tion. According to historian Brigham D. Madsen, the officer was also sent to gauge Mormon loyalty to the United States, which was already suspect before the Utah War.[4]

On nearing Salt Lake Valley, Stansbury heard reports that the Mor-mons feared that his survey was to be conducted "in the same manner that other public lands are surveyed, for the purpose of dividing it into townships and sections." He was further told that "they would never

3. Preemption was the preferential right of a settler on public lands to buy his claim at a modest price.
4. Madsen, *Exploring the Great Salt Lake*, xviii.

permit any survey of their country to be made," and "my life would scarce be safe" if he tried it.[5] The U.S. Army officer bravely shrugged off the threats, but decided it might be prudent to make a courtesy call at Young's office before going forward. He explained to the Mormon leader that the purpose of the project was to survey the lakes and their surroundings, not to divide the land to prepare it for public sale, and he showed him how this would benefit the new colonizers. Satisfied, Young gave the mission his blessing, but ever distrustful of federal authorities, he instructed Dartmouth alumnus Albert Carrington to be his personal representative on Stansbury's staff and keep an eye on the mapmakers.

The captain stuck to the mission he had described, but his second-in-command, Lieutenant John W. Gunnison, went beyond his own assignments, which included producing the only map showing the Indian names of creeks in the Salt Lake and Utah valleys. A close observer, he also wrote from personal experience a book containing the first detailed description of Mormon society in the Great Basin. With remarkable accuracy, he reported that it was self-governing in 1849, and the saints were "satisfied to abide their time, in accession of strength by numbers, when they may be deemed fit to take a sovereign position." He also reported that the practice of polygamy was "perfectly manifest to any one residing long among them."[6]

On the publication of Gunnison's book in 1852, the marriage doctrine could no longer be denied as it had been for so long. That August, Young called a meeting to tell how it had come about and to "deliver a prophecy on it." Confidently he predicted that it would be "fostered and believed by the more intelligent portions of the world, as one of the best doctrines ever proclaimed to any people."[7] The immediate effect of his pronouncement, however, was to sharply reduce the flow of new believers from overseas who were needed to boost Zion's population and uphold its sovereignty.

Meanwhile, faced with the need to reach an accommodation with the United States, Mormon leaders fumbled in deciding how best to do it.

5. Stansbury, *Exploration and Survey*, 84–86.

6. Gunnison, *The Mormons*, 23, 67.

7. See *Deseret News*, 14 September 1852, which includes these remarks and the full text of the revelation to Joseph Smith on 12 July 1843.

Shortly before his death, Joseph Smith had prepared a wordy petition to Congress asking it to bestow on Nauvoo "the rights, powers, privileges, and immunities belonging to Territories" and to give him, the mayor, the authority to summon U.S. troops to defend the city.[8] Later, Young thanked President Polk for his "friendly offer" to allow five hundred church members to serve as a battalion of infantry in the takeover of California during the Mexican War. "Should we locate within the territory of the United States, we should esteem a territorial government of our own," he said.[9]

Apparently following these precedents, the Council of Fifty in December 1848 approved a petition to Congress for a territorial government, provided that Young and the council members would appoint its officers. Signature collection began before the petition was finished and went on into March, when the names of those chosen as territorial officers were placed before the people, who unanimously approved them by raising their right hands. The territory claimed by the petition was immense, covering most of the land ceded to the United States by Mexico. John M. Bernhisel of the Council of Fifty left for Washington in May with a petition twenty-two feet long bearing the names of 2,270 signers.

In the meantime, Mormon leaders created in March 1849 "a free and independent government" named the State of Deseret, to stand until Congress should admit it into the Union.[10] Its name was taken from the word for a honeybee in the Book of Mormon, but it later became a synonym for the Kingdom of God. The constitution of Deseret called for an election in May, but this was handled before the constitutional convention met. An open election on 12 March in the bowery of Great Salt Lake City selected Young, who faced no opposition, as governor and chose the other officers unanimously. In Nauvoo, votes were cast by voice, but in the Great Basin they would be cast at first by uplifted hand.

Two months after Bernhisel had gone, Deseret's General Assembly met for the first time and in an emotional rush decided to change the petition he had carried east. First they resolved to ask for either state *or* territorial government, which evolved into a request that Congress ratify Deseret's

8. Smith, *History of the Church*, 6:131–32.

9. Young to Polk, 9 August 1846, BYC.

10. Morgan, *State of Deseret*, 29–37.

constitution and admit the aspiring entity into the Union "on an equal footing with other States, or such other form of civil government as your wisdom and magnanimity may award to the people of Deseret."[11] They rested their petition on the failure of Congress to provide any civil government in the new lands, which had reportedly allowed anarchy to prevail "to an alarming extent" and the "revolver and bowie knife" to rule in perhaps the most tightly controlled society in the nation.

Staked out by fewer than ten thousand inhabitants was a new nation about twice the size of Texas with a seaport in southern California.[12] The borders of Deseret reached from the Rocky Mountains, west of present-day Denver, to the Sierra Nevada peaks, and from the Wind River Mountains of Wyoming to the Gila River in southern Arizona. It encompassed all or parts of the future states of California, Colorado, Arizona, New Mexico, Oregon, Utah, Nevada, and Wyoming. The size of Deseret measured the area that an aspiring theocracy needed to accommodate the gathering of Israel in the Last Days.

Deseret's delegate and Council of Fifty member Almon W. Babbitt followed Bernhisel to Washington with the second memorial, but Congress refused to seat him because he professed to represent a political organization not recognized by national law, "the alleged State of Deseret." Faced with conflicting instructions, Bernhisel and Apostle Wilford Woodruff headed for Philadelphia to get advice from an astute and ambitious political advisor.

Thomas L. Kane was the son of the prominent judge and Democratic Party leader John K. Kane, and he had used his father's influence to build his own reputation in the political arena. In 1846, at the age of twenty-four, he was behind the strategy to win President Polk's approval to allow five hundred Mormons to enlist during the War with Mexico, and thereby won the faith's loyalty. Afterward the skilled propagandist and political tactician wrote fictionalized accounts of the Latter-day Saints to win public sympathy and support.

No government at all would be better than a territory, Kane told them. "I would prefer to see you withdraw the Bill than have a Territorial

11. Whitney, *History of Utah*, 1:406–407.

12. The constitution of Deseret projected a seaport at San Diego and empowered the governor to be commander-in-chief of the militia, the navy, and all the armies of the state.

government," he said, "for if you are defeated in the State Government you can fall upon it again at another session." Showing his complete understanding of the Mormon aim to establish God's Kingdom as a theocratic state, Kane shrewdly fingered two major points of conflict between the republican and theocratic systems. "They will also control the Indian Agency and Land Agency," he cautioned the pair, "and will conflict with your calculation in a great measure."[13]

Taking Kane's sage advice, Bernhisel and Woodruff shelved the territorial request. But hardly had Senator Stephen A. Douglas of Illinois introduced Deseret's petition for full statehood than Senator Joseph Underwood of Kentucky countered with a memorial by William Smith, brother of the slain Mormon prophet, and a dozen others. Prior to leaving Nauvoo, it alleged, some fifteen hundred followers of Brigham Young had sworn in the temple "to avenge the blood of Joseph Smith upon this nation, and so teach your children; and you will from this day henceforth and forever begin and carry out hostility against this nation, and keep the same a profound secret now and forever."[14]

Smith's memorial appeared to confirm reports by some of the two thousand or so California-bound emigrants who had attended observances at Great Salt Lake on 24 July 1850 to celebrate the third anniversary of Young's arrival in Salt Lake Valley. Franklin Langworthy heard one speaker "read a paper entitled 'Declaration of Independence of Deseret,' while another one read, 'The Constitution of Deseret.'" They said "many hard things against the Government and people of the United States," the Illinois emigrant reported. "They prophesied that the total overthrow of the United States was at hand, and that the whole nation would soon be at the feet of the Mormons, suing for mercy and protection."[15]

Another visitor, who did not belong to Langworthy's party, also described the Pioneer Day event at Salt Lake. Henry S. Bloom had stayed two weeks in the Mormon "half-way house" to work as a carpenter and earn some money before going on to California. "A great deal of ostentation and pomp was displayed," he wrote. "They bid open defi-

13. Kenney, *Wilford Woodruff's Journal*, 3:514.
14. Bancroft, *History of Utah*, 451–52.
15. Langworthy, *Scenery of the Plains*, 24 July 1850, 46.

ance to the United States, her government and her people." To this, the emigrant from Kankakee added: "They were also very insulting to the emigrants."[16]

With a respect for those who suffered for their religion that reached back to the Pilgrims and the Puritans, many Americans tended to view the Mormons and their ordeals with great sympathy. "They have struggled through prairies & mountains to reach this valley with a heroism which is beyond all praise," wrote an officer who entered Utah with the U.S. Army in 1858.[17] Emigrants' opinions of Deseret in 1849 and 1850 largely depended on when and how long they stayed, and whether their contacts were with ordinary settlers or Mormon authorities. If the former, transients usually volunteered favorable impressions of the new society. All of this changed when Congress ignored Deseret's bid for statehood. On 14 September 1850, the Assembly of Deseret voted to withdraw all requests to become a territory and remain independent. It was too late. Congress had already "passed an act to organize this state into a Territory called Utah," said Hosea Stout.[18] To add to this hurtful rebuff, federal lawmakers had bestowed on the new territory the unwelcome name of its Native inhabitants. Torn by the issue of slavery, Congress in 1850 had given little serious thought to the creation of territories in its newly acquired western domain.[19]

That year, about sixteen thousand emigrants passed through Deseret, roughly six times the number of new Mormon settlers. An unusually high number, nearly a thousand, elected to spend the winter in Mormon settlements. Asa Call, who had set out to walk to California from Wisconsin, said they "held out every encouragement to remain amongst them."[20] But hardly had cold weather cut off any escape, said the twenty-

---

16. Burroughs, "Tales of the Pioneers," California State Library.

17. Du Bois, *Campaigns in the West*, 6 July 1858, 74.

18. Brooks, *On the Mormon Frontier*, 2:382.

19. The five enactments, known as the Compromise of 1850, abolished the slave trade in Washington, D.C., admitted California as a free state, and divided the region acquired from Mexico, east of California, into the territories of New Mexico and Utah, making them open to settlement from both sides of the slavery issue.

20. Call, "The Mormons." Some overlanders thought that the invitation to stay was meant to inflate the population and justify Deseret's bid for statehood. One emigrant said that the Mormons "followed the emigrants 100 miles to take the census." See Unruh, *Plains Across*, 325.

five-year-old emigrant, "than they began to show the cloven foot."[21] The sudden freeze in Zion's hospitality coincided with arrival of the first report that Deseret was now Utah Territory.

After President Millard Fillmore on 9 September signed the act that established the territory, it took less than six weeks for the news to reach Salt Lake. People now braced themselves to hear that the president had named a political crony, not Brigham Young, as its first governor and *ex officio* Indian superintendent. Fillmore made his appointments only eleven days after he signed the measure, but a severe winter resulted in a three-month delay before the news reached the new territory of Utah. During that time, Mormon leaders made sure that wintering emigrants understood there was no place for them in Zion. Harassment took many forms—lawsuits, discriminatory taxation, exorbitant prices, spying, threats, and unpunished crimes against outsiders—but perhaps the deepest cut was hateful talk about the United States.

One of those most offended was Presbyterian minister Jotham W. Goodell from northern Ohio, who was moving with his wife, Annie, and their seven living children to make a new home in Oregon. Playing it safe, they took the Mormon Trail from Fort Bridger and arrived in Salt Lake Valley in September 1850. They camped in their two wagons near Farr's settlement on the north side of the Ogden River.

In January, Goodell heard Young declare that "they were not the territory of Utah, and never would be." The Mormon leader denounced the government "in no measured terms" and predicted its overthrow and downfall. "I am the governor of the state of Deseret," he made clear on another occasion. "I was elected for life, and no other person shall hold that office while I live." Goodell also heard Young say, "The United States may send a governor here and probably will send one," but "we will send him back or send him *duck hunting*." Another time, Young said, "If they send a governor here, he will be glad to black my boots for me."[22]

In a reply to Young's claim that no people existed who were more friendly to the government than Utah's, Goodell said, "What other people in the world, most friendly to the United States, would consider

21. Call, "The Mormons."
22. Bigler, *Winter with the Mormons*, 49–50.

the stars and stripes a *nuisance,* an *aggression,* an act of defiance!" To this, he added: "If the world can produce no better friends to the United States than the people of Utah, then I have only to say God save my beloved country!" He concluded: "The institutions of the Mormons are at antipodes with the republican institutions of the United States."[23]

Backing up Goodell was retired U.S. Army major William Singer, a Mexican War veteran, who was camped with his wife and three young children near Goodell's wagons. The emigrants were received at first with "kindness and good feelings," he said, but as soon as winter prevented them from leaving, "hate and prejudice against American citizens bursts forth." In a letter to the *St. Louis Intelligencer,* the officer wrote, "Many emigrants beside myself heard Brigham Young from the stand declare the most treasonable hostilities against the U. States." After a rumor started that he was a spy, Singer was arrested, his property was seized, and five of his cattle were shot. Only fear for his family forced him to suffer such treatment, the major said.[24]

This concern made Singer wait until his family was "out of their power" before describing his own and other emigrants' grievances. The Mormon practice, he later reported, was to "destroy letters containing anything against themselves, from communicating aught in relation to my own or the grievances of other emigrants."[25] Again and again in the lead-up to the 1857 Utah War, emigrants and federal officials would level this accusation. Goodell supported his "grave charge" that Mormon friends had told him *"no letters deposited in the post office, by either gentiles or Mormons, ever left the valley without its contents being known"* with the report of a man from his wagon train who had deposited a letter at the post office. "A day or two after, he was passing in the rear of some out houses near to the post-office, and his attention was arrested by observing a large pile of waste paper, and actually fished from that pile, *pieces of the identical letter he had mailed."*[26]

23. Ibid., 52.

24. William Singer, "About the Mormons," *St. Louis Intelligencer,* 7 August 1851, 2, reprinted in Bigler, *Winter with the Mormons,* 205–10. Singer was later elected mayor of Marysville, California, and practiced law until his death in 1901 in San Francisco.

25. Ibid., 207.

26. Bigler, *Winter with the Mormons,* 78, 79. Italics in the original.

By February 1851, wintering emigrants had grown desperate. The constant threats and intimidation to which they were subjected may have been intended to frighten former Mormon enemies. But without the protection of U.S. law, many took them seriously. "If citizens of the United States, while passing through that territory, have not been murdered in cold blood," wrote Goodell, "then the Mormons themselves are the most atrocious liars on God's footstool."[27] Giving substance to verbal menace was the murder of Dr. John M. Vaughn in February of that year at Manti in central Utah. Madison Hambleton shot the non-Mormon physician after church, in broad daylight, allegedly for seducing his first wife, thirty-three-year-old Chelnicia, not long after the polygamist married a second, Maria Jane, nineteen. Brigham Young himself appeared before Deseret's supreme court and pronounced Hambleton justified, and that was that. Young and everyone else knew that the bench had no legal standing because the State of Deseret had already become the Territory of Utah.

The people who were most intimidated by constant threats and divine justice were not the young fortune seekers rushing to the gold fields, but the emigrants with families heading west to make permanent homes in Oregon or California. Moved by fears for themselves and their families, about three dozen men met secretly, or so they thought, in the snow of northern Utah and pledged to act as one and share their resources to the last bite, if need be, to ensure that all got away safely. They selected Goodell to serve as chairman of a committee of three, apparently chosen for their literary ability, who were tasked with drafting a memorial to Congress. The other members were New York seminary teacher Nelson Slater and Asa Call. For taking on this role, Goodell became the target of arbitrary lawsuits and discriminatory taxation, which so impoverished him that he needed the help of other emigrants to leave Utah. In one of his nine descriptive letters, his indignation burst forth: "Were Brigham Young to come in person and tender back the money he robbed us of, there is not a man among us but would exclaim: '*Your money perish with you! In our distress and anguish of soul, you robbed us of our all, and exposed our wives and little ones to the danger of perishing with famine, amid the wastes of the desert!* Never, *never,* NEVER!'"[28]

27. Ibid., 79.
28. Jotham W. Goodell, "The Mormons," *Oregonian*, 26 July 1851, 1.

Even before these letters appeared in a Portland, Oregon, newspaper in 1852, Slater had carried out his assignment as a member of Goodell's committee. He compiled the personal accounts of dozens of outraged emigrants and published them in 1851 in the first book copyrighted in California. The emigrants' anger was still hot months after they had left Utah, when they signed ten resolutions charging that the court system was "a mockery," freedom of speech was being abridged, treasonable opinions were freely voiced against the United States, and "Mormonism as a system, is oppressive, unjust, and unworthy of confidence."[29] They called on Congress to impose military rule in the territory.

The experiences of wintering emigrants in 1850–51 provide a rich and often ignored source of information on the underlying causes of the 1857 confrontation with the United States. They also add to the growing body of evidence from the six years prior to the nation's first civil war in support of President Buchanan's decision to confront a defiant theocracy.

Meanwhile, Mormon fears regarding territorial appointments dissipated when the news came in January 1851 over the all-weather trail from Los Angeles that President Fillmore had appointed Brigham Young to a four-year term as governor of the new territory. Only then did the Legislative Assembly of Deseret authenticate what Congress had done the year before, and what Utah settlers had known for at least three months. On 28 March 1851, they "cheerfully and cordially" accepted "the legislation of Congress in the Act to establish a Territorial Government for Utah."[30]

In passing what became known as the Compromise of 1850, Congress cut back the size of the proposed "State of Deseret," eliminating its need for a navy. But the new territory was still big enough to encompass today's New England, Ohio, New York, and Pennsylvania. Its borders covered more than 220,000 square miles and took in all of present-day Utah, almost all of Nevada, the western slope of Colorado, and southwestern Wyoming, including Fort Bridger.

---

29. Slater, *Fruits of Mormonism*, 91. Slater became superintendent of schools in Sacramento County.

30. Whitney, *History of Utah*, 1:454.

So relieved were the leaders of Deseret by Young's appointment as governor that they created a territorial capital in central Utah and named it Fillmore, a city then unbuilt, and gave the president's first name to the county. For his part, the Whig president from New York had taken the appointment so lightly that less than a year later he could not remember the first name of the person who had urged him to recommend Young for the position, except that he was the son of John K. Kane, a prominent federal judge in Philadelphia. It was Thomas.[31]

Fillmore's other Mormon appointments were welcome in the new territory, no matter who had recommended them. They were Zerubbabel Snow from Utah, associate justice; Seth Blair of Utah, U.S. attorney; and Joseph L. Heywood, also of Utah and the Council of Fifty, U.S. marshal. But if the president's non-Mormon choices expected a friendly reception in the place where they would serve, they would be badly mistaken.

Hoping to get off on an obliging foot, Chief Justice Lemuel G. Brandebury of Pennsylvania arrived early that summer to swear in Young as governor, only to discover that it had already been done under higher authority. Daniel H. Wells, attorney general of the State of Deseret, had performed this necessary ceremony in February 1851, before Young had been officially notified of his appointment. The other outside appointees were Broughton D. Harris of Vermont, secretary; Perry E. Brocchus of Alabama, associate justice; and Henry R. Day, U.S. Indian agent.

Not long after their arrival, Brandebury and Harris attended the Pioneer Day celebration and heard Governor Young say, among other astonishing statements, "[President] Zachary Taylor is dead and gone to hell, and I am glad of it!" When asked how he knew it, Young reportedly shot back, "Because God told me so." At this, Heber C. Kimball, the first counselor in the church hierarchy, put his hand on Brocchus's shoulder and added, "Yes, Judge, and you'll know it, too; for you'll see him when you get there." Young also prophesied that any American president "who lifts his finger against this people shall die an untimely death, and go to hell."[32]

31. Fillmore to Kane, 4 July 1851, ibid., 1:478.

32. Millard Fillmore, *Message from the President of the United States: Transmitting Information in Reference to the Condition of Affairs in the Territory of Utah*, 32nd Cong., 1st sess., 1852, H. Ex. Doc. 25, serial 640. This document is reprinted as an appendix in Bigler, *Winter with the Mormons*.

Nor did the rhetorical assault end there. Wells rehearsed a familiar fable about the Mormon Battalion, in which the United States had "required a battalion of five hundred men to leave their families" in dire straits to fight its battles after refusing to protect them against the ruffians who had plundered, robbed, and murdered them. "The country that could have the *barbarity* . . . to make such a requirement," Wells said, "could have no other object in view than to finish, by utter extermination, the work which had so ruthlessly begun." On the following Sunday, Harris heard Salt Lake mayor Jedediah M. Grant declare from the pulpit "that now the United States could not conquer them by arms."[33]

Shortly before this verbal baptism, Fillmore wrote Thomas L. Kane in Philadelphia demanding to know whether an enclosed editorial from an opposition newspaper in his home state was true. Among other charges, the *Buffalo Courier* on 2 July 1851 accused Young of "wholesale abuse of the U.S. and our institutions . . . repeated insults to California emigrants in 1849–50 . . . and leagueing [*sic*] with the Indians to harass our people on the road to California." Finally, "this Young is now keeping over twenty degraded and prostituted females, under the appellation of spiritual wives, at Salt Lake."[34] Fillmore must have known about this before he made the appointment, the paper charged. "It was in bad taste and contemptuous of our national feelings, if not of morality and religion, to vest the government of one of the Territories of the United States in the person of the present ruler over Utah."[35]

"What about this?" the president asked. "I relied much upon you for the moral character and standing of Young," he reminded Kane. Having been blindsided, he demanded to know "whether these charges against the moral character of Governor Young are true." Not recollecting Kane's given name, he addressed the letter to Thomas's father, the eminent judge.

Forthrightly, Kane repeated his testimonial to Young's "patriotism, and devotion to the interests of the Union." He had assured Fillmore of Young's "irreproachable moral character," he said, "because I was able

33. Ibid.
34. "Executive Appointments," *Buffalo Courier*, 2 July 1851, 2.
35. Ibid.

to speak of this from my own intimate personal knowledge."[36] With his response, which he offered for publication, Kane oddly enclosed a note marked "private" in which he refuted specific accusations and called most of the charges against Young "a mere rehash of old libels." But he failed to answer charges of "high and unjust taxation" on emigrants, and his evasive response on the polygamy issue shows that his private note was less than candid.[37] Kane expected Fillmore to keep it secret, but the president sent a copy to Young.

Meanwhile, Secretary Harris landed in Utah with his wife, Sarah, and $24,000—some 150 pounds of gold—to pay legislative expenses. He also expected to certify the census, which the organic act required the governor to conduct, as well as subsequent elections to apportion legislative representatives. But he was told, he said, that "a census had been taken when the application was made by the State of Deseret for admission into the Union." The truth was that the census agent of Deseret, Brigham Young, had failed to conduct a count in 1850 "owing to the total miscarriage of instructions and blanks." Since the survey, now known as the 1850 census, is actually an "enumeration" taken during the first three months of 1851, its total of 11,380 includes nearly 1,000 wintering emigrants, some listed twice if they moved during that time. But whatever it showed, the secretary considered it "so false and exaggerated that a correct census would have betrayed the fraud."[38]

As for the election, he called it "a burlesque upon the order and decorum required by the organic act." Among the reasons he gave for this opinion, he failed to mention that all the candidates had won unanimously but one, who fell short of a clean sweep by a single vote.[39] Accordingly, the young secretary bravely defied Young's attempts to lay hands on the federal gold.

---

36. Fillmore to Kane, 4 July 1851, in Whitney, *History of Utah*, 1:477. The complete exchange of correspondence appeared in the *Millennial Star* 8:341–44, LDS Archives.

37. Young to Kane, 11 July 1851, in Roberts, *Comprehensive History of the Church*, 3:538–39.

38. Fillmore, "Information in reference to the condition of affairs in the Territory of Utah," 12–13, 28–32. Mormon population counts and estimates prior to 1860 were highly exaggerated.

39. Ibid., 12–13.

Judge Brocchus, the last non-Mormon appointee to arrive, hardly proved a peacemaking influence. As an agent for the Washington National Monument Society, he received Young's approval to address the people of the territory "when assembled in the greatest number." Brocchus found himself in the bowery standing before a congregation of at least three thousand. He spoke for two hours and conveyed the society's desire to obtain a block of marble or stone from Utah for the obelisk, then under construction in the nation's capital, "*as an offering at the shrine of patriotism.*"[40]

But Brocchus went further. He voiced in an "unreserved, yet respectful and dignified manner" his views on the disaffection of the Mormons and defended President Taylor against the "sacrilegious remarks of Governor Young." He expressed his "love of country" and the duty he felt to defend that country against unjust aspersions, trusting that if ever he "failed to defend her, my tongue, then employed in her advocacy and praise, might cling to the roof of my mouth; and that my arm, ever ready to be raised in her defence, might fall palsied at my side."[41]

Brocchus then may have stumbled. He said that if the people of Utah could not offer a block of marble in a feeling of fellowship with the people of the United States as brethren and citizens, "they had better not offer it at all, but leave it unquarried in the bosom of its native mountain."[42] He appeared not to know that the Assembly of Deseret had possibly passed a resolution earlier that year authorizing the governor to provide the marble block for the obelisk. If so, Young oddly failed to report it in his defense to Fillmore. Whenever it passed, a block of limestone in lieu of marble was sent as a gift from Deseret in 1853 and now rests in the monument.

Brocchus said that when he finished, Young denounced him and the government "in the most brutal and unmeasured terms." The effect was truly fearful: it appeared as if "the people (I mean a large portion of them) were ready to spring on me like hyenas and destroy me." Young exploded in response: "some persons might get their hair pulled or *their throats cut.*" He was "boisterous, passionate, infuriated in the extreme," his victim charged. If the governor had pointed his finger at him, he

40. Ibid., 5–7.
41. Ibid.
42. Ibid.

went on, "I would *in an instant* have been a dead man." Brocchus hoped to get away safely and expected Brandebury, Harris, and Day to go with him, "*to return here no more*," which they did. "I hope I shall get off safely," he reported on 20 September 1851. "God only knows."[43]

According to Sarah Harris, her husband told Young that he was leaving the territory, "taking the money with him—and that he should if need be defend it with his life." The secretary returned the gold to Treasury officials at St. Louis and went on to Washington, where he and the two justices informed President Fillmore about conditions in Utah in a report afterward published and since often ignored. Agent Day separately told the Office of Indian Affairs that he left with Harris and the judges over the unjustifiable conduct of Mormon leaders and "their seditious and violent expressions with regard to the United States."[44] The four were the first of a dozen or so federal officials who would take off in frustration or fright over the next six years.

No novices in the field of public controversy, Mormon leaders counterattacked the so-called "runaways." The effectiveness with which they parried the federal officer's charges may be the most revealing aspect of the incident. Jedediah M. Grant, a man of daunting rhetorical skills, headed east to consult with Thomas Kane and issue a stinging series of public letters rebutting the three. While the mayor ridiculed them and accused them of dishonesty, immorality, and worse, a reasonable Brigham Young wrote the president that upon learning "to my very great regret" of their intention to leave, he had called on them himself to find out why, "and if possible induce them to remain." He explained his actions and claimed "that no people exists who are more friendly to the government of the United States, than the people of this Territory."[45]

---

43. Ibid.

44. Day to Luke Lea, 2 June 1852, in Buchanan, *Utah Expedition*, 149–50.

45. Young to Fillmore, ibid., 28–32. Kane may have ghostwritten the letters, but there is no evidence that he did so. He had them published as a pamphlet in 1852, refuting the "absurd charges against the Mormon[s]." Historian David J. Whittaker called Kane "Brigham Young's closest non-Mormon friend and confidant," but this did not prevent Young from denying the practice of polygamy to his friend long after it was an open secret. Kane learned the truth from Jedediah M. Grant in December 1851; he likened the news to discovering a wife's infidelity, but the deception did not lessen his lifelong support for Young and his religion. See Whittaker, *Register to the Kane Collection*, 1:17, 351, 427.

As usually happened in public fights between the Mormons and their neighbors of whatever station, it was impossible for an impartial observer to figure out where the fault lay. Opposing accounts were highly convincing and mutually exclusive. Most of the time, an onlooker could conclude only that one side had engaged in orchestrated falsehood. But in the end both sides suffered, one with a damaged reputation, the other with a loss of credibility that would be felt when public confidence was needed.

The nasty quarrel with the runaway officials verified Kane's warning that a territorial form of government would subject the Mormons to direct rule by Washington. "Brigham Young should be your governor," he had said. "You do not want two governments."[46] Young was now governor, but two forms of rule were exactly what the Mormons had, a facade of republican institutions and a theocracy that governed behind the curtain. To keep control until the Kingdom was able to stand on its own as a state within the American Union or as a sovereign nation, Utah legislators passed laws to protect divine governance. Many would directly lead to a long confrontation with the American republic.

Especially divisive was an 1854 enactment that prohibited any law not approved by the territorial legislature or the governor from being "read, argued, cited, or adopted" in any court. It also specified that "no report, decision, or doings of any court" could be "read, argued, cited, or adopted as precedent in any other trial."[47] Cut down at a stroke were two pillars of the American judicial structure—legal precedence and common law. But in a society where perfect justice was divinely revealed, one did not place one's trust in manmade law.

As further evidence of this, Mormon legislators turned the intent of Congress on its head when it came to the territory's judicial system. Under the organic act, Congress established three district courts ruled by judges appointed by the president who formed the supreme court. The law also provided probate courts to settle estates. To get around it, the Utah legislature created probate courts in each county and vested them with original civil and criminal jurisdiction, powers never intended by Congress. The inventive 1852 law emptied district benches of standing, left the federal judges with no cases to hear, and touched off a continuing

---

46. Morgan, *State of Deseret*, 69.
47. *Acts, Resolutions and Memorials*, 32.

struggle over court jurisdiction. Not even the 1857 Utah War, which it helped to incite, would settle the fight before Congress restored its original intent in 1874.

Equally essential to theocratic rule was an election law that produced unanimous results. Section 5 of the territorial election law enacted in 1853 specified that each voter would hand his ballot "neatly folded" to the judge of elections, "who shall number and deposit it in the ballot box; the clerk shall then write the name of the elector, and opposite it the number of his vote."[48] Marked ballots protected revealed truth from human selfishness or folly. But they also led to "bitter hatred and unrelenting hostility," as predicted by the *Quincy Whig* editor, based on prior experience in Missouri and Illinois.[49]

Meanwhile, as Kane had foreseen, the first federal surveyor, who came to do exactly what Mormon leaders feared, soon learned that the land policies of the American republic and God's Kingdom were incompatible. David H. Burr, one of the nation's best-known and most respected cartographers, had produced charts for the U.S. Post Office, mapped many of the nation's states and counties, and drawn the first map of western America that incorporated the discoveries of Jedediah Smith. When the U.S. House of Representatives named an official geographer to map the growing nation, it selected him for the job.

However noted he was nationally, Burr would get no respect in Mormon country. He came in July 1855 with his son David A. to find the only place in the country where settlers on public land did not want a survey to enable them to acquire a preemption right to own their land at a minimum price without being exploited by crooks or speculators.[50] Instead, the fifty-two-year-old mapmaker discovered that steps had already been taken to frustrate the purpose that President Franklin Pierce had handed him under his appointment in 1854 as surveyor general of Utah Territory.

For one thing, lawmakers of the provisional State of Deseret and Utah Territory had already created the post of surveyor general and vested it with the authority to certify all land surveys in the territory. Moreover,

48. Ibid., 89.

49. *Quincy Whig*, 22 January 1842, in Hallwas and Launius, *Cultures in Conflict*, 83–84.

50. Another son, Frederick H. Burr, also an engineer, served in 1853 with the Stevens Expedition to survey a northern transcontinental railroad route. He stayed in Bitterroot Valley, where he had contacts with Mormon Indian missionaries at Fort Limhi.

they had ruled that only certificates issued by him or by a county surveyor under his authority could be "considered title of possession to the land." Control over property within a municipality was exercised by another law, which required county surveyors to issue as a title of possession a certificate countersigned by "one or more of the Selectmen."[51] One resident said that any unwanted person would find it impossible to satisfy these conditions and dangerous to try.

Another method of keeping outsiders outside took advantage of a provision in the 1841 law that exempted from entry any land within incorporated towns. Utah lawmakers drew town boundaries large enough to enclose all of the arable land for miles around. The city limits of Fillmore, the first territorial capital, enclosed a whole township, thirty-six square miles, or nearly one square mile for each of the town's original colonizers. Other laws gave control of creeks and timber in the canyons—critical resources—to trusted leaders, usually Council of Fifty members: anyone who wanted to cut firewood for the winter had to get their permission. Young received City Creek Canyon with its nearby timber and water resources.

The new federal surveyor general found that settlement patterns in Utah were unlike any he had seen elsewhere. Moreover, land measurements made before Burr arrived failed to square with the system adopted by Congress in 1785 or to complement the laws he had come to implement. They appeared designed instead to keep outsiders from gaining a foothold in the exclusive settlements of Zion.

Elsewhere in the nation, settlers made their homes on the land they farmed, which led to a widely dispersed population. Inhabitants had to travel some distance to visit neighbors and venture to town. Small towns to serve scattered farm families suited such conditions. To meet them, Congress in 1844 excluded from preemption more than enough land for the usual small town, 320 acres, or a half-section.[52] But exclusions that met the needs of landowners elsewhere did not square with Mormon settlement patterns. In Zion, worker bees were concentrated in the hive, or city, and went forth to harvest plots on the outskirts.

---

51. *Acts, Resolutions and Memorials*, 77–78, 81–82.

52. See "An Act for the relief of the citizens of towns upon the lands of the United States, under certain circumstances," in *Public Statutes at Large of the United States of America*, 28th Cong., 1st sess., 1844, chap. 17, 657.

Not long after he arrived, Burr reported that "the corporate limits of Salt Lake City extend several miles each way, but there are very few dwellings outside of the lines" on an enclosed map. It would be seen, he told the U.S. Land Office, that the 1844 law's provision of a half-section of 320 acres for a town would not cover the Mormon city because it "occupies more than three full sections," or roughly 2,000 acres, about six times the allowed amount. If the government desired to extend the right of preemption to holders of lots within the city, he said, "some special legislation will be necessary."[53]

Intentionally or not, Young had further added to Burr's worries by reinstituting the law of consecration in 1854. Given by revelation to Joseph Smith, it instructed church members to consecrate their property to the church's trustee-in-trust, now Young himself, "by a deed which cannot be broken." Under the law, someone who sinned and refused to repent would be "cast out of the church, and shall not receive again that which he has consecrated."[54] Burr did not know how many had obeyed, but he correctly figured that "nearly all of them will."[55] To make sure they did, Young reminded them who owned the place: "How long have we got to live before we find out . . . all belongs to the Father in heaven," he said, "that these mountains are his; the valleys, the timber and the soil."[56]

Most of his followers were no more eager to consecrate their property than their former counterparts in Missouri had been, but they would think twice before they ignored the law or took off to the California gold fields without permission. Territorial lawmakers in 1855 enacted a measure "for the management of certain property" that handed probate judges the authority to seize all property "left by any deceased or abscondent person" and give it to the fund for emigration.[57]

But oddities that Burr had never before encountered in a long and distinguished career were hardly worth mentioning compared with the perils his survey crews faced in the field. One of his deputies "was assaulted and severely beaten by three men under the direction of one

53. Burr to G. C. Whiting, 30 September 1855, in Buchanan, *Utah Expedition*, 123.
54. Smith, *History of the Church*, 1:148–54.
55. Burr to Whiting, 30 September 1855, in Buchanan, *Utah Expedition*, 123.
56. Young, "Discourse," in *Journal of Discourses*, 2:298–308.
57. *Acts, Resolutions and Memorials*, 50.

Hickman," he reported in August 1856.[58] He said authorities had refused to punish the offenders and justified what they had done on the ground that the victim had talked against their religion. "We, 'the Gentiles,' all feel that we cannot rely upon the laws for protection, and are only permitted to live here at the pleasure of the rulers," he said. Burr enclosed a letter from deputy surveyor C. L. Craig, "which will give you some idea of the feeling of this people toward us."[59]

As he worked in Juab Valley, Craig said, local Mormons tried to prejudice the Indians not only against Americans, "as they term us who are not Mormons, but also against the surveyors." Several chiefs had told the surveyor's interpreter that "we were measuring out the land in order to take possession of it, and would drive away the Mormons and kill the Indians," he went on.[60]

Since his arrival, Burr reported, he had been regarded "as an alien, an enemy, and an intruder upon their rights." The *Deseret News* had urged its readers to sue the surveyors for trespassing upon *their* lands, he said, but there had been no hostility toward him personally until Mormon officials intercepted a letter he had sent to the U.S. Land Office, charging Young with "extensive depredations upon the public lands." Three of them confronted the surveyor and bluntly informed him that he would "not be permitted to write such letters, declaring that all my letters would be examined," Burr charged. Unfavorable reports would never leave the territory, they told him, and warned "that the country, and all that appertained to it, belongs to them; that their exertions had made it what it was; that they had earned it, and were determined to keep it, and would permit no interference with their rights," Burr continued. From that day on, he said, "continued attempts were made to excite the populace against me."[61]

Young questioned Burr's motives and the permanence of his work. "Genl Burr has been watching for evil ever since he has been here," he

---

58. He no doubt was the noted Mormon gunman and enforcer William A. Hickman, who claimed that he acted on orders of Brigham Young. See Hickman and Beadle, *Brigham's Destroying Angel.*

59. Burr to Thomas A. Hendricks, 30 August 1856, in Buchanan, *Utah Expedition,* 115–16.

60. C. L. Craig to Burr, 1 August 1856, ibid., 116–17.

61. Burr to Hendrix, 11 June 1857, ibid., 120, 121.

told Bernhisel. In Young's opinion, the surveying was "a great humbug." "They stick down little stakes the wind could almost blow over, neither plant charcoal, nor raise mounts," he said. "Not a vestige of all they do will be left to mark where they have been in five years."[62] The governor's words proved prophetic.

Burr fled for his life in 1857 during events that led President Buchanan to send a military expedition to assert federal control in the rebellious territory. After the Utah War, he claimed that he had surveyed nearly two million acres before June of that year, but his successor, Samuel Stambaugh, reported in 1859 that there was no evidence the surveys had been conducted. Either the bur under Young's saddle had charged the government for work he had never performed, as Mormon leaders claimed, or someone had pulled up the stakes his surveyors had planted. A hint as to which it was came in 1861, when the General Land Office suspended further surveys because there was no demand for land in Utah.

62. Young to Bernhisel, 4 November 1856, BYC; and Larson, "Land Contest in Early Utah," 309–25.

CHAPTER 3

The Remnant of Jacob

The people do not realize what they have done by driving us into
the midst of the Lamanites. They prevented Joseph from associating
with the Indians, but they, through their ignorance, thought we
were going to Vancouver's Island, or on the borders of the Pacific,
but lo, they have driven us into the midst of the Lamanites.

—Brigham Young, 13 September 1857

Miss Clara E. Downes met a mail rider near South Pass in 1860 who told her that western Indians "say they have two fathers the president & Brigham Young. One lies where the sun rises & the other where the sun sets."[1] Years of experience had taught the tribes that while one of their two fathers was a distant abstraction, the second lived in their very midst. So when President Millard Fillmore in 1850 named Brigham Young governor and superintendent of Indian affairs in the expansive new territory, he placed a lion in the federal corral, an irony that Young himself appreciated. His intent to forge alliances between his followers and their Native cousins, the "remnant of Jacob" known as Lamanites, had little relation to the chief objective of the U.S. Office of Indian Affairs—keeping peace on the frontier. Instead it seemed more in keeping with the testimony of dissenters following the 1838 Mormon War in Missouri, who said the Mormons had rejoiced that "the time had arrived when all the wicked should be destroyed from the face of the earth, and that the Indians would be the principal means by which this object should be accomplished."[2]

1. Downes, "Journal across the Plains," 23 June 1860, Bancroft Library.
2. John Sapp and Nathan Marsh testimony, in LeSueur, *The 1838 Mormon War*, 71.

This allegation could be traced to Old Testament prophecies, repeated in the religion's essential scripture, the Book of Mormon, which state that a remnant of Jacob will "go forth among them; and ye shall be in the midst of them who shall be many; and ye shall be among them as a lion among the beasts of the forest, and as a young lion among the flocks of sheep, who, if he goeth through both treadeth down and teareth in pieces, and none can deliver."[3] These prophecies are no longer taken seriously. But in those days, people who lived on the western frontier and were sometimes in conflict with Indians took such beliefs *very* seriously.

Nor were such fears entirely unjustified. The patriarch of Zion's Cedar Stake in southern Utah had promised the commander of Mormon troops who committed the massacre at Mountain Meadows in 1857, the worst atrocity in the history of the Oregon-California Trail, that he would lead his people and the Lamanites "in the redemption of Zion and the avenging of the blood of the prophets upon them that dwell on the earth."[4] Before John Borrowman marched off with the Mormon Battalion in 1846, Patriarch John Smith promised that "when the remnants of Jacob go through among the Gentiles like a lion among the beasts of the forest, as the prophets have spoken, thou shalt be in their midst and shall be a captain of hundreds."[5]

From the outset, Young's position as *ex officio* head of Utah Indian affairs was at cross-purposes with the federal Office of Indian Affairs. It also put the approximately twenty thousand Utah natives at a severe disadvantage, for the new superintendent had little reason to look out for their interests. "Brigham Young never spent a dollar on the Indians in Utah, while he was Indian Agent," said John D. Lee, one of the men Young appointed as an agent to the Southern Paiutes. "The only money he ever spent on the Indians was when we were at war with them. Then they cost us some money, but not much."[6] Lee's charge was exaggerated, but as another agent reported, the fact that Young used "his office as superintendent and the money of the government to promote the interest of his

3. Book of Mormon, 3 Ne. 20:15, 16. Compare with Mic. 5:8.
4. Dame, Patriarchal Blessing, 1854, BYU Library.
5. Borrowman, Patriarchal Blessing, USHS.
6. Lee, *Mormonism Unveiled*, 257.

church" is undeniable.[7] This inherent conflict of interest was reflected in the travail of the earliest U.S. Indian agents in Utah.[8]

Subagent Henry R. Day arrived in Salt Lake with the first appointed territorial officials in 1851 and left with three of them later that year. He reported to his superior that he found it impossible to do his duties in the face of "the open hostility manifested publicly and privately by the governor and the Mormon community to the government of the United States and its officers." Further, the agent did not think "that any agent controlled by Governor Young can fully effect the objects of the government in their relations with the Indians."[9]

Also appointed in 1851, agent Jacob Holeman agreed that Utah leaders had "no sympathy or respect for our government or its institutions," and were "frequently heard cursing and abusing, not only the government, but all who are American citizens." Even so, he stuck to his post.[10] He soldiered on, despite being ignored by Young, as well as federal bureaucrats who had no idea what he was up against and would not have known what to do if they had. For three years, the agent sounded alarms over conditions in Utah. His superiors failed to see them for what they were—omens of pending conflict.

Holeman warned Washington that the Mormons would make every effort to prevent the United States from "peaceably extending her laws over the Territory." Consistent with this view, he reported that they drilled the militia weekly. The commanding officer had been overheard to say that they had drilled regularly in Nauvoo "when they had but one State to oppose them, but now they have the whole United States, they should be properly drilled and equipped." Others said they did not fear the United States. If they needed help, the agent said, "they can easily get it from England."[11]

Even more alarming was Holeman's report that white men were taking part in Indian attacks on emigrant trains. On 2 May 1852, he said

7. Jacob Holeman to Luke Lea, 29 March 1852, in Buchanan, *Utah Expedition*, 140.

8. Young has his defenders for his service as Utah's Indian superintendent, including Dale L. Morgan. See Morgan's essay "The Administration of Indian Affairs in Utah, 1851–1853," in his *Shoshonean Peoples*, 57–83.

9. Henry R. Day to Lea, 9 January 1852, in Buchanan, *Utah Expedition*, 132–33.

10. Holeman to Lea, 28 December 1851, ibid., 133–36.

11. Holeman to Lea, 29 March 1852, ibid., 139–44.

that Thomas S. Williams, a Mormon, had told him about a friend who belonged to a band of white men and Indians operating near Carson Valley whose object was "to plunder and rob the emigrants." According to this report, the friend warned Williams to "paint the horns of his cattle," as the Indians did not wish to molest the "brethren." "We ought to have troops here," the agent said in frustration. "These whites, associated with the Indians, are committing so many depredations on this route that something ought to be done."[12] To prevent interception, he had his report mailed at Fort Bridger.

By 1853, the agent was "at a loss to know how to act." He had so frequently asked for direction without a reply that he feared his letters had not reached Washington. Superintendent Young and Mormon sub-agent Stephen Rose concealed their movements, Holeman complained, and never consulted with him or paid any attention to his opinions. If things did not change, he did not feel that he could be of any real service to the Department of Indian Affairs.[13] "How I should like to see the reins of the general government, and an obedience and respect for the laws of the United States strictly observed," he wrote. "Sooner or later, depend upon it, it will have to be done."[14] Until then, his reports provide a case study of the many points of conflict between theocratic and republican forms of government.

Not one to follow federal direction, Young publicly expressed his own Indian policy in the seemingly sensible dictum that it was cheaper to feed them than to fight them. In practice, however, his policy appeared to define the extremes of a course that offered no middle ground. White newcomers gave cooperative Lamanites food from their own scarce supply, but if their Native cousins chose to defend their land and their way of life rather than be remade into obedient farmers, they were shot dead, often execution style.

The initial thrust of Mormon expansion led south of Salt Lake Valley along the line of what is today I-15 to the closest and most warlike

---

12. Holeman to Lea, 2 May 1852, ibid., 150–51. Holeman gave only the Mormon's last name, but historians agree that it must have been Thomas S. Williams. The "friend" was likely Return Jackson Redden.

13. Holeman to Lea, 5 March 1853, ibid., 160.

14. Holeman to Lea, 12 May [1853], ibid., 163–65. The year is mistakenly given as 1857 in the government document.

of Zion's Native neighbors, for whom the territory was named: the
Utahs, commonly called Utes. Their wider range extended into present-
day eastern Utah and southwestern Colorado as far south as the Navajo
country, but a large segment, called the Wasatch or Timpanogos Utes,
lived in the region bordering their primary food source, Utah Lake. This
freshwater body, near Provo, Utah, whose waters flow north via the Jordan River into Great Salt Lake, was then one of the West's richest fisher-
ies, yielding cutthroat trout, whitefish, and chubs.[15]

Between the lake and a sudden Wasatch Mountain uplift was Utah
Valley, home of scattered bands of the tribe. Among the most warlike
of these was a nomadic collection of marauders known as the Cheverets
or Cheveriches, under Walkara, better known as Walker. From their
mountain fastness, they raided as far as southern California ranches
for horses and preyed on their weaker desert relatives for children to
exchange with Mexican traders for animals. This mixed band of freebooters "roam through the whole of the other nations, and are confined
to no particular part of the Territory," said Indian agent Henry R.
Day.[16] Other groups fished and hunted in the mountains and from
time to time raided the territory of their old enemies the Shoshones on
the north.

The Utes were one of the West's proudest and most powerful peoples, but they had a mixed reputation among those who knew them
well. The renowned James Bridger told Young's 1847 Mormon pioneer
party that the "Utah tribe of Indians are a bad people; if they catch a
man alone they are sure to rob and abuse him, if they don't kill him."[17]
But a former U.S. agent who had lived among the tribe near Spanish
Fork in Utah Valley said, "there is not a braver tribe to be found among
the aborigines of America than the Utahs, none warmer in their attach-
ments, less relenting in their hatred, or less capable of treachery. So
complex is their nature that to trust them it is necessary to understand
them."[18] On the whole, the haughty and warlike Utes appeared unlikely

15. For the vital importance of Utah Lake to its Native population, see Jared Farmer's
prize-winning *On Zion's Mount*.

16. Day to Lea, 2 January 1852, in Buchanan, *Utah Expedition*, 130–32.

17. James Bridger, Journal History, 28 June 1847, LDS Archives.

18. Hurt to James H. Simpson, 2 May 1860, in Simpson, *Report of Explorations*, 461.

to convert or to cooperate with the Mormons enough to qualify for the feeding proviso of Governor Young's policy, which left as the only alternative what Holeman described as "a most brutal butchery of the Indians."[19]

The first fight with the Utes occurred in 1849, even before Mormon settlement had pushed southward into Utah Valley. During the season of hunger, a party of Indians slipped into southern Salt Lake Valley and stole cattle from Mormon herds along Willow Creek. A mounted company promptly followed them into Utah Valley, learning from other Natives where the culprits had holed up. At the mouth of a steep canyon, near present-day Pleasant Grove, the militia party cornered the Indians and shot the males dead on the spot. The women and children went to Mormon families for rehabilitation.

Ute Indian memories are long, and this episode was still fresh in their minds when the first Mormon company of thirty men entered Utah Valley to fish, farm, and teach the remnant of Israel about their Hebrew ancestors. Several miles before they reached the Provo River, Angatewats, a young Utah warrior, blocked their path with his horse and would not let them pass. Only after an extended parley and Mormon vows by uplifted hand that the newcomers "would not drive the Indians away, or take from them any of their rights," did the warrior allow them to go on.[20]

The arrivals built a fort on the Provo River within the limits of present-day Provo City. Warily the Natives watched as others rolled in, men, women, and children, to build a growing settlement. They broke ground for crops, harvested fish with nets rather than by hand, and killed deer in the nearby mountains.

The nervous truce was broken in January 1850, only a year after the first intruders had appeared, when three young Mormons quarreled with an Indian known as "Old Bishop." Mormon records say the men left Fort Utah "professedly to hunt cattle." Old Bishop was allegedly wearing a shirt stolen from one of them, and the whites shot the Ute through the head when he resisted their attempt to reclaim it. Thomas Orr, Jr., however, told a different story. The settlers, he recalled, made a treaty with the Utes, and "they agreed not to molest our cattle if we agreed not to

19. Holeman to Lea, 29 March 1852, in Buchanan, *Utah Expedition*, 139.
20. Morgan et al., *Provo*, 45.

kill the wild game which they depended on for a living." According to Orr, the men shot Old Bishop when he caught them poaching a deer.[21]

When the Natives discovered Old Bishop's body, peace with the Utahs was over. Angry Utes shot arrows into livestock, threatened settlers who ventured very far from their stockade, and stole horses and anything not tied down. Early in 1850, the frightened settlers appealed to Brigham Young to punish the saucy Utes and make them behave. The pendulum suddenly swung from feed to fight. On 31 January, Nauvoo Legion general Daniel H. Wells sent a company of one hundred picked men from the north; with the Utah Valley militia, they were told to march against the troublesome Natives, "exterminating such, as do not separate themselves from their hostile clans, and sue for peace."[22]

In a two-day pitched fight only recently given a name—the Battle of Provo River—both sides suffered light casualties, one Mormon and three to six Utes, but the Indians' body count rose sharply after they fled their crude fortification.[23] Legion forces killed Big Elk and an unknown number of his band between the stream and the mouth of Rock Creek Canyon and followed others to camps along Spanish Fork, where eleven men surrendered with their families but were dispatched "in the most summary manner," according to Wells. The long-accepted story was that the prisoners were killed while trying to escape across the frozen southern end of Utah Lake, but in fact they were simply executed. In all, as many as forty warriors died.[24]

Notably missing from these fights was the powerful Walkara, who preferred to mount his winter raids in the warmer climates of southern California or New Mexico. He would be on hand in spring 1853, however, when the next conflict with the beleaguered and resentful Utes broke out. It would prove fatal for him, but he would live forever in the name the victors gave it: the Walker War.

21. Journal History, 31 January 1850, LDS Archives; and Taylor, *Life History of Thomas Orr, Jr.*, 17.

22. Wells, Orders to George D. Grant, 31 January 1850, UTMR.

23. For the most recent account and the first use of this name for the battle, see Carter, *Founding Fort Utah*, 114–15, 163–95.

24. Wells, Report to Young, 13–14 February 1850, UTMR; and Carter, *Founding Fort Utah*, 178, 188, 206–10.

The dangerously unpredictable chief raged when Brigham Young put a stop to the trade in Indian children between the Utes and slave traders from New Mexico. A show of force, combined with conciliation, cooled his anger at the loss of loot and kept the Utes' resentment over growing settlements on Indian land from getting out of hand. On 25 July, Young sent Walkara a token of his friendship. The note, written in the almost illegible hand of General Wells, included a curious suggestion: "If you are afraid of the tobacco which I send you, you can let some of your prisoners try it first and then you will know that it is good."[25]

At the request of Holeman, a veteran Mexican trader named M. S. Martenas interviewed Walkara and other Ute leaders and reported his findings to Superintendent Young in July. Walkara said he had always been opposed to whites' settling on Indian lands, "particularly that portion which he claims; and on which his band resides and on which they have resided since his childhood, and his parents before him." The Mormons had been friendly with the Utes at first, "and promised them many comforts, and lasting friendship—that they continued friendly for a short time, until they became strong in numbers, then their conduct and treatment towards the Indians changed." They abused the Utes, who were "sometimes . . . treated with much severity—they have been driven by this population from place to place—settlements have been made on all their hunting grounds in the valleys, and the graves of their fathers have been torn up by the whites." He had always wished to be friendly, Walkara said, but now "he could not live in peace with the whites," for "the Indians were forced to leave their homes, or submit to the constant abuse of the whites." The settlers "seemed never to be satisfied—the Indians had moved time after time, and yet they could have no peace." As a result, he said "that his heart was sick—that his heart felt very bad."[26]

Walkara asked Martenas "to communicate the situation of the Indians in this neighborhood to the Great Father, and ask his protection and friendship," but if "his great father did not do something to relieve them, he could not tell what they would do." Ute leaders from Uinta Valley

25. Young to Capt Wacher [Ute chief Walkara], 25 July 1853, UTMR. For evidence that the militia used poison against Indians, see McBride, Report, UTMR.
26. M. S. Martenas, "Statement," 6 July 1853, BYC.

summarized the situation even more eloquently: "they say they cannot live with the whites, for they cannot live in peace—the whites want every thing, and will give the Indians nothing."[27]

Events spun out of control when one of the three young men who had killed Old Bishop now touched off a second Indian war. James Ivie intervened when a member of Walkara's band began beating his wife over a trade she had made with the settler's spouse, near Springville in Utah Valley. When they both turned on him, Ivie disarmed the man and broke his skull with the barrel of his own gun. Efforts to save the injured Native failed, and the shaky peace ended. As Howard Keele stood guard at the hollow square of cabins at Fort Payson, two apparently peaceful Natives rode by and shot him dead at point-blank range. To the Utes, it was a life for a life. To white settlers, it was treachery that called for swift punishment.

What happened over the next three months was a series of atrocities by both sides. At Manti and Nephi, friendly Natives were invited into the settlements, and the males were shot down in the streets. Ute warriors raided Mormon herds; murdered four men at Uinta Springs, today's Fountain Green, who were delivering a load of wheat to Great Salt Lake; ambushed four others hauling wood at Parley's Park, now Park City; and killed careless settlers on roads and in canyons.

Young's response was a strategy called "forting up," concentrating isolated farms and small settlements inside adobe-walled strongholds. "Active preparations are now in operation to wall in the cities and all the considerable settlements throughout the Territory," Mormon leaders announced. Even Great Salt Lake City was to be fortified. "Next Week, we commence making a substantial ditch & wall around the whole city, the wall to be 12 feet high with Gates & Bastions; this will be something of a Job, but we deem it one of the best means we can now make for our temporal salvation," Young reported in August 1853. "It was usual for our people to protect themselves by building what we called a fort—a place the people could get into in the event of a raid," Daniel H. Wells explained years later.[28] The policy did little to suppress the violence of the war against the Utes, and it made independent settlers who

27. Ibid.
28. Bagley, "A Great Wall," B1.

were forced to abandon farms and towns resentful and Indian leaders suspicious.

Into this far-flung guerrilla war came another federal surveyor. His tragic story reveals the benefits available to Lamanites who avoided the iron fist of Young's Indian policy and chose the open hand, aligning themselves with their white cousins of Israel. John W. Gunnison served as a lieutenant on the Stansbury Expedition, and later published a sympathetic but revealing book about the Mormons. In October 1853 he returned as a captain in command of his own expedition. Like Stansbury, he did not come to survey the land into townships in preparation for public sale, but instead was conducting a survey for a proposed transcontinental railroad. Unlike the prudent Stansbury, Gunnison did not inform Young of his purpose beforehand. Nor did he follow the main route into Great Salt Lake from Fort Bridger. He came instead over the Spanish Trail well to the south. At daybreak on 26 October, the forty-year-old officer and seven of his command were surprised and killed on a bend of the Sevier River.

What made the atrocity stand out from others was that the Natives who killed the surveyors were Pahvants who had played no part in the Walker War. They belonged to a distinctive band of about five hundred that lived on Corn Creek, near present-day Fillmore. Shortly after the Mormons arrived in central Utah, they had replaced the Pahvants' belligerent leader, Chuick, with Kanosh, the "white man's friend," who believed it was pointless to resist white power. He even had his new followers baptized into the Mormon faith. Acknowledging Kanosh as a valued ally, Young rewarded him with wives and property.[29] John D. Lee invited the Pahvant leader to speak to the Southern Paiutes and said he had done "much good among the Lamanites in this country, and behaved himself like a gentleman."[30] Emigrants camping at Corn Creek on the southern route to California had killed a Pahvant war chief, and the attack on Gunnison was apparently a simple case of Indian vengeance that had nothing to do with Ute grievances.

Reaction to the massacre was wide and strong. Gunnison was publicly admired and had been engaged in a project of national interest. Stories of

29. Paul Padilla, "Kanosh," in Powell, *Utah History Encyclopedia*, 297, 298.
30. "Harmony—Kanosh's Visit to the Piedes," *Desert News*, 16 July 1856, 148.

Mormon collusion with the tribes were well known and widely believed. Charges that the Mormons were behind his murder were leveled at the time and can still be heard: Anson Call of Fillmore was less than forthright with Gunnison about the nature of the threat from the Pahvants, but there is no proof that Mormons were involved in the attack. At the same time, the aftermath provides convincing indications of an orchestrated scheme to subvert justice and frustrate any punishment of Lamanite allies of God's Kingdom.

An unhappy victim of the scheme was Major Edward J. Steptoe, who was ordered to investigate the massacre and, as a lieutenant who accompanied him wrote, whose "principal object" was "to avenge the death of Captain Gunnison [and] punish any guilty Indians."[31] Steptoe was getting ready to march from Fort Leavenworth to deliver horses, mules, and replacements to the West Coast when he received orders to stop in Utah with his troops, spend the winter there, and dispense justice to the Indians who had murdered his West Point classmate the previous year. On arriving in 1854, he did not have to look very far for them. For nine months after the massacre, they and their band had lived on Corn Creek under the nose of Utah's governor and Indian affairs superintendent on the trail to California. Had it not been for Steptoe, they would have continued to do so with impunity. For the Indians, the implication was that it was all right to kill American soldiers, but not Mormons.

The winter stay in Salt Lake City was turbulent for Steptoe and his men. The locals were suspicious of the troops and vice versa. Suspicion quickly escalated into real conflict, especially over Mormon women. One of Steptoe's officers notoriously pursued a daughter-in-law of Brigham Young, and additional conflicts eventually led to brawling between the troops and Mormon youths. Then in February 1855, Steptoe received a letter from President Franklin Pierce that caused a "good deal of excitement throughout the City."[32] Pending his acceptance, the president had named the Mexican War hero as Utah's governor, to replace Young, whose term had expired. If he was not replaced by presidential appointment, the territorial organic act allowed him to remain in office. In only four years, however, he had made himself unacceptable to the president

---

31. LaRhett L. Livingston to James G. Livingston, 16 September 1854, Beinecke Library.
32. Kenney, *Wilford Woodruff's Journal*, 4:304.

and the U.S. Senate. Not only had Pierce, a stiff Mexican War general and fellow Democrat, ignored Kane family influence, he had now named a U.S. Army officer to take charge of a territory that had grown steadily more defiant toward the United States since Congress created it in 1850.[33]

The four mountaineers who delivered this stunning message to Utah also escorted a new U.S. Indian agent who would play a minor part in the Gunnison affair, but a major role in making clear the difference between a republic and a theocracy. Garland Hurt, a thirty-five-year-old former Kentucky legislator and self-taught physician, came at just the right time to mount an audacious challenge to win the loyalty of the suffering Ute tribe for the United States. In so doing, he provided convincing evidence to support the resolution of a future president to impose federal control over the territory.

Hurt came too late to help Walkara, who had died unexpectedly following a visit from Mormon Indian missionary David Lewis. Rumor, accepted by many as fact, was that the chief had been poisoned on order of Brigham Young.[34] Dimick Huntington, Young's emissary to the tribes, found that "Wahker's Death has been a good thing, for I tell them they must harken to Brighams words or they will go like Walker Did for he would not hear Brigham when he talked."[35]

Meanwhile, respectful of civil authority, Steptoe took Governor Young's advice to allow Young's interpreter, George Bean, to negotiate with Kanosh for the surrender of Gunnison's killers. After lengthy talks and great delay, the Pahvant chief reluctantly turned over six Natives he said were the ones who had done it. They included two blind old men, one woman, and three males for whom Kanosh apparently had no use. As others snickered, Steptoe knew that the joke was on him.

The trial of the six scapegoats in March 1855 at Nephi, some eighty miles south of Great Salt Lake, was a staged comedy. When U.S. attorney Joseph Hollman demanded indictments, the grand jurors, under local bishop Jacob Bigler, threw out the charges against three Natives and drew

33. Steptoe held the regular rank of major but won brevet promotion to lieutenant colonel for "gallant and meritorious conduct" in the Battle of Chapultepec.

34. Chandless, *Visit to Salt Lake*, 184, iii; Burton, *City of the Saints*, 650; Charles Wandell, writing as "Argus," "Open Letter to Brigham Young," *Daily Utah Reporter*, 12 September 1870, 2; Gottfredson, *History of Indian Depredations*, 78.

35. Huntington to George A. Smith, 1 September 1856, BYC.

up an indictment charging the prosecutor with being drunk and abusive. Kanosh denied that he had told the other three to confess, but simply "threw them away" because George Bean told him to.[36] Defense attorney Almon W. Babbitt contended that Native custom allowed the right to avenge the murder of one of the tribe's members "by taking life" and called on his fellow Mormon jurymen to bring a verdict of manslaughter.

Utah Chief Justice John F. Kinney instructed the jurors that a manslaughter verdict would be unlawful: they could only find the three Pahvants guilty of murder or acquit them. However, "to the astonishment of the Court," the jury pronounced the trio guilty of manslaughter, an offense that called for them to spend three years in Utah's new adobe prison. "The verdict is a strange one; in violation of law and the instruction of the Court," Kinney told the U.S. attorney general, "and can only be accounted for upon the ground that the authority of the Priesthood is paramount to the law of the land." But even this penalty was deliberately shortened. As soon as Steptoe had gone, someone forgot to lock the prison door, and the three inmates, who had allegedly killed one of the U.S. Army's most promising officers, walked out and went back home to Corn Creek.[37]

Well before the curtain came down, Major Steptoe knew that he had played the fool in a production designed to protect Kanosh's band rather than investigate the crime and punish those who committed it. He described the duty as "one of excessive embarrassment and annoyance to me." The officer called the jury's performance "lamentable" and gave his opinion that Young had told the tribe that any member it surrendered for trial "would escape any serious penalty." In an obvious reference to Young, Steptoe expressed his regret that there were "citizens of our country so disregardful of their high obligations to the laws as many connected with this affair have shown themselves to be."[38]

The officer told George W. Manypenny, the commissioner of Indian Affairs, that he had had "no idea whatever" that Mormon authorities would support U.S. military operations against the Indians. Nor did he

36. Miller, "Impact of the Gunnison Massacre," 182.

37. Kinney to Caleb Cushing, 1 April 1855, USHS. Young later claimed that he had the escapees rounded up and returned to jail, saying he had sent word of their recapture just after Steptoe left. See Young, "Discourse," 15 July 1856, *Deseret News*, 16 July 1856, 146.

38. Steptoe to Samuel Cooper, 26 March and 15 April 1855, USHS.

believe that Governor Young's Indian policy was proper. Instead he recommended the advice of Garland Hurt. The Indians had "undoubtedly
learned from Dr. Hurt and myself, *for the first time*, what relation they
hold to the government," Steptoe added. He urged the commissioner
to support the course of the Indian policy that Hurt had adopted—
teaching them "to cultivate the soil"—and grudgingly gave Young's
followers deserved credit, "whatever may have been their motive," for
having "done *something* towards this end."[39]

Steptoe had no doubt about who would rule Utah, no matter who
might be appointed to replace Young. The officer left without accepting
President Pierce's gubernatorial appointment. Instead, he recommended
that a military force be stationed in Utah. Knowingly or not, two years
later, Pierce's successor would adopt the major's recommendation.[40]
Meanwhile, if the trial farce humiliated Steptoe, it also imposed a financial burden on Hurt, who had paid for the presents that motivated the
Pahvant chief to surrender the three members of his little band. After
this costly lesson, he turned his attention to the condition of the Natives
under his charge.

Bloodied by Nauvoo Legion troops, displaced from their homeland
by spreading settlements, and pushed away from Utah Lake and their
mountain fish and game food sources, the once-haughty Utah tribe had
become "exceedingly destitute . . . and turned upon the white settlers to
beg for their subsistence."[41] Fearfully they watched as newcomers used
advanced methods to catch and pickle fish in wooden barrels for shipment to feed mouths other than their own. The tribe gathered along the
Provo River and the lakeshore each spring to catch fish, "known as the
mountain trout," Mormon subagent George Armstrong told Governor
Young, by trapping or shooting them with bows and arrows. But the
chiefs now complained that "they could not catch their usual supply of
fish, in consequence of some of the citizens using sein[e]s and nets to their
disadvantage." The agent asked one of the Mormon "fishing companies"
to catch some fish for them, too, which he said it did.[42]

---

39. Steptoe to Manypenny, 5 April 1855, in Buchanan, *Utah Expedition*, 178–79.
40. Ibid.
41. Hurt to Young, March 1855, USHS.
42. Armstrong to Young, 30 June 1855, 34th Cong., 1st sess., 1855, vol. 1, no. 1, S. Ex.
Doc. 1, serial 810, 521–28.

In addition, Armstrong said, the chiefs had become resentful that they no longer had safe places for their horses to feed because so much of the land had been "improved and fenced in by the settlers." They demanded that a pasture be reserved for them, bordering on the Provo River near their fishing grounds, where they could fish and at the same time "protect themselves and animals from the Shoshonee, or Snake Indians, with whom they are almost constantly at war and in continual dread of," the agent said. "Measures should be taken in some way to appease their hunger," Armstrong warned.[43]

As he tried to help the angry Utes, Hurt also moved at first to improve relations between the theocratic territory and the federal government. Invited to address the Fourth of July observance at Great Salt Lake, he said that he had not been surprised at the "delicate relations that exist between the United States and the little colony of Utah," considering the persecution his listeners had suffered. And he stood "ready and willing," he pledged, to "consecrate his life and his feeble energies for the conciliation of your rights."[44] Hurt also attempted to achieve a cooperative relationship with Young. Soon after his Independence Day oration, he acknowledged Young's "general supervisory role over his agents" and promised his cooperation "in all your efforts to advance the interests of the Territory."[45]

While apparently working with Young as governor, Hurt at the same time took actions in opposition to Young. In an audacious scheme, he first plotted a course between the extremes of feeding and fighting. Instead he was determined to teach the suffering Utes to feed themselves and thereby win their loyalty to the United States. At the same time, he collaborated with the surveyor general's son, David A. Burr, to satisfy the requirements for making public lands in Utah eligible for entry under existing federal law—which would break the Mormon monopoly on landownership.

Hurt's scheme was based on provisions of the 1841 Preemption Law that withheld the right of entry by preemption on "lands included in any reservation, by any treaty, law or proclamation . . . or other Indian reservation on which the title has been or may be extinguished." The

43. Ibid.
44. Hurt, "Remarks," 4 July 1855, BYC.
45. Hurt to Young, 6 July 1855, ibid.

law approved several ways to create an Indian reserve.[46] Hurt's opening gambit was to propose to Governor Young the establishment of reservations, where Natives "whose lands the whites have occupied," reducing them to "a state of dependency on the white settlements," could learn to become farmers. Rather than employ outsiders to run these operations, as other federal officials had done, he gave his opinion that it would be best to hire Mormon settlers to teach the Indians. To this diplomatic suggestion he added a tactful question. He asked for Young's opinion "in regard to this enterprise as well as his advice as to the best locations." For a time even the governor was taken in, but not entirely.

Young's initial reaction to Hurt's proposal was prompt and unqualified. "I can truly say that I highly approve the suggestions therein contained," he said. He had recommended a similar approach himself as the best way to pacify the troublesome Utes, but he understood that the Indians were resistant to the change in their way of life. Now he believed that if the idea was "presented to them in its proper light, they may be induced to comply." Young knew by Hurt's performance in drafting a treaty with the Natives along the Humboldt that he was a man who could get things done.[47] But his suggestions revealed his usual mistrust of federal officials and showed that his idea of a "farm-reservation" differed in scale and purpose from what Hurt had in mind.[48]

Young thought, first, that there should be "a small reservation" in Utah, Juab, Sanpete, Millard, and Iron counties. As to specific sites in those areas, he recommended as the most promising locations the left bank of Spanish Fork in Utah County "between Palmyra and Payson"; Chicken Creek in Juab County, "quite a favorite resort of the Indians"; New Mill Creek below Manti, as the "most suitable point" in Sanpete County; Corn Creek, "already occupied by them," in Millard County; and Coal Creek below Cedar City in Iron County. "There should be a farmer at each of those points whose business should be, not to farm for the Indians," he went on, "but to learn them to farm raise grain cattle &c and to keep and preserve property."[49]

---

46. *The Public Statues at Large of the United States of America*, 5:453–58. Preemption was the preferential right of a settler on public lands to buy his claim at a modest price.

47. Young later said that he forwarded the treaty to Washington, but it never arrived.

48. Hurt to Young, 15 September 1855, Utah State Archives.

49. Ibid.

With Governor Young's seemingly enthusiastic but hardly all-out approval, Hurt launched his project with a self-confidence that perhaps lacked sufficient respect for the shrewdness of the man he was working with. On 27 November 1855, he and a party of six, including David A. Burr, left Salt Lake "to select suitable places to establish and locate Indian reservations, with a view to persuade the poor unfortunate Indians to forsake their nomadic [ways] for a civilized life."[50] What they did was hardly in keeping with Young's idea of a small farm-reservation.

Over the next three weeks, Hurt and Burr's crew of surveyors made it clear they had more in mind than locating farms where Natives could be taught to grow their own crops. At Corn Creek, some ten miles south of present-day Fillmore, they laid out a whole township, thirty-six square miles, for a reservation that offered only enough water and soil resources to farm at most a thousand acres out of the more than twenty-three thousand they provided at the site. The projected reservation for Kanosh's Pahvants was at least twenty times larger than what Brigham Young probably had in mind.

In Sanpete County, the tribal homeland of Walkara's half-brother Arapeen and his followers, they quadrupled the size of the Corn Creek spread, measuring off four townships, or 144 square miles, reaching from five miles south of present-day Manti to the mouth of the San Pitch River. Bordering the Sevier River, the reservation was big enough to encompass today's towns of Gunnison, Mayfield, Richmond, and Centerfield, as well as Arapeen's favorite hunting ground in the rugged canyon of Twelvemile Creek. Less ambitious at first was the 640-acre farm-reservation marked off on the west bank of Spanish Fork in Utah County, which became Hurt's headquarters. But even this was surveyed the following April into a "reservation" covering 12,380 acres, or more than nineteen square miles.[51]

In his year-end report, Hurt briefed the governor on his work and threw away any pretense that the sites he had surveyed were anything

50. See report by Lyman S. Wood, Indian interpreter, Journal History, 14 December 1855, LDS Archives.

51. The Spanish Fork reservation-farm reached from a point about two miles west of Spanish Fork to West Mountain and Utah Lake and encompassed today's town of Lake Shore. See Burr, "Map of a Survey," BYU Library.

less than reservations with farming instruction added. The agent told Young he planned "to stock these reservations during the ensuing season with such stock and implements . . . as may be necessary to carry on a vigorous system of agriculture." He also said, "I wish through you to have an act passed by Congress confirming these reservations as the future home of these bands." And the ambitious federal emissary to the Indians called on the governor to arrange for an appropriation of as much as $100,000 to finance his plans, plus $30,000 to pay for his commitments to tribes other than the Utes.[52]

Not only did all of this go far beyond what Young had had in mind when he approved Hurt's plan, but the head of God's Kingdom was not accustomed to being told what to do by Gentile Indian agents. This may explain why he forwarded the proposals on to Washington without any recommendations, and it took nearly four months for them to arrive. He also sent the agent on a thousand-mile journey to Carson Valley in 1856. Young's correspondence made it appear that Hurt insisted on making the trip himself.[53] But this was not how Hurt recalled its origins.

Hoping to maintain Young's apparent support for his farm-reservation scheme, the agent kept up a cooperative front in his relations with the governor. In February 1856 he even allowed himself to be elected, unanimously as usual, as one of sixteen delegates from Salt Lake County to that year's pivotal statehood convention. At the same time, the self-taught physician began to study law. On his return from Carson Valley in August, he was stunned to learn that Washington had refused to honor his drafts for costs he had already incurred to initiate his project. He was responsible to make them good out of his own pocket.

Hurt fought back. He explained to the commissioner of Indian affairs how he had been led to make the payments and said he blamed Young for his financial ruin.[54] He successfully appealed to an influential friend in Congress for an appropriation to make up his $20,000 cost overrun, but after this incident the agent and Young dropped any affectation of a cooperative relationship.[55]

52. Hurt to Young, 31 December 1855, USHS.

53. See Young to Hurt and Armstrong, 11 and 12 February 1856, Utah State Archives.

54. Hurt to Manypenny, 30 August 1856, in Buchanan, *Utah Expedition*, 179–81.

55. Hurt to John M. Elliott, 1 October 1856, USHS.

A short time later, Hurt was plainspoken in protesting an incident that happened when he was going from Fillmore to Corn Creek. Hearing that Kanosh had become ill, he went with his interpreters, Richard James and James White, and Ute guide Pin-tuts from Spanish Fork to see the ailing Pahvant chief in his capacity as a physician. On the way, they saw two men on horseback "going in the direction of the Indian lodges at full speed." After they camped, Hurt asked Pin-tuts if the Pahvants had said anything about the riders. "The Mormons had sent them word that the Americans were coming to tie them," the Ute guide replied, "but he told them that they were great fools." He later heard that Fillmore bishop Lewis Brunson had sent the two men "to tell the Indians the Americans were coming to their camp to arrest the murderers of Captain Gunnison, and to advise them to look out."[56]

Afterward, Edwin Pugh invited White and James to stay at his house in Fillmore, Hurt told Young, but they had not been there long before "some persons began to stone the house." Pugh rushed out and asked why they were bombarding his home. They turned on him and demanded to know "what he was doing with those damned Americans about his house." White and James were not Americans, Pugh told them, but Mormons. At this the attackers said, "They were no better than Americans, or they would not be with them."[57]

If the national identity was despised by some Mormons, to the Utes "the American" was an appellation of affection that set Hurt apart from Utah's earliest settlers. As Brigham Young prepared to send hundreds of missionaries to forge alliances with the tribes across the western United States, the American friend of the Utes undermined Young's position with an important Native people in the Kingdom's own backyard.[58] Not only would Hurt sound an alarm heard from the Mississippi River to Puget Sound, but his writings would also justify President Buchanan's decision to order the U.S. Army to impose federal authority on a defiant territory.

56. Hurt to Young, 31 October 1856, in Buchanan, *Utah Expedition*, 181–82.
57. Ibid.
58. Hurt to Manypenny, 2 May 1855, cited in Brooks, "Indian Relations," 17.

CHAPTER 4

A Terror to All Nations
The Crusade for Sovereignty

They are determined to make us an independent State or
Government, and as the Lord lives it will be so. (The Congregation
shouted, amen.) I say, as the Lord lives, we are bound to become
a sovereign State in the Union, or an independent nation by
ourselves, and let them drive us from this place if they can,
they cannot do it. I do not throw this out as a banter.

—Brigham Young, 31 August 1856

As Thomas Kane had foreseen, by 1855 Congress's imposition of a territorial system of government on God's Kingdom had put the Mormon
theocracy in an intolerable position. To throw off the federal yoke,
Brigham Young began a coordinated drive on many fronts to win independence either as a sovereign state within the American Union or, preferably, as a sovereign dominion, no longer part of the United States. The
move to independence began with a dramatic declaration.

"Twenty five years to day this Church was organized," Lorenzo
Brown wrote in his diary. Thousands gathered on 6 April in the open-
air tabernacle at Great Salt Lake to attend the annual general conference
on this momentous anniversary. The brush-covered bowery provided
ample space for such a large turnout, but little protection from the
blustery spring weather in a city on the western slope of the Wasatch
Mountains. The chilling wind was quickly forgotten in the thrill of an
unexpected announcement: "The Gentiles had rejected the truth & lo
we turn to Israel," Brown reported.[1] Rufus Allen carried word of this
dramatic news to the Southern Indian Mission: "Prest. Said the day has

---

1. Lorenzo Brown, Journal, 8 October 1855, 56, BYU Library.

come to turn the key of the Gospel against the Gentiles, and open it to the remnants of Israel, the people shouted, Amen, and the feeling was such that most present could realize, but few describe."[2]

A portentous moment in the history of all mankind had at last arrived, a moment charged with millennial expectation. The hour had struck, Young told his enthusiastic followers, for the Lamanites to hear and accept the gospel of their Hebrew ancestors, as foretold by the Book of Mormon prophets. American Indians were to gather with their white cousins of Israel, and "they shall build up a holy city unto the Lord, like unto the Jerusalem of old."[3] Two days later, he said, "It has been remarked that the Gentiles have been cut off, and I doubt whether another Gentile ever comes into this Church."[4]

Young's listeners knew at once the millennial significance of his announcement and what it required of them. To carry out this purpose, Jacob's white descendants must take this message to their cousins in the wilderness. On arriving in Salt Lake Valley, Young had described in plain language how his followers would bring this prophecy to pass. They would teach the natives English, farming, and the gospel of their Hebrew ancestors. Like mountaineers, they would connect themselves with every tribe in America, live with them, marry their women, and have children by them, a mission made possible by the practice of polygamy, which in time would make the Indians "white and delightsome."[5] But unlike mountaineers, they mistakenly persisted in seeing American Indians as one people, the Lamanites, and failed to grasp an essential fact of survival in the wilderness: Native peoples were not all alike.

Young's proclamation also revealed that the time had come to reject the colonial government Congress had imposed on God's Kingdom. For Israel to fulfill its destiny in the Last Days, it must rise and stand on its own, either as a sovereign member of the Union, as statehood was understood at that time, or as an independent state in the world of nations. The way finally decided would be not an end in itself, but the first tumble of the prophet Daniel's little stone destined to destroy all man's kingdoms

2. Brooks, *Journal of the Southern Indian Mission*, 21 April 1855.
3. Book of Mormon, Ether 13:8.
4. Brigham Young, "Discourse," 8 April 1855, in *Journal of Discourses*, 2:266–71.
5. Kenney, *Wilford Woodruff's Journal*, 3:241.

and give the "greatness of the kingdom under the whole heaven" to the "saints of the most High."[6]

To begin the transformation of American Indians, the 1855 conference called 160 missionaries to leave their new homes in the Great Basin and seek out their Native brethren from the Mississippi River to the Pacific Shore. They would be the first of hundreds sent over the next three years to the Delawares, Cheyennes, Cherokees, Kiowas, Comanches, Wacos, Witchitas, Lakotas, Choctaws, Moquis (Hopis), Mojaves, Nez Percés, Goshutes, Shoshones, Utahs, Paiutes, Omahas, Flatheads, Navahos, Shawnees, Bannocks, Creeks, and other North American tribes.

This important prelude to the millennium followed the success of some twenty-one missionaries sent the year before to the Southern Paiutes along the tributaries of the Virgin River in present-day southern Utah and Nevada. There they had protected the poor desert tribes from the depredations of their Ute relatives to the north, who kidnapped their children and traded them to New Mexican slave dealers for horses. Besides removing the brutal Ute heel from Southern Paiute necks, they helped the Indians improve their ancient irrigation systems and crops. In return, the Southern Paiutes along the Santa Clara, Muddy, and Virgin rivers flocked to the waters of baptism by the hundreds.

The unprecedented harvest was a clear sign of the times. It notified God's people that the remnant of Jacob in America were ready to receive the gospel of their fathers and to fulfill their destiny to build New Jerusalem on the North American continent. By late 1857, at least three hundred Mormon missionaries had been called to go alone, in pairs, or from newly constructed mission forts or farms to live among the tribes. They were instructed to learn the Natives' language, teach them to farm, and preach the gospel to them in words they would understand. In less than three years, fortified Mormon outposts took shape on almost every major trail and wagon road approaching the Great Basin from any direction. They controlled almost every major artery of transportation between the eastern and western seaboards of the United States.

The strategic location of these sites revealed the Kingdom's move to fortify and defend a sovereign position. They included Fort Limhi on the Lewis and Clark and Flathead trails between Bitterroot Valley

6. Dan. 3:44–45, 8:27.

and Fort Hall, some nineteen miles south of today's Salmon, Idaho; Fort Louisa at present-day Parowan, Fort Harmony near what is now Cedar City, Las Vegas Springs at today's Las Vegas, Nevada, and the Elk Mountain Mission at what is now Moab, Utah, all on the Spanish Trail; Mormon Station in Carson Valley on the California Trail; Fort Malad, or Barnard's Fort, and Call's Fort on Hensley's Salt Lake Cutoff, other California Trail cutoffs, and the Fort Hall Road; and Deer Creek Station, near present-day Douglas, Wyoming, and Fort Supply, near Fort Bridger, Wyoming, on the Oregon-California-Mormon Trail. Related to this expansion was Young's offer in 1856 to purchase Fort Hall on the Snake River, near present-day Pocatello, Idaho, from the Hudson's Bay Company and the construction the following year of Fort Lookout near present-day Blackfoot, Idaho. At various times before 1857, these outposts also overlooked John C. Frémont's trails of 1845 and 1854 and John W. Gunnison's 1853 route. Their location on the main avenues of communication and travel during the floodtide of America's western migration bore serious implications in light of Mormon doctrines relating to American Indians.

Even as the fortified outposts began raising their mud and log walls, one man sensed the potential danger these developments presented to the rest of the country and sounded an alarm. Garland Hurt alerted the commissioner of Indian affairs to the mass call of missionaries. "There is perhaps not a tribe on the continent that will not be visited by one or more" of this "class of rude and lawless young men such as might be regarded as a curse to any civilized community," he reported. On arriving in Utah, the agent went on, he had discovered that "these saints" had created "a distinction in the minds of the Indian tribes of this Territory between the Mormons and the people of the United States" prejudicial to the interests of the latter. He recommended that "these Mormon missionaries be subjected to the strictest scrutiny" to ensure that federal laws to preserve peace on the frontier were enforced.[7]

Acting commissioner Charles E. Mix in turn told the secretary of the interior that he considered Hurt's report to be a "subject of importance" and informed him of federal law making it a crime to "alienate, or attempt to alienate" Indians from the U.S. government. The law

---

7. Hurt to George W. Manypenny, 2 May 1855, in Buchanan, *Utah Expedition*, 176–77.

further allowed the president to use military force to apprehend anyone "found in the Indian country in violation," Mix said. He urged "as a precautionary step" that Indian superintendents and agents across the nation be instructed to watch "the Mormons and all others suspected of having a design to interrupt the peace and tranquility between the Indian and the government."[8] Hurt's recommendation touched off a number of reports by agents and others of Mormon tampering with the tribes in other parts of the country.[9]

For the missionaries called to venture forth from Utah, it was the worst of times to leave their families in the care of others. A devastating drought struck the West in 1855, and the gaunt visage of hunger stared out from Mormon fields ravaged by the rapacious grasshopper called the Mormon cricket. In 1848, flocks of California gulls had come just in time to feast on the destructive horde of hard-shelled Huns and save at least part of the settlers' life-saving first crop. But the birds had failed to deal with the waves of pestiferous grasshoppers that annually threatened "to destroy all vegetation as fast as it appears" during Utah's starving times.[10] Still, the determination to build a sovereign state in the Great Basin never rested on the black-tipped wings of noisy shore birds: it depended instead on the alliance of American Indians, a population large enough to sustain independence, and a vital, self-contained economy.

"The Kingdom of God [cannot] rise independant of the Gentile nations until we produce, Manufacture & make every article of use, convenience, or necesity among our own People," Brigham Young said on arriving in Salt Lake Valley in 1847. "We do not intend to have anny [sic] trade or commerce with the Gentile world, for so long as we buy of them we are in degree dependant upon them."[11] Despite the Gold Rush, he persisted in trying to create an exclusive society, free of greed, corruption, and outsiders. "We should have only one mess chest, one place of deposit, one storehouse, one 'pile,' and that is the kingdom of God upon

8. Ibid.
9. For examples, see Bigler, "Garland Hurt," 156n28.
10. For the best description of this disaster, see D. Robert Carter, "Fish and the Famine of 1855–56," 95–97.
11. Barney, *Mormon Vanguard Brigade*, 229.

the earth," he later said. "All who contend for an individual interest, a personal 'pile,' independent of the kingdom of God, will be destroyed."[12]

True to Young's words, the drive for economic independence began with a campaign to promote home industry. He called on his followers to "dispense with every article of manufactured goods, except such as were manufactured in their own families, until they could be produced by Manufactories established among themselves."[13] God's people must be able to produce everything they needed to achieve a fully independent position.

To build a growing economy, Mormon leaders relied on centralized planning and control, in contrast to the economic principles on which the rest of the country operated. The communal industries that Young tried to create lay directly in the path of a dynamic nation founded on individual freedom and enterprise. The beehive blueprint of Salt Lake City symbolized the agrarian sector of his philosophy of command and control. Work to establish industries along the same lines began in 1849 with the discovery of iron ore and coal near present-day Cedar City.

For two decades, Young tightly controlled how the community developed its resources. As he said in 1867, "the man whom God calls to dictate affairs in the building up of his Zion has the right to dictate about everything connected with the building up of Zion, yes even to the ribbons the women wear; and any person who denies it is ignorant."[14] Cooperative endeavors using this model—irrigation, settlement projects, and rescue efforts—showed success, but such a system lacked a competitive edge and failed to encourage individual initiative. Young's command economy also yielded a grossly uneven distribution of wealth.

In keeping with these communitarian ideas, Young called on territorial lawmakers to enact supportive legislation to encourage home manufacturing. "Clothing, of every description, sugar, candles, soap and many other articles," which enabled Gentile merchants to siphon off the territory's money, should be produced at home, he said, to form the basis of a free and independent state.[15] Mineral deposits in southwestern Utah

12. Brigham Young, "Remarks," 14 June 1863, in *Journal of Discourses*, 10:210.
13. Journal History, 5 January 1852, LDS Archives.
14. Brigham Young, "Discourse," 3 February 1867, in *Journal of Discourses*, 11:298.
15. Brigham Young, "Governor's Message," *Deseret News*, 25 December 1852.

seemed divinely placed for this purpose. Prior to the Utah War, Young expended huge amounts of money and human resources to produce iron, pottery, paper, sugar, lead, and other commodities. Made at great sacrifice, such investments were largely wasted. By 1857, the church had lost a $12,000 investment to make pottery, at least $8,500 spent on a paper mill, and more than $100,000 on the failure of the "Damn Miserable Company"—the Deseret Manufacturing Company—to make sugar from beets. By the time the Deseret Iron Company folded, it had spent at least $150,000 "to produce nothing more than a few andirons, kitchen utensils, flat irons, wagon wheels, molasses rolls, and machine castings."[16] Virtually all of these ventures proved to be neither competitive nor viable within the free market economy of the West.

Such failures, and the dire poverty that wracked Utah, made some doubt the infallibility of their prophet. "The people must know that I know how to handle money and means," Young said defensively, "and I never supposed that anybody had a doubt of it."[17] The problem, Mormon leaders assured their followers, lay not with the shepherds but with their sinful flock, whose transgressions had called down divine wrath. To establish God's Kingdom, Young became ever more convinced, would require an obedient people, untempted by personal gain, willing to make the sacrifices necessary to achieve an expanding economy.

Besides economic independence, the way to world dominion called for an "overflowing and abundant population," as foreseen by the original borders of the free and independent State of Deseret, which claimed roughly fifty square miles for each of its founding settlers. John M. Bernhisel, Deseret's Washington spokesman, admitted that its size did appear somewhat immodest, but if land suitable for farming was taken into account, "it is not so large." Since less than 4 percent of it was arable, he was right, but his claim that Deseret's settlers outnumbered California's by five to three was immensely overblown.[18]

---

16. Arrington, *Great Basin Kingdom*, 114–15, 117–20, 127. According to Elias Morris, Mormon stalwart A. O. Smoot coined the DMC's popular name on Green River while greeting the company that had hauled the machinery across the plains and sympathizing with its "wretched condition" after "suffering from snow, hunger[,] stampedes and other unpleasant visitations." See Whitney, *History of Utah*, 4:487.

17. Brigham Young, "Remarks," *Deseret News*, 12 November 1856, 283.

18. Morgan, *State of Deseret*, 85.

To bring wishful numbers to pass, one of the first actions of the Deseret lawmakers had been to create the Perpetual Emigrating Fund Company in 1850 "to promote, facilitate and accomplish the emigration of the poor."[19] Money was advanced from the fund to needy converts, mainly in England, where some thirty thousand church members outnumbered the Mormons in Utah by nearly three to one. (The public announcement of polygamy two years later reduced that number and dramatically limited new conversions.)

Recipients agreed to pay the money back as soon as possible after arrival. In theory, the system was perpetual, in that it was self-sustaining and grew in relation to the number it helped. In practice, Utah's barter economy and lack of growth potential made it hard for emigrants to reimburse the fund—and the contract they signed made them promise "that, on our arrival in Utah, we will hold ourselves, our time, and our labour, subject to the appropriation of the Perpetual Emigrating Fund Company until the full cost of our emigration is paid, with interest if required."[20] This—and an interest rate that compounded the debt by 10 percent annually—gave many of them the status of indentured servants. Debt repayment was a high priority, as Young made clear in September 1855: "I want to have you understand fully that I intend to put the screws upon you, and you who have owed for years, if you do not pay up now and help us, we will levy on your property and take every farthing you have on the earth."[21] Despite such efforts and several ingenious attempts to convert resources to cash, the fund became a constant drain on the Kingdom's coffers.

Facing the need to move more people in a shorter time at lower cost, Young, a creative thinker in the field of transportation, came up with an answer. Most westering emigrants walked virtually the entire distance rather than place an added burden on the teams that hauled their wagons, goods, and supplies. Young's solution was to hook the emigrants up to light vehicles and have them walk across the heart of the continent pulling their belongings in handcarts. So out of the need to build a population large enough and quickly enough to support the bid for independence, the epic of the Mormon handcart migration was born.

19. *Deseret News*, 21 September 1850, 114.
20. "Emigration Department," *Millennial Star* 18:2, 12 January 1856, 26, LDS Archives.
21. Brigham Young, "Discourse," 16 September 1855, in *Journal of Discourses*, 3:6.

In October 1855, Young announced his plan. To those who could not afford the journey, he said, "let them come on foot, with handcarts or wheelbarrows; let them gird up their loins and walk through, and nothing shall hinder or stay them."[22] Those able to pay their own way were urged to exchange their money for drafts from the church, payable on arrival in livestock or other necessities, and go by the new method.

After a campaign to promote the new scheme, nearly two thousand signed up in England in 1856. Ahead of them was a journey of six months and more than five thousand miles by sea and land. The hardest leg of the trip would be the last thirteen hundred miles, from the end of the railroad at Iowa City to Salt Lake Valley. At this jumping-off place, they would stop and pick up their handcarts or build them at the lowest possible cost and weight.

In design, the carts featured two wheels some five feet in diameter and far enough apart to fit the wagon ruts of the heavily traveled Oregon Trail. The open bed, or box, was designed to carry a few provisions and seventeen pounds of baggage for each of the four or five persons it served. Extending about three feet in front was the crossbar or singletree for one or two persons to push against and thereby pull the cart. To lift their spirits as they rolled along, a new song was written just for the handcart pioneers: "Some must push and some must pull as we go marching up the hill, as merrily on the way we go until we reach the Valley, oh!"[23]

If the 1852 announcement on polygamy curtailed the flow of converts and cash from Europe, the marriage doctrine made possible another method of population growth that was announced to the same general conference as the handcart plan. On 19 October 1855, settlers who attended the meetings returned to Manti to report that Heber C. Kimball, Young's first counselor, had counseled "young men to get married at sixteen, and take two wives and a dozen if they wished." Kimball moreover had told girls that "they were old enough to get married at fourteen," Azariah Smith said.[24] Lorenzo Brown especially liked the humor the apostle put into the teaching. He "wanted all the girls 14 & boys 16 to go to it and get married or rather get married and go to it,"

---

22. "Thirteenth General Epistle, Church of Jesus Christ of Latter-day Saints," 29 October 1855, *Deseret News*, 31 October 1855.

23. Hafen and Hafen, *Handcarts to Zion*, 66.

24. Azariah Smith, Journal, 19 October 1855, Authors' Collection.

he said. Brown also said that Brigham Young had explained that "there were spirits of a nobler class waiting to take bodies & it was the duty of every man to be taking to himself more wives."[25] Since the population count just four years earlier in 1851 had shown that males outnumbered females, it was unlikely there would be enough women of childbearing age to make this approach noticeably productive.

There were, however, other methods to achieve the numbers needed. These included padding the census count by including passing emigrants, as was the case in 1850–51, or, even quicker, inflating census returns arbitrarily, the method employed during the great statehood campaign of 1856. Overland visitors were skeptical about local population estimates even as they admired what the Mormons had accomplished. "They are walling in the city also building a large Temple," Thomas Dorsey of Michigan commented in 1854. "They claim 30,000 population [but] I think 10,000 would not be out of the way." Dorsey added, "I think it will be a great town when it is walled in."[26]

In 1856, Mormon leaders made their most determined bid for statehood prior to the Civil War. Territorial lawmakers had repeatedly requested Congress to authorize a constitutional convention. Congressional permission to prepare and submit a proposed charter for approval represented an invitation to enter the Union and initiated a process designed to bring this to pass. As with Oregon, Congress each year had simply looked the other way. But God's Kingdom would not be brushed off so lightly. This time Deseret presented Congress with a take-it-or-leave-it proposition: take us as a state or get out and leave us alone.

This was the choice Governor Brigham Young laid down on 11 December 1855 in his annual message to the last legislative session held in the statehouse at Fillmore, Utah. He called "odious and anti-republican" the requirement of the territory's organic act that all laws enacted by the Legislative Assembly and governor be submitted to Congress for approval. To put his people on a "platform of equal rights, constitutional sovereignty, and free government," Young called on lawmakers to have a census of Utah taken and "hold a convention for the formation and adoption of a constitution," whether Congress liked it or not. As for

25. Lorenzo Brown, Journal, 8 October 1855, BYU Library.
26. Dorsey, Journals and Letters, 7 July 1854, 33, Beinecke Library.

territorial rule, he thought federal lawmakers should have the wisdom to abolish "that odious, tyrannical, and absurd system of colonial government which emanated from the British throne."[27]

As Young directed, Utah legislators immediately called for an election of delegates from each county to draft a constitution and submit a memorial to Congress. Typical of all the counties, the eighteen delegates from Salt Lake had been chosen before the election was held on 16 February 1856. To give the constitutional exercise an appearance of inclusiveness and point up the republican nature of Deseret's forthcoming charter, the county lineup included three federal officers: district judges John F. Kinney and George P. Stiles and U.S. Indian agent Garland Hurt. Six of the fifteen Mormon luminaries listed belonged to the secret Council of Fifty, the governing body of God's Kingdom. The election caused no "stir or excitement," Hosea Stout said, since even the federal officials were elected unanimously.[28]

But the atmosphere changed dramatically when the delegates met on 17 March in Great Salt Lake City, about to become Utah's new capital. The American flag flew from stores, church buildings, and the governor's residence, and "the day was celebrated by the firing of cannon nearby," Stout wrote.[29] The day before, Young had made clear what the occasion signified. While the world did not understand, he said, "the Lord is building up his kingdom on the earth, is gathering his Israel for the last time, to make a great and mighty nation of this people." Before long, He would "give them a free and independent State, and justly make them a sovereign people," he said.[30]

The constitution of a state that equaled the sweep of Young's vision in size, if not in population, was completed eleven days later. While the true number of its inhabitants, not counting Indians, probably did not exceed forty thousand, its borders followed those set for the Territory of Utah, which would make Deseret large enough in area to place third among today's states. The constitution of the free and independent state

27. Brigham Young, "Annual Governor's Message," 11 December 1855, *Millennial Star* 18:257.

28. Brooks, *On the Mormon Frontier*, 16 February 1856.

29. Ibid., 17 March 1856.

30. Brigham Young, "Discourse," 16 March 1856, *Deseret News*, 26 March 1856, 18.

was eminently republican in nature and differed little from Deseret's 1849 charter, which was patterned in turn after the constitutions of other states. Apostles George A. Smith and John Taylor, editor of the newspaper *The Mormon* in New York City, were chosen to present the document and memorial to Congress. In all these proceedings, no dissenting voice was heard.

In high spirits, Young alerted John M. Bernhisel, Utah's congressional delegate, to these developments on 1 April and gave him a good reason to cooperate with Smith and Taylor. "If we gain our admission as a state we intend to elect you and Bro Geo A to the Senate and Bro Taylor to the house," he said.[31] Alert to what was going on, the erudite physician had already sounded a note of caution about entering the Union. "I am sorry to say that the prospects are dark and gloomy," he told Young. Ostensibly, polygamy had caused the "bitter and cruel prejudice against us as a people," he said, but he added without elaboration, "the true cause probably lies much deeper."[32]

Meanwhile, an orchestrated promotion on many fronts opened on 2 April in the *Deseret News*, the territory's only newspaper. The church-owned weekly challenged "all ye inhabitants of the States" to read the founding charter "and see if you can find a single item incompatible with other State Constitutions, with the Constitution and laws of the United States and the genius of republican institutions." If they could not find anything, "was there any good, fair, valid reason why Utah should not be speedily admitted into the Union as a free, sovereign and independent state named Deseret?" Not one, it concluded. "Hence it is but fair to infer that Senators and Representatives in Congress will grant the prayer of Utah for admission as unanimously as she presents it."[33]

On 10 April, Young informed Apostle John Taylor of his election as a delegate to Congress. The only difficulty he would have to overcome, he told the hard-pressed editor, was the "bitter, unyielding partisan spirit" that prevailed in Congress and across the country. People would not listen to counsel from "High Heaven's King," he went on, but would go to their destruction. In the meantime, he expounded, the Mormons were

31. Young to Bernhisel, 1 April 1856, BYC.
32. Bernhisel to Young, 18 March 1856, ibid.
33. "Convention and Constitution," *Deseret News*, 2 April 1856, 29.

"seek[ing] to place ourselves in as favorable position as possible" to avert the blow not only against themselves, but on the country as well, "for upon us at last will its destiny depend."[34]

Young avoided such lofty predictions four days later when he asked Thomas L. Kane to help his old friends in the mountains. "What do you think?" he asked his much-esteemed advisor. "Shall we gain admission into the Union this session of Congress in time to vote for President of the United States next November?" His question carried the hint that the presidential candidate who favored Deseret's statehood bid could rely on its electoral votes, recalling the political bargaining that had ignited a storm of opposition at Nauvoo. "May we rely on your aid and influence in effecting this desirable object?" Young asked. To support his case, he said the census put the population of Utah, "alias Deseret," at "nearly 80,000."[35]

As Young knew, Utah's population that spring was less than half that many, and the number of mouths at Zion's communal table was getting smaller every day. On 25 May, Major William H. Hoffman at Fort Laramie reported that the 1855 crop failure and the "increasing discontent of the people with the state of things there" were driving many of Young's people back to the states, "quite destitute of provisions." The commander of the U.S. Army's most important overland trail post, near present-day Torrington, Wyoming, issued them rations of hardtack and bacon to sustain them until they reached Fort Kearny.[36]

The ugly horde of grasshoppers that had destroyed Mormon crops in 1855 returned in the spring to threaten the plan to achieve rapid population growth. While the ravenous invaders did less damage the second time, it was enough to put many settlers on a near-famine diet. To ease the hunger, Mormon leaders took the Old Testament example of Ruth and ordered bishops to make certain that "every grain raiser permits the poor to glean his fields." Should anyone "not seasonably and properly glean his field, nor permit the poor to do so, let his Bishop deal with him according to the law of Zion," they said. The warning meant harsh

34. Young to Taylor, 10 April 1856, BYC.

35. Young to Kane, 14 April 1856, BYC. The first reliable count four years later put the population at 40,273. See Powell, *Utah History Encyclopedia*, 431.

36. Hoffman to Samuel Cooper, 27 May 1856, National Archives.

punishment for offenders. At Salt Lake, a frost on two nights in mid-July did not help Deseret's prospects for survival, let alone independence.[37]

The specter of famine was not enough, however, to dampen an all-out display of patriotism on Independence Day as part of the campaign to win support for statehood and dispel Gentile fears that the Mormons were disloyal to the United States. Normally the Fourth of July was yawned at in Utah Territory—as it still is in today's state—while all of the excitement was reserved for Pioneer Day, twenty days later, which celebrated the anniversary of Brigham Young's arrival in Salt Lake Valley. But in 1856 it was the other way around.

"Celebration of July Fourth and Grand Military Review in Great Salt Lake City," bannered the *Deseret News*. The firing of a "national salute of 13 guns from the arsenal" broke the stillness at sunrise to signal "the ringing of bells and the hoisting of flags." A huge flag of the United States was hoisted upon the Temple Block, other flags were unfurled over buildings throughout the city, and "a great variety of displays and mottos was displayed at the different stores and private residence." The mounted Nauvoo Brass Band led two other bands through the main streets of the city "discoursing beautiful and harmonious strains of music" to show that "the anniversary of American Independence was to be celebrated with joy and thanksgiving."[38]

Afterward, a Nauvoo Legion honor guard of mounted lancers, a band, Life Guards, light infantry, and more Life Guards marched to Young's residence, where the governor and his guests climbed into carriages and were escorted to the parade ground on Union Square, today the site of West High School. Honored among Young's guests were David H. Burr, Utah's surveyor general, and Associate Justice George P. Stiles. All took their places on a reviewing stand "beautifully decorated with flags, banners, mottos and evergreens." Since the event was all about Deseret's bid for sovereignty, not a celebration of the nation's birthday, the program opened with a reading of the U.S. Constitution rather than the Declaration of Independence.[39]

37. "Gleaning," *Deseret News*, 25 June 1855, 125, LDS Archives; "Gleaning and Saving," 9 July 1856, ibid., 141; Young to Bernhisel, 17 July 1856, BYC.

38. For extended coverage of this celebration, see *Deseret News*, 9 July 1856, 140.

39. Ibid.

Governor Young then sat quietly and listened as his clerk, Thomas Bullock, read his oration. He had the Constitution read instead of the Declaration of Independence, he said, to contrast many of the political movements of the day "with the guiding principles contained in that inspired governmental system." Reflected in his remarks was the belief that God had inspired the Constitution's founders to prepare the ground for God's Kingdom to take root and grow, not the current corrupt man-made system of rule. So it was that he proclaimed in one breath his fidelity to the Constitution and in the next scored "tyrannical governments," which "establish a system of espionage, appointments and military rule." He warned, "Let not the Federal Government presume upon the same suicidal policy." A nine-gun salute of cannon fire "echoed a response to the spirit and sentiments" he expressed, said the *Deseret News*.

Meanwhile, the distance of more than two thousand miles between Zion and the nation's capital, and the time it usually took for a letter to cover this distance, enhanced the contrast in mood between them. On arriving in Washington, George A. Smith found that "there was no probable chance" Deseret's statehood petition would even be considered, he wrote Young. The Republican Party had won control of the House, on a platform that "prohibits the admission of States without a positive prohibition of Slavery and Polygamy." Moreover, Bernhisel had told him that "there was the most bitter feeling in Congress towards us there had been since he has been a member." Therefore, "To present our Petition now would be sure defeat, and such a defeat as would keep us out of the Union for years to come."[40]

On 12 July 1856, Apostle John Taylor, Deseret's other constitutional delegate, added his own assessment of conditions in Washington. Knowing that Democrats favored the Mormon position, he said, the Republicans had "introduced opposition to Polygamy, as well as to Slavery," in their platform and stamped them the "*twin* relics of barbarism," which had thrown "the onus of protecting & sustaining both onto the Democratic party." It was a "mean dastardly act, in good keeping with other political moves of the present day; it is greedily swallowed by religionists of all parties," he added. In the battle over slavery, "polygamy now

---

40. Smith to Young, 30 June 1856, BYC.

is shook at the Democrats as one of the institutions which they must defend, in conjunction with slavery."[41]

If these statements were less than heartening, the words that Bernhisel penned on 17 July cleared one man's mind of any illusions that Washington looked favorably either on him or on his bid for statehood. Bernhisel had heard that "an effort was being made to procure your removal from office," he told Young. The territorial delegate hurried to call on President Pierce and find out if it was true. The president said that he had not been recently approached, Bernhisel reported, but he "complained of what he called your meddling with matters there." When Pierce was asked what matters he was referring to, he said, "with the juries, and that your organ [meaning the Deseret News] which he said he had seen, had requested the people to keep away from the gentiles." Bernhisel never saw the president "in so ill a mood, but he said that he did not know that he should remove you."[42]

Bernhisel's report and letters from Apostles Taylor and Smith arrived in record time from the East. On the evening of 28 August, Young and Apostles Woodruff and Kimball strolled over to Temple Square to inspect the new baptismal font being built in the Endowment House. As they left the walled block, "We saw the Eastern Mail drive up the earliest arivel [sic] we have ever had," Woodruff said. With the others, he continued to Young's office and listened while Daniel H. Wells read the mail aloud until well after 10 P.M. "We find the Nation in great Confusion & discord & a vary strong feeling against Utah," Woodruff said. "Our delegates have not yet presented our memorial to congress & probably will not this session."[43]

The four-week mail delivery was indeed "unusually good time," confirmed the Deseret News, but the tidings it bore did not brighten the remaining hours of 28 August for those who heard them.[44] The Republican House of Representatives would take up a law to ban polygamy in the territories, and President Pierce knew all about the Gunnison farce

41. Taylor to Young, 12 July 1856, ibid.

42. Bernhisel to Young, 17 July 1856, ibid. President Franklin Pierce was obviously referring to reports he had received about the Gunnison trial from Major Steptoe, Judge Kinney, U.S. Attorney Hollman, and possibly others.

43. Kenney, *Wilford Woodruff's Journal*, 4:440–41.

44. "The Eastern Mail," *Deseret News*, 3 September 1856, 205.

and was thirsting to replace Young. The well-planned operation to push statehood through Congress had accomplished nothing.

Even so, Young was typically defiant. The next Sunday the angry prophet "spoke by the spirit & power of God," Apostle Woodruff wrote, and he promised that the Gentiles "could not drive us from this valley. He was still governor & should be untill the Lord saw fit to remove him."[45] Young informed his allies that he found much in "the signs of the times" that caused his soul to rejoice: he may have taken such encouragement from events in "Bleeding Kansas." Pro-slavery Border Ruffians there had raided Lawrence three months before, looting and burning buildings, and three days later, near the Missouri line, zealot John Brown and his sons had cut down five men on Pottawatomie Creek with drawn swords. For the Mormon prophet, the news was filled with portents showing that the Kingdom of God would soon take its place on earth as a free and sovereign power. "We absolutely do not care about the result" of the statehood quest, Young told the three delegates on 30 August. "We desire admission but simply for the recognition of political rights, for the independent sovereignty which the act of admission carries with it." This would "place us on a better footing when the fabric splits asunder," he went on, but either way it made no difference, for "it will all be right whether we gain our admission or not *into the Union*."[46]

The United States was going to "destruction at rail road speed, and it behooveth us to be prepared for the great events shortly to come to pass," Young said.[47] He based this belief on Joseph Smith's Civil War revelation of 1832, in which Smith had predicted that the South would be divided against the North, "war will be poured out on all nations," slaves would rise up against their masters, and "the remnants," meaning American Indians, would "vex the Gentiles with a sore vexation" to usher in Christ's return.[48] As for a law against polygamy, "it is an Ex Post Facto, hence unconstitutional," he pronounced. "It is a law prohibiting the free exercise of the rights of conscience and religion, hence

45. Kenney, *Wilford Woodruff's Journal*, 4:441.

46. Young to Smith, Bernhisel, and Taylor, 30 August 1856, BYC.

47. Ibid.

48. Joseph Smith, Jr., "Revelation on the Civil War," in Smith, *History of the Church*, 1:301.

again unconstitutional." And finally, it was "the exercise of a power not granted in the Constitution hence unlawful."[49]

"Therefore let them howl—or as our poets have it 'Let them rip and let them roll while the devil pops them through,' for truly their time is short," he told Deseret's delegates.[50] His defiant letter of 30 August signaled a change in policy toward the federal government and a stand more in keeping with his attitude all along. If Washington would not recognize sovereignty through statehood, the Kingdom would break the federal bands and stand on its own.

Also on 30 August, Surveyor General Burr posted a letter at Salt Lake reporting to the Land Office the severe beating of one of his deputies during the elections there on 4 August. His deputy, Joseph Troskolawski, either had attempted to vote or had protested the balloting process that produced unanimous outcomes. For this, the notorious William A. Hickman and two young men had "knocked him down, then kicked him, and beat him with a butt end of a loaded horsewhip," Burr reported. His deputy had been so badly hurt that "for several days his life was despaired of." Hickman admitted that "he only obeyed counsel," Burr said.[51]

In a curious coincidence, Young mailed a rebuttal to Burr's accusation, his second letter to Bernhisel on the same day, warning that the surveyor general might come to Washington to report the attack. He called the victim "one of the foulest worthless and profane individuals ever found in this region." Burr's deputy "happened to get a cow hiding one afternoon in the public street for his abuse of some boys who were in from the country," Young said. Federal officials considered "all this country" to be "*Public Domain* and every body except themselves are trespassing that they can throw down fences and even houses if they choose to, graze their animals upon the grain fields and use the fence poles for fuel abuse and insult every body and everything and no person has any right to say a word," Young complained.[52] This letter, written on the same day Burr reported the incident, seems to confirm the charge that Salt Lake postmaster routinely opened federal officials' mail.

49. Young to Smith, Bernhisel, and Taylor, 30 August 1856, BYC.
50. Ibid.
51. Buchanan, *Utah Expedition*, 115–16.
52. Young to Bernhisel, 30 August 1856, BYC.

Young's defiant attitude was displayed again the following day in an appearance in the bowery that was less notable for what he said than for what he chose not to say. After building expectations about statehood for some nine months, he failed to mention the bad news he had received from Washington three days earlier. Instead he vowed that Deseret was bound to become a sovereign state in the Union or an independent nation, and he began to ready his followers for the preferred alternative. From the beginning, God's Kingdom had been "a terror to all nations," he said. But it was destined to "revolutionize the world and bring all under subjection to the law of God, who is our law giver."[53]

Affronted by Washington's hostility, Young crossed the Rubicon and moved to fulfill this vision. On 14 September he touched off a fiery revival, now remembered as the Reformation, to sanctify the body of Israel and present to the Lord a righteous people worthy of divine favor in the impending conflict with the American republic, which he foresaw and even encouraged.

As the great revival gathered intensity, Young began to cut his ties to the United States and sought to establish a new relationship based on mutual sovereignty and respect. In a bristling letter to Bernhisel in December 1856, he noted that a government surveying party had come to "Box Elder Pass" and planned to visit Salt Lake Valley for supplies in 1857.[54] "Now what we wish you to understand is this [—] we have not got any wheat, corn, flour, or other provision to spare to them or any body else," he wrote.[55] "We shall prevent any provision from going out of the Territory or being furnished to strangers within."

Noting that all say that Mormons do as Young says, he went on. "Let them rest assured that Brigham Young will keep all the provision there is in the Territory of Utah for the use of its inhabitants." His congressio-

53. Brigham Young, "Sermon," 31 August 1856, *Deseret News*, 17 September 1856, 219–20.

54. Young was apparently referring to a party led by Lieutenant F. T. Bryan that included a geologist, a topographer, a barometer expert, several assistants, and two rod carriers, sent to locate a military supply route from Fort Riley to Bridger Pass, also known as Box Elder Pass, in the Medicine Bow Mountains, south of present-day Rawlins, Wyoming, on the Continental Divide.

55. Quotes in the following four paragraphs are from Young to Bernhisel, 10 December 1856, BYC, 231, 235.

nal delegate should inform President Pierce or Secretary of War Jefferson Davis "or anyone else interested not to send any parties of surveyors troops or any explorers or parties of men under any pretence with the expectation of their being supplied from our rations," Young made clear, "for it will not be done."

Furthermore, it appeared that "some of our outside friends resident at present in territory, officials &c are combined to use an influence against us with the government," he said, referring to the federal officials. He told Bernhisel to demand the "privilege of perusing Dr. Garland Hurt's correspondence especially that mailed by this mail." He directed him not to be put off with some report or anything of the kind, "but get his correspondence and if possible obtain a copy and forward [it] to me." He also ordered the delegate to become acquainted with Congressman John Elliott, who had helped Hurt overcome his deficit spending for Indian reservations. "Ascertain if he is acquainted with Dr. Hurt," Young said, "and has correspondence with him, and how he feels disposed toward us."

"The facts are, they are as corrupt as hell, and we know it, and they would cut our throats, and destroy this people if they had the power, and they are endeavoring to stir up some kind of mess, between us and the General Government," he said. "They should all walk the plank next spring when this new administration comes into power," he went on, "and we hope this may be the case; we mean Hurt, Burr & Co." Unless Young got the word by private express, he could not have known so soon that James Buchanan had defeated Republican John C. Frémont and American Party candidate Millard Fillmore in the 4 November presidential election. But it mattered little who would be inaugurated on 4 March 1857.

Not until 18 December did Young make public the outcome of the campaign for statehood. The delegates, he said, had advised him that the application was not presented because of "intolerance evinced by the predominant party in the House of Representatives." The 1856 census of "near 77,000," plus a "presumed" increase of 20,000 more since the count was made, had removed any objection to admission on the score of insufficient population, he said.[56]

56. Brigham Young, "Annual Governor's Message," *Deseret News*, 24 December 1856, 333.

By this time, Brigham Young knew that his handcart scheme had resulted in the deaths by starvation and exposure of hundreds of faithful converts. The spiritual firestorm known as the Reformation was about to roar out of control, as the great crusade to prepare Young's followers to become obedient citizens of a sovereign Kingdom of God took on a fearful life of its own. Launched as a prelude to independence and Christ's return, the flaming revival instead would introduce war with the United States and lead to consequences that even Brigham Young could not foresee.

CHAPTER 5

The Cleansing
Blood of Sinners

The Reformation

> There are sins that can be atoned for by an offering upon
> an altar as in ancient days; and there are sins that the blood
> of a lamb, of a calf, or of turtle doves, cannot remit, but
> they must be atoned for by the blood of the man.

—Brigham Young, 21 September 1856

Shortly after receiving word that Deseret's statehood aspirations were dead on arrival at Washington, Brigham Young ignited the most fearful spiritual upheaval since the 1642 Salem witch hunts. Known as the Reformation, the movement to cleanse Israel aimed to flush out "nasty apostates" and Gentiles of every stripe, especially federal officials and merchants. Above all, it meant to reform the people of God, who had failed to meet millennial standards for sacrifice and obedience.[1]

The Mormon eruption of uncontrolled religious emotion was neither spontaneous nor unplanned. Young and his second counselor, Jedediah M. Grant, touched it off at separate locations on the same weekend. On 14 September, Apostle Wilford Woodruff reported, Young "spoke in the power of God" in the bowery at Great Salt Lake. He "chastised & rebuked" his followers "for lying, stealing, swareing, commiting Adultery, quarelling with Husbands wives & children & many other evils."[2]

---

1. Brigham Young, "Discourse," 27 March 1853, in *Journal of Discourses*, 1:83.
2. Kenney, *Wilford Woodruff's Journal*, 4:448.

In Davis County, north of the capital, Grant the day before had "worked up the people with his tongue," demanding that they "purify their lands, their houses, their persons, and dedicate themselves and the substance to the Lord."[3]

The following Sunday, the two leaders joined together to throw the fear of God into their Salt Lake followers and cut loose a flood of confession, repentance, and rebaptism throughout Zion: five years later, Young's own son characterized the Reformation as a "reign of terror."[4] Young rebuked "the sins of the people," Woodruff wrote. He "said that the blood of Heifers lambs Doves &c would again be offered for certain sins but for some sins no blood would be acceptable except the life & blood of the individual." Doubtless understating listeners' reaction, the apostle noted, "He made the Harts of many tremble."[5] If so, Grant in turn offered little comfort. "We have those amongst us that are full of all manner of abominations, those who need to have their blood shed, for water will not do, their sins are of too deep a dye."[6]

It was a day of red letters that spelled "blood atonement," a doctrine indirectly referred to before, but now pronounced publicly and made operative for all members of the church. The fearful teaching called for the shedding of human blood for the remission of certain sins not covered by Christ's atonement: adultery, apostasy, and possibly others. As Young stressed, its purpose was to save sinners, not to punish them. He knew that his followers would think it was "strong doctrine" when they heard about "cutting people off from the earth," he said, but he assured them that it was "to save them, not to destroy them." He even had men come to him and "offer their lives to atone for their sins."[7]

Chosen to lead the cleansing of Israel was a puritanical figure uniquely qualified for the task. Known as "the sledgehammer of Brigham," forty-year-old Jedediah Morgan Grant stood more than six feet tall, bore not an excess ounce on his lanky frame, and was utterly untroubled by doubt.

3. "Great Reformation," *Deseret News*, 24 September 1856, 228.
4. Brigham Young, Jr., Diary, 15 December 1862, cited in Jensen, "Without Purse or Scrip?" 6.
5. Kenney, *Wilford Woodruff's Journal*, 4:451.
6. Jedediah M. Grant, "Remarks," 21 September 1856, *Deseret News*, 1 October 1856, 235.
7. Brigham Young, "Discourse," 21 September 1856, ibid.

An enigmatic character, he loved his home and his wives, all six of them, and was deeply loyal to Young. What made him exceptional, however, was the fire that burned in his belly at the sight of uncleanliness, personal and spiritual. Grant was the voice of Leviticus with a tongue sharpened by years of verbal combat with evangelical ministers, a hellfire preacher who scared the congregation out of any proclivity to doze off. Only weeks after he delivered a searing sermon on the need to shed sinners' blood as the only way to save them, Young picked him to be the third member of Mormonism's highest triumvirate.

Grant made certain that every listener understood that he might have to take this bloody road to glory, not the sinner next door. "If the arrows of the Almighty ought to be thrown at you we want to do it," he aimed, and "make you feel and realize that we mean you." His advice to wrong-doers was to go to Young "and ask him to appoint a committee to attend to their case; and then let a place be selected, and let that committee shed their blood." The fiery oracle of reform never relied on logic or common sense to encourage the people to clean up and put on the armor of righteousness; he set out instead to scare them into standing right before God. "Brothers and sisters, we want you to repent and forsake your sins," he cried, "and you who have committed sins that cannot be forgiven through baptism, let your blood be shed and let the smoke ascend, that the incense thereof may come up before God as an atonement for your sins, and that the sinners in Zion may be afraid."[8]

The luckier sinners, whose offenses were treatable by baptism, were cut off from the church only until they had confessed their faults in public, undergone rebaptism for remission of their wrongdoing, and been reconfirmed as members of the church. From then on, however, they would come under the law of God, a more demanding moral standard. "The Saints have the privilege of their sins being forgiven by making restitution to those we have injured & then renew our Covenants before God," Lorenzo Brown wrote. After that, he added ominously, "all sins must be atoned."[9]

To prepare believers for that day, Grant ordered spiritual authorities to wake up and enforce righteousness. Bishops were commanded to "repent

8. Grant, "Remarks," 21 September 1856.
9. Lorenzo Brown, Journal, 1 April 1857, BYU Library.

and wash them, cleanse their premises, their Houses, back houses," and everything else about them. "Get the Holy Ghost and go from house-to-house," said Grant, "and purify the whole city." If they did not do it, "the Marshall shall receive orders to send Policemen round to wash the Bishops and people and cleanse every house," he said, for God's wrath "burns against us, owing to the filth and abomination that exists here."[10] The steady drumbeat on obedience to one's "file leader" would produce fearful consequences.

Grant gave wives in polygamy a special "working up." Referring to plural marriage, he said, "We have women here who like any thing but the celestial law of God." "If they could break asunder the cable of the church of Christ, there is scarcely a mother in Israel but would do it this day," he railed on 21 September. "They want to break up the church of God, and to break it from their husbands and from their family connections."[11] As he spoke, national lawmakers were taking up legislation to ban polygamy, the second of the "twin relics of barbarism," in the Republican-controlled U.S. House of Representatives.

Perhaps the most invasive characteristic of the Reformation was the "catechism," a long list of intrusions into a person's conduct meant to uncover violations of righteous behavior and cleanliness. Grant told bishops and teachers to visit every home and "find out those who are not disposed to do right." The reformer instructed, "Let their names be written down and let the offence and place of residence be written against the name, that we may know who are living in sin, where they live and what their offences are."[12] Drawn up by Grant, the first list grew as local officials added questions of their own to probe the private lives of members under their charge.

Hannah Tapfield King, a forty-nine-year-old Englishwoman from Cambridge, described the ordeal: "The Bishop and at least 2 teachers went around and catechized the people in every house, taking some members into separate apartments! How well I remember them coming to our house. There was no one at home but Tom Owen and me. They asked if I desired to be questioned in a separate room. I said no, and

10. Bishops' Meeting, 30 September 1856, cited in Sessions, *Mormon Thunder*, 219.

11. Grant, "Remarks," 21 September 1856.

12. Grant, "Discourse," 2 November 1856, in *Journal of Discourses*, 4:83–87.

smiling at Tom I asked if he did. Poor boy, he was but 16, he looked as guileless as a child and said no. They then proceeded with me. It began, Have you committed murder, ditto, ditto—adultery? Ditto-ditto—robbed?—Spoken slander of your neighbor?—Broken down your neighbor's fences?—Brought your children up in principles of righteousness, etc. It was over a foot in length!! Blessed were those who could answer in innocence. But I do believe men in those times were frightened into praying and confessing sins they never committed. It was a fearful time for all. Whether it did good or was instituted by the spirit of God is not for me to judge. I leave an open verdict in my heart of hearts. Only I know it was a fearful ordeal, and fear is a slavish passion and is not begotten by the spirit of God!"[13]

Garland Hurt said that peace and good order had prevailed before the Reformation; then "the Lord's anointed" commanded the people "to bow at the Confessional, and repair to the streams of the mountains and be rebaptized forth with." The agent had seen men and women "weeping in the utterest agonies of soul." When he tried to console them, "they abhorred the idea of being forced into a confessional but dare not refuse."[14]

Into this boiling cauldron marched the first Zion-bound handcart companies from England, some five hundred strong. Sunburned and tired, they rolled in on the same day, 26 September, to finish the thousand-mile final stretch of a six-month journey at an average of fifteen miles a day, "oxen not being able to keep up with them."[15] Young, the Nauvoo Legion band, and mounted lancers met them in Emigration Canyon and escorted them as they pulled their carts into the city and lined up at the public square. "No pen Can write, the sensation it created," Woodruff said.[16] Soon after, a third company of some three hundred arrived from Wales, having rolled over the trail at the extraordinary rate of sixteen miles a day.

---

13. King, Diary, 8 October 1856, USHS. Hannah Tapfield King came to Utah in 1855 and died in 1886. Her journals are an important source on Utah society and events in this period.

14. Hurt to Cumming, 17 December 1857, USHS.

15. Woodruff to Pratt, 30 September 1856, *Millennial Star* 18:50, 13 December 1856, 794–96, LDS Archives.

16. Kinney, *Wilford Woodruff's Journal*, 4:452–53.

But as their leaders knew, there were still more than a thousand hand-cart emigrants somewhere in the mountains. Thus far, the new low-cost method to boost the Kingdom's population had proved remarkably successful. For many of the arrivals, however, what they saw and heard was not what they had been led to expect. As historian Polly Aird has shown, the Reformation and doctrines such as blood atonement hardly helped attract, much less retain, incoming citizens.[17] The great revival was cleansing Zion, as intended, but it was reducing the number of new converts needed to establish Deseret's sovereignty. Moreover, it was not easy to get out, and not everyone who wanted to was brave enough to try. "Every possession and object of affection will be taken from those who forsake the truth, and their identity and existence will eventually cease," Young warned.[18]

The Reformation had hardly gotten off to a good start when Zion was suddenly shocked to reality. With innocent faith, and with the operation's managers exhibiting reckless disregard for frontier realities, the last two handcart companies had left the Missouri River far too late in the season. As they labored up the North Platte River in October without warm clothing or adequate supplies, blizzards struck. There were no settlements, army posts, or travelers to render assistance, no telegraph to wire for help, no federal emergency relief programs. All alone on the open plains, hundreds of miles from their destination, more than a thousand men, women, and children faced death by exposure and starvation. The greatest disaster in America's westward migration loomed.

Fortunately, the one man who possessed the power to help them was ever at his best at such times. "Many of our brethren and sisters are on the plains with hand carts, and probably many are now 700 miles from this place," said Brigham Young. "That is my religion; that is the dictation of the Holy Ghost that I possess, it is to save the people." He immediately ordered the bishops to provide forty veteran teamsters, sixty outfits of "good horses and mules" (oxen were too slow), twelve tons of flour, and many wagons. "I shall not wait until tomorrow," he said.[19] His early October call launched a desperate winter rescue operation that saw two

17. For this groundbreaking study, see Aird, "'You Nasty Apostates,'" 129–207.
18. Young, "Discourse," 17 August 1856, in *Journal of Discourses*, 4:31–32.
19. Young, "Remarks," 5 October 1856, *Deseret News*, 15 October 1856, 252.

months of heroism and heartbreak before a line of wagons carried the last survivors, some with frozen limbs that needed amputation, into Salt Lake Valley. More than two hundred were left behind in unmarked graves, mostly older members and men who had sacrificed their own lives for their families.

But when it came time to assess blame, Young could not accept his role in creating the disaster: it had been his idea from the start, and despite the warnings of some of the church's veterans, he had allowed the operation to move forward without the cows, support wagons, or relief supplies that could have made the handcart experiment a success. As it was, by early November, Apostle Heber C. Kimball had to denounce the "spirit of murmuring among the people" and chastised them because "the fault is laid upon br. Brigham." At the same meeting, Young asked, "What is the cause of our immigration's being so late this season? The ignorance and mismanagement of some who had to do with it, and still, perhaps, they did the best they knew how." He was reluctant to "attach blame to either" Daniel Spencer or Apostle Franklin D. Richards, the men who had dispatched the handcarts dangerously late, but "if even a bird had chirped it in the ears of brs. Richards and Spencer, they would have known better than to rush men, women and children on to the prairie in the autumn months, on the 3d of September, to travel over a thousand miles."[20]

"There is not a person, who knows anything about the counsel of the First Presidency concerning the immigration, but what knows that we have recommended it to start in season," Young insisted. He admitted that this was not a formal policy, but warned, "If any man, or woman, complains of me or of my Counselors, in regard to the lateness of some of this season's immigration, let the curse of God be on them and blast their substance with mildew and destruction, until their names are forgotten from the earth." Young's two counselors loyally agreed. Kimball blamed Satan: "The devil has tried to hedge up the way, so that we should not bring about the wise plans devised by our President, and has tried to make those plans look as disagreeable and as miserable as possible." Kimball threatened, "Not one of you will ever go through the straight gate into the kingdom of God, except those that go through by that

20. Heber C. Kimball, "Remarks," 2 November 1856, *Deseret News*, 12 November 1856, 282–83; Brigham Young, "Remarks," ibid., 283.

THE CLEANSING BLOOD OF SINNERS: THE REFORMATION   101

man." Grant extended Young's defense to the whole First Presidency: "I do not believe that the biggest fool in the community could entertain the thought that all this loss of life, time, and means, was through the mismanagement of the First Presidency."[21]

What the audience who heard all this could not know was that Young had other priorities on the overland trail that fall. He had sent a wagon train east in the spring with orders to bring back nails, glass, dry goods, a threshing machine, and a steam engine that weighed some thirteen thousand pounds. The train's captain, A. O. Smoot, reached Fort Bridger between the two hardest-hit handcart companies and informed Young that he might leave some of the freight at the fort: one of his teamsters recalled that they left behind eight wagons and marched on to Echo Canyon.

Here Smoot "received a letter from Bro Young directing him to bring all the goods in and if he had not enough teams to call upon the brethren who were out in the mountains with ox teams to assist the hand cart emigrations" and bring in the wagons. Twenty-two-year-old Frank Woolley was assigned to do the job. On 4 November he found the survivors of James G. Willie's company at Bear River. They learned "that President B. Young had sent word that some freight still lying at 'Fort Bridger' was to be brought in this season & that some teams and men of our company were needed." Willie's train was still eighty miles from Salt Lake: eight more members of the company, ranging in age from eight to sixty-six years, would die before they reached the valley. The last handcart company was still trapped more than 340 miles from Great Salt Lake near Devils Gate.

Despite causing the worst disaster in the history of the Oregon, California, and Mormon trails, Young's cut-rate emigration scheme was used again in 1857, 1859, and 1860 before being replaced with a more efficient system. The handcart veterans themselves identified the key problem with making men and women do the work of oxen and mules: "What have you brought us to, you, yourself in shafts drawing like beasts of burden, your children hungry and almost naked, myself will soon be gone, and My God, what will become of you and the children?" Joseph

21. Brigham Young, "Discourse," and Jedediah M. Grant, "Discourse," both 2 November 1856, *Deseret News*, 12 November 1856, 282, 284.

Sermon asked his wife as he lay dying of starvation. Like Sermon, John Taylor identified the problem: "it looked too much like hard work for men to perform labor that has hitherto only been considered proper for beasts of draught and burden." And when Young tried to lay the blame on Taylor, who had sent explicit warnings about the plan, he replied simply, "I did not consider that a few dollars were to be put in competition with the lives of human beings."[22]

Too sick to watch the tragic parade of the last of the 1856 handcart trains as they entered Salt Lake on 30 November was Reformation leader Jedediah Grant. While other leaders had turned their attention to the plight of the pilgrims, Grant had worn himself out in his zeal to cleanse Israel. Ignoring the approach of winter, he had preached too often in unheated halls and baptized for too many hours in mountain waters without sufficient rest or support. Suddenly his voice was silenced. The troubler of Israel was struck down by typhoid and pneumonia, probably brought on by exhaustion, on the day after the last handcart victims arrived. "A mighty man in Israel has fallen," lamented Woodruff.[23]

Grant was silenced, but his passing did not end the mission he gave his life for. After mourning his loss and relocating the handcart veterans, often in remote settlements, Brigham Young and top Mormon leaders took up the torch Grant had laid down and brought it to full flame with a vengeance. This time there would be no way for sinners to hunker down until the storm had passed or for some leaders to moderate the Reformation's most extreme impact on their local church or settlement.

In early December 1856, Juab County bishop Jacob G. Bigler traveled south sixty miles through the snow to attend the last meeting of the Legislative Assembly in the unfinished statehouse at Fillmore. The Utah lawmakers met just long enough to vote, as directed, to "move the seat of Government" from the central Utah settlement to Great Salt Lake City. Bigler headed back north nearly 150 miles past his home settlement at Nephi to the newly designated capital. There he found himself in an assembly that threw away any pretense of being a legislative

---

22. For the latest studies of the disaster and sources for the preceding quotes, see Bagley, "'One Long Funeral March,'" 50–115; and Roberts, *Devil's Gate*.

23. Kenney, *Wilford Woodruff's Journal*, 4:498.

proceeding of a republican form of government under the authority of the United States.

During the meeting of legislators on 23 December, the Social Hall at Great Salt Lake City became "filled as with consumeing fire," Woodruff said. Members of the body spoke until sundown, and "the House was filled with the spirit of God almost to the consuming of our flesh," the apostle reported. That night he attended the meeting of bishops, who did triple duty as lawmakers and judges, and "the fire of God still burned in us."[24] Hosea Stout participated in an emotional meeting and said that the "power and testimony of the Elders of Israel exceeded anything" he had seen. "It was truly a pentacost."[25]

The forty-three-year-old Juab bishop was shaken. "My eyes have not been open but I begin to see as through a glass dimly," he confessed.[26] "The fire of God is burning here and I command you and your Quorums to scour up your armer both temporally & spiritually," he told Nephi's priesthood leaders. "What I say I me[a]n you to understand literally," he instructed. "For your sake & for my sake also," he told them "to Wake Up Wake Up Wake Up." Go to scripture, he said, and "see what the men of God has done under the influence of the holey Ghost, when it cleansed Israil put the gavaline [javelin] to the hearts of wicked rulers [and] kicked out the bowels of a Judas."[27]

Bigler now understood what the Reformation was all about and the part he must play in it. "Prepare your selves to stand by me when Israil is to be cleansed," he said, "for this has got to be done that the Gentile bands may be Broken." He also saw "as through a glass dimly" that the cords between God's Kingdom and the United States were about to be cut and that the move to independence anticipated an armed confrontation. "The Saints in Carson & Sanbernidino [sic] are called to Come Home Come Home Come Home," he said.[28] As early as 24 December 1856, Mormon colonies in southern California and western Nevada were called home to defend Zion.

24. Ibid., 4:520.

25. Brooks, *On the Mormon Frontier*, 2:611.

26. Bigler to Miller, Foote, Bryan, and Hoyt, [23] December 1856, cited as "Minutes of Nephi Branch" in Brough, *Freely I Gave*, 97.

27. Bigler to Pyper, Webb, and counselors, 23 December 1856, BYU Library.

28. Ibid.

The next day, Christmas, "a young woman by the name of Williams committed suicide by cutting her throat," Stout said without comment.[29] But Garland Hurt told the rest of her story. She had come with the handcarts and been told that she would be denied subsistence and denounced as a prostitute if she did not become the polygamous wife of the man with whose family she was living, Hurt reported, "and the fatal razor was brought to its relief."[30]

As the flames of reform roared, legislators on 30 December met in joint session on "the state of the Reformation and passed an unanimous Resolution to repent of and forsake our sins and be rebaptized for their Remission," Stout wrote. After dinner they "repaired to the *Font* filled it with water and some fifty-five were Baptized."[31] The lawmaker did not say whether his sins included taking part in the disciplined "mob" that had broken into the offices of district judge George P. Stiles the night before. They dumped his books and documents into a nearby privy and pretended to burn them. A former Mormon, Stiles had been excommunicated a week before for alleged adultery, but equally likely was his offense of defending the superior jurisdiction of district courts over Mormon probate benches.

Shortly after the new year began, Young told John Taylor that Stiles "has been cut off from the Church corrupt and wicked Course of life." In sermons and letters like this one, Young's voice roared with such fire and venom, and made the Mormon case of persecuted and abused righteousness with such single-minded passion that his followers called him "the Lion of the Lord." At the same time, what many historians have long downplayed as "rhetoric" makes clear why representing federal authority under Governor Young was impossible. With very few exceptions, Young believed that "the chief delight & business" of the president's appointees was "to Stir up strife between us and the General Government" for their own selfish purposes. They acted as if "they were sent here to quarrel and create difficulties." With their "foul and false statements," they wretchedly abused the "good feelings, confidence and respect" of a people taught by bitter experience and persecution "to view strangers with a jealous eye." Surveyor General Burr was

29. Brooks, *On the Mormon Frontier*, 2:611.

30. Hurt to Cumming, 17 December 1857, USHS.

31. Brooks, *On the Mormon Frontier*, 2:213.

a swindler and "a snarling puppy, snapping and biting at everything that comes his way." Burr, Hurt, and district judge William W. Drummond, who had arrived from Chicago in July 1855, were "dogs and skunks." But the good news was that the Reformation burned on, and "We do not expect the current crop [of officials] to remain any longer than Spring."[32]

Flush with the same zeal, Utah legislators drew up a memorial to president-elect James Buchanan. They began with a long rehearsal of Mormon persecution that left unmentioned no source of resentment, real or imagined, before or after Utah became a territory. Among other abuses, U.S. presidents were accused of appointing men to territorial positions "who seek to corrupt our community, trample upon our rights, walk under foot our laws, rules and regulations, who neither fear God nor regard man and whenever checked in their mad career, threaten us with death and destruction by United States troops."[33] The officers they were so upset about were three district judges and four others, whose offices the lawmakers had already duplicated and filled with men chosen by Young. Under the best of circumstances, the alleged offenders had little power to oppress anyone because no one paid much attention to them.

Even so, the emotionally overheated legislators held them up as justification to declare political independence from the American republic. In a parade of defiant resolutions, they vowed to "resist any attempt of Government Officials to set at naught our Territorial laws, or to impose upon us those which are inapplicable and of right not in force in this Territory."[34] As for presidential appointees, they would "send them away, asking no odds either of political demagogues or bigots." Less provocative was a companion memorial listing candidates for each office they would approve of, starting with Brigham Young.

The defiant memorial was unwise and ill-timed, and did more to bring on the United States Army than all the complaints of federal appointees

---

32. Young to Taylor and George A. Smith, 3 January 1857, BYC.

33. "Memorial & Resolutions to the President of the United States, concerning certain Officers of the Territory of Utah and Memorial to the President of the United States," Memorials and Resolutions, Utah State Archives. Also printed without names and titles in the *Deseret News*, 7 October 1857, 244–45.

34. Ibid. The claim of power to nullify federal law is based on Section 10 of the 1850 Act to Establish a Territorial Government for Utah, which declares the laws of the United in force in Utah "so far as the same, or any provision thereof, may be applicable."

over the prior six years. Under Young, the Mormons had always been devout Democrats—"The Democratic banner floats again triumphant over our Country," Young wrote to a follower after James K. Polk's election. "God grant that it ever may." Through their agents in the East, they hoped to continue the amicable relationship with the new executive. Buchanan's statement in his inaugural address that the territorial question had been "settled upon the principle of popular sovereignty—a principle as ancient as free government itself" surely warmed the hearts of his fellow Democrats in Utah. But the Constitution authorized Congress to build military roads, the new president observed, when "absolutely necessary for the defense of any State or Territory of the Union against foreign invasion." He reasoned that there was no way to protect "California and our Pacific possessions except by means of a military road through the Territories of the United States." Since Great Britain could easily sever seaborne communications with the West Coast, a transcontinental military road would be the only way federal troops could reach the Pacific territories "in sufficient time to 'protect' them." If nothing else, Buchanan's statement reminded the Mormons that they stood astride an essential American highway.[35]

When John M. Bernhisel, Utah's well-mannered delegate to Congress, presented Utah's combative memorial to the president on 18 March, two weeks after his inauguration, Buchanan said that he was too busy with office-seekers to read it and sent it to Interior Secretary Jacob Thompson for consideration. Two weeks later, Thompson called Utah's courteous emissary to his office and gave him a dressing-down more deserved by others, starting with Young. Thompson flatly branded the Mormon nullification doctrine "a declaration of war." He told Bernhisel that "it breathed a defiant spirit, that if we got into trouble with the General Government that we would have nobody to blame but ourselves," the delegate told Brigham Young. The interior secretary had no objection to the recommendation of candidates for Utah offices, but said the memorial "tells us that we must appoint these men, and if we do not, and appoint others, that you will drive them out of the Territory." The government wanted "to live in peace with us," Thompson said, "and inquired whether we did not intend to set up an independent

35. Young to Rogers, 5 December 1844, Beinecke Library; Buchanan, Inaugural Address.

Government."[36] The diplomatic Utah delegate tried to mollify the secretary, but he would have none of it. Thompson said "he knew nothing of our religious principles, but if the[y] lead to such pra[c]tices, they must be very bad," Bernhisel reported. Buchanan's cabinet member also said "he did not know how the memorial would strike the President, but that it had made a very unfavorable impression on his mind."[37] Not before June would Young learn that he had burned his bridges to Washington.

In the meantime, the flames of reform burned on in Deseret into 1857. Spring would see a flight of "such as cannot abide righteousness and the purifying influence of the Spirit of God," Young wrote George Q. Cannon on 7 January. It was better to have them go than "fail us in times of trouble," when "their treachery might cost some of us our lives," he wrote the editor of the Mormon *Western Standard* newspaper in San Francisco. "We hope the fire will continue to burn and grow hotter, until wickedness and iniquity shall be consumed, and truth triumph over the whole earth."[38]

Stiles, upset by the fire that appeared to have burned his court papers and fearful for his life, was the last of three judges appointed by President Franklin Pierce who took to their heels and left justice in Utah wholly in the hands of the probate courts, which meant Brigham Young. He was also the last of eight federal justices who escaped between 1851 and 1857, five out of fear, two by death, and one not reappointed.[39] Given handicaps of distance and communication, the turnover was a significant record for a U.S. territory.

William W. Drummond "& lady" came with the eastern mail in July 1855.[40] The most controversial of Pierce's judicial appointees, the new judge had Mormon relatives in Utah and no doubt had heard about polygamy, but since the woman who accompanied him was not his wife,

36. Bernhisel to Young, 2 April 1857, BYC.

37. Ibid.

38. Young to Cannon, 7 January 1857, in "Letter from Pres. B. Young," *Western Standard*, 21 February 1857, 2.

39. The others were Perry E. Brocchus, Lemuel G. Brandebury, John F. Kinney, and William W. Drummond, fled; Leonidas Shaver and Lazarus Reid, died. Zerubbabel Snow, a Mormon, was not reappointed.

40. Brooks, *On the Mormon Frontier*, 2:558.

he seemed not to know that adultery was a capital offense in Utah. The Midwesterner arrived just six months after territorial lawmakers had bestowed original civil and criminal jurisdiction on the probate courts, thereby neutering the Second District bench he was to rule. When his court convened in November that year at Fillmore, he announced that the legislature had no power to grant such jurisdiction and told the Mormon grand jury that if any probate judge exercised that authority, "it was their duty to indict not only the judges, but all jurors and officers who had acted under them."[41]

For this impertinence, he would receive his comeuppance. The next January, when Drummond met in Fillmore with the two other district judges as Utah's supreme court, he found himself and a black servant, Cato, indicted by the Millard County grand jury for assault "with intent to kill" one Levi Abrams.[42] He was then arrested under a warrant issued by the probate judge at Fillmore, a court he had stamped illegal. In Utah, in contrast to Illinois, where he had practiced law, Drummond had no power to enforce his rulings. The contest between duplicate court systems ended when the other district judges agreed not to rule on the legality of probate benches and the county grand jury dropped the charges.

It had all been a farce, like the pretended burning of Stiles's books and papers, but it scared Drummond. On 17 May 1856, he and his mistress took off, ostensibly to hold court in Carson Valley, but they kept going all the way back to Chicago. However, he was not one to let an injury to his self-esteem pass. He would be heard from again.

In the meantime, so-called "apostates" had also begun to feel the Reformation's heat. "Last night Jarvis['s] House was broken into and his family drove out, the House set on fire in two or three places and he beaten and drove off and hell played generally," Hosea Stout said on 14 January 1857.[43] Unless mentioned in personal journals or letters, crimes in Utah during this time went unreported since there was no newspaper in the usual sense of the term. In vain, readers could search the church's

41. Ibid., 2:565.
42. Ibid., 2:583.
43. Ibid., 2:618.

newspaper, the *Deseret News*, for crime news in what had become a virtual police state, where the police often committed the crimes.

Unreported was what happened in late January 1857, when David H. Burr looked up from his maps and saw James W. Cummings, former Nauvoo police chief Hosea Stout, and territorial marshal Alexander McRae standing before him. They handed him a copy of the letter he had sent to the General Land Office on 12 May 1856 reporting "certain trespasses on the public lands" and demanded to know if he had written it. He said he had. They then told the surveyor that "*the country was theirs, that they would not permit this interference with their rights, and this writing letters about them would be put a stop to.*" Burr could figure no reason for their visit, "unless it was to intimidate me and prevent my writing," he told Thomas Hendricks, commissioner of the General Land Office.[44]

Several weeks later, Burr tried to follow his superior's advice and seek through federal law a corrective for the opposition that his surveyors were encountering in the field. He and Indian agent Garland Hurt appeared before Judge Stiles in the district court at Great Salt Lake and asked for a ruling upholding the primacy of federal laws over territorial statutes. Mormon attorney Hosea Stout and marshal James Ferguson called this "a contest for the supremacy of our laws in our own courts over the unlawful usurpation and rulings of the District Courts." A shouting match and scuffle followed, and the pair of Gentiles "went out of the house in the form of a sled, using the seat of their honor for runners," Apostle Woodruff wrote.[45]

The air was filled with threats and rumors, but there was little reliable information about the perils Burr might face. Then he heard a report from Springville, some sixty miles south of Great Salt Lake, that inspired fear in the hearts of outsiders and dissenters across the territory. Unknown assailants had ambushed and killed three men who tried to escape from the town, a hotbed of religious fanaticism. Moreover, no attempt was being made to bring the murderers to justice.

44. Burr to Hendricks, 5 February 1857, in Buchanan, *Utah Expedition*, 118.
45. Brooks, *On the Mormon Frontier*, 2:622; Woodruff to George A. Smith, Journal History, 1 April 1857, LDS Archives.

Two years later, protected by U.S. soldiers, witnesses told what happened. Alvira Parrish testified that she had heard Bishop Aaron Johnson and others threaten from the stand that if any apostates tried to leave the town, "hogholes would be stopped up with them." But her husband, William, did not believe in "killing to 'save' as taught by the teachers," she said. The forty-nine-year-old Parrish decided to leave with his sons William Beason, twenty-two, and Orrin, eighteen. On 14 March, he and his guide, Gardner G. Potter, an alleged friend, slipped out through the fort's east gate and headed south across Hobble Creek to Dry Creek, where they watched for his sons and their own "friendly" guide to come. Before they arrived, gunfire tore through the darkness, and Potter was hit and went down. He had lured Parrish into the ambush, but was ironically shot and killed by mistake. Then a man, later identified as William Bird, sprang forward and struggled with Parrish. Bird stabbed the older man repeatedly, and after Parrish fell, he bent down and cut his throat.[46]

Near an opposite corner of the fort, Orrin Parrish heard the shot but hardly had time to think what it meant when another gun sounded close at hand and his brother Beason fell at his side, mortally wounded. Then his guide, another "Judas goat" named Abraham Durfee, pointed a revolver at him and pulled the trigger. The gun misfired, and the younger Parrish jumped over the wall and ran to his uncle's house, where he feigned not to know what had happened.[47]

Everyone in town knew who had done it, but no local officials opened an investigation worthy of the name or made any arrests. Territorial authorities from Governor Young on down appeared to consider the murders justified under a higher legal code that applied in such cases. The episode seemed to send a calculated message to local Mormon leaders about what to do with apostates; to outsiders, it seemed a graphic illustration of what to expect. At the very least, it was intimidating to everyone, and it especially terrorized federal officials, whose work and safety depended on common respect for federal law.

---

46. "Testimony of Alvira L. Parrish and Orrin E. Parrish and Confession of Abraham Durfee," *Kirk Anderson's Valley Tan,* 19 April 1859; Cradlebaugh, *Utah and the Mormons,* 43–60.

47. For more on the Parrish-Potter murders, see Aird, *Mormon Convert,* 171–87.

Now thoroughly alarmed, David H. Burr reported, "there is no tribunal here to enforce [the law]." On 28 March, he told the General Land Office, "The United States courts have been broken up and driven from the Territory, and the Utah courts, with their usurped power, will not recognize the United States laws, and scarcely their own, when they conflict with their schemes."[48] With fear and desperation in every word, his report moved an American president to take immediate action:

> Judge Stiles, the only United States judge remaining here, intends trying to make his escape from the Territory as soon as it is possible to get over the mountains, but he fears attempts will be made to "cut him off." Knowing that our correspondence through the mails was examined, he has been afraid to write an account of affairs here, but intends reporting in person if he can get away. *The fact is, these people repudiate the authority of the United States in this country, and are in open rebellion against the general government.* I have sent all of my letters, excepting those relating purely to business matters, by private hands, and believe that most of them have gone through without being opened. Brigham Young has declared openly that the surveyors shall not be suffered to trespass on *their* lands as they did the last season, and threats are frequently made that any party attempting to survey will be "cut off." In their public meetings the Mormons have been told not to engage in the service of the surveyors, for they would be destroyed. They have hitherto failed in their endeavors to excite the Indians against us, and we think will not succeed hereafter. We have from the beginning had no fear except from the Mormons.
>
> So strong have been my apprehensions of danger to the surveyors, that I scarcely deemed it prudent to send any out; but Mr. Mogo, anxious to be at work, concluded he would venture to make the attempt. He took twenty-seven men with him, all well armed. Reports are already coming here that the party have been cut off, but I am satisfied that the reports are at least premature. If he is vigilant, with the force he has, I think he may avoid an attack.
>
> For the last three months my friends have considered my life in danger. I have been cursed and denounced in their public meetings, and the most diabolical threats made against me. I have remained at my post, partly

---

48. Burr to Hendricks, 28 March 1857, in Buchanan, *Utah Expedition*, 118.

to protect the office, but more for the reason that I have been hemmed in by the mountains of snow, and could not get away. Several houses of "apostate Mormons" have been pulled down, and at one time an attack was contemplated on the office, to destroy its contents and "wipe me out." I got notice of it in time, and kept well guarded. Several friends volunteered to protect me. I had five or six men in the office for nearly four weeks, and have not had less than three any time this winter. The Mormons, knowing we were prepared for defence, hesitated to make an attack, and we have thus far escaped. Affairs are rather more quiet now.

We are all, "Gentiles" and Mormons, waiting the arrival of the next mail from the States with much anxiety. If it should bring no tidings or assurance of protection from the United States, every "Gentile" officer may be compelled to leave the Territory. We find our position a critical one. We are by no means sure that we would be permitted to leave, for it is boldly asserted we would not get away alive. The same threats have been made against disaffected Mormons. We were inclined to think them idle menaces, until a few days since, when three men were killed at Spring-ville, sixty miles from this place, for making the attempt. They were shot, *their throats cut, and their bowels ripped open.* Another party was fired upon, and three of them wounded, one of them seriously.[49] "These out-rages are perpetrated by Mormons, and we have every reason to believe by the orders of Brigham Young No efforts are made by the authorities to bring the perpetrators to justice.[50]

Burr's report was not the only verbal bomb that exploded that spring on the president's desk. The first was a resignation letter from William W. Drummond, penned a year after he and his mistress had abandoned his post and only three weeks after the president was inaugurated. Among other things, he charged that supreme court records had been destroyed "by order of the Church"; federal officers were daily offended at hearing "the American government traduced"; men were imprisoned without

---

49. An apparent reference to the attack on four men, including John Tobin, son-in-law of San Bernardino founder Apostle Charles C. Rich, and John C. Peltro, described as a government surveyor, on the Santa Clara River on 18 February 1857. Tobin was seriously wounded, and two others were slightly hurt. In "'Pursue, Retake & Punish,'" Ardis E. Parshall offers convincing evidence that the attack was a case of mistaken identity.

50. Burr to Hendricks, 28 March 1857, in Buchanan, *Utah Expedition*, 118–20.

"having violated *any criminal law in America*"; Brigham Young instructed juries how to vote; Captain John W. Gunnison and others of his party had been murdered by the Indians "under the orders, advice, and direction" of the Mormons; and his predecessor, District Judge Leonidas Shaver, "came to his death by drinking poisoned liquors."[51]

The former judge gave no evidence for these charges but said that "much good would follow" if a non-Mormon was appointed governor and "supported by a *sufficient* military aid." As it was, he said, it was "noonday madness and folly to attempt to administer the law."[52] He soon followed his letter to Washington, no doubt to offer himself for the task, but the president, a peacemaker by nature, selected someone less controversial and more like himself.

How many crimes occurred during the Reformation period, after Drummond had left, will never be known, but one fearfully underscored his and David Burr's charges of lawlessness in Utah. In Sanpete Valley, Manti bishop Warren S. Snow led a party of men who castrated Thomas Lewis at Willow Creek that winter as he was being escorted to the prison at Great Salt Lake for alleged sexual crimes. The thirty-eight-year-old bishop and his companions took the young man "into the willows" and emasculated him "in a brutal manner Tearing the Chords right out," Samuel Pitchforth said. They left Lewis bleeding and senseless on "a bitter cold night."[53] When found two days later, he was crazed and almost dead.

The unpunished crime prompted Joseph Young to tell his younger brother, Brigham, that he disapproved of this act and "would rather die than to be made a Eunuch." To which Governor Young replied that the day would come when thousands would be made eunuchs "in order for them to be saved in the Kingdom of God." As for Bishop Snow, he said, "when a man is trying to do right & do[es] some thing that is not exactly in order I feel to sustain him & we all should."[54] John D. Lee said that Lewis was castrated because he refused to give up a young woman whom

51. Drummond to Jeremiah Black, 30 March 1857, ibid., 212–14.

52. Ibid.

53. Pitchforth, Diary, 31 May 1857, BYU Library. See also Peterson, "Warren Stone Snow."

54. Kenney, *Wilford Woodruff's Journal*, 5:55.

Snow wanted to make one of his polygamous wives.[55] The bishop on 20 April took seventeen-year-old Sarah Elizabeth Whiting as his fourth. Four days later, she and six other teenage plural wives accompanied older church officials who went with Young on his tour to Fort Limhi, the Mormon Indian mission in Oregon Territory.[56]

Meanwhile, as Burr watched for a way to escape, he and others would get no help from the territorial militia, known as the Nauvoo Legion. To prepare for the anticipated confrontation with the American republic, its commander, Lieutenant General Daniel H. Wells, theoretically equal in rank to the U.S. Army's commander-in-chief, Winfield Scott, announced on 1 April a reorganization of the theocracy's military arm to comply with the "good old Bible rule of Captains of 10's 100's &c," said its new judge advocate, Hosea Stout.[57] All able-bodied white males between the ages of eighteen and forty-five were ordered to enroll for duty in companies patterned after the hosts of ancient Israel.

General Wells issued General Order 1 at the same time, notifying Nauvoo Legion members that they now belonged to the armed forces of God's Kingdom. The order divided Utah into thirteen military districts and designated leaders in each who were ordered to enroll recruits from their areas into companies. Named general officers in command of the Sanpete and southern Utah County military districts were Bishops Warren Snow and Aaron Johnson, respectively.[58]

On 15 April, the way out of Utah at last opened, and David H. Burr, district judge George P. Stiles, and U.S. marshal Peter K. Dotson "with nearly all the gentile and apostate Scurf in this community left for the States," Hosea Stout said. To this, he added the next day, "The fire of the reformation is burning many out who flee from the Territory afraid of their lives." Stout saw this as scriptural: "The wicked flee when no man

55. Lee, *Mormonism Unveiled*, 285–86.

56. They were Margaret Ann Boyce Andrus, 17, ninth wife of Milo Andrus, 43; Sarah Texana East Blair, 16, sixth wife of Seth M. Blair, 38; Charlotte Campbell Dunn, 17, third wife of Thomas Dunn, 35; Nicoline Erickson Farr, 18, fifth wife of Lorin F. Farr, 36; Mary Bell Heywood, 18, fourth wife of Joseph L. Heywood, 41; and Emily Hoagland Little, 19, second wife of Jesse C. Little, 41.

57. Brooks, *On the Mormon Frontier*, 623.

58. For the new organization, see "Militia of Utah," *Deseret News*, 1 April 1857, 28.

pursue and so with an apostate Mormon he always believes his life in danger and flees accordingly," he said.[59]

As Stout admitted, not all the "scurf" had gone. Either braver or less wicked than his associates, Garland Hurt, a devout Methodist, stuck to his post, the last federal officer remaining in the breakaway territory. Before heading for a sanctuary that he had established, Hurt blew the whistle on Utah's superintendent of Indian affairs, Brigham Young. "Brigham Young, Heber Kimball, and other heads of the Church propose to leave here in April for a trip to the North," wrote an anonymous *New York Times* correspondent—probably Hurt—in early March. He reported that the names of between two hundred and three hundred men "were read off publicly in the Tabernacle" in February. "Where they are going or with what design is a profound mystery." He had also talked with Arapeen, the Northern Wasatch Ute chief and a half-brother of the late war leader Walkara. He had been "very assiduous in endeavors to ascertain what the Mormons were going to fight the Americans for. He said they had been urging him to join them in such a war, but declared that he had refused absolutely to have anything to do with it."[60]

In a subsequent private letter posted at Fort Bridger, Hurt alerted Washington that Young planned to visit tribes outside his jurisdiction. Even then, the governor was preparing an outfit of Indian goods for an "exploring expedition through the Territories of Oregon, Washington, and perhaps British Columbia."[61] Then Hurt picked up and moved to the Ute Indian Farm on the Spanish Fork River in Utah Valley, entrusting his life to the Natives he had befriended, and waited for the trap he had set to go off.

Young's northern expedition in spring 1857, the longest of his career in the West, was no pleasure jaunt, as Hurt suspected. It was a vital part of planning for the coming showdown with the United States. Young announced the journey on 22 February, less than a week after four worn-out horsemen, "whose trail could be followed by the blood from our horses legs," arrived at Great Salt Lake after a winter ride of some

59. Brooks, *On the Mormon Frontier*, 625.
60. Utah, "Highly Interesting from Utah," 5 March 1857, *New York Times*, 19 May 1857. Hurt often used the penname "Utah."
61. Hurt to Manypenny, 30 March 1857, USHS.

four hundred miles from Fort Limhi, the northernmost Indian mission on Salmon River.[62]

The news and the map they bore were riveting. In October 1856, Young had ordered northern Indian missionary Pleasant Green Taylor to contact Hudson's Bay agent Neil McArthur in Bitterroot Valley and investigate the purchase of Fort Hall on the Snake River, overlooking the Oregon Trail. The strategic location of the abandoned trading post drew Young's interest as he looked for ways to strengthen the Kingdom's defenses. That November, Taylor and three other Fort Limhi missionaries crossed the Continental Divide through the 1805 Lewis and Clark Pass and rode north to the great valley of the Bitterroot, now in southwestern Montana.[63]

The magnificence of the homeland of the proud Flathead Indians stunned Young's emissaries from the arid Great Basin. From its southern end at Ross's Hole, the twenty-mile-wide valley of the Bitterroot River stretched due north for nearly a hundred miles to the river's mouth at what is now Missoula, Montana. Guarded on three sides by soaring mountains, the valley was open only on the north and presented an imposing barrier to any invader. Nature had created a defensive bastion for the Flatheads to defend, and they had done so fiercely.

Of particular interest to the Mormon agents was the valley's agricultural potential. The ground was richly fertile and lay a thousand feet below Salt Lake Valley in elevation, thus offering a longer growing season. Streams of fresh, clear water rushed on every side, and the timber resources seemed endless. The three rode over rich prairie land to Cantonment Stevens, near present-day Hamilton, where they located McArthur, who was noncommittal about a price for the trading post, but said he would pass Young's bid along to Hudson's Bay.

As the others talked, Benjamin F. Cummings gave his attention to what may have been the real purpose of their trip from the beginning. The Nauvoo Legion officer saw at once the military and agricultural advantages of the region. He learned that the northern railroad survey from Fort Benton on the Missouri River followed the Clark Fork River,

62. Shurtliff, "Life and Travels," in Bigler, *Fort Limhi*, 137.
63. The other two were Benjamin Franklin Cummings and Ebenezer Robinson. For more on this exploration, see Bigler, *Fort Limhi*, 115–34.

then known as the Hell Gate, past the mouth of the Bitterroot at today's Missoula. He also saw that there was a wagon road that could take emigrants who came to Fort Benton by steamboat the rest of the way to Bitterroot Valley. "When considered with Mormonism," Cummings was struck by what he had learned. He and his two companions "could not help thinking that some day Bitter-Root valley as well as other portions of the country over east of the mountains would become the abode of the saints," he reported.[64]

Brigham Young thought so, too. Less than a week after the spent horsemen from Fort Limhi delivered Cummings's journal and map, he announced that he would go north as soon as the weather allowed to the Northern Indian Mission, then in Oregon Territory. As the *New York Times* noted, Young made public that Sunday the names of a "large number" of the theocracy's top civic, military, and religious leaders who were to go with him. Later that day, as he met with his close advisors, he listened as Cummings's journal was read aloud and studied his map. "The price of freight will come down when settlements are made in the Land," he told them.[65]

Young knew, too, that Bitterroot Valley and the upper Missouri River country would place latter-day Israel in the midst of the most powerful Lamanites in North America. As potential allies, the Great Basin tribes hardly compared with the Lakotas, Blackfeet, Flatheads, Bannocks, Nez Percés, Shoshones, and other Native peoples of the Northwest. He would see for himself. On 24 April 1857, Young led the long line of people, animals, wagons, and carriages that headed north from Great Salt Lake to begin a journey north of nearly four hundred miles to Fort Limhi. The parade extended more than a mile and numbered 115 men, 22 women, and 5 boys. It also included 168 horses and mules, 54 carriages and wagons, and two light boats with decking for crossing the Snake River.

Since 1851, when the Hudson's Bay agent at Fort Colvile had reported that there was "no room to doubt" that the Flathead country would be "largely colonized by Mormons" that summer, there had been repeated

64. Cummings, Biography and Journals, 16–19 November 1856, BYU Library.
65. Kenney, *Wilford Woodruff's Journal*, 5:26.

rumors that the Mormons would move north, even as far as Alaska.[66] Now a closer look at the makeup of Young's northbound cavalcade seemed at last to confirm these reports. At its head were all three members of the ruling triumvirate, making up the First Presidency: Young, Heber C. Kimball, and Nauvoo Legion commander Daniel H. Wells, chosen to fill the office of second counselor left vacant by Jedediah Grant's passing. Traveling with this high-ranking trio were the Kingdom's top military, political, and religious leaders.

An especially notable member of the party was Hurt's informant Arapeen, who like many Natives had learned the benefits of playing both ends against the middle. Having concluded that it was better to cooperate with his white cousins than to fight them, he was going to take part in Young's powwows with northern tribal leaders. As evidence of the benefits of cooperation, the chief and his wife, Wispit, rode in a special wagon of their own, escorted by U.S. Indian interpreter Dimick B. Huntington, Young's personal ambassador to the tribes.

Over the next thirty-three days, Utah Territory's superintendent of Indian affairs met with the Indians of Oregon Territory and gave them "many presents of blankets" and other gifts in violation of federal law.[67] Afterward, he accounted for them to the Office of Indian Affairs by reporting them as presents to Indians in Utah, as Garland Hurt had anticipated.[68] Possibly also taking part in the sessions was the Pahvant chief, Kanosh. If so, both he and Arapeen would have given convincing testimonials on behalf of their hosts if it would encourage them to leave their territory.

Young and members of his entourage inspected the Lewis and Clark Trail over the Continental Divide that led to the waters of the Missouri River and a rough wagon trace to Bitterroot Valley. They selected a location on Salmon River's east fork, now the Lemhi River, for a second fort in a planned expansion of the mission into a full settlement. Young told the missionaries that the Oregon outpost marked an overall shift in

---

66. Alexander Anderson to George Simpson, 21 April 1851, Simpson, Incoming Correspondence, Hudson's Bay Company Archives, 635–36.

67. A number of participants reported on the meetings, including Lewis Shurtliff, John D. T. McAllister, and John Brown. For the latter's account, see Brown, *Autobiography*.

68. See Smith, *Accounts of Brigham Young*.

Mormon colonization from south and west to the north. Said a member of his party, "[Young] felt well toward the brethren in this place and said the settlements must go north instead of south."[69]

Young's interest in the north was not a well-kept secret. His meeting with the Indians and the ostentatious nature of his visit set off rumors that the Mormons were coming, and reports of their tampering with the tribes rolled across the Northwest and beyond: a year later, the president of the United States would ask Utah's congressional representative what Brigham Young was doing in Oregon that spring.[70] George Gibbs in Washington heard from Indians near Steilacoom that "the Klikatats had told them that Choosuklee, (Jesus Christ,) had recently appeared on the other side of the country, and all would be well for themselves." It was no stretch for Gibbs to connect "this second advent with the visit of Brigham Young to the Flathead and Nez Perces country."[71]

General Newman S. Clarke, Department of the Pacific commander at San Francisco, passed Gibbs's report on to U.S. Army headquarters and included a "private" letter from Captain Ralph W. Kirkham at Fort Walla Walla. "The Snakes tell our Indians that they are well supplied with ammunition, and that they can get from the Mormons any quantity that they wish," the officer said. "They further tell our Indians that the Mormons are anxious to supply them, to wit: the Nez Perces, the Cayuses, and Walla Wallas, with everything they wish."[72]

The flood of similar stories prompted James W. Nesmith, superintendent of Indian affairs for Oregon and Washington, to investigate the "large colony of Mormons" on Salmon River. He sent Flathead agent Richard H. Lansdale to check into reports that the Mormons at Fort Limhi were "supplying the Indians with arms and ammunition and inciting them to hostilities."[73] The agent went as far as Bitterroot Valley in August 1857, but found little or no evidence to sustain such stories. At the same time, he did report that "the leading Flathead chiefs have serious

69. Dame, Journal, 18 May 1857, Dame Papers, BYU Library.

70. Bernhisel, summary of interview with President Buchanan, Spring 1858, BYC.

71. Clarke to L. Thomas, 1 January 1858, in Floyd, *Annual Report, 1858*, 335–36.

72. Ibid.

73. Nesmith to V. W. Denver, 1 September 1857, 35th Cong., 1st sess., 1857–58, vol. 2, S. Ex. Doc. 11, serial 919, 1858, 612.

fears lest the Mormons, being driven from their present settlements by the government, should overrun and occupy their lands in force."[74]

The Bible-reading Lansdale did his best to calm the Flatheads' alarm, but such rumors persisted until General Clarke notified the U.S. Army post at Walla Walla on 12 January 1858 that information from across the frontier indicated that "through the Mormons the Indians are being inclined to hostility." Moreover, he said, "a conflict in Utah may be the signal for trouble on the frontier, and it is not improbable that the Mormons may move north."[75]

74. Lansdale to Nesmith, 22 September 1857, ibid., 663–69.
75. W. W. Mackall to Edward J. Steptoe, 12 January 1858, in Floyd, *Annual Report, 1858*, 336.

This portrait shows Utah's territorial governor and the president, prophet, seer, and revelator of the Church of Jesus Christ of Latter-day Saints after the time he challenged the authority of the United States. Authors' collection.

Mounted Rifleman Joseph Heger's 24 July 1858 pencil sketch of the Sanpete Valley
settlement of Manti shows one of the best surviving images of a Mormon frontier fort.
Courtesy Yale Collection of Western Americana, Beinecke Rare Book and Manuscript
Library.

This September 1858 image from *Harper's Weekly* shows the adobe hall, now known as
the Old Tabernacle, where Mormon leaders made many of the speeches that called their
loyalty to the U.S. government into question. Courtesy Rick Grunder.

This engraving from *Ballou's Pictorial Drawing-Room Companion*, 20 September 1856, is one of only two known contemporary images of Mormon handcarts. Courtesy Rick Grunder.

As a member of the First Presidency, Mormonism's ruling triumvirate, Jedediah Grant was called the "sledgehammer of Brigham." He stoked the fires of the Reformation before his untimely death in December 1856. Authors' collection.

The dilapidated adobe fort typical of Mormon frontier outposts is at the center of Mounted Rifleman Joseph Heger's 23 July 1858 pencil sketch of Ephraim, Utah. It also shows better-kept private homes, half-starved livestock, and the settlement's irrigation ditch, which made survival possible in the arid West. Courtesy Yale Collection of Western Americana, Beinecke Rare Book and Manuscript Library.

Allegedly "taken about 1859—Bee Hive House and Lion House," this photograph shows the Brigham Young estate, with LDS Church offices in the foreground and Salt Lake's city wall in the background. Courtesy Yale Collection of Western Americana, Beinecke Rare Book and Manuscript Library.

Brevet Lieutenant General Winfield Scott is pictured in a Mathew Brady studio portrait in civilian dress about the time "Old Fuss and Feathers" commanded the U.S. Army during the Utah War. Daguerreotype Collection, Library of Congress Prints and Photographs Division.

This unpublished image shows apostle and LDS Church historian George A. Smith about the time he toured southern Utah and set the stage for the massacre at Mountain Meadows in 1857. Smith's subsequent "investigation" of the atrocity blamed it on the Indians. Courtesy Old Rock Church Museum, Daughters of Utah Pioneers, Parowan, Utah.

Known to the Native people he served as "the American," Dr. Hurt was the last non-Mormon federal officer to leave Utah in 1857. The Indian agent carried first word of the Mountain Meadows massacre to the advancing army in October. Authors' collection.

Porter Rockwell was immortalized by biographer Harold Schindler as "Man of God, Son of Thunder." His exploits during the Utah War were not as colorful as often depicted, but they did encompass key assignments from Brigham Young. This portrait is by noted Utah artist Alvin Gittins. Courtesy Utah State Historical Society.

Bill Hickman did not formally hold the offices described in the title of his autobiography, but he was indeed one of Mormonism's most notorious serial killers. Despite Brigham Young's later insistence that he barely knew Hickman, Utah's territorial legislature recommended Hickman as a possible U.S. attorney for Utah Territory. From *Brigham's Destroying Angel; Being the Life, Confession, and Startling Disclosures of the Notorious Bill Hickman, the Danite Chief of Utah* (1872).

CHAPTER 6

To Cut the Thread

Independence

The time must come when there will be a separation between this
kingdom and the kingdoms of this world, even in every point of view.
The time must come when this kingdom must be free and independent
from all other kingdoms. Are you prepared to have the thread cut now?

—Brigham Young, 2 August 1857

Unaware of the fears his junket to Fort Limhi had spread, on returning to Utah Brigham Young applauded the progress of the Reformation
while he was away. "Our city looks as though it had taken an emetic
and vomited forth apostates, officials, and in fact all the filth which was
weighing us down," he said.[1] He had little good to say publicly about
the northern country he had seen. As they journeyed over the Snake
River Plain, he had begged his companions not "to take all of the rock
out of the road, for if they did there would be nothing to travel on."[2]
He told his followers that he had done what he set out to do in going to
Oregon to "rest the mind and weary the body." On the eve of his fifty-
sixth birthday, five days after coming back, he said, "I have renewed my
strength, renewed the vigor of my body and mind; and I believe that I
am as ready to act in any capacity now as ever I have been in my life."[3]
He would need all the mind and muscle he could muster to pilot the ship

1. Young to Parley P. Pratt and Ezra T. Benson, 30 June 1857, *Millennial Star* 19, 29
August 1857, LDS Archives.
2. Brigham Young, "Remarks," 31 May 1857, *Deseret News*, 10 June 1857, 107.
3. Ibid.

of Zion through the storms that now threatened the course he himself had charted.

To trusted associates he told a different story. "We saw much good land some little of it good soil, much good grazing land, but the best soil we are told 'lies still ahead' in the Bitter root valley and in the vallies [*sic*] still further east on the head waters of the [Missouri River]," he told Apostle Orson Pratt in England.[4] He later advised Pratt "to turn our emigration to the Canadas." Referring to the map, he pointed to "the north of Lake Superior, and along the chain of small Lakes dividing the United States and British possessions." There the apostle would find an "abundance of space for settlements as that country has none at present."[5]

Early signs of trouble ahead came only three days after his return, when four wagonloads of letters and newspapers from the East rolled in. With the heavy delivery on 29 May also came Apostle George A. Smith and John M. Bernhisel. The following Sunday they joined the other members of Young's prayer circle to corroborate hostile reports on conditions in Utah, which they read aloud from eastern papers. "We find that all hell is boiling over against us," said Wilford Woodruff.[6]

Adding to the apostle's alarm was a letter from the trusted president of the faith's Eastern Mission. William I. Appleby in New York City relayed unofficial reports that General Winfield Scott had ordered Brevet Brigadier General William S. Harney and some twenty-five hundred officers and men to take positions along the Oregon Trail from Fort Leavenworth to Fort Laramie.[7] According to Appleby, James Gordon Bennett of the *New York Herald* speculated that the government intended to "send them to Utah and appoint a Governor to follow." Provoking this punitive action, he said, were the "burning of the Records & Laws of the United States" and the widely published letters of former judge William W. Drummond.[8]

More shocks came a month later with the news from the East. On 23 June, expressmen Ephraim Hanks and Feramorz Little arrived from Fort Bridger, the last leg on the thousand-mile journey from Independence.

4. Young to Pratt, 29 May 1857, *Millennial Star*, 15 August 1857, 524–25.
5. Young to Pratt, 12 September 1857, ibid.
6. Kenney, *Wilford Woodruff's Journal*, 5:53–54.
7. Harney's regular rank was colonel, U.S. Second Dragoons.
8. Appleby to Young, 13 April 1857, BYC.

Their arrival rang up a new record for delivery from the Missouri River—just twenty-three days. The Mormon pair also shared a less wanted honor by making the last delivery by the short-lived Brigham Young Express and Carrying Company (BYX), whose contract had not been renewed by the U.S. Post Office.

The news they brought shocked the faithful. On 13 May 1857, a cuckolded husband had murdered Parley P. Pratt, one of the faith's original apostles, in northwestern Arkansas. The popular theologian and missionary had taken as his twelfth polygamous wife the emotionally unbalanced Eleanor McLean, who had left her husband and been "sealed" to Pratt. The furious Hector McLean had begun a pursuit of the fifty-year-old apostle. The press closely followed the unfolding drama, involving adultery, Mormons, and polygamy.

In a carefully planned operation, Eleanor McLean reclaimed her children from the custody of her parents in New Orleans on the pretense that she had seen the error of her ways. She then headed north to meet Pratt in Indian Territory. Her abandoned husband got wind of the design and pursued her to Fort Gibson in what is now Oklahoma, where he had the apostle arrested for stealing the McLean children's clothes. Five hundred spectators jammed the U.S. circuit court in Van Buren, Arkansas, to hear the husband tell how Pratt had stolen his wife. Lacking evidence to convict on the charges, the judge released Pratt the following day and had his horse quietly brought to the jail. Whether he intended to or not, he had given the apostle a death sentence.

When Hector McLean learned that Pratt had fled, he pursued the apostle, and overtook him near the Arkansas state line. There, as two companions looked on, he shot and stabbed Pratt from horseback. He afterward paraded the streets as if he had done something worthy of adulation, then took his children and left. No attempt was made to arrest or punish him for killing the unresisting apostle. Many in western Arkansas appeared to consider Pratt's murder justified. But to the faithful in Utah, where the Reformation still burned brightly, Pratt had been killed for his religious beliefs. Like Joseph and Hyrum Smith, he was now a martyr of the faith.

Word of Pratt's death was apparently not the only blow that landed on 23 June with the eastern mail. Even if it was anticipated, the second hit was even more stunning. Frederick H. Burr, another of runaway surveyor general David H. Burr's sons, was fishing near present-day Montpelier, Idaho, on 24 June when he wrote in his journal, "News of troops coming to Salt Lake."[9]

If Burr heard the news on 24 June, the day after the eastern mail arrived at Great Salt Lake, it seems highly unlikely that Young was unaware that President Buchanan in late May had decided to unseat him as governor and ordered the U.S. Army to escort his successor to Great Salt Lake to restore federal authority in Utah. On 28 May, Lieutenant General Winfield Scott ordered "not less than 2,500 men," nearly one-third of the officers and enlisted men available for frontier service, to carry out this duty. Scott told Harney, the expedition's commander, that his force was to serve as a *posse comitatus* in aiding a new governor and federal officers to keep the peace and enforce the law. He was directed not to "attack any body of citizens whatever, except on such requisition or summons, or in sheer self-defense."[10]

Scott's orders fell on a military already stretched to the breaking point by the failure of Congress to increase its strength in line with unprecedented national growth. The period of rapid expansion began with the annexation of Texas in 1845, followed a year later by the settlement of the Oregon border issue. In 1848, after the invasion and defeat of Mexico, the treaty of peace added virtually the entire present Southwest to the U.S. domain, over a half-million square miles, an increase second only to the 1803 Louisiana Purchase. The acquisition produced calls for protection from thousands of emigrants who crowded the trails west, seeking land in Oregon, gold in California, and Zion in Utah. Additional demands rose from the "bleeding Kansas" border war over slavery.

The guerrilla war developing in Kansas was a direct result of the triumph of the popular sovereignty doctrine implemented in Illinois senator Stephen A. Douglas's Kansas-Nebraska Act of 1854. It preceded the trouble brewing for the army in Utah. The act created the territories of Kansas and Nebraska, opened new Indian lands to settlement, and repealed the Missouri Compromise of 1820, which had maintained a delicate balance between slave and free states. The Supreme Court's

9. Frederick H. Burr, Diary, 24 June 1857, Beinecke Library.

10. George W. Lay to Harney, 29 June 1857, in Buchanan, *Utah Expedition*, 4–9.

Dred Scott decision, issued two days after Buchanan's inauguration in March 1857, essentially required all states to enforce the hated Fugitive Slave Act, further exacerbating the growing tensions between North and South, while the subsequent murderous battles between Yankee jay-hawkers and Southern border ruffians added immensely to demands on the army's limited manpower. The bloodletting in Kansas complicated the president's need to win popular support for enforcing federal law in remote Utah Territory. And reports from Kansas traveled with tele-graphic speed, while news from Utah was hardly news when it finally reached the eastern press weeks if not months after it happened.

Expected to police this huge area was an army limited by law to some eighteen thousand officers and men. Recruitment during the years before the Civil War failed to make up for losses from death, disease, and desertion.[11] As a result, the army never gained its authorized strength from 1848 to 1861. In addition, coast defense and other eastern duties took about one-third of its line and staff manpower. As a consequence, said historian Robert M. Utley, "Never in the years before the Civil War did the little regular army succeed in fielding more than seven or eight thousand officers and enlisted men for duty in a frontier west of two million square miles."[12]

If the army's strength failed to strike fear into Indian hearts, the qual-ity of some seven hundred line officers, who led its nineteen combat regiments—ten infantry, five mounted, and four artillery—did much to compensate for its lack of manpower. Most were West Point gradu-ates and possessed the qualities that an education at the military academy imparts. For dedication to duty, honor, and performance, they were a distinctive class, and many were experienced veterans of the Mexican War or had learned the art of leadership from making life-and-death decisions for small units scattered over vast areas, beyond supporting dis-tance. Richard S. Ewell caught a steer in 1862 and drove it to camp to feed his men. When he was reminded that his division numbered eight thousand, the former U.S. Army captain, now a Confederate general, said, "Ah, I was thinking of my fifty dragoons!"[13]

11. Ball, *Army Regulars on the Western Frontier*, xxi.
12. Utley, *Indian Frontier of the American West*, 40. See also Utley, *Frontiersmen in Blue*.
13. Freeman, *Lee's Lieutenants*, 1:348.

When it came to enlisted men, immigrants outnumbered native-born Americans by two to one in 1857. The majority came from European countries and in most cases had joined the army for five years out of dire economic necessity. By far the largest number came from Ireland, followed by Germany, England, and Scotland. As new recruits, they received little or no basic training, but learned the skills of soldiering from noncommissioned officers or just by doing. While most were laborers, enough tradesmen signed up to do the unmilitary work of building their own posts and quarters. In character, they ranged from reliable soldiers who took pride in their profession to the misfits who contributed to an annual desertion rate of about 10 percent.

In many ways, officers and enlisted men confronted similar conditions. Both groups suffered inadequate compensation for the service they performed, and both enjoyed few opportunities for advancement. Brevet promotions, honorary advances in grade for battlefield performance, had been awarded to many during the Mexican War, but they hardly made up for the lack of regular advancements in grade. In addition to low pay and slow promotion, officers and enlisted men shared danger, exposure, a diet lacking in fresh vegetables and fruit, and primitive medical care. Posing a deadlier threat were alcohol and monotony. Sectional loyalty among officers toward the North or South was prevalent, while enlisted men almost to a man identified with the Union. In summing up the state of America's frontier army at this time, historian Durwood Ball said: "Year after year, the United States deployed its army, underfunded, undermanned, and ill-trained, into frontier war zones and demanded the work of a legion from a mere battalion."[14]

So it was not surprising that Brigham Young laughed when William A. Hickman confirmed on 25 June the news, which Young had probably first heard the day before, that the U.S. Army was coming.[15] In his memoir, Hickman claimed to have warned Young and the other leaders gathered in his office that troops were on the way; but he "was laughed at, tantalized, and treated scornfully for making such an assertion. I told them I had been there and ought to know as well as those who sat at home and

14. Ball, *Army Regulars on the Western Frontier*, 85.
15. Kenney, *Wilford Woodruff's Journal*, 5:62.

knew nothing," he recalled. "All hands agreed they were not coming, and Brother Brigham said neither should they come so this ended it."[16]

The apparent failure of the government to notify Young that he was being replaced as governor later became a major issue. Ironically, the War Department *had* notified him, at least in a backhanded way, that the army was coming. The Utah Expedition was carrying seventeen copies of the latest *General Regulations of the Army*, which had appeared in March 1857. In a May 1857 letter addressed to "His Excellency The Governor of Utah Territory," the secretary of war, John B. Floyd, wrote that he was sending them for distribution to the territorial militia "in such manner as you may deem advisable." The secretary added a postscript: "The army will deliver them."[17] The letter, now in Utah's state archives, probably arrived with the June mail delivery.

Having repeatedly spoken of his contempt for the government and prophesied of the imminence of a war between the Lion of the Lord's Kingdom and the American eagle, Young seems to have found the reality of pending conflict disquieting. Whatever the Mormon leader knew or believed as June 1857 ended, he kept it quiet for a month. He apparently had decided to make the public announcement in Utah fulfill an unrecorded prophecy that he later claimed to have made on 24 July 1847 upon his arrival in Salt Lake Valley: "If the people of the United States will leave us alone for ten years, we will ask no odds of them."[18]

If indeed he had said it, the announcement of coming federal troops on the tenth anniversary of his arrival could not have been better timed. The 1857 celebration was held at what is today the Brighton Ski Resort, high in the Wasatch Mountains, before an invited audience of Mormon stalwarts. Stagecoach passengers informed a reporter for the *New York Daily Tribune* that "contrary to previous practice, Gentiles were carefully excluded."[19] Access to "the "Pic-nic party at the Head Waters of Big Cottonwood" was tightly controlled; at least two elaborate invitations were printed, containing a detailed list of restrictions: "Bishops will,

16. Hickman and Beadle, *Brigham's Destroying Angel*, 117

17. Floyd to Young, 11 May 1857, UTMR.

18. Young, "Remarks," 13 September 1857, *Deseret News*, 23 September 1857, 228. We know of no contemporary source to confirm this prediction.

19. A. G. Browne, Jr., "Dispatch," Fort Kearny, 23 August 1857, *New York Daily Tribune*, 10 September 1857, in MacKinnon, *At Sword's Point*, 1:217.

before passing the first mill, furnish a full and complete list of all persons accompanying them from their respective Wards, and hand the same to the Guard at the gate."[20] For two days, traffic almost stood still in Big Cottonwood Canyon as lathered teams dragged hundreds of carriages and wagons up the winding wagon road a few feet at a time.

On the evening of 23 July, a bugle summoned the early arrivals to what Young called "the Secret chambers of the mountains" to hear him make a short speech. "He had things on his mind to tell that he had never told to any people before. The time had now come he could have the privilege of revealing them," Ira Ames recounted. "We have had men ranging these mountains ever since we have been here," Young was reported to have said, "hunting for secret retreats, and mountain passes. The formation of the mountains around this place are such that they are calculated to ward off the traveler on the outside from coming down in here."[21]

At nearly five thousand feet above the valley floor, frost still covered the ground when Pioneer Day 1857 opened the following morning. Twenty-five hundred or so invited participants were reluctant to leave their warm sacks, but "a few rounds from a howitzer soon had everyone in motion," Hosea Stout said.[22] The fresh mountain breezes resonated with "music, singing, praying, addresses and each one enjoyed himself," Wilford Woodruff enthused. "Many trout were caught in the Lake," said the apostle, an avid fisherman. Five brass bands enlivened the affair, and a platoon of mounted lancers and companies of light artillery and infantry gave a military touch to the celebration in the scenic mountain valley guarded on three sides by jagged peaks.[23]

Young had organized the elaborate festivities to inform his most devout followers that the U.S. Army was marching on Utah and to rally them to his cause. About noon, five dusty men rode dramatically into the camp with astonishing news. Two of them, Judson Stoddard and Bishop A. O. Smoot, had reached Salt Lake the day before in a record-breaking twenty days from Independence. The only mail they bore was a letter from the Post Office Department notifying Hiram Kimball that his fail-

20. Cooley, *Diary of Brigham Young*, 46.
21. Ames, Journal and Record, 24, USHS.
22. Brooks, *On the Mormon Frontier*, 2:634.
23. Kenney, *Wilford Woodruff's Journal*, 5:69.

ure to execute the mail contract in time, and the "unsettled state of things at Salt Lake," had made it necessary to reject Young's bid for renewal.[24] Mail conductor Porter Rockwell had joined them at Fort Laramie, and the party picked up Salt Lake probate judge Elias Smith before heading for Silver Lake the following morning.

"They informed Us that the United States had taken away the mail Contract & that a New Governor & judges & 2,500 troops would start for Utah soon," Woodruff said tersely. Mormon leaders had gathered in Young's spacious tent, where "questions were asked and answered," the apostle went on. At first, Young seemed conciliatory. He said that if the governor and officers behaved themselves, they would be well treated, but he would not let soldiers enter the valley. But by sunset he had grown belligerent when a trumpet called the revelers to an eminence inside the campground, and he announced the news. Never again would he "submit to oppression either to individuals, towns, Counties, states or Nation," he made clear.[25] Moved to unaccustomed eloquence, Daniel H. Wells "then spoke a few moments full of the spirit of prophecy and predicted many things in relation to the United States, and these troops that are coming toward Utah," Ames wrote. "He then made a prayer so solemn and powerful that all were effected. Many tears were shed."[26] Afterward, many "passed the evening in the joyous dance" in three spacious boweries with planked floors, George D. Watt reported in the *Deseret News*.[27] But if the road home was downhill, the mood of all the next day was somber.

Of the inner circle that met in Young's spacious tent on 24 July, only Elias Smith recorded other surprising news that otherwise went unannounced.[28] The buckboard from Independence had also delivered Eleanor McLean, the widow of Parley Pratt. More emotionally unhinged than ever by the apostle's death, the troubled woman cried for the apostle's innocent blood to be avenged, and gave church historian Wilford Woodruff a heart-rending if overheated account of Pratt's murder on 1 August. Just two days later, Alexander Fancher and John T. Baker led a wagon train of more than one hundred farm families, most of them women and

24. "No Eastern Mail," *Deseret News*, 5 August 1857, 173.
25. Kenney, *Wilford Woodruff's Journal*, 5:59–60.
26. Ames, Journal and Record, 25, USHS.
27. "The 24th of July," *Deseret News*, 29 July 1857, 165.
28. Thomas, *Elias Smith's Journal*, 23 July 1857.

children, into Great Salt Lake on their way to make homes in California. They were from northwest Arkansas, where Pratt had been killed.

Two days after Pioneer Day, Young opened his Sunday remarks with a scripture reading, something he rarely, if ever, did. That he did so on 26 July, when his followers desperately wanted to hear why an American army was marching to Utah, was significant. His choice of scripture revealed a deep conviction that Buchanan's move was the fulfillment of prophecy. A secretive man who knew how keep his plans to himself, Young signaled that the time had come for God's Kingdom to rise up and fulfill its destiny. The verses he read revealed that a separation from the United States was at hand. Those who heard him that day understood the reason for the coming confrontation, as many others since have failed to grasp, because the power of religious belief to shape human actions is too often underestimated.

Young opened his Bible to the Book of Daniel and read from chapter 2, verses 27 to 49. They tell how Daniel went before Nebuchadnezzar to interpret a dream that had deeply troubled the king and mystified his wise men. But Daniel told the Babylonian ruler there was a God in heaven who had made known to him "what shall be in the latter days." In that time, he said, a stone would be cut out of the mountain without hands, which would break in pieces all worldly kingdoms and become "a great mountain" and fill the whole earth. Then would "the God of heaven set up a kingdom, which shall never be destroyed," the young prophet said, "*but* it shall break in pieces and consume all these kingdoms, and it shall stand forever."[29]

He had established the Kingdom that God revealed to the king of Babylon, Young assured his people. They need not be afraid because it would never be destroyed, "and that is my testimony," he promised. "This is the kingdom of heaven—the kingdom of God which Daniel saw," he stated. "This is the kingdom that was to be set up in the last days."[30] Such a kingdom could never compromise or coexist with man-made dominions, but would consume them, starting with the American republic. Its destiny was universal dominion. This was Young's belief

29. Young, "Remarks," 26 July 1857, *Deseret News*, 5 August 1857, 172–73. See also *Journal of Discourses*, 5:73–79.

30. Young, "Remarks," 2 August 1857, *Deseret News*, 12 August 1857, 180. See also Young, "The Coming Crisis," 2 August 1857, in *Journal of Discourses*, 5:99.

and purpose. He would do it in his lifetime: it was the reason for the Mormon rebellion.

Young and other Mormon leaders breathed defiance at the U.S. Army units at Fort Leavenworth preparing to march west on the Oregon-California Trail. "I shall take a hostile move by our enemies as an evidence that it is time for the thread to be cut," roared the Lion of the Lord. "I think that we will find three hundred who will lap up water, and we can whip out the Midianites."[31] During early August, Young outlined his war policy. On the ninth his councilors agreed that since the government had failed to provide any explanation of its intentions, Utah had "a right to put upon" any forces it sent. "Fixed my detirmintation not to let any troops enter this territory," Young confided to his diary on 11 August. "And unless the Government assumes a more pacific attitude, to declare emigration by the overland route Stopt. And make every preparation to give the U.S. a Sound drubbing. I do not feel to be imposed upon any more."[32]

Those who heard the sermons Young delivered during August and September 1857 had little doubt about his regard for the American republic. A Gentile merchant told Arkansan S. B. Honea during a brief stop in Salt Lake that on 16 August "Brigham Young had declared, in the Temple, that henceforth Utah was a separate and independent Territory, and owed no obedience or allegiance to any form or laws, but those of their own enactment, and called upon the people to stand together, and support him in maintaining the cause of God and the church."[33] Devout Mormons heard the same definitive statements: "This people came out and declared their independency of the United States from this very time," George Brown Bailey recalled. "The Presidency put it to the people wither they would maintain it to the last and it was carried by unanimous vote of uplifted hands and a shout of Yea which made the place echo."[34]

31. Ibid. For the story of Gideon and the three hundred who lapped water and defeated a great Midianite army, see Judg. 7:5–25. In this sermon, Young claimed that members of the British Parliament "know all about us" from studying "those *Journals of Discourses*." He speculated that they "keep them from the Queen, for fear that she would believe and be converted." Ibid.

32. Cooley, *Diary of Brigham Young*, 57–58.

33. "Declaration of Independence," *Los Angeles Star*, 24 October 1857, 2.

34. Bailey, Journal, 23 August 1857, Authors' Collection.

With his usual bluntness, Heber C. Kimball announced in early September, "We commenced last Sunday to declare that we are a free people, and we will be free from this day henceforth and for ever; and we never will come under that yoke again."[35] Hosea Stout heard the governor declare that "the thred was cut between us and the U.S. and that the Almighty recognized us as a free and independent people."[36] On another occasion, Young made clear, "If they can send a force against this people, we have every Constitutional and legal right to send them to hell, and we calculate to send them there."[37]

So Brigham Young could tell Wilford Woodruff that the time had come to sell his coat and buy a sword, for the Mormons had "to go & deliver ourselves from our enemies & the Lord will help us. He will fight our battles & we will become an independant kingdom."[38] Yet at the same time, the Mormon press was usually careful to make such statements conditional: "I shall take it as a witness that God designs to cut the thread between us and the world," Young said in a printed sermon, "*when* an army undertakes to make their appearance in this Territory to chastise me or to destroy my life from the earth."[39]

The erstwhile governor of Utah Territory was equally determined to keep up the pretense that he was still a dedicated if defamed servant of the federal government. Young's ability to believe that he was both at war with the United States and an officer of its government, along with his repeated declarations that Mormon arms would destroy the U.S. Army while resolutely keeping open an escape route should he have misread the mind of the Lord, reflected his lifelong ability to believe two contradictory notions with equal conviction.

Understanding the striking paradoxes in Young's conduct of the Utah War requires an appreciation of how the Mormon leader saw his role as prophet. "I don't profess to be such a Prophet as were Joseph Smith and Daniel, but I am a Yankee guesser," he said in July 1857. His mentor "had the keys to get visions and revelations, dreams and manifestations, and the Holy Ghost for the people." Joseph Smith had begun his revelations

35. Kimball, "Discourse," 6 September 1857, in *Journal of Discourses*, 5:217.

36. Brooks, *On the Mormon Frontier*, 2:636.

37. Young, "Remarks," 13 September 1857, *Deseret News*, 23 September 1857, 229/2.

38. Kenney, *Wilford Woodruff's Journal*, 26 August 1857, 5:83.

39. Young, "Remarks," in *Journal of Discourses*, 5:99. Emphasis added.

with a simple "Thus saith the Lord," but Young only "received the spirit of Christ Jesus, which is the spirit of prophecy."[40] He had to rely on signs, portents, and the promptings of "the still small voice," rather than the direct communication that Smith claimed to have with the Almighty. This lack of certainty led him to continually second-guess himself—and made him always careful to provide a back door should a visionary policy go astray.

Young's role as a Yankee guesser created a fundamental contradiction in his character. From start to finish, his career seemed to testify to his status as a true believer entirely dedicated to doing "the work of Joseph." But his devotion to the cause conflicted with his other Yankee attributes, most notably his fundamentally practical and pragmatic nature. However much he believed that the approach of the army in 1857 signaled the beginning of "the winding up scene," he could not be sure. So while his public statements repeatedly spoke of "cutting the thread" that bound Utah Territory to the United States, his printed sermons and official correspondence always cast such declarations as conditional.

Both publicly and in private, Young's words reflected a singular understanding of the nation's charter, to which he often vowed eternal allegiance, and how it authorized him to transport American soldiers to the nether regions. "The United States had turned mob & were breaking the Constitution of the United States & we would now have to go forth & defend it & also the kingdom of God," he preached in mid-August. "If General Harney Came here with an armey to destroy this people we would destroy him & his armey."[41] He believed that God had inspired the Constitution to create a land of religious freedom where His Kingdom would be restored and prevail, superseding the American republic and all other earthly realms, as a prelude to Christ's return. The nation's charter was a steppingstone to higher, millennial rule, not an end in itself. He cherished the Constitution as a founding document of God's Kingdom and considered himself its true defender.

Equally original was Young's view of republican government. "Parties in our government have no better idea than to think the Republic stands all the firmer on opposition," he said. But he did not agree.

40. Young, "Remarks," 26 July 1857, *Deseret News*, 12 August 1857, 172.
41. Kenney, *Wilford Woodruff's Journal*, 16 August 1857, 78.

"A Republican government consists in letting the people rule by their united voice, without a dissension; in learning what is for the best and unitedly doing it," he said. "This is true Republicanism." The founding prophet of the faith had paradoxically called this kind of government a "theodemocracy." By any name, theocratic rule had already led to violent opposition in Missouri and Illinois. Now, under Young, it had brought on a civil war with the United States.[42]

Meanwhile, an old Mormon friend put himself in line for a shortcut to Hades by backing Buchanan's action to impose federal sovereignty on the theocratic territory. In a typically blunt speech at Springfield, Illinois, Senator Stephen A. Douglas charged that "the Mormon Government, with Brigham Young at its head, is now forming alliance with Indian tribes in Utah and adjoining territories—stimulating the Indians to acts of hostility." Like earlier denials of polygamy, the Mormon refutation of Douglas was equally lacking in nuance. The senator's "frenzy for office" had placed him "in the ranks of the foul libelers and maligners of a people loyal and patriotic far beyond the short ken of your dark and feeble comprehension," the *Deseret News* said in early September.[43]

Weeks before this denial, however, word had gone out to the tribes that gainsaid the indignant profession of innocence. On 13 August, Lieutenant General Daniel H. Wells ordered the Nauvoo Legion's district commanders to tell "the Indians that our enemies are also their enemies & how they are continually fighting against them somewhere and that it will be come upon them as the Sioux & Cheyennes in due time." The commanders were to inform the Natives that "they must be our friends and stick to us, for if our enemies kill us off, they will surely be cut off by the same parties."[44] In September, Dimick B. Huntington, a salaried government interpreter and Young's personal envoy to the tribes, told Chief Ammon and other Utes that the soldiers "have come to fight us & you for when they kill us they will kill you."[45]

42. See "The Government of God," *Times and Seasons*, 15 July 1842, 855–58.

43. "Comments upon the Remarks of Hon. Stephen Arnold Douglas," *Deseret News*, 2 September 1857, 204–207.

44. Wells to Dame, 13 August 1857, Sherratt Library; and Wells to David Evans, 13 August 1857, USHS.

45. Huntington, Journal, 1 September 1857, LDS Archives.

Not only did Mormon actions corroborate Douglas's words, they also exposed an almost irrational trust that American Indians would unite and take an active part in the Kingdom's struggle for independence from the United States. Publicly Brigham Young only hinted at this partnership, warning that Americans "must stop travelling through this country," for the "outrageous treatment" the Indians received from emigrants made it impossible for him to keep the peace on the overland trail.[46] But in the teeth of all evidence to the contrary, he made no bones about his conviction that the Indians would be willing to fight and die for their professed Hebrew cousins and play a decisive role in the Kingdom's defense. His assurance may have risen from the success of John D. Lee and Mormon missionaries in southern Utah in winning the loyalty of the Southern Paiutes on the trail to southern California.

"The gospel has begun to go to the Lamanites & the Lord is about to remember his Covenant with that people," Woodruff said in a chilling prediction. "The Judgments of our God must now soon be poured out upon the Gentile world," he said, and "the Children of Jacob & the House of Israel," referring to American Indians, "must go forth & fulfill their destiny & help build up Zion."[47] His pronouncement on 28 August was followed three days later by the arrival of the southern Utah chiefs, whose bands had previously raided but never directly attacked Americans moving west.

The unreasonable dream of an alliance with the tribes was behind Young's plan of last resort if the United States were to send "an army of 50,000 or 100,000 men" in 1858. In that event, no longer would he give in "to their Ungodly persecutions," but he would "lay waste this whole Territory & flee into the mountains," he swore. "There was no way to know where this people would go, is there?" Apostle Orson Hyde had asked. "No," Young replied. "I will leave it for you to read in the Book of Mormon and guess at."[48] For one familiar with this Mormon scripture, the story of King Limhi, who had preserved a colony of fair-skinned Nephites in the wilderness among the Lamanites, would jump

---

46. Brigham Young, "Remarks," 13 September 1857, *Deseret News*, 23 September 1857, 229.

47. Ibid., 5:85. See also the Book of Mormon, Ether 13:1–10.

48. Young, unpublished discourse, 16 August 1857, BYC.

off its pages.[49] The high places of refuge that Young had in mind were not the arid Great Basin ranges. The mountains that promised a new home in more fertile locations were most certainly to be found in the midst of some of the most powerful tribes in North America. He had seen such country on his trip that year to Fort Limhi, the Salmon River Indian Mission, then in Oregon Territory.

On 6 September, Young again signaled his intentions to the members of his prayer circle, his most trusted associates. Thomas S. Smith was presiding at Fort Limhi, he reminded them. "Now do we not want a station about half way from here say near Fort Hall," he inquired. "He said that the north is the place for us & not the South," Woodruff said. "This is the [key] of this Continent & I think we had better keep near the lock & keep the [key] in our own hand."[50]

In October, Nauvoo Legion colonel Andrew Cunningham led a company of fifty men north to the Snake River to establish Fort Lookout a few miles east of Fort Hall on the Blackfoot River, close to present-day Blackfoot, Idaho. Near the Flathead Trail's ford on the Snake River, they built cabins, planted grain, and cached food. If all else failed, the new colony on the route to Fort Limhi would serve as a resupply point for a staged move north to Bitterroot Valley and the headwaters of the Missouri River.

In the meantime, a messenger from the real world interrupted Young's dreams of a grand alliance between Manasseh and Ephraim.[51] During the Mexican War, Stewart Van Vliet had led the charge of his company that won the day at Monterrey, but he was now more peacemaker than warrior. He had earned the trust and friendship of the Mormons through his even-handed dealings with them at Winter Quarters and Fort Kearny. General William S. Harney, commander of the Utah Expedition, ordered the forty-two-year-old captain and assistant quartermaster to go in ahead of his force and line up forage and supplies for troops and animals nearing the territory. He was also to find a place for a post close

49. See the Book of Mormon, Mosiah 7–8 (21:22–23).

50. Kenney, *Wilford Woodruff's Journal*, 5:90. Where the word "key" appears, Woodruff drew a key.

51. Mormons believed that they and American Indians shared the same lineage, the Indians through Joseph's son Manasseh, and white believers through Manasseh's younger brother, Ephraim.

enough to the capital to aid civil officials in enforcing the law, but far enough away to prevent any "improper association of the troops with the citizens—an object in this selection of primary importance."[52]

As the officer approached Zion's stronghold, mountaineers warned that the Mormons might kill him. His orders were to keep a close rein on his escort of twenty-five men from the Tenth Infantry under Lieutenant James Deshler and "treat the inhabitants of Utah with kindness and consideration."[53] So as not to endanger his escort, Van Vliet left it with six mule-drawn wagons at Hams Fork, some thirty miles east of Fort Bridger. There he met Mormon plainsmen Nathaniel V. Jones and Bryant Stringham, returning from the abandoned Deer Creek mail station, who led his carriage over the last 150 miles. They reached Salt Lake City on 8 September. That evening, Young and other Mormon leaders called on the officer at the residence of William H. Hooper, acting territorial secretary under an appointment by Young of doubtful legality, where they exchanged "mutually frank and friendly" views.[54] It was the day after Mormon Indian missionaries and Southern Paiutes had opened fire on the Arkansas emigrants at a peaceful stop on the Spanish Trail known as Mountain Meadows.

Unaware of these events far to the south, Van Vliet met the next morning with the LDS First Presidency (Young, Heber C. Kimball, and Daniel H. Wells); the apostles then in the city; John M. Bernhisel, Utah's congressional delegate; and a hundred or so leading citizens. He handed General Harney's letter to Young, addressed to "President of the Society of Mormons," not to the governor. It politely informed Young that the U.S. government had decided to form Utah and other western territories into separate military departments. Harney said he had been appointed to command the Utah Department, and he went on to describe Van Vliet's mission and its benefits.[55]

The captain asked "if there was lumber to be bought & grain & hay" he could acquire. Young allowed that "there was a plenty in the country"

52. A. Pleasanton to Van Vliet, 28 July 1857, 35th Cong., 1st sess., 1857–58, vol. 2, H. Ex. Doc. 2, serial 943, 27–28.

53. Ibid.

54. Others participating in the talks were Heber C. Kimball, Daniel H. Wells, John M. Bernhisel, James Ferguson, and Albert Carrington. *Deseret News*, 14 September 1857, 221.

55. Harney to Young, 28 July 1857, USHS.

and inquired "if there was any one present who could supply capt Van Vliet any lumber." The others were supposed to keep still, but there was always somebody who failed get the word. Samuel Snyder, who ran a sawmill at Parley's Park, today's Park City, piped up and "said He could supply [40/47,000] feet of Lumber. No other one said any thing."[56] The others wisely kept their mouths shut.

The following day, 11 September 1857, Hooper and territorial surveyor general Jesse Fox escorted Van Vliet to Rush Valley, where he inspected Major Steptoe's 1854–55 winter camp. He concluded what the army already knew—a location more than fifty miles from the capital was unsuitable. As he rode back to Great Salt Lake, three hundred miles to the south, Mormon militia and Indians decoyed the Arkansas emigrants into the open at Mountain Meadows and murdered all except seventeen children.

While he was gone, Young put in writing his reply to the officers' request for supplies and forage for Harney's command. He admitted that the items Van Vliet had specified were available in the amounts needed, but he doubted that the troops would arrive "in consequence of the lateness of the season." Young's response was cooperative in tone and did not mention that he intended to see to it that the soldiers would not enter the valley. But he did make a point to sign his letter "Governor and ex-officio Sup't of Indian Affairs."[57]

In face-to-face talks, however, Young left no doubt that "the *troops now on the march for Utah should not enter the Great Salt Lake Valley,*" Van Vliet afterward reported. The captain replied that they might stop the small military force now approaching, but the United States would then send troops "sufficient to overcome all opposition." As an answer, Apostle John Taylor treated the officer to a demonstration that never failed to impress newcomers. At a church meeting on Sunday, 13 September, Taylor asked worshipers "who would put the torch to their own buildings, cut down their trees, and lay waste their fields," and four thousand hands went up in the same instant.[58]

---

56. Kenney, *Wilford Woodruff's Journal*, 5:91. Pioneer industrialist Samuel Snyder bought Apostle Parley P. Pratt's claim in Parley's Park, where he built one of the territory's first sawmills. For many years he was the only settler there.

57. 35th Cong., 1st sess., 1857–58, vol. 2, H. Ex. Doc. 2, serial 943, 36–37.

58. Ibid., 24–27.

That evening, Van Vliet had his last interview with Young, who as usual was surrounded by a large group of top Mormon leaders. Young wished to talk to Van Vliet "in a plain manner," and talk he did. "The intention of the Government is to destroy us & this we are determin[ed] they shall not do. If the government of the United States [persists] in sending Armies to destroy us in the name of the Lord we shall Conquer them," he insisted. "And even should an Armey of 50,000 men get into this valley when they got here they would find nothing but a Barren waste." The government "must stop all emigration across this Continent for they Cannot tread in safety. The Indians will kill all that attempt it," Young warned. He then issued a darker threat: "If the Government Calls for volunteers in Calafornia & the people turn out to come to destroy us they will find their own buildings in flames before they get far from home & so throughout the United States."[59] Seven days later, Nauvoo Legion surgeon general John L. Dunyon clarified the nature of Young's threat to an emigrant he met east of Salt Lake. If the army entered the Mormon settlements, Dunyon told John Aiken of Mississippi, "*every city, town and village in the States of California, Missouri and Iowa should be burned immediately—that they had men to do this who were not known to be Mormons!*" The Saints "would cut off all the emigrant trains, army stores, stock." No man, woman, or child would cross the plains without being scalped, and the Mormons "expected the Indians to perform this infernal and cowardly part of their designs."[60]

Van Vliet left Salt Lake at 3 A.M. on Monday, 14 September, convinced that "Governor Young and the people of Utah will prevent, if possible, the army for Utah from entering their Territory this season." He was accompanied by Utah's congressional delegate, John M. Bernhisel, "the Captain having kindly proffered our delegate a seat in his carriage and a plate at his mess table," the *Deseret News* said. They would "journey together to the frontiers and, perhaps, to Washington."[61] As they went, Bernhisel would send detailed reports back to Young on U.S. Army supply trains and military units and their officers and locations.

59. Kenney, *Wilford Woodruff's Journal*, 5:96–97.

60. "The Late Outrages on the Plains—Further Particulars," *Los Angeles Star*, 7 November 1857, 2. Emphasis in original.

61. Ibid.

Later, in Washington, the captain told Secretary of War Floyd some things not included in his official report. Young "exercises absolute power, both temporal and spiritual, over the people of Utah," he said, "both of which powers he and the people profess to believe emanate directly from the Almighty." Before a congregation of more than four thousand, Van Vliet had heard John Taylor say that "the Almighty had appointed a man to rule over and govern his Saints, and that man was Brigham Young." And Young had told him "that should Governor Cummings [*sic*] enter the Territory, he would place him in his carriage and send him back."[62]

The day after the officer left Great Salt Lake and four days after the massacre at Mountain Meadows, Young took a final and momentous step. He knew by now that President Buchanan had named a new governor, his own appointment having expired three years before. He also knew from multiple sources, including Van Vliet, that U.S. soldiers had been ordered to respect the rights of all inhabitants, act only in self-defense, and serve only to assist federal officials in upholding the law. In spite of this knowledge, on 15 September he issued an inflammatory and already printed declaration of martial law.

"CITIZENS OF UTAH," he proclaimed. "We are invaded by a hostile force, who are evidently assailing us to accomplish our overthrow and destruction." After rehearsing the obligatory litany of Mormon grievances, he blamed this latest confrontation with an elected system of government on the "corrupt officials" and "hireling priests and howling editors, who prostitute the truth for filthy lucre's sake." "Our duty to our country, our holy religion, our God, to freedom and liberty," he told his people, "requires that we not quietly stand still and see these fetters forged around us which are calculated to enslave, and bring us in subjection to an unlawful military despotism."[63]

The unelected territorial governor, whose appointment had expired, declared martial law "in the name of the people of the United States, in Utah Territory," forbade all "armed forces of every description" from entering the territory, and ordered the Nauvoo Legion to repel an imagined invasion of American soil by soldiers of the republic. The proclamation's most provocative decree, however, was that "no person shall be

62. Van Vliet to Floyd, 20 November 1857, in Buchanan, *Utah Expedition*, 37, 38.
63. "Proclamation by the Governor," ibid., 34–35.

allowed to pass or repass into or through or from the Territory without a permit."[64] To enforce this command, on 18 September a General Order reminded Mormon soldiers that "many and deep were the scars which the knife of the legalized assassin has inflicted upon us." Now, "God will avenge our many wrongs," it said. "To guard the portals and bar the entrance of the polluter," Legion headquarters instructed military district commanders "to see that the requirements of the Proclamation are strictly carried out."[65]

If Young had wanted to start a war, this was a sure way to do it. By his action, a territory with a population not over forty thousand had virtually cut in half a nation of more than thirty million. He justified this unprecedented action on the pretext of protecting travelers from a few impoverished desert Natives, who could never have seriously threatened overland travel without outside help. Ironically, the measure left open the southern route across the southwest deserts, much of it controlled by the infinitely more dangerous Apaches.

As historian Michael N. Landon's research has revealed, classic trail studies have seriously underestimated the number of people heading west in 1857. George Stewart guessed the total at only about four thousand, while Merrill Mattes revised his original 1969 estimate of five thousand to perhaps six thousand; both blamed fear of Indians for the low numbers. Contemporary sources tell a different story: Henry Buckingham described "the largest overland emigration that has ever been known for years." Many old Californians, he said, "were returning with their families to spend the remainder of their days in the Golden State, with a 'right smart sprinkling' of young ladies." On 22 August 1857, the *San Francisco Bulletin* described the influx of newcomers as "greater than any since 1853," while the *San Joaquin Republican* reported an "overland emigration from 25,000 to 30,000 strong, of which two-thirds are women and children." According to one Arkansas traveler, "The number of emigrants killed this year on the plains it is said far exceeds that of any previous year": he had seen the upsurge in violence along the Humboldt River that followed the commencement of hostilities in Utah.[66]

---

64. Ibid.
65. James Ferguson, General Orders No. 3, 18 September 1857, UTMR.
66. Landon, "Continuous Line," Will Bagley notes.

No American president could let stand an arbitrary shutdown of communications across a vast area of western America that reached from the Continental Divide in present-day Colorado to California's Sierra Nevada. Westerners considered Young's threat to close the overland road intolerable. Referring to the massacre at Mountain Meadows and other atrocities, California governor John Weller protested the impact of "Mormons and Indians" on immigration, "so essential in developing the resources of the state." The state's newly elected fifth governor said, "Our people are certainly entitled to protection whilst traveling through American territory." To secure it, he said, "the whole power of the federal government should be invoked."[67]

Indian agent Garland Hurt, known to the Natives he served as "the American," would surely have agreed with this opinion. He was the only federal official left in Utah. His only friends for hundreds of miles were a handful of sympathetic but terrified Mormons and the Indians he had worked with, and he relied on them alone for his protection. From his sanctuary at the Ute Indian Farm on the Spanish Fork River, the thirty-seven-year-old Virginian watched with growing concern as Mormon military companies mobilized in nearby Utah Valley settlements.

Hurt was also aware that he, in turn, was being closely watched. His location some sixty miles south of Great Salt Lake in a thickly settled central valley made him a thorn in the side of Mormon military leaders in planning the Kingdom's defense. While they reached out to area Natives to enlist their support, or at least keep them from joining the American side, Hurt claimed for the United States the allegiance of the region's most powerful tribe in the Kingdom's own backyard. His very presence was enough to tie down Nauvoo Legion companies in Utah Valley and make Young wish that his treatment of the Utes in prior years had been less brutal. But up to mid-September, Hurt was mainly a nuisance.

Then on 14 September, a Native from the farm brought word that a large wagon train had been destroyed in southern Utah. Hurt sent a young Indian boy, called Pete, to find out what had happened and who was responsible. The youth returned on 23 September with word that the story was true. He said the Southern Paiutes had admitted taking part in the massacre, but claimed that "the Mormons persuaded them

67. Weller, "Inaugural Address," 75.

into it." Other Indians "insisted that Mormons, and not Indians, had killed the Americans."[68]

The agent now faced real danger. Only he knew of possible Mormon participation in a reported atrocity of almost unimaginable magnitude. Since he had close contact with the Natives, it was also reasonable to assume that his enemies were aware that he knew about it. Under the best of circumstances, he was too proud to suffer the "humiliating ceremony of applying to Brigham Young for a passport" to travel in his own country.[69] He was also afraid to put his life in Young's hands. He had to get out, he knew, but how? From the Ute farm, the way was hemmed in by Mormon settlements in three directions. Only to the east was there a possible opening, but it would require help from his Native friends.

Hurt decided to go that way, but his plan was soon discovered. On 26 September, Nauvoo Legion colonel Charles B. Hancock sent word from Payson to Brigadier General Aaron Johnson, the district military commander, that an Indian had informed him that Hurt meant "to leave the Territory within five or ten days, for the states, taking with him some few Indians, and go by the way of Uinta Valley," the site of today's Ute Indian Reservation. "Keep all *still*, and *watch*, the movements, not only at the Farm, but that *no such one* leave as contemplated, without our knowing it," Johnson said, while he went to Salt Lake to find out what to do about the troublesome agent.[70]

But Hancock would not wait. Johnson was on his way back the next afternoon with Young's instructions "pertaining to the Indian Farm" when he met express riders from Utah Valley with reports of what had taken place. On hearing that Hurt intended to take off, Hancock and Nauvoo Legion officers from other Utah Valley towns jumped the gun and determined to make him "*a prisoner this day.*" Expecting the Indians to fight for their agent "at the drop of a hat," they raised some three hundred men from Spanish Fork, Payson, and Springville, enough "to cow them into submission."[71] Or so they thought: on approaching the farm, they found that "the Indians were there armed, and much excited,

---

68. Hurt to Forney, 4 December 1857, in Buchanan, *Utah Expedition*, 202–204.

69. Hurt to Forney, 24 October 1857, ibid., 205–208.

70. Hancock to Johnson and Johnson to Hancock, 26 September 1857, in Johnson, Report to Wells, UTMR.

71. John S. Fullmer to Johnson, 27 September 1857, ibid.

about 150 of them in all." Twenty mounted men were sent to the mouth of Spanish Fork Canyon to block the trail along Diamond Fork to the Uinta Basin, but they encountered more Indians, "who would not let them pass."

Lieutenant George A. Hicks from Spanish Fork said that about 250 Natives appeared between his company and the Indian farmhouse. "They uttered yells of defiance and daring us to come on, yelling and whooping in the most terrific manner," the officer said.[72] Other Mormon leaders tried to negotiate with the Indians, but they would not let them come within eighty rods of the farm. "So the Indians are in possession of the Farm, armed," the Springville militia adjutant said. "The Dr. is reported gone!"[73]

That was not what Bishop Johnson wanted to hear. He arrived the following day to find the Indian farm a "perfect scene of Waste and confusion," he regretfully reported. "The bush had been shook and the bird flown."[74] But Hicks was glad "we did not get him for more than likely he would have been killed if we had."[75]

The "bird" later told how he had managed to fly.[76] On 27 September, Hurt was meeting with some chiefs from Uinta Valley when a half-dozen Indians rushed into his office at the adobe farm building shouting, "Friend! Friend! The Mormons will kill you!" He looked outside and spotted a hundred armed dragoons in the road to the east. Another Indian ran in to say that the Spanish Fork Canyon was "full of Mormons armed with guns and pistols," and they were going to kill him.

At this point, Richard James, his Mormon interpreter, came "in an apparent state of excitement, and exclaimed: 'Doctor, you're gone in!'" He carried a note from Spanish Fork bishop John L. Butler saying that he had discovered that the agent planned to escape in violation of the martial law and that he would be arrested. The friendship both men had shown to Hurt suggests that they tried to warn him in time for him to get away. The agent's reaction was typical of his courage: "To think that an officer of the government should be thus menaced in the peaceful

72. Hicks, "Family Record and History," Authors' Collection.
73. Wilbur Earl to Johnson, 27 September 1857, in Johnson, Report to Wells, UTMR.
74. Johnson to Wells, 28 September 1857, ibid.
75. Hicks, "Family Record and History," Authors' Collection.
76. For Hurt's account of his escape, see Buchanan, *Utah Expedition*, 205–208.

discharge of his official duties, could not fail to excite in the bosom of any one possessed of a spark of patriotism feelings of the most indignant scorn." He resolved "to escape or die in the attempt."[77]

Hurt ran to the door to call for his horse, but the chief's son had already brought the animal up. As this "sprightly boy" saddled the agent's mount, Hurt stuffed his papers and clothing into some meal sacks, threw them to his Native companions, and stepped into his saddle. Escorted by three young Utes, Pete, Sam, and Showers-hockets, he took off, but instead of heading east, as the Mormon troops expected, he rode in the opposite direction and went across West Mountain to the other side of Utah Lake, where he hid in a hollow in the Lake Mountains.

Before long, a Ute warrior brought word from the chief that Hurt should return to the farm after dark. A hundred or so Indians greeted him when he came back that night and "manifested great joy" upon seeing him alive. When he asked where the Mormons were, "twenty voices shouted 'cotch carry Mormon' (not here Mormons).'" Bishop Butler had ordered the troops disbanded. He justified this move under his earlier orders to avoid trouble with the Indians, but General Johnson suspected that he did so to allow Hurt to escape without being pursued.

The way was now open. Hurt and his faithful Ute lifeguards rode up Spanish Fork Canyon to Diamond Fork, where they turned left and went a hundred miles or so east on the 1776 Escalante Trail to Uinta Valley. As they crossed the rim of the Great Basin, they drove into a heavy snowstorm that "pelted without mercy the naked skins of my shivering escorts," he said. Later, crossing the mountains, they "waded through snow knee deep, subjecting my party to the utmost degree of privation and suffering," but the loyalty of his Native guides was unremitting. Often, around their campfires, they assured him that "if any attempt was made to take my life, they would die in my defense."[78]

The Indian agent stayed a week or two in the Indian camps along Ashley Creek, near present-day Vernal, Utah, until the way was clear for him to cross Diamond Mountain into Brown's Hole on the line of the Outlaw Trail, later popularized in western movies. He then rode up Green River to reach the Oregon-California Trail at the mouth of the

77. Ibid.
78. Hurt to Forney, 24 October 1857, ibid.

Big Sandy River, north of the present-day town Green River, Wyoming. From there it was an easy ride over South Pass to meet advancing elements of the U.S. Army on the Sweetwater River.

Ten days after the agent's escape, Young on 7 October reported to the commissioner of Indian affairs that Garland Hurt "saw fit to leave the field of his duty on the 26th of September last, in company with some Indians, whom it is said he had hired to escort him to the United States troops." He enclosed a copy of a letter he allegedly had sent to Hurt, dated 26 September, in which he noted Hurt's plan to take off by "some unfrequented route, and in company with certain Indians." He allegedly called this course "very unsafe and highly improper" and offered the agent "speedy and safe transportation."[79]

As examples of whose word should be believed in the often conflicting accounts during this time, Young's report and alleged letter to Hurt are instructive. Both are deliberately false and intended only to deceive. In his report, Young backdated the agent's escape from 27 September to 26 September, and he placed the earlier date on his fabricated invitation of safe transportation. But he had met with General Johnson and given him orders to arrest Hurt on 26 September.[80] This report appears to have been intended to destroy the agent's credibility and discredit any justification he might give for his escape, as well as to cover up Young's own role in the episode.

Young signed both letters as governor and *ex officio* superintendent of Indian affairs, despite being aware by 7 October that the president had appointed a new governor, Alfred Cumming, who was even then on the way west to assume his duties. Young also knew that Congress in March had authorized the president to appoint one superintendent of Indian affairs for Oregon and Washington territories and one for each of the territories of New Mexico and Utah, thereby stripping this function from the governors.[81] He was aware, too, that his successor in this office, Jacob Forney, was also on the road to his new post. All this he knew from

---

79. Young to V. W. Denver, 7 October 1857, ibid., 209–10.

80. Johnson, Report to Wells, UTMR.

81. See "An Act making Appropriations for the Current and Contingent Expenses of the Indian Department, etc.," 3 March 1857, in *Statutes at Large and Treaties of the United States*, 34th Cong., 3rd sess., vol. 11, chap. 90, sec. 3, 185.

a number of sources, not least of which was Utah's delegate to Congress, John M. Bernhisel.

Yet Young still claimed these positions. He justified this pretense on the ground that he had not been officially notified, but the territorial organic act imposed no obligation on the president to inform Utah's governor that he was being replaced. He also claimed the offices because no replacements had arrived. But acting as if he were governor, Young himself had ordered the territorial militia to stop the new appointees and their military escort from coming in.

Most revealing of all was that Brigham Young knew at least by 27 September, and probably days before, that a mass murder of emigrants had occurred at Mountain Meadows in southern Utah, and that Mormon militia and Southern Paiutes had committed the crime. Yet, acting as governor and superintendent of Utah Indian affairs, he considered it more important to discredit an Indian agent than to report this terrible massacre or investigate it. He took the trouble to call official attention to the agent's alleged misdeed, sending his report overland to Los Angeles, then to Washington, via Panama, but he did not mention an unprecedented atrocity in which Indians had participated under his claimed direction. As far as he was concerned, it was a non-event.

But Garland Hurt was not a man to engage in pretense or falsehood. He remained with the army during its tortured winter march to Fort Bridger. There, in December 1857, relying on information from his Ute friends, he wrote the first essentially accurate report of the butchery on the Spanish Trail of Arkansas farm families on their way to make new homes in California.

CHAPTER 7

Come Forth to Slay the Wicked
Mountain Meadows

Skulls and bones, most of which I believed to be those of women,
some also of children, probably ranging from six to twelve years of
age. Here, too, were found masses of women's hair, children's bonnets,
such as are generally used upon the plains, and pieces of lace, muslin,
calicoes, and other material, part of women's and children's apparel.
I have buried thirteen skulls, and many more scattered fragments.

—Assistant Surgeon Charles Brewer, U.S. Army, 6 May 1859

When they set out on the long road west in April 1857, the closely inter-
connected families—the Fanchers, Bakers, Camerons, Joneses, Dunlaps,
Mitchells, Huffs, Tackitts, Millers, and Woods—who had left northwest
Arkansas trailing a large cattle herd had not the slightest notion that they
might have trouble with the Mormons. They knew little and perhaps
nothing about the strange crisis that had led to the Utah conflict. They
were simply passing through Mormon country on their way to California, some to sell cattle there, others to make their home in the new state.
Most were women and children.

But when the Arkansans reached Great Salt Lake City and began forming what became known as the Fancher party, the weary sojourners must
have felt as if they had stepped into a nest of angry hornets. They had
come to the wrong place from the wrong place at the wrong time. In the
summer of 1857, Utah Territory was unlike any other place in America,
before or since, a frontier afire with war fever and unchecked religious
passions. Nor did the prayers of Brigham Young at that time offer any
comfort or promise of safe travel across his Great Basin kingdom: "We

pray our Father to turn the hearts of the Lamanites even the sons of Jacob unto us that they may do thy will & be as a wall of defense around us."[1]

After four months on the trail, largely without access to news from the outside world, the members of the Fancher train were quickly becoming aware of the multitude of dangers they now faced. The wagons from Arkansas reached Salt Lake only days after an emotionally unhinged widow, Eleanor McLean Pratt, had provided Mormon leaders with an overwrought account of Apostle Parley P. Pratt's murder by her estranged husband.[2] The train had left Arkansas weeks before Pratt was killed, but it came from roughly the same part of the state where her jealous husband had struck him down, and it arrived in Utah only days after Young's dramatic announcement that an American army was on its way to invade Utah and once again drive the Latter-day Saints from their homes.

Shortly before the Arkansans arrived, on 2 August 1857, Colonel George A. Smith gave one of the folksy and self-deprecating discourses that so endeared him to many Mormons—and his long-winded stem-winder rained pitchforks on outsiders. He loved his friends, he said, "and God Almighty knows that I do hate my enemies." The rotund apostle and church historian was not afraid to die and promised to fight as long as he had one finger left. Reports said that the government's plan for Utah was "deep, and it is laid with the intention of murdering every man that will stand up for 'Mormonism.' But the evil which they design towards us will fall upon their own heads, and it will grind them to powder," Smith promised, while the righteous would "laugh at their calamities, and mock when their fear cometh."[3]

"If the United States send out troops to fight us this season we shall whip them out," Young said the same day. If more troops were to be sent the following year, he said, then "we shall have the Lamanites with us & the more the United States send out the wors[e] off they will be for they will perish with Famine."[4] In the eight days since the dramatic arrival of Porter Rockwell and the widow Pratt, Mormon leaders had decided to launch a military response to Buchanan's dispatching of the army. As

1. Kenney, *Wilford Woodruff's Journal*, 13 August 1857.
2. McLean, "Account of the Death of Parley P. Pratt," LDS Archives.
3. Smith, "Discourse," 2 August 1857, *Deseret News*, 12 August 1857, 184.
4. Kenney, *Wilford Woodruff's Journal*, 5:71–72.

August began, their words made clear that they had decided to wage a guerrilla war, and they were banking on the tribes of the Great Basin to help them fight it. So when Colonel Smith set out to arouse resistance in the settlements of southern Utah, one of his key assignments was to implement Young's war policy and enlist the support of the desert tribes against the United States.

Smith, one of the youngest of the Mormon apostles, took off on 3 August on a flying visit to the string of settlements along the Spanish Trail near Cedar City. Smith had led the first colonizing party there in 1850, had organized Iron County and its militia, and was celebrated as the father of Utah's impoverished southern frontier. As his faith's overseer in the region, he was known and trusted as Young's spokesman. Traveling in a horse-drawn carriage, Smith covered the nearly 250 miles from Great Salt Lake to Iron County in six days. Even at this swift pace, he took time to instruct settlement leaders along the trail to southern California and hand them Young's written orders "to save all their grain, nor let a kernel go to waste or be sold to our enemies." If anyone persisted in "selling grain to the gentiles," Young threatened, "I wish you to *note* as such."[5] He also told them to preserve their guns and ammunition and to drill and prepare their military companies for active operations to repel the approaching U.S. Army.

Wherever he went, Smith fanned the flames of the Reformation. Legend has it that he told settlers at Parowan that bones make good fertilizer for fruit trees. As for American soldiers, Smith could "think of nothing better that they could do than to feed a fruit tree in Zion." At New Harmony on 17 August, a few miles south of Cedar City, he "*delivered a discourse on the spirit that actuated the United States*" toward Mormons as a people, the church minutes said, and it was "full of hostility and virulence." Smith's fiery orations stirred up "a craze of fanaticism," recalled John M. Higbee, the officer whose verbal order would initiate a mass murder. "Excitement was at fever heat."[6]

The message Smith carried was a volatile brew of resentment, defiance, fear of the approaching U.S. Army, and an unfounded belief that the Mormons could forge the Indians, that "remnant of Jacob," into "the battle ax of the Lord." As the apostle scurried about, laying the groundwork for an atrocity, in Great Salt Lake Lieutenant General Daniel H. Wells sent orders to district military leaders, including Colonel William H. Dame, commander of the Southern District, which included Beaver, Iron, and Washington counties. "Instruct the Indians that our enemies are also their enemies," the top Mormon officer ordered, "that they must be our friends and stick to us, for if our enemies kill us off, they will surely be cut off by the same parties."[7]

Known as a hotbed of religious fanaticism, the south hardly needed the apostle's vitriol to inflame the region. Its spiritual head, Elisha Grove, patriarch of the Cedar Stake of Zion at Cedar City, regularly gave blessings to members of his faith that breathed resentment and vengeance for past wrongs, real and imagined. The zealous patriarch gave Colonel Dame a prophetic blessing that would meet even the strict standard set in Deuteronomy for true prophets:[8] "Thou shalt be called to act at the head of a portion of thy brethren and of the Lamanites in the redemption of Zion and the avenging of the blood of the prophets upon them that dwell on the earth . . . the angel of vengeance shall be with thee."[9] David Lewis, the farmer to the Paiute Indians whom John D. Lee had replaced in 1856 as the leading federal Indian official in the southern settlements, saw the Indians as a weapon to be used to avenge past wrongs. "Ephraim is the battle ax of the Lord," he told his fellow Indian missionaries at Harmony in May 1854. "May we not have been sent to learn to *use* this ax with skill?"[10]

Meanwhile, when it came to fanaticism, the mayor of Cedar City played second fiddle to none. New Yorker Isaac C. Haight, a member of the "Old Police" at Nauvoo, had returned from a mission to Britain in 1853 with $37,000 in church funds and two new brides. Young rewarded him for his successful management of that year's overland emigration with a job he did not want: manager of the struggling Deseret Iron Company in Cedar City. Unable to rescue the impractical venture, Haight fanned the flames of the Reformation and proclaimed, "the

---

7. Wells to Dame, 13 August 1857, Sherratt Library.

8. "If what a prophet proclaims in the name of the Lord does not take place or come true, that is a message the Lord has not spoken." Deut. 18:22.

9. Dame Papers, 20 February 1854, BYU Library.

10. Brooks, "Indian Relations," 21.

pruning time has come." The day was near "when the servants of God will come forth to slay the wicked," he warned. In addition to serving as mayor, Haight was president of Zion's Cedar Stake and head of his town's Nauvoo Legion battalion. Equally zealous was his first counselor, John M. Higbee, who also served as the major of Cedar City's militia outfit. He told people there to prepare themselves "for every thing, and to every thing required at our hands."[11]

Apostle Smith, who had been the Iron County Brigade's first colonel, met with local leaders and gave them instructions, both written and verbal. He stayed overnight in the home of the man who would play the key role in the coming atrocity. John D. Lee and the apostle were fellow members of the ultra-secret Council of Fifty, the ruling body of the earthly Kingdom of God. Ostensibly a lowly Indian farmer, Lee was also an adopted son of Brigham Young under a long since discontinued sealing ordinance, which stressed loyalty and obedience to one's adoptive parents.

Lee conducted much of Smith's "pleasant but somewhat arduous journey of 185 miles" through Santa Clara Canyon to Mountain Meadows.[12] After meeting several Paiute leaders, Smith privately observed to Lee "that these Indians, with the advantage they had of the rocks, could use up a large company of emigrants, or make it very hot for them." He asked a hypothetical question: "Brother Lee, what do you think the brethren would do if a company of emigrants should come down through here making threats? Don't you think they would pitch into them?" "They certainly would," Lee said. "This seemed to please him, and he again said to me, 'And you really think the brethren would pitch into them?'" Lee was no fool, and he warned Smith "that he had better say to Governor Young that if he wants emigrant companies to pass without molestation that he must instruct Colonel Dame or Major Haight to that effect, for if they are not ordered otherwise, they will use them up by the help of the Indians."[13]

Southern Utah leaders who met with Colonel Smith knew what was expected of them. They "concluded that the dividing line had been drawn between Mormons and gentiles and all that came in the Territory

11. Cedar Stake Journal, 29 January and 29 March 1857, Sherratt Library.

12. James H. Martineau, "Trip to the Santa Clara," Deseret News, 23 September 1857, 227.

13. "Lee's Last Confession," San Francisco Daily Bulletin Supplement, 24 March 1877, reprinted in Bigler and Bagley, Innocent Blood, 337.

must be cut off," John Hawley recalled.[14] Peter Shirts, Lee's independent neighbor, later told a federal official that the Mormons "intended killing all parties who came on to here."[15] Smith also carried out Young's order to dismiss the moderate head of the Santa Clara Indian Mission and replace him with frontier zealot Jacob Hamblin, who could be trusted to do as he was told. The apostle ordered Hamblin to round up the Southern Paiute leaders and escort them with him back to Great Salt Lake to meet with Young. Young's emissary had arrived in southern Utah with a single traveling companion. He would return to the Mormon capital with an entourage of Indians.

As Apostle Smith was preaching and counseling far to the south, in the brush bowery on Temple Square Young graphically laid out his war policy to his most devoted followers and a few curious outsiders. Though he was a true believer in the apocalyptic prophecies of Joseph Smith, Young was painfully aware of how little actual power he could deploy against the vast resources of the United States. His native political genius latched on to the central geographic position held by his beleaguered Kingdom at the crossroads of the West: that reality looked like his ace in the hole, and he played it. The overland road, he pronounced, was closed.

"I now wish to say to all Gentiles send word to your friends that they must stop crossing the Continent to Calafornia for the Indians will kill them," Young warned. He said that emigrants wantonly shot Indians, and that without the Mormons, the Natives would "cut off" nineteen out of twenty of the more than twenty thousand emigrants who would travel to the West Coast that year. Playing on the fears of potential emigrants, Young's threat was obviously exaggerated, since well-organized parties hardly faced deadly peril from Great Basin tribes.[16]

Yet no longer would he serve as defender of the trails. "If the United States send their army here and war commences," he menaced, "the travel must stop; your trains must not cross this continent. To accomplish this I need only say a word to the[m] for the Indians will use them up; unless I continually strive to restrain. I will say no more to the Indians,

14. Ibid., 103.

15. Bagley, *Stones, Clubs, and Gun Barrels*, 14.

16. Kenney, *Wilford Woodruff's Journal*, 5:79.

let them alone, but do as you please. And what is that? It is to use them up; and they will do it."[17] Young knew the consequences of his policy: as reported by Apostle Woodruff, that evening he privately told church leaders that the government was "driving [his] people to war sooner than is for their [the nation's] good for we are civilizing the Indians & they would have some Judgment & not kill women & Children & those who ought not to be killed."[18]

For Granville Stuart and his brother James, Young's closure of the trails was life-changing. Traveling east from California on Hudspeth's Cutoff in present-day southern Idaho, they reached the aptly named Malad River, some twenty miles north of today's Malad City, where Granville was stricken on 17 July by fever.[19] While the rest of their party went on to Soda Springs, for seven weeks he lay too sick to travel. By the time he could mount a horse, all overland routes were guarded, "and we could neither go forward to the States nor back to California." To try, he said, "would cause us to be arrested as government spies and that meant sure death."[20] The only direction open was north, but they needed supplies to reach the Beaverhead Valley on the Missouri River headwaters, as proposed by Jacob Meeks, a mountaineer camped nearby.

Granville stayed behind while James and Meeks traveled some forty miles south to Barnard's Fort, a Mormon outpost near today's Plymouth, Utah, where John Porter Barnard, "as was always the case among the Mormons," fell victim to the temptations of a free market. He would sell them the food and ammunition they wanted, provided they picked it up at midnight and got "far away before day dawned." On 11 September, the Stuart brothers packed up to head north. Had they known of the "dreadful deed" being done at Mountain Meadows that day, Granville later said, they would have traveled day and night "to get as far away as we could in the shortest space of time."[21] They reached their new destination, imposed

17. Young, unpublished discourse, 16 August 1857, BYC; and Unruh, *Plains Across*, 185. The overwhelming majority of emigrants to California or Oregon had little incentive to shoot Indians. Most feared the Natives and would hardly have wished to invite retaliation in country they controlled.

18. Kenney, *Wilford Woodruff's Journal*, 5:84.

19. In French, *malade rivière* means "river of sickness."

20. Phillips, *Forty Years on the Frontier*, 120, 121

21. Ibid., 124.

on them by Young's closure of the trails, and would be numbered among Montana's most renowned early pioneers.

Not so lucky were several hundred overland emigrants who faced the likely result of Young's threat to "say a word" to the Indians, who would then "use them up." Years later, Malinda Cameron Thurston testified that her Arkansas train numbered about one hundred on 3 August when it reached the Mormon city, where other families joined it. Her husband decided to take the northern route west rather than follow the corridor of settlements through southern Utah on the trail to Los Angeles. Her father and mother, her brothers Tillman, Isom, Henry, James, and Larkin, and her sister Martha took Mormon advice and went south. She would never see them again.[22]

Dozens of Arkansas farm families arrived at Great Salt Lake in the first days of August along with the Camerons. Several sources say they were told to leave at once. Like other overland companies, the Fancher party expanded or contracted as people joined or left based on which trail they believed offered the best prospects of getting them to their destination safely. Others sought refuge with the train as it moved south through a long string of Mormon settlements. Some have claimed that a band of land pirates traveled with the company; a legend first told long after the fact claimed that they called themselves the Missouri Wildcats, and their reckless belligerence provoked the massacre that followed. But this is one of many myths created years later to explain or excuse the murders. More probably the newcomers to the emigrant party were disaffected Mormons, afraid to leave the territory alone after others who tried to flee had been "righteously slain in order to atone for their sins" at Springville and Provo.[23]

Twenty years later, Young said that Apostle Charles C. Rich, who had come from San Bernardino over the southern trail that summer, claimed to have urged the Arkansans to go by the northern route, but Young's memory did not square with Malinda Thurston's recollection.[24] She said her father was "advised" and "persuaded" to go south because

22. Indian Depredation Claim 8479, *Malinda Thurston v. United States and Ute Indians*, National Archives.

23. The phrase is from Cradlebaugh, *Utah and the Mormons*, 11, quoting Brigham Young.

24. "Interview with Brigham Young," *Deseret News*, 23 May 1877, 242. Young's claim was later repeated in Bancroft, *History of Utah*, 547.

the Mormons told him that "the food for their stock was better and more plentiful" there. He acted on their advice, she said, "and did take the southern route."[25]

Documentary evidence establishes that the Arkansas company consisted of prosperous farm families seeking a better life on the West Coast. Its members were not inclined to misbehave like some of the parties of undisciplined young men, still celebrated in Mormon lore, who were hell-bent on reaching the gold fields. The party was instead an orderly train of relatives and friends, led by mature captains who had been over the trail before. Fifty-two-year-old John T. Baker, his son George W. Baker, twenty-seven, and Alexander Fancher, forty-five, were family heads, responsible for the safety of the women and children who made up most of the party. Fancher had taken his family through Utah to San Diego in 1850. He clearly had no fears about returning to Mormon settlements. Much of the train's wealth was tied up in the large cattle herd, but it included thirty or so wagons, fine horses and mules, tools, firearms, and a considerable amount of cash to start a new life on the West Coast.

About 140 persons made up the Fancher party by the time they reached their last campground, but once the Arkansans headed south, reliable information about their fate is so scarce that they might as well have fallen off the edge of the earth. All that can be known with certainty is that by mid-September 1857, every man, woman, and child among them over the age of six years had been brutally murdered. Everything they owned had been stolen, even their clothing, and not by Indians.

"One of the most pathetic things connected with the case is that none of the Arkansas company of emigrants survived who were competent to relate the events as they saw them take place, since all were killed who could have had any certain memory of the circumstances," said the great Mormon historian B. H. Roberts. So their story "must be pieced together from the admissions and confessions of their murderers, Indians and white men, told at different times and under varying circumstances." Roberts acknowledged that these murderers' tales were "prompted sometimes by self-interest, admissions and confessions alike, made in the hope of escaping censure, sometimes in the hope of avoiding the just consequences of participation in the crime; sometimes told in

---

25. Indian Depredation Claim 8479.

despair; and then again in the bitterness of revenge against some fellow participant who had betrayed the deed of blood; sometimes told haltingly, to shield those who may have been unwillingly brought into the wretched affair." The adult eyewitnesses all colored their confessions "to their own interested or biased views of the subject."[26]

Roberts, however, overlooked a considerable body of evidence that his fellow LDS historians have long ignored—notably the contemporary newspaper accounts, reports of the earliest government investigations, and the recollections of the surviving children. Long-suppressed and closely held church records and journals that are only now becoming available to scholars cast considerable light on the entanglement of Mormon leaders in the atrocity, from Brigham Young on down. Within a month of the crime, California newspapers began printing reports from those who had traveled with the three or so "Gentile" companies and a Mormon freight train that followed immediately in the Fancher party's wake. These passersby carried a story carefully packaged by Deseret's military, civil, and religious authorities of how the Arkansans had insulted local citizens and poisoned the local tribe, provoking the Paiutes to exact Indian vengeance. None of the non-Mormons who repeated this unlikely tale believed a word of it. One said, "these threats seemed to be made with the intention of preparing the mind to expect a calamity, and also when a calamity occurred, it should appear to fall upon transgressors, as a matter of retribution."[27]

Unaware of the gathering danger in their path, the Baker-Fancher train followed Apostle Smith's trail south along the route of today's I-15, but at a much-reduced pace. Slowed by their herd, the Arkansans covered a little more than seven miles a day. As they went, Fancher may have marveled at the changes that had taken place since his trip over the same route seven years before. And he may have wondered why it had been recommended to a company driving a large herd of cattle.

South of Salt Lake City, the valley of the Jordan River was mostly settled and cultivated. The big communal fields offered little opportunity for livestock to graze as the train went along. When Fancher had crossed the low range and entered Utah Valley in 1850, there was only a modest

26. Roberts, *Comprehensive History of the Church*, 4:139–40.
27. "The Late Horrible Massacre," *Los Angeles Star*, 17 October 1857, 2.

fort on the Provo River. Now, for forty miles, a string of settlements, each with its own communal fields and herd grounds, followed the crescent of fertile land between Utah Lake on the west and a sharp uplift of the Wasatch Mountains on the east. The fortified settlements ran from Lehi on Dry Creek on the north to Summit Creek, today's Santaquin. After that, they were widely separated, with mostly sagebrush and little grass in between.[28]

The nature of the terrain and Mormon communal land-use patterns made the large cattle herd and its need for forage a point of dispute over who owned the land—Uncle Sam or the Almighty? Speaking for the latter was the acting city marshal of Provo, Simon Wood, who told the intruders they had parked their "near 400 head of livestock" on the hay meadow reserved for the settlement's winter range. Move on, he ordered. The Baker-Fancher train herder spoke up "with some feeling" and said, "This is Uncle Sam's grass." When they refused to go, Wood gave them an hour "to decide whether you want to fight or pull up stakes."[29] They pulled up stakes to avoid trouble.

A similar dispute broke out near Nephi on Salt Creek, some forty miles south of Provo, where the train camped on Willow Creek, near today's Mona. "There is a company of Gentiles at Millers Springs who have 300 head of cattle," Samuel Pitchforth said on 15 August. "The Bishop sent out to them requesting them to move for they were destroying our Winter feed. They answered that they where [sic] American Citizens and should not move." Two days later, the settler reported, "The company of Gentiles passed through this morning—they wanted to purchase Flour."[30]

The settlements' refusal to sell them any, however, was another source of friction. After four months on the trail, the emigrants needed flour and fresh vegetables, especially for their children. They had probably chosen to go through Utah in order to supply this need. The settlers had food, and they were starved for money in an economy driven to barter by the lack of it. To the emigrants, the refusal to sell them supplies at

---

28. For a detailed description of this region in 1856, see Burr, *Annual Report*.

29. Anonymous undated statement, in Collected Statements on Mountain Meadows, LDS Archives.

30. Pitchforth, Diary, 15 and 17 August 1857, BYU Library.

any price, or only surreptitiously under cover of darkness, revealed a hostility beyond understanding. Even in the Old Testament, the Israelites had not been allowed to deny food to aliens in their land. But virtually without exception, settlement leaders enforced Young's order, delivered by Apostle Smith, not to sell so much as "a kernel" of grain "to our enemies"—and to keep a record of anyone who did.

Three weeks after leaving Great Salt Lake, on 25 August the Fancher train camped on Corn Creek, home of the small Pahvant band under its Mormon chief, Kanosh, whose members had murdered Captain Gunnison and seven members of his survey party four years before. That night George A. Smith rolled in on his return to Salt Lake and camped "within forty yards of them."[31] With him were Jacob Hamblin, the new head of the Santa Clara Indian Mission, and the dozen Native leaders he had collected to visit Young.

According to Smith, the emigrants were fearful at seeing Indians and Mormons traveling together and doubled their guard. Three of them, including the "Captain of the company," perhaps Jack Baker, came to his camp and asked if there was "any danger from the Indians who were encamped near us," the apostle later said. "I replied that if their party had not committed any outrage upon the Indians there would be no danger."[32] He later claimed that the Arkansans poisoned the Pahvants, which led them to attack the train, but there was no truth to this story. According to the unanimous testimony of participants, no Pahvants joined in the atrocity that would occur a few days later over a hundred miles to the south.

As Hamblin described the meeting, Smith's party camped on Corn Creek near "a company of emigrants" from Arkansas "on thare way to Calafornia." He thought, "Thare was a Strang[e] atmosphere Serounded them." The apostle spoke of it, Hamblin said. Unable to resist the temptation to prophesy what he may have known was coming, Smith said he believed "Some evle [evil] would befall them before they got through."[33] Hamblin in 1859 described the emigrants as "ordinary frontier 'home-

31. George A. Smith to St. Clair, 25 November 1869, in Bigler and Bagley, *Innocent Blood*, 271. This letter was part of Smith's evolving alibi.

32. Ibid.

33. Hamblin, Daybook, August–September 1857, BYU Library.

spun' people," hardly the kind to carry poison across the plains to murder unsuspecting Indians who had done them no harm.[34]

When Jacob Forney, who replaced Young as superintendent of Indian affairs, investigated the poison claim two years later, he concluded that it was entitled "to no consideration."[35] The same is true of other stories, still repeated today, that malign the emigrants and make it appear that what happened to them was their own fault. While verbal conflict occurred at Provo and Nephi, evidence shows that the train's leaders backed away from confrontation or provocative behavior at both places, as one would expect under the circumstances. Nor do contemporary Mormon journals verify later claims of disorderly or threatening conduct.

Up to this point, halfway between the Mormon capital and Mountain Meadows on the southern rim of the Great Basin, the Arkansans had traveled an average of eight miles a day. Over the ten days before reaching Corn Creek, they journeyed at an even slower pace to allow their cattle to feed along a trail with plenty of sagebrush and little grass. After the encounter at Corn Creek, they boosted their rate of travel to more than twelve miles a day, about as fast as an ox train with a large cattle herd could go after more than four months on the trail. This party, consisting mainly of women and children, led by mature captains, had not come to Utah to persecute the Mormons; they were only passing through. After camping at Corn Creek, they were trying to get away from trouble, not cause it.

Smith delivered the Paiute chiefs to Salt Lake, where they met on 1 September with Young and his personal interpreter, Dimick B. Huntington. Huntington had just returned from giving loads of corn and melons and four beeves to 120 lodges of Shoshones camped north of Salt Lake, where he had delivered a message. "I told them that the Lord had come out of his Hiding place & they had to commence their work," he wrote. "I gave them all the Beef Cattle & horses that was on the Road to California [by] the North Rout" and advised them to hide the stolen cattle in the mountains. "They sayed it was some thing new" and "they wanted to Council & think of it." Ben Simons, a Delaware Indian who

34. Carleton, *Special Report of the Mountain Meadows Massacre*, 2–3.

35. Forney to A. B. Greenwood, August 1859, in Buchanan, *Presidential Message Communicating Correspondence, Etc., on Massacre at Mountain Meadows*, 75–80.

had assumed leadership of a mixed band known as the Weber Utes, said that his father had told him "they would have to rise up to fight but he did not think it was so near." Long practiced in telling white leaders what they wanted to hear, Simons "said tell Brother Brigham that we are his friends & if he says the soldiers must not come it is anough. The[y] wont come in, he said. Tell B that he can Depend upon us & I come down to see & if he talk as you do it is enough."[36]

Simons immediately reported his conversation to Indian agent Garland Hurt, who learned that Huntington had "told the Indians that Brigham wanted them to run off the emigrants' cattle, and if they would do so they might have them for their own." Simons assured Hurt that he had advised his comrades to have nothing to do with the cattle, but he implied that the Mormons had hired Chief Little Soldier to seize about four hundred animals from a Missouri emigrant named Squires.[37]

A round of attacks on civilian trains on Hensley's Salt Lake Cutoff followed Huntington's generosity. Richeson Abbott complained that emigrants had to run "the gauntlet of Indian attacks and Mormon treachery" for three hundred miles. Raiders ambushed his party at City of Rocks: he was "satisfied the attack was led by Mormons, as they heard them cursing in regular Mormon slang, and calling out to them to get out of the country, as they had no business there." The Saints boasted that they would kill them all.[38] It was "an undoubted fact that the Mormons were at the head of most of these outrages, and instigated the Indians to commit the murders," California newspapers reported. White men had led an Indian attack on an Arkansas train near City of Rocks that killed Oliver Bailey. Among the embattled emigrants, the general conviction was that "the Mormons led the Indians in their attacks and murders."[39] Bishop Elias Blackburn of Provo confirmed emigrant suspicions that Mormons were behind this violence when he told his congregation that twenty-five Shoshones had stampeded six hundred cattle and horses, leaving an emigrant company on foot. "As

36. Huntington, Journal, August 1857, 12–13, LDS Archives.

37. Hurt to Forney, 4 December 1857, in Buchanan, *Presidential Message Communicating Correspondence, Etc., on Massacre at Mountain Meadows*, 96–97.

38. "More Mormon Massacres," *Daily Alta California*, 1 November 1857, 2.

39. *California Farmer*, 30 October 1857, California State Library, 128:1–2.

soon as this word went out they have commenced upon our enemies!" the bishop blustered.[40]

What Young discussed with the Pahvants and Paiutes on 1 September is unknown, but in his diary he claimed that he could "hardly restrain them from exterminating the 'Americans.'"[41] Huntington's explosive record shows that Young did nothing of the sort: speaking for Utah's superintendent of Indian affairs, Huntington said he gave them "all the cattle that had gone to Cal[ifornia] by the south rout. It made them open their eyes." The Native leaders "sayed that you have told us not to steal so I have but now they have come to fight us & you for when they kill us they will kill you they sayd the[y] was afraid to fight the Americans & so would raise grain and we might fight."[42] Whatever Governor Young believed about Lamanites from his reading of apocalyptic scriptures, Utah's Indians had no desire to get in the middle of a Mormon fight with the U.S. Army.

Since the Fancher, William C. Dukes, Nicholas Turner, and Wilson Collins trains were the only parties driving cattle "by the south rout," the handout from Utah's governor and Indian affairs superintendent was an invitation to attack the California-bound companies with an implied promise of help if it was needed. The Southern Paiutes knew just what cattle Huntington had in mind because they had seen them a week earlier at Corn Creek. "The Indians must have started for home immediately," historian Juanita Brooks concluded, "for in seven days they were

40. Utah Stake Minutes, 30 August 1857, 671, LDS Archives. Punctuation added. Blackburn specifically identified emigrants as "our enemies."

41. Cooley, *Diary of Brigham Young*, 71.

42. Huntington billed Brigham Young $33.90 on 11 September 1859 for lodging Indians "on a visit to the superintendent of Indians affairs at Great Salt Lake City," including $20.40 incurred on 1 September for "Kanosh and fourteen of the band, Ammon and wife, four days, at thirty cents." See Smith, *Accounts of Brigham Young*, 22, 85. German emigrant P. M. Warn reported conversing at Corn Creek (where the Fancher train allegedly left a poisoned ox for the Indians) on 5 September with "an Indian said to be the war chief Ammon, who spoke good English. . . . His manner, and that of all his people towards us, was not only friendly, but cordial; and he did not mention the [Fancher] train which was doomed." "The Duty of the Government," *Los Angeles Star*, 17 October 1857, 2. Emigrant S. B. Honea of Arkansas reported that shortly after an Indian attack on the Turner-Dukes train at Beaver, Ammon came to the camp "in company with the Bishop . . . and demanded cattle. We gave him six head." "More Outrages on the Plains," *Los Angeles Star*, 24 October 1857, 2.

harassing the emigrants at Mountain Meadows, and in ten days they participated in the massacre of the company."[43]

Whether any of the Indians who met with Young in Salt Lake were on hand six days later at Mountain Meadows to fire the opening volley is uncertain, but Thomas L. Kane and several historians include Tutsegabit on their list of those who were present. One of them, Walker's brother Ammon, extorted cattle from a wagon train after Indians allegedly assaulted and seriously wounded two of the party's leaders while a third was "grazed by two or three bullets." This singular attack took place in broad daylight in the streets of the Mormon settlement at Beaver on Wednesday morning, 9 September.[44] What is clear is that in "giving" tribal leaders under his jurisdiction the property of other people, Superintendent of Indian Affairs Brigham Young violated the law and endangered the lives of emigrants on all the roads to California.

Meanwhile, the Fancher party passed Cedar City. Small contingents may have gone on ahead of the train to scout the trail or gather tar for the wagons, but the main party crossed the gradual swell that divided the waters of the Great Basin and the Colorado River on Sunday, 6 September. They camped at the scenic mile-high Spanish Trail grazing ground known as Mountain Meadows, where weary travelers took advantage of the abundant water and grass to prepare their animals for the long, hard drive across the Mojave Desert. Here, some five miles from the nearest tiny Mormon settlement and two miles from Hamblin's Ranch, they felt so safe they did not corral their wagons. But the place they selected was "shut in by smooth, rounded hills," said U.S. Army major Henry Prince, who mapped the spot two years later.[45] Their campsite was exposed to concealed fire from all sides and was too far from water.

That same Sunday, Cedar Stake president Isaac C. Haight was in a militant mood and wanted to "feed to the Gentiles the same bread they fed to us."[46] He met with the highest local priesthood leaders to have

43. Brooks, *Mountain Meadows Massacre*, 42.

44. Moorman and Sessions, *Camp Floyd and the Mormons*, 133; Alexander, *Utah*, 131; "Diary of Colonel Thomas L. Kane," in Bigler and Bagley, *Innocent Blood*, 168; and Walker, Turley, and Leonard, *Massacre at Mountain Meadows*, 177.

45. A copy of the Prince map is in Backus, *Mountain Meadows Witness*.

46. Cedar City Ward Records, 6 September 1857, cited in Brooks, *Mountain Meadows Massacre*, 52.

them approve the actions already set in motion. To Haight's surprise and aggravation, someone suggested that they send an express rider to ask Brigham Young what they should do about the Arkansan intruders. Before the courier was dispatched, however, John D. Lee had already triggered the events leading to the tragedy.

Early Monday morning, a deadly burst of gunfire killed or wounded as many as ten men silhouetted by the campfire in the predawn darkness. Since the Southern Paiutes had few firearms and little skill in using them, the first volley's destructive power revealed the involvement of a large force of white marksmen and whatever Indian "freebooters" they could enlist.[47] The emigrants chained their wagons together, dug rifle pits, and fought back, killing several Indians whom Lee had persuaded to lead the attack. Faced with resolute men with Kentucky rifles, "the Indians could not do the work," Lee realized, "and we were in a sad fix."[48]

The standoff led to a highly significant episode in the Utah rebellion story and a bizarre chapter in western annals of heroic rides for help. Late Monday afternoon, Haight finally dispatched a thirty-two-year-old Englishman, James Haslam, on a five-hundred-mile round trip to Great Salt Lake to ask Young what to do about a wagon train under attack by Indians. Elsewhere in the West, settlers knew what was required to rescue a besieged wagon train, and without so much as a "by-your-leave," they would do it.[49]

On Wednesday night, two young volunteers slipped out of the besieged emigrant camp and tried to backtrack to a following train. One of them, William Aden, had joined the train at Provo to escape from Utah. Guards confronted the pair at a nearby spring and killed Aden. According to Lee, the guards also wounded his companion, but he escaped and warned his party that whites were involved in the attack, thus forcing the Mormons to take drastic measures to end the confrontation. However, the fact that

47. Two years later, participants in the ambush confessed that "fifty or sixty Mormons" had been involved in the attack. See Carleton, *Special Report of the Mountain Meadows Massacre*, 20.

48. Lee, *Mormonism Unveiled*, 228.

49. The annals of Mormonism present Haslam's ride as a desperate, hell-bent-for-leather enterprise. In fact, Haslam had a hard time getting horses and needed almost a week to complete his mission, taking exactly six days to cover approximately five hundred miles, the distance a well-organized relay system such as the Pony Express covered in two.

the besieged emigrants surrendered to the Mormons casts doubt on Lee's claim that the Arkansans knew that white men were acting in concert with the Indians.

The next night, Major John M. Higbee returned with more militiamen from Cedar City and new orders. Surrounded and under fire, the emigrants could not move, but they clearly would fight to the death if the Mormons and their allies launched a direct assault. It was necessary to decoy them into the open, where they could be killed with little risk to the attackers, Mormon or Indian.

Haslam reached Young's office just after daybreak on Thursday, 10 September, and handed him the message from Haight. But the Englishman was not the only unexpected visitor Young received that week. Three days before, U.S. Army captain Stewart Van Vliet had come to arrange supplies for the American soldiers ordered to Utah by President Buchanan. The officer was still there when Haslam, at 1 P.M., rode off on a fresh horse with Young's reply. It is highly revealing that Young did not tell the captain that a wagon train filled with women and children was under Indian attack within his professed jurisdiction as governor. Nor did he show the officer his order to the Mormon soldiers under his command not to interfere.

By themselves, the two messages—Haight's request for guidance and Young's reply—offer little help in determining Young's involvement in the atrocity. Haight's letter was reported lost and has never turned up. Young swore that his own reply could not be located, despite a diligent search, but after his death Mormon officials found the letter and published it in 1884. If its authenticity is problematic, the carefully crafted document does appear to be genuine—and it is a textbook example of the Mormon leader's communications style.

Typically, Young began his reply to the urgent request for guidance as if couriers galloped in every day with news of wagon trains under Indian attack. In no apparent hurry, he took the opportunity to send a report on current events. When he returned to the subject, he avoided a direct reply to Haight's presumed request to be told what to do about a certain wagon train under immediate siege. "In regard to the emigration trains passing through our settlements we must not interfere with them until they are first notified to keep away," Young said. "You must not meddle with them. The Indians we expect will do as they please but you should try and preserve good feelings with them. There are no other trains going south that I know of. If those that are there will leave, let them go in peace."[50] In the end, his reply made no difference because the express rider failed to get back in time. Two days after the massacre, Haslam reached Cedar City and handed Young's note to Haight, who allegedly burst into tears. He knew from reading it who would wind up holding the bag.

If this story is true, Young's absolute religious authority, and even his official position as civilian chief of the Nauvoo Legion, presents a baffling problem: Why did southern Utah's leaders not wait for his orders to arrive? The emigrants trapped at Mountain Meadows were not going anywhere. What made it imperative to kill them rather than wait for Haslam's return with the purported orders? These men acted as if they already had their orders and hesitated to delay in executing them. Emigrant George Powers met Colonel Dame at Parowan on Wednesday, 9 September, and asked him why he did not send solders to rescue the besieged train. Dame replied that he "could go out and take them away in safety, but he dared not; he dared not disobey counsel."[51] Many years later, Bishop Charles Adams of Parowan recalled that as a teenage boy he watched the Legion's officers emerge from Dame's house after a meeting at 2 A.M. on Thursday. "You know what the council decided," Higbee said, referring to the Stake High Council's decision to wait for word from Salt Lake. "I don't care what the council decided," said Dame. "My orders are that the emigrants *must be* done away with."[52]

On Thursday, the day Haslam began his return journey from Great Salt Lake, three of the Arkansas train's best men slipped out of the fortification in a desperate attempt to reach California on foot. While little is known for certain about their fate, the best sources indicate that Indian missionary Ira Hatch helped Indian trackers follow them and kill them

50. See Brooks, *Mountain Meadows Massacre*, 63, citing Church Letter Book, no. 3, 827–28.

51. Lee, *Mormonism Unveiled*, 233–34; and "The Late Horrible Massacre," *Los Angeles Star*, 17 October 1857, 2. As the presidents of Parowan and Cedar Stakes, respectively, Dame and Haight were the senior priesthood authorities in southern Utah. No local authority could give them "counsel"—orders—they were obliged to obey. The last man they had met whose priesthood outranked them was Apostle George A. Smith.

52. Brooks, *Mountain Meadows Massacre*, 80.

one by one. The last was reportedly stripped and his throat cut at Las Vegas Springs as he struggled in the sand.

On Friday, 11 September, John D. Lee and William Bateman drove two wagons into the little stronghold under a white flag. They found the emigrants almost out of ammunition and out of water. Lee told them that their only hope was to give up their arms, so "as not to arouse the animosity of the Indians," and to entrust their lives to the protection of the Mormon military.[53]

Soon after, the saddest parade ever staged on American soil emerged from the camp. Leading was a wagon filled with children under seven years old. Next came Lee on foot, followed by a second wagon carrying several wounded men and one woman. Some distance behind walked the women and older children. After them, a quarter-mile or so to the rear, the disarmed men marched in single file, each flanked by an armed guard. It was all carefully planned. As the women and children entered a narrow place in the hills, heavy with brush, Major Higbee on horseback called out: "Halt. Do your duty."

Each of the guards shot the disarmed man next to him. At the firing, painted white men and a few Indian freebooters swarmed out of the brush to kill the women and children with knives, guns, and rocks. A place of peace and rest was filled with gunfire and the screams of women and children under murderous attack. Girls begged for their lives and cried out loud as they were dragged away to have their throats cut. As he murdered two wounded men in the wagon with one shot, Samuel McMurdy reportedly cried, "O Lord, my God, receive their spirits, for it is for thy Kingdom that I do this."[54] Some seventy Nauvoo Legion members from Cedar City did most of the killing, not the Southern Paiutes as was claimed for many years afterward.

Bishop Philip Klingensmith, who participated in the slaughter as a private in the Iron County brigade, testified that he watched as Major Higbee approached a wounded man "and drew his knife and cut his throat. This man begged for his life, and he was lying on the ground when that was done." The man, apparently an apostate Mormon, said, "'Higbee, I wouldn't do this to you.' He knew Higbee, it appears," Klingensmith

53. Lee, *Mormonism Unveiled*, 240
54. Ibid., 241.

recalled. "And the reply was that, 'You would have done the same to me, or just as bad.'"[55] The accounts of Mormons, Indians, and survivors all report that the assailants cut the throats of the women and children.

What happened that dark day at a remote oasis on the trail to California was much more than typical western violence: in the region's entire history, there is no other example of white-on-white savagery that even comes close. Where else did frontiersmen brutally murder scores of American women and children? "I saw my mother shot in the forehead and fall dead. The women and children screamed and clung together," recalled survivor Nancy Saphronia Huff Cates. "Some of the young women begged the assassins after they had run out on us not to kill them, but they had no mercy on them, clubbing [them with] their guns and beating out their brains."[56] Spared by the doctrine of "innocent blood," seventeen children survived, all under the age of seven. For their mothers and fathers, brothers and sisters, it was all over in minutes. For the seventy or so deeply religious men who took part in the slaughter, it would never be over. Most were God-fearing men, devoted husbands, caring fathers. The wounds they bore from that day were soul-deep and ever open.

As Nephi Johnson, an old Indian missionary, lay dying, he preached in Native tongues, sang hymns, and prayed. Suddenly the old man's eyes opened, staring at the ceiling, and he cried, "Blood! Blood! BLOOD!" More than sixty years before, he had led the killing of the women and children. At age eighty-four, he was still reliving the horror; he was afraid to die, and for good reason. Fifty-one years after the murders, Johnson said "that when they rested from the killing," he had gone to keep the Indians from looting the wagons. The senior officers "gathered up the children together, and Klingen Smith, selected seventeen of the smallest children together, and handed the older ones over to the Indians who killed them."[57] This long-suppressed statement substantiates Nancy Huff Cates's much earlier account. "At the close of the massacre there was eighteen children still alive, one girl, some ten or twelve

55. Backus, *Mountain Meadows Witness*, 137.

56. Nancy Huff Cates, "The Mountain Meadow [*sic*] Massacre: Statement of One of the Few Survivors," *Daily Arkansas Gazette*, 1 September 1875, in Bigler and Bagley, *Innocent Blood*, 426–27.

57. Johnson, "Affidavit," 22 July 1908, in Turley and Walker, "Mountain Meadows Massacre Documents," 140.

years old, they said was too big and could tell, so they killed her, leaving seventeen," she said.[58]

An accurate count of the number slain will never be determined because no one knows for sure how many were in the emigrant camp that day. Judge Roger V. Logan of Boone County, Arkansas, compiled the names of most of the company members from his state, but the number does not include all of them or those who joined the train as it passed through Utah. A reasonable estimate would come to 140, including 40 or 50 men, 30 or so women, and 50 or more children between the ages of seven and eighteen. In terms of lives lost during America's western migration, the massacre at Mountain Meadows was second only to the Mormon handcart disaster the year before. And it was three times the number who died in the Donner party.

The day after the massacre, Mormon leaders rode out to the field of slaughter. Colonel Dame, the Iron County military commander whose orders had authorized the slaughter, was overcome by what he beheld. "Horrible, horrible," he said over and over. "I had no part in this. I had nothing to do with it."[59] After they stopped quarreling, those who had taken part dumped the dead into ravines and covered the bodies with a layer of dirt too light to keep the coyotes from feasting on them. They then formed a prayer circle and thanked God for delivering their enemies into their hands. And they swore to keep their role secret from everyone except Brigham Young, to always say that the Indians alone did it, and to kill anyone who broke the oath. To justify their Indian allies, the initial story put the blame for what happened on the victims. According to this falsehood, the emigrants had poisoned Pahvants and Paiutes on Corn Creek, 140 miles to the north, and brought it all on themselves. The lie is still repeated today.

Lee waited nearly three weeks to report personally on the massacre to Young, who by then knew all about it. On Monday evening, 28 September, Lee went to Young's office and told him all there was to tell, including the names of those who took part. The next day, Young ordered him to tell no one else and to send him a letter in his capacity as Indian farmer, putting the blame on the Indians. Lee repeated the alibi before

58. Bigler and Bagley, *Innocent Blood*, 426–27.
59. Lee, *Mormonism Unveiled*, 241.

witnesses, including Wilford Woodruff, who recorded it in his journal to exonerate Mormon leaders forever after. It took two more months for Lee to get around to writing the letter to the superintendent of Utah Indian affairs, an office Young held only by his refusal to acknowledge his displacement.

This account of the Mountain Meadows massacre is as accurate as three decades of intensive research in a gradually expanding range of sources can make it. But as with the nineteenth-century Mormon wars in Missouri and Illinois, the shifting, church-approved versions of the atrocity cannot be reconciled with this account. The latest attempt to exonerate Brigham Young of responsibility, *Massacre at Mountain Meadows*, by noted Mormon scholars Ronald W. Walker, Richard E. Turley, Jr., and Glen M. Leonard, restates the church position, which is that Mormon leaders in southern Utah ordered the massacre without Young's knowledge and then success-fully conspired to hide the truth from him for more than a decade.[60]

Like other historians who have studied this horrific event in detail, we have concluded otherwise. To claim that Young ignored "the appalling business of the massacre is to deny the supreme and minute control that he habitually exercised over all the affairs of church and state in Utah," and naïvely assert that a man "who kept himself as fully and completely informed on all matters that went on in the 'Kingdom of the Saints' as absolute authority and human ingenuity made possible would choose to remain complacently ignorant of an incident that threatened to bring stark ruin to the whole Mormon dream of spiritual and temporal sover-eignty in the State of Deseret," wrote Juanita Brooks and Robert Cleland in 1955. "Brigham Young was not a credulous simpleton: he was not duped or hoodwinked: he was not misinformed. He knew the true story of the Mountain Meadows Massacre . . . as well as any man in Utah; and he knew the names of the individual Mormons, whether prominent or obscure, who participated in the wholesale atrocities,"[61]

When considered in the light of Mormon religious beliefs at that time, the evidence shows that the Arkansas party was a marked train in a planned operation that went forward from the time it left Great Salt

60. Walker, Turley, and Leonard, *Massacre at Mountain Meadows*.

61. Robert Glass Cleland and Juanita Brooks, eds., *A Morman Chronicle: The Diaries of John D. Lee, 1848–1876* (San Marino, Calif.: Huntington Library, 1955), xiii–xiv.

Lake, chosen to demonstrate Young's ability to unleash the "battle ax of the Lord" and stop overland travel. A telling moment came during the visit of U.S. Army captain Stewart Van Vliet, who had come to line up supplies for Buchanan's advancing army. In the midst of Van Vliet's discussion with Young, James Haslam rode in at dawn on a Thursday with Isaac Haight's urgent request for guidance from his spiritual leader and the territorial governor. Militia leaders at Cedar City wanted Young to put his order to destroy the train in writing. The express rider handed their request to him personally.

For Young, it was a time of decision. Would he inform an experienced U.S. Army officer about the emigrant train of more than a hundred American citizens, most of them women and children, in deadly peril? Would he welcome the assistance and advice of a veteran combat officer, as any other territorial governor in the same circumstances would do? Would he seize this moment to demonstrate his professed loyalty to the federal government? Or would he conceal all and never let Van Vliet discover that he, acting as governor, had ordered the territorial militia under his command not to interfere? Young's answer bares his culpability in the atrocity.

"Terrorism" is not a word to be taken lightly. But the evidence, coupled with long-forgotten Mormon doctrines, demonstrates that the purpose of the Mountain Meadows atrocity was to strike fear into the hearts of intruders and show Young's power to sever the transcontinental overland lines of travel and communications. The Arkansas train was the chosen example because it was large enough to command attention and its members came from the part of Arkansas where the Apostle Parley P. Pratt had been murdered just a few months before. Vengeance played no small part in the deed.

At Mountain Meadows, Brigham Young served notice to the rest of the nation that he would defend with arms the sovereignty of God's Kingdom in the West as it opened its march to universal dominion, as foretold by the Prophet Daniel. The atrocity was a self-fulfilled prophecy of what could happen to anyone who violated its borders without a "permit," a synonym for passport.[62]

With God's help and the Indians, he would prevail.

---

62. Young, "Proclamation by the Governor," 15 September 1857, in Buchanan, *Utah Expedition*, 34, 35.

CHAPTER 8

The Want of Cavalry
The U.S. Army Stumbles to War

The want of cavalry is severely felt, and we are powerless on
account of this deficiency to effect any chastisement of the
marauding bands that are constantly hovering about us.

—Colonel Edmund B. Alexander, 9 October 1857

Determined to prevent bloodshed if United States troops tried to enter
Salt Lake Valley that fall, Captain Stewart Van Vliet left Utah's territorial capital before dawn on 14 September, escorted by Mormon plainsmen Nathaniel V. Jones, Porter Rockwell, and Stephen Taylor. Applying
"all diligence to make a short trip to Washington City," the officer and
his Mormon escort averaged more than forty miles a day to reach his
camp on Hams Fork, a pace the quartermaster would maintain throughout his return. Van Vliet detached Tenth Infantry lieutenant James
Deshler and a dozen enlisted men with orders to hold up all supply trains
and cattle herds at that point and guard them there under the unilateral
understanding he had reached with Brigham Young to stop U.S. troops
short of Echo Canyon. At first light on 17 September, he and ten soldiers
took the best animals and hurried east.

Van Vliet began encountering separate units of the American army
coming west, spread out along the trail without cavalry support. He
alerted their commanders of threatened Mormon resistance. On 21 September, near Ice Spring on the Sweetwater River, west of Devils Gate, he
and John M. Bernhisel met the advance element of the federal army, the
Tenth U.S. Infantry. Colonel Edmund B. Alexander was in command.
Alexander, whose unremarkable military career following the War with

Mexico had hardly readied him for the military and political challenges he now faced, led his troops by proxy. General William S. Harney, originally appointed to lead the expedition, had been ordered to Kansas with the Second Dragoons to deal with the sectional bloodshed, in response to a plea from the governor of that territory. Now senior officer, Alexander would command all U.S. forces on the field of operations if fighting broke out. And the endless vistas of plains and mountains ahead made the colonel feel lonely and rightly worried about his lack of cavalry support.

More than four hundred miles east of his encounter with Alexander, Van Vliet met Colonel Albert Sidney Johnston, who belatedly had been picked as Harney's replacement as commander of the expedition, and his dragoon escort on the South Platte River crossing near what is now Ogallala, Nebraska. Van Vliet briefed Johnston on his Salt Lake meetings. Young would not allow Johnston's command to enter Salt Lake Valley that fall, he reported. Even a small force could stop Johnston's passage through Echo Canyon, he said, and he suggested Jim Bridger's trading post on Blacks Fork as the best place to winter. Agreeing with this opinion was the mountain man himself, who was serving as Johnston's guide and wanted to recover the property a Morman sheriff's posse had confiscated when it seized his trading post in 1853. Fort Bridger on the original Oregon Trail was also accessible to early spring supply.

Van Vliet's report was the last thing the expedition's new commander wanted to hear. Having replaced General Harney only seventeen days before, the colonel of the Second U.S. Cavalry now found himself leading an armed force much reduced from its paper strength of twenty-five hundred officers and men. The expedition was scattered over the Oregon Trail from the Missouri River almost to Fort Bridger, with its supply wagons and infantry in front and the commanding officer and cavalry in the rear. In the event of hostilities, the backward lineup would present an irresistible target.

To get the U.S. Army's largest body of men strung out over a thousand miles of desert and mountains with food and foot in front and commander and horse in back was not an uncommon display of the ineptitude with which a republican form of government often treats the unexpected. To achieve such a muddle required bureaucratic foul-ups on every level. Most rested on the assumption that Young and his forty thousand followers would never be foolish enough to cross swords with a nation of more than thirty million. Most smiled when Young boasted that one would chase a thousand and "two will put ten thousand to flight," echoing the biblical story of Gideon and his three hundred.[1] Apostle Heber C. Kimball, Young's first counselor, even crowed, "I have wives enough to whip out the United States."[2]

One who did not forget the biblical lesson was the army's commanding general. Known as "Old Fuss and Feathers," Brevet Lieutenant General Winfield Scott had joined the U.S. Army a half-century before and never attended a military academy. But he knew enough by age seventy-one to measure an adversary on what he was capable of, not on what seemed to make sense. When the newly inaugurated president at last got around to asking Scott's advice, the overweight Mexican War hero said that the Mormons could field four thousand troops on short notice—there was not enough time to assemble and equip a force large enough to deal with that number before winter set in—and supply lines would be dangerously exposed. Wait until next year, the old fusser fussed, and do it right.

The Virginian, a gifted planner and a brilliant general, had trouble getting along with presidents. In 1846, President James K. Polk wanted to name Missouri senator Thomas Benton to head the invasion of Mexico at Veracruz, but he had to admit that Scott was the best man for the job. Scott had also run as a Whig for president in 1852 against Buchanan's fellow Democrat Franklin Pierce, which hardly endeared him to Pierce's successor. But presidents commonly know more than generals, and his advice was ignored. Good soldier that he was, Scott did his best to mount the expedition and put it on the road. Elsewhere, preparations to assert federal sovereignty in the theocratic territory reflected the prevailing notion: the Mormons would not be so foolish as to mount armed resistance.

If that idea had held up, missteps made in haste by a young administration would have made little difference. The purpose of sending a military force was to escort a new governor and other officers to the territory and back them up in enforcing the law. The experience of federal officers

---

1. See Judg. 7.

2. Kimball, "Remarks," 26 July 1857, *Deseret News*, 12 August 1857, 179; and Young, "Remarks," 13 September 1857, *Deseret News*, 23 September, 228. See also Deut. 32:30.

since the first batch had arrived there in 1851 and left soon after scarcely generated a flood of applicants for the honor to black Brigham Young's boots. The president wasted a month trying to enlist Ben McCulloch to replace the Mormon leader as governor, but the renowned Texas Ranger captain was not interested. *Harper's Weekly* later said that Buchanan's "affinity for traitors" was the only reason he considered McCulloch.[3]

It took until July for Buchanan to find another southern sympathizer to fill Young's seat. He was Alfred Cumming, the massive and self-important superintendent of Indian affairs for the Upper Missouri Agency at St. Louis, later described by Utah citizen Milton Hammond as resembling "a whiskey barrel more than the Governor of an intelegent [*sic*] community."[4] The former mayor of Augusta, Georgia, the portly bureaucrat insisted on taking his wife, Elizabeth. Other offices were no easier to fill. Not until August were the appointments of Delana R. Eckels, chief justice; John Cradlebaugh and Charles E. Sinclair, associate justices; John Hartnett, secretary; Alexander Wilson, U.S. attorney; and Peter K. Dotson, marshal, made public.

After several false starts, Buchanan appointed Jacob Forney, from his home state of Pennsylvania, to replace Young as Utah's new superintendent of Indian affairs. Forney's only fitness for this important position was that he had worked for Buchanan's election. At least Frederick W. Lander, chief engineer of the Pacific Wagon Road Survey, thought so. He told Young that the hard-drinking Forney was "a kind and quiet gentleman," but "a little too slow for this country."[5]

To escort these worthies, elements of the expedition arrived at Fort Leavenworth during June and July in various states of readiness, most below an acceptable condition. There they were outfitted for the march west. From Minnesota came Colonel Alexander with eight companies of his Tenth Infantry, well under strength and composed mainly of recruits. What the regiment lacked in numbers and experience, however, it made up for in the quality of its officers, who would make it one of the force's most efficient commands. Debilitated from chasing elusive Seminoles

---

3. *Harper's Weekly*, 7 September 1861, 571. McCulloch became a brigadier general in the Confederate Army and was killed at Pea Ridge, Arkansas, in March 1862.

4. Hammond, *Journal Kept by Milton D. Hammond*, 6 May 1858, USHS.

5. Lander to Young, 23 September 1858, BYC.

through the fever-ridden Florida Everglades, the Fifth Infantry needed time for rest and refitting at Jefferson Barracks in St. Louis.

Though they were the first to reach Fort Leavenworth, the Second Dragoons were the last to march west with the expedition. General Harney's horse soldiers had arrived in June at the Missouri River post, but were quickly detached, with Harney, at the urgent call of territorial governor Robert J. Walker to stop the bloodshed over slavery along the eastern border of Kansas. Some have wrongly accused Harney of seeking duty in Kansas to avoid going to Utah.[6] Either service offered many career pitfalls and scarce opportunities for promotion. In the end, Governor Walker got his way, and the Army of Utah lost its first commander—and for far too long its mounted elements.

Not until mid-July, nearly two months after Buchanan had ordered troops to Utah and already dangerously late in the season, did eight companies of the Tenth Infantry become the first soldiers to march west from Fort Leavenworth. Trailing them separately over the days and weeks to come were other elements of the Utah Expedition: the Fifth Infantry under Lieutenant Colonel Carlos A. Waite; two more Tenth Infantry companies under Lieutenant Colonel Charles F. Smith; Captain John W. Phelps's Battery, Fourth Artillery; Captain Jesse L. Reno's Battery; additional infantry and dragoon segments under Lieutenant William D. Smith; and other units and supply trains, all marching separately without cavalry support.

By the time the War Department at last acted to straighten out the disorder caused by expediency and false assumptions, it was almost too late. Less than three weeks before Young declared martial law and shut down transcontinental travel, General Scott on 28 August ordered Colonel Johnston of the Second U.S. Cavalry to take command of the expedition

---

6. Kimball, "Discourse," 6 September 1857, in *Journal of Discourses*, 5:217. As Kimball noted, orders "have made him stop to aid the Governor of Kansas." He added, "and, it is likely, to kick up jack. But we do not care anything about it or them." A surprising number of historians have repeated Mormon charges that army leaders intended to hang LDS leaders without trial, based on a single less-than-credible sentence in an 1878 biography: "[Harney] would capture Brigham Young and the twelve apostles and execute them in a summary manner and winter in the temple of the Latter-day Saints." See Reavis, *Life and Military Services of Harney*, 277–78. Not a single known contemporary source reports Harney making such comments.

to Utah without delay. At the same time, he formally relieved Harney from this duty and ordered him to recall six Second Dragoon companies from Kansas and reassign them to the expedition under Johnston.

The man named to replace Harney was one of the army's two most promising officers, both of whom belonged to the same regiment. When Congress created the Second Cavalry in 1855, the argument raged in army circles over which man, Robert E. Lee or Johnston, would become the new regiment's colonel and which its second officer. Lee was favored by Winfield Scott, on whose staff he had served during the War with Mexico, while Secretary of War Jefferson Davis supported Johnston, who had commanded one of the Texas regiments in that conflict. It was a measure of the character of both men that the choice could have gone either way without rancor between them. As it was, Johnston won the appointment and in 1857 left the regiment in the capable hands of its second-in-command, Lieutenant Colonel Robert E. Lee.

The new commander of the U.S. forces, still known in Utah as "Johnson's army," deserved better than to have his name misspelled. A native of Kentucky, Johnston was a graduate of West Point and former secretary of war of the Texas Republic, his adopted state. At age fifty-four, standing more than six feet tall, he was athletic in build, temperate in habit, grave and dignified in manner, and energetic and decisive. His devotion to duty was total. It was said that his self-controlled decorum subjected affections, will, and passions to its performance. Yet Johnston was no martinet. His son recalled his many lessons "that a man has no right to inflict upon any creature unnecessary pain."[7] When he left for West Point, he gave his horse to his sister rather than sell it, fearing that another owner might mistreat the animal.

Two weeks after receiving orders from General Scott to report without delay, Johnston reached Fort Leavenworth from San Antonio to take command of the Utah Expedition. His exercise of leadership made an immediate difference in ending the uncertainty and lack of direction that had stalled the movement. The morning after he arrived at the Missouri River post, he notified the War Department that he intended to station twenty mounted infantrymen at Fort Kearny on the Oregon Trail to put a stop to raids by the Cheyenne Indians on cattle herds destined for his

7. Johnston, *Life of Gen. Albert Sidney Johnston*, 9.

command. He even reminded General Scott to ask Congress for funds to build barracks for his troops in Utah and gave him an estimate of the cost.

Within a week, Johnston had assembled the officials he was ordered to escort, including Governor Cumming and his wife. He made arrangements for their comfort on the trail, and organized the last units of the expedition for the journey west. He even made sure that measures were taken to protect mail delivery to his force in Salt Lake Valley. These acts showed that he anticipated no resistance.

When Lieutenant Colonel Philip St. George Cooke and companies A, B, C, F, G, and L joined Johnston's command on 16 September, the colonel ordered him to ride west from Fort Leavenworth the next day. The Second Dragoons officer resented being called from the field and allowed only three or four days to get ready to march over a thousand miles across an "uninhabited country and mountain wilderness."[8] But he had done better than that as commander of the Mormon Battalion during the Mexican War in 1846.

Cooke was one of the army's best frontier field officers—some say *the* best—accustomed to hardship and demanding duty, as Johnston no doubt knew. Even so, he saw to it that the tall Virginian got moving as ordered. Johnston planned to take forty dragoons himself as an escort and travel fast to reach the head of his new command. The civilian officials chose to go with Cooke, which required him to care for their comfort and travel at a slower rate. To make certain that Cooke did not dally at the fort, Johnston ordered the dragoons to march on 17 September and waited until the following day to make sure they were under way before leaving himself. Irked by this, Cooke coolly moved on the day ordered, but went only three miles before camping and waiting for Johnston and his escort to pass.

This prideful display was all too typical of the complacency that marked virtually every step of the planning and preparation of the hastily called expedition, and would lead to near-disaster. Nearly four months after President Buchanan ordered it and three days after Brigham Young halted all travel on the overland trails and mobilized the Utah militia to repel an imagined "invasion," the cavalry at last got moving. The republic's largest body of soldiers was finally under way, but scattered from

8. Buchanan, *Utah Expedition*, 92–99. See also Gardner, "March of 2d Dragoons," 43–59.

eastern Kansas to western Wyoming and as unready for combat operations as could be imagined.

Even so, favorable weather conditions would allow enough time to correct past mistakes, its commander thought. There were no indications of an early winter, Johnston reported from Fort Kearny on 24 September, "and I see no reason to apprehend it."[9] He also reportedly said that the only reliable weather forecaster is one who lives in a house with a leaky roof, and Johnston's roof was in good repair. The climate that fall would soon seem to confirm his opponents' faith that the Lord ruled the weather and He was on their side.

Not that Young relied only on divine favor. His direction of the conflict that he had started displayed his belief in preparation as well as in petitioning the Lord's help. On the day he landed in the Great Basin, Young knew that a confrontation with the country of his birth could not be avoided if God's Kingdom was to fulfill its prophesied destiny, and he had planned for that day. His actions over the past decade in the Great Basin were fully consistent with his defiant attitude toward the federal government.[10] They reflected expectation, strategic vision, and a clear-eyed grasp of the Mormon theocracy's weaknesses, as well as its advantages.

For ten years he had struggled, with uneven success, to create a self-sufficient economy; sent missionaries to gather the "blood of Israel" in Great Britain and to forge alliances with the Indians; employed drastic measures, such as handcarts, to build a population large enough to sustain sovereignty; created an army far exceeding any call for defense against Utah's Indians; and flushed from the body of latter-day Israel the corrupting influences of Gentile merchants, apostates, and federal officials. Like Moses on the Plains of Moab, he had reformed his people and instructed them how to live under God's law. Now the signs of the times revealed that the Almighty was ready to fulfill His part of the covenant with Israel.

The millennial factor on which Young heavily relied was revealed in a letter of 4 August 1857 to one of his most capable commanders. The coming of the U.S. Army was a strong indication that the Lord was hastening his work and the "Redemption of Zion draweth nigh," he told

9. Johnston to Irvin McDowell, 24 September 1857, in Buchanan, *Utah Expedition*, 23, 24.

10. Young, "Discourse," 13 September 1857, *Deseret News*, 23 September 1857, 228.

Andrew Cunningham. Conciliate the Indians, he said, "and make them your friends for the prospect is *that all Isreal* [*sic*] will be needed *to carry on the work of the last days.*"[11] The border war over slavery in "bleeding Kansas" would lead, he believed, to the breakup of the Union, as Joseph Smith had prophesied.[12] "If we can avert the blow for another season," Young added, "it is probable our enemies will have enough to attend to at home without worrying about the Latter Day Saints."[13]

These were the elements, practical and spiritual, of Young's strategy to seize a 220,000-square-mile slice of the western United States. Its immediate objective was fully within the capability of Mormon manpower and resources. As Young forthrightly told Captain Van Vliet, this was to stop the American army from entering Utah's settlements that fall, forcing the Utah Expedition to go back whence it had come or survive the winter on the high plains. Either way, it would hold up the army's advance for at least eight months and allow enough time for the fighting over slavery in Kansas to spread to other states, forcing Washington to turn its attention elsewhere.

Typical of Brigham Young, his plan also had a fallback provision. In the unlikely event that the U.S. Army should manage to force its way into Salt Lake Valley in 1857, as Colonel Johnston intended to do, or that the Lord should fail to follow Young's timetable for breaking up the Union, his people would reduce their homes and farms to ashes, Young had told Van Vliet, give no food to the invaders, and follow their leaders out of the Great Basin in a planned evacuation that could go on for months. No longer would he compromise with the United States. But he did not tell him or anyone else where they would go. Far to the north in Bitterroot Valley, Chief Victor and other Flathead leaders feared that the Mormons would move their way, as did their mountaineer neighbors.[14]

---

11. Young to Cunningham, 4 August 1857, BYC.

12. Smith visited New York City in 1832 and found excitement running high over South Carolina's threat to leave the Union. He then prophesied a great war between northern and southern states that would spread "until the consumption decreed hath made a full end of all nations." See "Revelation given through Joseph Smith," 25 December 1832, in *Doctrine and Covenants*, sec. 87, 532–33.

13. Young, "Remarks," 13 September 1857, *Deseret News*, 23 September 1857, 229.

14. Richard H. Lansdale to James W. Nesmith, 1 September 1857, 35th Cong., 1st sess., 1857–58, vol. 2, S. Ex. Doc. 11, serial 919, 663–69.

In the meantime, a theocratic command structure functioned with an efficiency that made Washington's fumbling performance look almost comical by comparison. In conflict or crisis, the Mormon system worked efficiently because authority flowed from the one who conveyed the divine will through subordinates who executed orders rather than engaged in independent planning or decision-making. If the man at the top was effective, as the leader of latter-day Israel indeed was, there would be few missteps in organizing Utah Territory's manpower and resources on a wartime basis. Young had anticipated a possible military showdown with the United States for a decade, and now God's Kingdom had rejected territorial rule and would fight for its independence.

In preparation for war, production of Colt revolvers began at the Public Works in Salt Lake City about the same time the territorial legislature's nullification of unwanted federal laws landed on the desk of the newly inaugurated president, James Buchanan. In addition to "pistols furnished and in production," work was under way to convert muskets from flint to percussion lock and repair rifles, reported Colonel Thomas W. Ellerbeck, chief of ordinance of the Nauvoo Legion and Young's clerk. At Cedar City, Eleazer Edwards made "an unglazed musket powder" that proved "equal to 2/3rds as strong as the Kentucky Rifle Powder sold in cannister," Ellerbeck said, and "a somewhat improved sample of lead" was smelted at Cedar City from Las Vegas Springs deposits contaminated by the less desirable silver.[15]

In 1862, General Thomas J. "Stonewall" Jackson would order iron pikes, "six or more inches longer than the musket with the bayonet," as a substitute for scarce muskets in arming Confederate infantry.[16] Five years earlier, resourceful Mormon military leaders had beaten Jackson to the punch. In a singular development in U.S. military annals, Colonel Ellerbeck in 1857 observed some experiments with steel crossbows and pronounced the weapon "so good as desirable." Noting that bows could not compare with a rifle "for range and accuracy," the twenty-nine-year-old Englishman advised that a few men be picked who "can use the bow and arrow" when ammunition could not be obtained.[17]

---

15. Ellerbeck, Report to Ferguson, 14 January 1858, Beinecke Library.
16. Freeman, *Lee's Lieutenants*, 1:323.
17. Ellerbeck, Report to Ferguson, 14 January 1858, Beinecke Library.

On the day Buchanan was inaugurated, 4 March 1857, Young published a proclamation as governor of Utah that a special plebiscite would be held on 6 April to elect a lieutenant general of the Nauvoo Legion, ostensibly the territorial militia.[18] The election would be a formality since it would be conducted by a show of hands during the general conference of the church on the anniversary of its founding in 1830. This meant that the territory now boasted two lieutenant generals, the other being Young, while the rest of the nation had only one, General Winfield Scott, whose elevation to this grade was by brevet only. It would also give the Nauvoo Legion a three-to-two edge over the U.S. Army in general officers of this grade.[19]

Since the election was ritualistic, the winner felt unconstrained to wait until 6 April before issuing his first general order. On 27 March, Lieutenant General Daniel H. Wells reorganized the Nauvoo Legion into companies of ten, one hundred, five hundred, and one thousand. The new organization would "strike all as being more congenial because of its perfection and simplicity than anything heretofore," said Young's second counselor.[20] He meant that the army of latter-day Israel would be patterned after the Army of Israel of old. He ordered all able-bodied white males in Utah between the ages of eighteen and forty-five to enroll for military duty unless they were exempt by law.

Wells divided the territory into thirteen military districts on 11 April and designated officials in each district to enroll all eligible men into platoons and companies. As soon as these units were formed, he ordered elections to choose officers to command them. He ended his General Orders No. 1 with words that seemed to reflect his awareness of the mighty challenge that lay ahead: "I pray my Father in Heaven for His Holy Spirit to strengthen me to discharge the duties [now] devolved on me to the honor of His good cause."[21]

Even without divine help, the commander of this unique American army already enjoyed a number of strengths in accomplishing the responsibility he apparently had foreseen. First, a governing system that

---

18. Brigham Young, "Proclamation," *Deseret News*, 4 March 1857, 413.

19. The score: Nauvoo Legion, Joseph Smith, Brigham Young, and Daniel H. Wells; U.S. Army, George Washington and Winfield Scott by brevet.

20. Wells, "Militia of Utah," 27 March 1857, *Deseret News*, 1 April 1857, 28.

21. Wells, "General Orders No. 1," 11 April 1857, *Deseret News*, 22 April 1857, 48.

could produce tightly disciplined emigrant companies and an army on short notice also benefited from interior lines of communication and supply, an important advantage. It had taken two days for Van Vliet to journey the 113 miles from Great Salt Lake to Fort Bridger, where the U.S. Army expedition would spend the winter. But it took him more than two months to cover the distance to the nation's capital and deliver his report to Secretary of War John B. Floyd.

Nauvoo Legion troops and animals were also in better condition to conduct active operations on the high plains because they had a relatively short distance to go to meet an enemy exhausted by a thousand-mile journey overland from Fort Leavenworth. Nor were they tied to a supply line that ultimately reached at least that far. For the Utah Expedition, the nearest source of provisions would be Fort Laramie, nearly four hundred miles to the east on the far side of the Continental Divide.

Enhancing the benefit of interior lines was a landscape that appeared shaped by a divine hand to guard against unwelcome intrusion from the east. The Wasatch Mountains stretched four hundred miles from the Snake River on the north to southern Utah as an almost impassable barrier for wheeled vehicles. The only direct passage to Mormon settlements along its western front was Echo Canyon, a winding corridor on the Mormon-California Trail from Fort Bridger to Salt Lake Valley. From early fur traders to Interstate 80, the spectacular red-walled canyon has channeled travel and communications over its twenty-three-mile length to all points west.

Echo Canyon in 1857 gave an advantage to the Mormon side because it was the only feasible entry to Salt Lake Valley for a large U.S. Army expedition with extensive supply trains coming from the east over the Oregon-California Trail. The narrow defile was highly defensible, with towering rock walls almost impossible to flank on either side. Its strategic value was incalculable. The corridor through the mountains funneled wagons to major routes to Oregon, northern California, and Los Angeles. As Mormon resistance showed, it could be readily plugged, disrupting communications and travel over some two hundred thousand square miles from the Wasatch Range to the West Coast.

Of less value was another historic passage through the Wasatch Range farther south, now followed by I-70. Opened by Mexican traders in 1829, the Spanish Trail reached from New Mexico to Los Angeles. From Green

River it entered the Great Basin at Emigrant Pass and ran down Salina Canyon to meet and follow the Sevier River south to the southern Utah settlements of Parowan and Cedar City and the alpine oasis at Mountain Meadows before heading across the southwestern desert to Los Angeles. As C. Gregory Crampton and Steven K. Madsen have shown, the Spanish Trail was a horse-and-mule trade route.[22] Not even during the Gold Rush did it become a wagon road, and, like the route Captain John W. Gunnison surveyed for a railroad through central Colorado and Utah, the trace had no value as a pathway for a military expedition.

More than a hundred miles north of Echo Canyon, Bear River opened another entry to Salt Lake Valley. From Fort Bridger, the Oregon Trail followed the river north to Soda Springs, where the stream passes through the mountain wall of the Wasatch and reverses course to flow south toward Great Salt Lake. While the Oregon road continued north to Fort Hall, the Bidwell-Bartleson party in 1841 followed the river south from Soda Springs to open an easy but roundabout avenue to Salt Lake Valley from the north.[23]

Adding to the Mormons' advantage of terrain was the quality of officers and men in the Nauvoo Legion. Some of them had marched two thousand miles in 1846 from Fort Leavenworth to Los Angeles as members of the Mormon Battalion to occupy Mexico's northernmost province during the War with Mexico. What most lacked in military training, they made up for in leadership skills gained from building settlements and leading closely organized overland companies to Salt Lake Valley, some from as far away as Denmark. They knew the land they defended and were hardened to the conditions it imposed.

The "tall, angular figure" who commanded Mormon forces in the field was an asset by himself. Forty-three-year-old Daniel H. Wells was austere by nature and physically as hard as nails, but Brigham Young's oldest son said that he suffered from severe attacks of "congestion of the brain," which the general's nephew said had afflicted him even during his days as a non-Mormon alderman at Nauvoo. An undoubting

22. See Crampton and Madsen, *In Search of the Spanish Trail.*

23. The Bidwell-Bartleson party of thirty-two men and one woman, Nancy Kelsey, who carried a baby on one arm and led a horse with the other hand, was first to travel overland from the Missouri River to California. Without a map or compass, all made the journey safely by following the sun west.

believer, the New York native left a wife and child in Illinois to follow Young and later replaced both with six and twenty-four, respectively. Wells once said that anyone who professed the right to differ with Young "might as well ask whether one had the right to differ honestly with God."[24] A dismal speaker, he was the reverse image of Jedediah M. Grant, the fire-eating preacher he replaced as Young's second counselor. His all-but-illegible handwriting revealed limited schooling, but he was highly capable, possessed a passion for knowledge, and had an instinctive understanding of the value of intelligence. He usually knew what his opponents were going to do almost as soon as they decided to do it. At the same time, Young allowed his top commander little freedom to make decisions on his own. The almost daily reports and orders between them show that Wells, like every other official in the Mormon hierarchy, did largely what he was told.

While the strengths of terrain and leadership offered promising prospects over the short run, there were two handicaps that would indeed require divine favor to overcome if the confrontation continued after 1857. Young had known what they were from the beginning, but even he had failed to surmount them. The first was the lack of a population large enough to sustain a claim of sovereignty over much of western America. Ten years before, Young had told his pioneer company that they would find a place to raise the Standard of the Kingdom of God and fulfill the prophecy of Isaiah that in the last days "all nations shall flow unto it."[25] But the announcement on polygamy in 1852 had sharply reduced the flow of new believers from abroad, and many of those who did come fled during the Reformation. In December 1857, Young boasted that the population was nearly one hundred thousand, but the actual count was less than half that many.

To make up the difference, Young's military strategy relied heavily on the Lamanites, American Indians who would give up their way of life and

---

24. Whitney, *History of Utah*, 4:178; *Utah Magazine*, 30 October 1869, 406–12; and Joseph A. Young, Journal of a Mission, 9 March 1864, Marriott Library. "Congestion of the brain" was a catchall term for a variety of ills. A contemporary authority said that with the condition, "all the great functions of life are in a state of severe vital depression." See Forbes Winslow, *On Obscure Diseases of the Brain, and Disorders of the Mind* (Philadelphia: Blanchard & Lea, 1860), 514.

25. Isa. 2:2.

join their fellow Children of Israel to usher in the Last Days. "The door has already been unlocked to the Lamanites in these mountains," Wilford Woodruff had predicted in February. "They will begin to embrace the gospel and the records of their fathers, and their chiefs will be filled with the spirit of God, and they will rise up in their strength and a nation will be born in a day."[26] Such an alliance of Mormons and Indians would force the United States to submit and build New Jerusalem, the City of Zion, in Missouri. This hope was in contradiction to all the practical knowledge the Mormons had accumulated about their Shoshonean neighbors over a decade, but it revealed their devotion to the apocalyptic prophecies of Joseph Smith. What the strategy lacked in practicality, it made up for in its propaganda value: "There can no longer be any doubt but that all the central routes will be unsafe as an emigrant highway for a very long time. The Mormons will resist," a San Francisco newspaper proclaimed. "They number at least ten thousand fighting men, and are in close alliance with at least fifty thousand hostile Indians."[27]

Related to the population shortfall was the inability to establish a self-sustaining economy in the Great Basin. The bed of ancient Lake Bonneville, a vast region of interior drainage, was hardly the best place to build a growing economy based on agriculture. The high-altitude desert gave Zion's farmers a short growing season, plenty of rocks and gravel, hordes of voracious Rocky Mountain locusts, and too little arable soil and water. The great expanse of mountain ranges running north to south held unlimited promise for mineral development, but the lack of transportation sharply reduced its value. Costly attempts to jump-start the production of iron, pottery, sugar, clothing, arms, and munitions repeatedly failed. Except for trade with emigrants, sources of hard cash were almost nonexistent. After a decade, the economy still struggled for growth on a barter footing.

These strengths and weaknesses shaped the tactics that Young and Wells employed to stop the U.S. Army expedition from reaching Mormon settlements in 1857. Preferably this would be accomplished by burning grass, the fuel of travel on the plains; rustling cattle; destroying unguarded supply trains; raising night alarms; and spreading propaganda to hurt morale and encourage desertion. Up to a point, the campaign

26. Woodruff, "Discourse," 22 February 1857, *Deseret News*, 4 March 1857, 411.
27. *San Francisco Herald*, 17 October 1857, 2.

would be carried on without bloodshed. But the Nauvoo Legion would stand and shed the blood of American soldiers if they tried to advance beyond Echo Canyon or Soda Springs.

To carry out this strategy, the Nauvoo Legion mobilized smoothly. A week after the announcement of the threatened "invasion," General Wells organized "the Eastern Expedition" and ordered the Legion to prepare for winter operations in the mountains. By 8 September, when Van Vliet arrived, hundreds of men were already in the Wasatch canyons. Many more were ready to join them, camped on Union Square, where Hensley's Salt Lake Cutoff left the city to head north to the California Trail. The foot soldiers of Zion labored to make Echo Canyon and other mountain defiles as impassable as Van Vliet feared they would be for a force as small as the one Buchanan had sent, while fast-moving mounted companies ranged far to the east, employing classic guerrilla tactics to slow the progress of the coming army.

On 15 August, Nauvoo Legion colonel Robert T. Burton led a mounted company of some seventy men to deliver food to the Devils Gate station on the Sweetwater River for emigrant companies still on the road. Upon fulfilling this task, the Canadian officer was ordered to burn grass, watch the enemy's movements, and report back to Legion headquarters. By chance, Burton met Colonel Alexander's Tenth Infantry on the same day as Captain Van Vliet, 21 September, at the Ice Spring, near what is now Jeffrey City, Wyoming. While Burton and Colonel James W. Cummings kept their men out of sight, Captain Jesse Gove of the Tenth U.S. Infantry saw a damaging sign of the Legion's presence along the river west of Devils Gate. "They have burnt the grass for many miles along the road," he protested.[28] The two Mormon officers would shortly give him even more to complain about.

In the meantime, Burton was not the first to spy on the U.S. Army's advance and tell Young what he saw. That distinction goes to eastern mail carriers Samuel W. Richards and Bryant Stringham, who left Great Salt Lake City three days before the colonel and reported five days later from the Deer Creek Station, at present-day Glenrock, Wyoming. A few miles east of Independence Rock, they met "Bros [Israel] Evans, [Jesse B.] Martin, and [Benjamin] Ashby with their companies of Handcarts," trying to keep ahead of federal troops. Also on 17 August, they

28. Gove, *Utah Expedition*, 60.

met John M. Moody and the Texas Company with "with good teams and able to travel fast" a few miles west of the North Platte River.[29]

Later that day, they spotted "the first company of Government Wagons loaded with freight designed for the Troops." The train "consisted of 26 wagons with 6 yokes of cattle to each wagon," they noted. "There were only two or three extra men with the train in charge, and everything appeared very civil and quiet." That night, "we passed the 2nd Government train in camp," they reported, "14 miles above the crossing of the Platte, and judged them to be of about the same size and character of the first company."[30]

At the upper North Platte ford at what is now Casper, Wyoming, the mail carriers met and camped with the last handcart company under captains Christian Christiansen, Matthias Cowley, and James Park. Short on food, the Danish and English converts were going to Zion, pulling their few belongings along in handcarts and depending "upon the station at Devils Gate for their entire breadstuff to last them from that point into the Valley," Park said. He judged that "they would require about 600 lb per day."[31] Whatever supplies Burton may have brought with him proved entirely inadequate to feed the approximately 330 members of Christiansen's train. Ironically, on the Sweetwater River it fell to Uncle Sam to help feed the struggling emigrants. "We appreciated the fact that at one time when our company was nearly without food, almost like a miracle, the Army came to our rescue," recalled Carl Dorius, a member of the company. The army train's captain "approached us and said in a kindly way, that one of his oxen had a crushed foot. If we could use it we were welcome to have it. This came as a blessing, because the company had been without any meat for several weeks. It was a real treat," Dorius wrote. "We ran out of food and sent to Salt Lake City for provisions which came too late to help. One tenth of the company died for want of care and nourishment."[32]

John M. Bernhisel sent Young the most detailed and literate reports on the U.S. Army's movements. Traveling in Van Vliet's comfortable

29. Richards and Stringham to Young, 18 August 1857, BYC.
30. Ibid.
31. Ibid.
32. Dorius, "Autobiography."

carriage, the University of Pennsylvania graduate returned the captain's hospitality by serving as Young's eyes in the enemy camp. He reported that the Tenth Infantry numbered about 750 after losing about 100 to desertion, while unauthorized leave-taking had reduced the trailing Fifth Infantry companies to about 475. He confirmed that Colonel Johnston was the new "Commander in Chief of the Utah Expedition," describing his long train of light spring wagons, each drawn by four mules. On the Platte River, he met Young's slow-moving successor as governor, Alfred Cumming, and the other new officials being escorted by Colonel Cooke's Second Dragoons. "I have had quite a pleasant & prosperous journey across the plains," Bernhisel told Young from Fort Leavenworth. "Captain Van Vliet is an agreeable and gentlemanly man," he said. "His report will be favorable."[33]

Adding to the flow of information about the U.S. Army's advance over the direct route to Salt Lake Valley, scouting parties in August and September watched other trails through the mountains to guard against surprise. Captain James S. Brown and a party from Weber Military District invaded Oregon Territory to circle Bear Lake on the Utah-Idaho border. And Nauvoo Legion major Marcellus Monroe commanded a party sent to scout the trails on the upper stretches of Bear River and give Indian chiefs the "necessary instructions."[34] The "instructions" that other Mormon officers gave Native leaders at the time informed them that "they have either got to help us or the United States will kill us both."[35]

Meanwhile, violence flared on the Great Plains. "Indians, supposed to be the Cheyennes," attacked a small party of Arkansas emigrants on the Republican Fork some eighty miles west of Fort Riley, killing four of the men and burning their wagons, Missouri newspapers reported. "This may be looked upon as the commencement of the Cheyenne war," the press said. Responding to raids along the Platte River in 1856, including one that killed Utah's secretary of state and Council of Fifty member Almon W. Babbitt, Colonel Edwin V. Sumner of the First U.S. Cavalry

33. Bernhisel to Young, 17 October 1857, BYC. Quartermaster Van Vliet consistently gave Mormon leaders this impression, while his official reports are strictly objective and professional.

34. Monroe, "Report of a Party of Observation," UTMR.

35. Young to Jacob Hamblin, 4 August 1857, in Brooks, *Mountain Meadows Massacre*, 34, 35, cited as Church Letter Book, no. 3, 737–38.

was already on the tribe's trail, but frontier editors feared that the "well mounted" Indians had "a fine chance of slipping in between and getting in his rear, which, it appears they have done."[36]

They need not have worried, for the hard-bitten officer, known as "Bull" Sumner, and six cavalry companies met three hundred warriors drawn up in a line across the valley of a Solomon River fork in western Kansas on 29 July. To prepare for the upcoming battle, the Cheyenne soldiers all bathed in a small blue lake that two shamans, Ice and Dark, had promised would make them invulnerable to the soldiers' bullets. True to his nickname, the sixty-year-old Sumner wheeled his men into line and ordered his buglers to sound two commands: draw sabers and charge. Suddenly, the confident warriors' sacred invulnerability vanished. "They had been assured of safety from the usual threat, a rain of bullets, not against the slash of sabers," historian Elliott West observed. The Indians stood it as long as they could while the horse soldiers came straight at them, then broke and scattered in every direction.[37]

Sumner was doing what nervous frontier citizens wanted the army to do: kill Indians. But the destruction of the Arkansas train on the Republican Fork aroused fears that "there will be a great loss of life and property" among the very large "emigration crossing the plains this year" unless the government promptly dispatched more horse soldiers to deal with the threat. Instead, the press complained that the government was sending "an unnecessarily large number of troops to Utah, a portion should be sent to chastise the Indians who are murdering and robbing our citizens at our very doors." As General Harney informed army headquarters, "This business will complicate very much the movement upon Utah."[38]

Far to the west, rumors that the army would "invade" Utah Territory over the Spanish Trail raised repeated alarms. Just the thought of Colonel Sumner charging around Utah kept people on edge. West Coast newspapers were already reporting that Sumner and eighty-six dragoons had swooped down on Salt Lake on 25 June "and took Brigham Young

---

36. "Indian Hostilities on the Plains," *Kansas Weekly Herald*, 16 June 1857.

37. West, *Contested Plains*, 3–4.

38. "Indian Hostilities on the Plains"; and Harney to J. Thomas, 25 June 1857, National Archives.

prisoner, on a charge of treason and other crimes, and started with him for Washington city, within two hours after his arrival, meeting with no opposition on the part of the Mormons."[39] The newspapers knew that Sumner had been in Kansas on that date, but the rumors apparently rattled Mormon leaders in Deseret enough for Daniel Wells to order Colonel William Dame in southern Utah "to keep one or two tens out in the mountains upon the approaches to the settlements as a corps of observation that we may not be taken at any point by surprise."[40] On 24 August, Samuel Lewis from Parowan led a party to scout the Spanish Trail entry into the Great Basin at Emigrant Pass and Salina Canyon, retracing Gunnison's 1853 railway survey. New alarms led to more excitement. Captain James H. Martineau of the Nauvoo Legion's Iron County Brigade led a scouting party on 4 September over the Spanish Trail's alternate route that ran by Fish Lake from Emigrant Pass along Otter Creek to the Sevier River, "having heard the cavalry under Col. Summer would enter the country that way."[41] Still fearful that Sumner was coming, General Wells sent Andrew Love from Nephi and nine men from Manti "on a trip in the Mountains to watch the Gunison trail to see if he had passed into the Territory."[42] They met heavy snow and a bear, but no "Bull."

As early as December 1856, Brigham Young had foreseen the military confrontation with the United States and sounded a recall of Mormon colonies in Carson Valley and San Bernardino. "For some cause or other, *The Mormons* at San Bernardino and all the surrounding settlements had been called in to Salt Lake City," travelers from Utah reported in early April 1857.[43] The order to return and defend Zion became urgent in August 1857 and included a plea to acquire arms and ammunition for possible use against Mormon soldiers. Apostle Charles C. Rich initiated the return of the southern California colony in June, when he arrived in

39. "Important News from Salt Lake. Brigham Young Arrested for Treason. Young Carried off a Prisoner by Col. Sumner to Washington," *Daily Evening Bulletin*, 22 August 1857, reprinted in Ekins, *Defending Zion*, 356.

40. Wells to Dame, 13 August 1857, Sherratt Library.

41. Martineau, "My Life," Huntington Library.

42. Love, Journal, 12–19 September 1857, Authors' Collection.

43. "From Utah," *New-York Daily Times*, 22 May 1857, 2, reprinted from *St. Louis Republican*, 18 May 1857.

Salt Lake City and reportedly delivered a load of powder and lead. William Mathews, a freighter from San Bernardino, also hauled gunpowder to the rebellious theocracy for a "war with Uncle Sam."[44]

In August 1857, as Colonel Burton headed east to meet the U.S. Army, Peter W. Conover and Oliver B. Huntington rode west across the Great Basin to deliver Young's order to Carson Valley settlers to abandon their homes there, return to Zion, and "bring as much ammunition as you can."[45] Raising more than $12,000 from church coffers and Mormon contributors in Carson Valley and California, they acquired gunpowder and lead in San Francisco and shipped them by steamboat to Stockton, where others picked up the munitions and hauled them over the Sierra Nevada. The covert operation ended at Genoa, where a wagon train of returning Mormons moved out on 23 September with the hidden delivery in tow.

A rare glimpse into Young's financial records suggests that BYX agent Nicholas "Big Nose" Groesbeck delivered "1,617 pounds of gunpowder, a half-ton of ballistic lead, and tens of thousands of percussion caps," and perhaps an additional 1,216 pounds of powder, 207 pounds of lead, and 10,000 more caps to Salt Lake in November. Groesbeck had been compelled to hide the rifles he was carrying west for Young at the North Platte Crossing, which Johnston ordered seized after learning of Mormon attacks.[46]

At the same time, Young was aware that secret acquisitions delivered by wagon over long distances could never supply enough ammunition to take on the U.S. Army. If shooting broke out, he would rely on a more promising supplier of guns and powder at no cost—the U.S. Army itself. On 4 August, he ordered Andrew Cunningham at the Genoa mail station on the Loup River in today's east-central Nebraska to arm himself with "guns and plenty of ammunition and if you can send us a little, although we expect to make those who cause us trouble to supply us in this respect."[47] Young gave similar assurance to the head of northern Utah's Cache Valley settlement. "In relation to ammunition, we cannot

44. Bagley, *Blood of the Prophets*, 77.

45. Young to Chester Loveland and the Brethren in Carson County, in Owens, *Gold Rush Saints*, 329.

46. MacKinnon, *At Sword's Point*, 1:262–63.

47. Young to Andrew Cunningham, 4 August 1857, BYC.

part with any as we have not enough to supply this district," he advised. "Save what you have, and the Lord will move upon those who cause us trouble to haul our powder and lead."[48]

Once again, Young was telling less than he knew. Not one to leave securing such a critical war-making materiel as gunpowder to Divine Providence, early in 1857 he had directed his son-in-law (and future Utah congressional delegate) William H. Hooper to contract with the firm of Russell, Majors & Waddell, who later that year won the army's main freight contract, "to bring out several thousand pounds of freight for Mr. Hooper." The company sent Hooper's order with their other wagons hauling army supplies. That fall, soldiers impounded the boxes marked as dry goods, hardware, crockery, "etc." at Fort Bridger. Upon examining the shipment, "it was found that every box contained, hidden among and surrounded with dry goods and other articles, one or more kegs of powder, the whole amounting to eight thousand pounds," a newspaper correspondent reported early in March 1858. He suggested that the mercantile firm at St. Louis that had assembled the goods should be identified so the public could "know the traitors who are aiding in this rebellion."[49]

From almost every point on the compass, Brigham Young's faithful followers came, some with guns and ammunition, most not, to concentrate in the main Mormon settlements along the Wasatch Mountain front and defend God's Kingdom in the Last Days. From as far as Europe and Hawaii, missionaries would return to make the cause of latter-day Israel with powder and lead in place of scripture. Handcart companies from England would come from the east and settlers from outlying colonies to the southeast, west, and southwest. In only one direction was a Mormon company outbound that fall.

On 1 October, a new colonizing party of some seventy men, women, and children left northern Utah and journeyed due north. Their destination: Fort Limhi, the Kingdom's colony in Oregon Territory on the eastern fork of Salmon River. The Indian mission overlooked the Lewis

48. Young to Peter Maughn, 4 August 1857, ibid.
48. Young to Peter Maughn, 4 August 1857, ibid.
49. "Movements in the Utah Expedition—Reports of Mormon Preparations, &c.," 5 March 1858, *New-York Times*, 18 May 1858. Our thanks to John Eldredge for sharing this insight.

and Clark Trail and a covered escape route to the headwaters of the Missouri River and Bitterroot Valley, now in southwest Montana. Their purpose: to strengthen the existing settlement and prepare it as a place of rest and supply in a staged movement from the Great Basin to a new gathering place.

CHAPTER 9

Pitch into Them

Brigham Young Orders Bloodshed

You are at liberty to return a fire in self defence, and if they leave the ["Fort Hall" crossed out] Oregon road, pitch into their picket guards and sentinels, and among them all you can, but avoid the open ground.

—General Daniel H. Wells, 17 October 1857

Without cavalry, a foot soldier, who packs a load that would be heavy even for a mule, cannot hope to overtake or guard against an enemy on horseback. So when Nauvoo Legion colonels Robert T. Burton and James W. Cummings received orders on 24 September to stampede the U.S. Army's animals, they moved that same night. They did not have far to go: their mounted command on the Sweetwater River was brazenly located between the federal army's two advance units, little more than a dozen miles from either one. And the absence of cavalry made both vulnerable when Brigham Young became alarmed at the progress of Colonel Edmund B. Alexander's quick-stepping infantry and ordered the first attack on American forces to slow them down.[1]

To raid both enemy camps the same night, the Legion colonels ordered Mormon Battalion veteran Captain Joseph Clark to take thirty men and attack Captain John W. Phelps's Battery of the Fourth U.S. Artillery on Willow Creek, a few miles east of the Oregon Trail's last crossing of the Sweetwater at what is now Burnt Ranch, Wyoming. Camped with Phelps's cannons were William M. F. Magraw and a Pacific Wagon Road

---

1. Cummings and Burton, Report to Wells, 27 September 1857, BYC.

Survey party with mules and wagons.[2] Burton and Cummings led the remaining forty-five men some twelve miles across South Pass to the first waters on the Pacific side of the Continental Divide, where Alexander and his Tenth Infantry had camped on Pacific Creek.

There Captain Jesse Gove of Company I slept with a candle and matches by his head, as he always did while in the field. "I am ready, as you know," he had told his wife before leaving. "I always am." The ambitious young officer was also always proud of his company. "No one has to wait for the 'I's,'" he said.[3] To set them apart, he made them all wear gray hats. But Gove and the "gray hats" were caught in the early hours of 25 September, not ready.

"This morning about 2 o'clock several shots were fired immediately behind my tent," he told his wife, "and immediately the whole herd of mules stampeded with a terrific rush." As the herders hallooed "Soldiers turn out, we are attacked," Gove struck a light, pulled his pants on, and ran "to turn out my company," dressing as he went. But by the time he reached it with sword and revolver in hand, "ready for a fight," the regiment's "bell sharp" mules had already saved Company I's honor. The bell mule's picket rope got caught in the sagebrush, the captain said, "stopping him, and with him most of the herd stopped."[4]

The frustrated Burton and Cummings knew they had failed but never did figure out why, and they vowed it was not their fault. "We sent 6 men direct through their camp into the midst of their animals," they said, with "bear Skin 'Rattles' 'Dum[b] Bells" and other noisemakers, while the rest lined up along the creek, making all the racket they could, but the mules refused to move. They kept trying, but when "the Bugle Sounded the 'call to Arms,'" they rode off for Green River "as fast as possible." They had not heard from Captain Clark, who had been ordered to

2. In March 1857, President Buchanan named William M. F. Magraw superintendent of the Fort Kearney [sic]–South Pass–Honey Lake stretch of the Pacific Wagon Road project, to the chagrin of the more qualified Frederick W. Lander. Magraw was an outspoken Mormon enemy, and his 1856 letter to President Pierce was among the documents Buchanan handed to Congress to justify sending an army to Utah. See MacKinnon, "Buchanan Spoils System," 127–50.

3. Gove, *Utah Expedition*, 13, 15.

4. Ibid., 64, 65. "Bell sharps" were mules trained to follow a bell mule, as opposed to animals whose tails had been shaved to warn herders that they were inexperienced and untrustworthy. Hence enlisted men called new second lieutenants "shave tails."

stampede the Fourth Artillery's camp, but assumed "he was Successful or he would have been here ere this."[5]

If so, Phelps was unaware of it. The erudite artillery captain later heard that some Mormons had run through the Tenth Infantry camp and "by yells and discharges of firearms succeeded in scattering the mules," but he had no idea that his own camp was targeted.[6] If it had been struck, the Vermonter might not have known it anyway. He was always more fascinated by cloud formations and nature than by military matters.[7] If Alexander seemed to pay little attention to the Pacific Creek raid, as well, his rate of march spoke otherwise. Since meeting Captain Stewart Van Vliet on 21 September, his Tenth Infantry had advanced more than twenty miles a day. After the mule fiasco, Alexander's "foot cavalry" marched even faster.

During his Salt Lake visit, Van Vliet gave his Mormon hosts the impression that he was on their side. He said that if the federal government "made war upon us He should withdraw from the Army," Apostle Wilford Woodruff reported. "On his own responsibility," the captain promised Young that he would stop the army's supply trains on Hams Fork "and leave them there," which would force U.S. troops to halt their advances indefinitely more than 30 miles east of Fort Bridger and more than 150 miles from Salt Lake Valley. "I do think that God has sent you out here," Young answered. "If you will speak in favor of us & I think you will, the Lord will bless you for so doing," he promised. "He will require it of you."[8]

Van Vliet was as good as his word. He told Alexander that the Mormons would never allow him to enter Salt Lake Valley, but not to worry about supplies. There was a train of more than a hundred wagons parked on Hams Fork. Although "they contained provisions and supplies which would have been of great use to the Mormons," they did not molest it. Nor did they bother a herd of eleven hundred cattle along the stream.[9] The quartermaster urged Alexander to stop and camp his column at Hams

---

5. Cummings and Burton, Report to Wells, 27 September 1857, BYC.

6. Phelps, Diary, 25, in Hafen and Hafen, *Utah Expedition*, 133–34.

7. When the Hafens published the Phelps Utah War diaries, they omitted most of his extensive descriptions of cloud formations.

8. Kenney, *Wilford Woodruff's Journal*, 26 September 1857, 100.

9. Alexander to S. Cooper, 9 October 1857, in Buchanan, *Utah Expedition*, 31.

Fork in keeping with Young's plan to prevent the army from reaching Salt Lake Valley that fall. But Alexander's apparent answer to Van Vliet's proposal had been a "a forced march, which was repeated with such good success by them day after day that not only did all attempts to deprive them of their animals fail," but it was all that Burton and Cummings and their companies on horseback could do to keep from being run over by soldiers on foot, Nauvoo Legion adjutant general James Ferguson told Brigham Young.[10]

On reaching Green River, the two Mormon officers had sent a party back to seize "a train of supply wagons."[11] The twelve wagons were under Tenth Infantry lieutenant William Clinton, who had been sent ahead to Green River to pick up a load of forage for the livestock and was on his way back. Hardly had the mounted party taken off to capture this imagined prize than they unexpectedly ran into Alexander's footmen, making what Captain Gove proudly hailed as "one of the most extraordinary marches on record." The foot soldiers saved the lieutenant and his wagonloads of animal feed just as "some 60 armed and mounted Mormons" were getting ready to pounce on them. "When the troops came, they went off in great haste," Gove said.[12]

After rescuing their fellow officer, the Tenth Infantry marched on to Green River, while Burton and Cummings rode as fast as they could for Fort Bridger to raise the alarm. They had seen the difference between part-time militia and regular troops, and it left little room for complacency. The invaders were coming on fast and showed little inclination to stop at Hams Fork, despite "the reported recommendation of Captain Van Vliet for the army to pause and reflect."[13]

In the meantime, Alexander's infantry unknowingly dispelled some of the threats that Young had leveled during his talks with Van Vliet two weeks before. If the federal government tried to enlist volunteers in California "to destroy us they will find their own buildings in flames before they get far from home & so throughout the United States," he reportedly had said. He would rein in the Indians no longer. "I shall Carry the war

10. Ferguson, Report to Young, 7 January 1858, UTMR.
11. Gove, *Utah Expedition*, 65, 66.
12. Ibid.
13. Ferguson, Report to Young, 7 January 1858, UTMR.

into their own land and they will want to let out the job before they get half through," he threatened.[14] As he spoke, Mormon agents were telling the Natives that "our enemies are also their enemies . . . they must stick to us, for if our enemies kill us off," they would suffer the same fate.[15] In early October, Young suggested that two veteran Indian missionaries be sent to "have a conversation with" Chief Washakie to learn "what they can of his views and plans," in the hope that "Lott"—the Shoshones— would *"genteely escort* Genl Harney under, if found on the road."[16]

At Green River on 27 September, the Tenth Infantry found that the region's most powerful tribe had no intention of taking part in Young's menacing campaign. On the contrary, the "great number of Shoshonee or Snake Indians" gathered at the crossing of the Colorado River's main tributary were eager to join the American soldiers in fighting the Mormons. "They are a splendid set of men," Gove said. Their chief wanted to lead more than a thousand warriors into the field, he said, but "the old woman," his name for Alexander, "never will do any such thing."[17] Nor would Colonel Albert S. Johnston allow Indians to join in operations against an American territory. Unwilling to fight for the Mormons, unwanted to fight against them, and unable to understand either side, the Shoshones headed north to their favorite wintering ground. When General Daniel H. Wells sent a Shoshone interpreter to Green River "to endeavor to talk to the Snakes," he discovered that they had left for the Wind River Mountains.[18]

Mormon policy—at least officially—was to avoid bloodshed, but when the "Governor and Commander in Chief of the Military of Utah" issued private orders to his military commanders, they often conveyed an entirely different message. "When the troops occupy the roads our forces must be in ambush behind the cliffs on the sides of the mountains or in the brush," Young instructed Colonel P. C. Merrill in late September. "You are already aware of our mode of warfare, to stampede animals, cut off scouting parties, and use every other means to wipe out our enemies."[19]

14. Kenney, *Wilford Woodruff's Journal*, 13 September 1857.
15. Wells to Evans, 13 August 1857, USHS.
16. Young to Wells, Taylor, and Smith, 7 October 1857, BYC.
17. Gove, *Utah Expedition*, 66.
18. Wells to Young, 17 October 1857, BYC.
19. Young to Merrill, 28 September 1857, ibid.

While claiming that he was "highly pleased with the bloodless success which has so far attended your labors," Young told Wells to prepare men for "operating in the night, picking off picket guards and sentinels and rousing up the camp as often as it becomes quiet" so "the enemy will be in sorry plight for marching or fighting fresh forces on the succeeding day and will doubtless soon surrender or be subdued."[20]

Continuing his advance, Alexander sent the "always ready" Captain Gove and Company I on a night march from Green River to Hams Fork to strengthen the guard on the army's cattle under Lieutenant James Deshler, while he followed with the rest of his command. But on reaching the mouth of Hams Fork at present-day Granger, Wyoming, Alexander headed his command north up the stream some sixteen miles to establish Camp Winfield. To the disgust of his young officers, the colonel of a regiment that covered ground without stragglers at a rate that would gladden the heart of Stonewall Jackson now settled down to await further developments. The "old woman" took the quartermaster's advice and lost the opportunity to march into the Mormon stronghold and end the rebellion at a stroke.

Mistakes in planning and needless delays that put the hastily called expedition on the road in reverse order had led to an even bigger fiasco. Young, in effect, was now directing the army's operations through a supply officer and an infantry colonel, who knew how to march a column "by platoon fronts with regular intervals, at the rate of 96 or 100 steps per minute," but who lacked enterprise and judgment.[21]

By now, Colonels Burton and Cummings had reached Fort Bridger and reported the regiment's quick march from Pacific Creek to Green River. First light on 28 September next revealed Gove's Company I, which had left at 2 A.M., approaching Hams Fork as if it had flown from Green River. Not far behind Gove came Alexander and the other seven companies. Their travel speed touched off a rumor that the Tenth Infantry had not stopped at Hams Fork, but was determined to tramp ahead into Salt Lake Valley. Alarmed, Young ordered Wells to stop them.

From East Canyon, some twenty miles from Salt Lake on the road to Fort Bridger, at 5 A.M. on 29 September, Wells sent word that U.S.

20. Young to Wells, Taylor, and Smith, 9 October 1857, ibid.
21. Alexander to S. Cooper, 3 September 1857, in Buchanan, *Utah Expedition*, 19.

troops had indeed left Hams Fork. He did not know yet what route they might take to the city, but if they came by Echo Canyon, he had directed Nauvoo Legion forces there to give them a warm reception. "They seem determined to force their way into the city anyhow," he said, "and we know no other way than to fight and destroy them." If that was incorrect "in any particular," he said, "we wish to be informed immediately as there is now no time for delay."[22] Wells was ready to fire on U.S. troops, but he did not want to take the sole responsibility.

John D. Lee was also dodging responsibility. The day before Wells entered his pointed request, Lee had reported to Young the details of the massacre of well over a hundred men, women, and children at Mountain Meadows. On two fronts Young suddenly faced the possibility of serious consequences from his overheated rhetoric.

A later opponent once said that Young was not of much consequence as a lion, but when he took on the role of a fox, "he is very formidable."[23] Young now showed his nimble skills in escaping culpability for both blunders on the same day. On 29 September he ordered Lee to "write a long letter" to him as Indian affairs superintendent charging the atrocity to the Indians.[24] Eighteen years later, he would turn this excuse on its head at Lee's first trial, entering a deposition in which he swore that the reason he did not investigate the crime or punish the guilty was that he was no longer governor. The president had appointed his successor, he said, and he did not know when the new man would arrive, failing to mention that as governor he had ordered the territorial militia to keep his replacement out and accepted his salary as a federal officer until 21 November 1857.[25]

Young's response that same day to General Wells's request for authority to open fire was to avoid implicating himself in any bloodshed and to try to stop the U.S. infantry in their tracks with a volley of words. He prepared a letter for Wells to deliver to "The officer commanding *the forces now invading Utah Territory*." With it, he sent a copy of his martial law proclamation, plus a copy of Utah Territory's laws. Wells

22. Wells to Young, 29 September 1857, BYC.

23. Baskin, *Reminiscences*, 56.

24. Lee, *Mormonism Unveiled*, 253.

25. Brigham Young, Deposition, 16 September 1875, LDS Archives, cited in Brooks, *Mountain Meadows Massacre*, 284–86.

then ordered Quartermaster General Lewis Robison to take all this to Alexander. Robison, in turn, dropped this potentially dangerous assignment on a mountaineer, Madino Mariano, asking him to deliver it and simultaneously spy on the federal camp. In the latter role, Mariano counted the U.S. soldiers on parade, putting at every fifty "a match in his box to make sure." His exaggerated report to Wells gave the total as twelve hundred, but he thought "there were some four or five hundred more that he did not count."[26]

As Mariano miscounted his men and cannons, Alexander read the letter from Young. "I am still the governor and superintendent of Indian affairs for this Territory," Young began. Alexander had violated his proclamation "forbidding the entrance of armed forces." He ordered him to "retire forthwith." Should the officer "deem this impracticable," an apparent reference to his orders, Young would permit his encampment to remain on Blacks Fork or Green River until spring, provided that Alexander deposit his arms and ammunition with Quartermaster General Robison.[27]

The officer who received this sharp volley of words now had cause to regret the rapid march of his regiment in which he had taken so much pride. The backward lineup of the Utah Expedition and his own success in moving troops overland now placed him far ahead of the rest of the army with no idea of why he was there in the first place or how he should respond to an apparently authoritative order from the governor of a U.S. territory. He was "in utter ignorance of the objects of the government in sending troops here," he later confessed, "or the instructions given for their conduct after reaching here."[28] Accordingly, he limited his reply to what he knew. The president of the United States had sent his troops there, he said, and they would move only "upon orders by competent military authority." But the badly flummoxed officer addressed his reply

26. Wells, Taylor, and Smith to Young, 2 October 1852, BYC. Since the mountaineers were then engaged in their own war with the Mormons, Mariano may have purposely exaggerated these numbers.

27. Young to Officer Commanding *the forces now invading Utah Territory*, 29 September 1857, in Buchanan, *Utah Expedition*, 33–35.

28. Alexander to "Officers of the United States Army Commanding forces en route to Utah," 8 October 1857, ibid., 38–40.

to Brigham Young as "*Governor of Utah Territory*," thereby inviting a war of words in which he would be hopelessly outgunned.[29]

Even before he ordered the delivery of Young's letter, Wells knew the report that had prompted it was false. But he expected federal forces to concentrate and advance that fall and was sure he could stop them with the troops he had. In the meantime, he aimed to "hedge up" their path in every possible way, short of killing them, "until they reached Echo Canyon." He feared only that "they will take the open Country by Soda Springs." If Alexander had pushed past Hams Fork, he said, "Bros Cummings & Burton would have attacked them from the brush near this place."[30]

The record of this pair at Pacific Creek and Green River hardly promised that they would have slowed the Tenth Infantry much, but there was one man in Wells's command who would deliver a blow that would have far-reaching consequences for both sides. On 2 October, Wells ordered Major Lot Smith with a mounted force of forty-seven picked men to cut Alexander's supply line and "serve the Government trains yet in the rear of the troops in the same way."[31] The order was just what the fiery-bearded zealot had been waiting for.

The next day, Wells ordered Colonel Burton to burn Fort Supply, a Mormon Indian mission and emigrant station about nine miles south of Fort Bridger. More than a hundred log houses, a sawmill, and a gristmill, within a log palisade, went up in flames, as did sixteen cabins and a gristmill at the new Supply City station nearby. Later that day, the Legion torched most of the buildings at Jim Bridger's trading post, leaving a rock wall built by Mormon settlers around the ruins. As ordered by Young, the families at these locations decamped in late September and returned to Salt Lake Valley.[32]

As dawn broke over Green River on 4 October, Lot Smith watched from his island camp as a small federal battery headed west. The major divided his forty-four men, dispatching a scouting party to Blacks Fork

---

29. Alexander to Young, 8 October 1857, ibid., 35.

30. Wells to Young, 30 September 1857, BYC.

31. Wells to Young, 2 October 1857, ibid.

32. For more on Fort Supply, see Gowans and Campbell, *Fort Supply: Brigham Young's Green River Experiment*.

and leading the rest east toward South Pass. That evening, three scouts reported that a train of twenty-six freight wagons was camped on the mouth of the Big Sandy River, within what is now the Seedskadee National Wildlife Refuge. Smith called a council to determine "whether it would be wisdom to go back to Green River and burn the wagons," Legionnaire James Parshall Terry reported when he rewrote his 1857 journal. "It was decided to try it."[33] Smith struck with some two dozen men about midnight, capturing the train's captain and his slumbering teamsters. The Mormons then seized a second train camped nearby, taking what they wanted and burning the rest. "The country was lit up for miles around and we returned to Big Sandy and camped till morning," Terry reported.

As the best-remembered event of the Utah War, Smith's raid naturally created its own mythology, culminating twenty-five years later in the major's personal recollection of the exploit, embellished by years of retelling before admiring audiences. According to Smith, the wagon master stepped forward and implored, "For God's sake, don't burn the trains." To this Smith allegedly replied, "It was for His sake that I was going to burn them." He may not have actually said this, but he surely would have had he thought of it.

The next day, Smith's men surprised another unguarded supply train stopped for noon west of what is now Farson, Wyoming. When Major Smith told the wagon master that he intended to burn the wagons, Lewis Simpson conceded, "Well you have got the advantage of me. I guess you will have to burn them." Terry recalled that the Mormon major suggested an alternative: "There is your guns . . . stacked at the head of the corral, you can take them and we will try for it." Something about Lot Smith persuaded Captain Simpson that none of the Russell, Majors & Waddell wagons was worth dying over. The only casualties of the strike were incurred during a dispute over the spoils, when an accidental shot from a captured weapon grazed Philo Dibble's head and "crashed through O. P. Arnold's left thigh smashed the bone and made a terrible wound."[34]

---

33. The quotes from Smith in this and the following paragraphs are from Wells, "The Narrative of Lot Smith," published serially in the magazine *The Contributor*, 1882–83, reprinted in Hafen and Hafen, *Utah Expedition*, 220–46.

34. Terry, Autobiography, BYU Library, cited in MacKinnon, *At Sword's Point*, 1:347–49; and Wells, "Narrative of Lot Smith," in Hafen and Hafen, *Utah Expedition*, 220–46.

Aside from this unfortunate accident, Smith and his men, in less than twenty-four hours, destroyed seventy-six wagons with enough supplies to serve the federal expedition for about two months.[35] By early November, the army still would have enough food at Fort Bridger to feed two thousand men for seven months. But it would be barely enough, if it lasted that long, to serve the command until spring opened the wagon road from Fort Laramie and allowed fresh supplies to get through. If the supply shortfall was serious, however, it was the least of the repercussions from Lot Smith's destructive raid.

On 5 October, the day Smith burned the third train, Colonel Johnston reached Fort Laramie. There he found two companies of dragoons and forty-seven men, left there by Lieutenant Colonel C. F. Smith of the Tenth Infantry to escort the governor's party in the mistaken assumption that their protection had not already been provided for. Johnston ordered these men to march at once under Second Dragoons lieutenant William D. Smith and join the forces in advance. Still expecting an extended autumn, he vowed, "The troops will enter the Valley of Utah this fall." But he rested this commitment on two conditions: "concentrating the troops, and properly securing the supplies for the army."[36]

Eight days later, Johnston's hope to meet both was blasted. At Three Crossings of the Sweetwater, two messengers from Alexander's camp reported that mounted Mormon raiders had destroyed the army's supply trains between its front and rear elements on the Green and Big Sandy rivers. The messengers on 13 October also delivered the surprising news that Colonel Alexander had marched north up Hams Fork to enter Salt Lake Valley by way of Bear River and had sent word to following U.S. forces on the Oregon Trail to join him at the junction of Sublette's Cutoff and Hams Fork.

From this day forward, Johnston surrendered any hope of entering Salt Lake Valley that fall. Alexander's move north might not make it impossible to concentrate his troops in time to enter Salt Lake Valley, as he reported. But it was certain that the distance from the army's supply

---

Until recently, accounts of the raids on Green River have relied almost exclusively on Smith's ghostwritten account: MacKinnon provides an excellent analysis of problems with Smith's narrative using a wide range of sources.

35. For a full accounting, see Buchanan, *Utah Expedition*, 63.

36. Johnston to Irvin McDowell, 5 October 1857, ibid., 28, 29.

sources made it impossible for the small army under his command to fulfill this objective in the face of determined opposition, as demonstrated by the loss of three supply trains almost within hailing distance of American forces.

Johnston now devoted his full attention to preserving his little army, gathering its scattered parts, safeguarding its supply trains, and reaching a protected location to spend the winter. In his rush to reach the head of his command, he traveled in only twenty-eight days from the Missouri River to Pacific Creek, near South Pass, where he decided to stop and concentrate his command. From the same location, the Tenth Infantry had marched to Hams Fork in only four days. It would now take Johnston nearly three weeks to cover the same distance.

Johnston's decision to concentrate his command at South Pass rather than push on to join Alexander on Hams Fork, where he would be within striking distance of Echo Canyon, measured the impact of Lot Smith's attack on the supply trains. The Nauvoo Legion major had struck the decisive blow in fulfilling Young's strategy to keep the federal expedition from occupying Mormon settlements west of the Wasatch Mountains in 1857. And Colonel Johnston, like Colonel Alexander before him, lost his own opportunity to end the Mormon rebellion at a stroke.

Nor was this the only consequence of Smith's audacious attack on the Green and Big Sandy rivers. He also demonstrated the vulnerability of U.S. Army supply lines over the vast distances of the Mountain West. Moreover, the daring action appeared to confirm Young's claim that the Lord of Hosts stood with the armies of latter-day Israel, which gave a needed lift to Mormon morale. As if bestowed by a divine hand, Johnston's pause at South Pass provided precious days to continue fortifying the Echo Canyon entry into the Mormon heartland and other defenses in the mountains. And it infuriated the young officers with Alexander on Hams Fork, who wanted to push on but had to stand idle under an officer in whom they had no trust. They roundly damned William S. Harney, the expedition's initial commander, not knowing that Johnston had replaced him.

Still, not all of the consequences of Smith's raid were a blessing for the Mormon side. Like a strong dose of reality was the reaction of Lieutenant Colonel C. F. Smith upon getting this news a few miles in advance of Johnston on the Sweetwater River. The threats of Mormon leaders to

Van Vliet, Smith said, "coupled with the burning of our supply trains—in itself an act of war—is evidence of their treason." He henceforth would "regard them as enemies," he added, "and *fire* upon the scoundrels if they give me the least opportunity."[37] Johnston shared his opinion. He ordered Captain Barnard Bee to secure government stores on Green River, instructing him that if any armed mounted men were to approach his party, "you will knock them out of their saddles." He told Bee to "treat as enemies all persons who molest you or appear in arms on your route." That would be his policy from 13 October on.

The treatment of Mormons as enemies was not the only negative consequence of Smith's daring exploit. Colonel Johnston told Washington that a protracted war would be inevitable unless a larger force was sent. But he went on to put forth a better alternative. Moving troops from California and Oregon by the overland trail "would terminate a war with the Mormons speedily and more economically than if attempted by insufficient means."[38] Not the least unfavorable result of Smith's raid would come when Brigham Young, Heber C. Kimball, Daniel H. Wells, and others were indicted for treason, a charge also lodged against the faith's leaders after the Mormon wars in Missouri and Illinois.

Before that day came, the bedeviled Colonel Alexander waited on Hams Fork for orders while Nauvoo Legion scouting parties hovered about his force like gnats, staying out of sight, but near enough to watch every move. More welcome than Mormon spies were the "thousands of rabbits within gun shot of the camp," Captain Gove said.[39] "Everybody dines on the rabbits." On 29 September, Phelps's Fourth Artillery Battery joined the growing body of troops. Lieutenant Colonel Carlos A. Waite's undermanned U.S. Fifth Infantry and Lieutenant Jesse L. Reno's Battery arrived on 4 October with a large wagon train, plus "6 Carriages & Several ladies," Mormon scouts told General Wells.[40]

Morning ice appeared on the water buckets. It was a warning to Alexander that he could not dither forever, waiting for orders that might never arrive. The Articles of War placed the burden of command squarely on

37. Smith to Assistant Adjutant General, Headquarters Army of Utah, 13 October 1857, ibid., 40–42.

38. Johnston to McDowell, 18 October 1857, ibid., 35–38.

39. Gove, *Utah Expedition*, 68.

40. Thomas Callister, Report to Wells, 5 October 1857, BYC.

him, whether he wanted it or not, and he knew what he was supposed to do. But to avoid the sole responsibility, he delayed until Waite's infantry and Reno's siege train joined him before calling a meeting of the senior officers on 5 October to ask them what course he should take. He listened, pondered, and at last made a decision. It was one that brought joy to Captain Gove and the other young officers of his regiment.

On 7 October, Alexander assumed the command that was already his. Two days later, he reported to Washington that he would lead his forces, now the largest concentration of troops in the U.S. Army, up Hams Fork to Sublette's Cutoff, near what is now Kemmerer, Wyoming, and follow the Oregon Trail over the Bear River Divide. On reaching the trail at today's Cokeville, he would march north to Soda Springs, brush aside any opposition he met there, and follow Bear River into Salt Lake Valley from the north. If he failed to overcome Mormon defenses, he would head for the Wind River Mountains, which "offered valleys for wintering the troops," a questionable notion.[41]

Alexander rested his strategy on other assumptions that proved false. Unaware of conditions in his rear, he wrongly thought that Tenth Infantry lieutenant colonel Smith with two dragoon companies and about fifty infantrymen were not far behind and ordered them to meet his command at the junction of Sublette's Cutoff and Hams Fork. But Smith had left these units at Fort Laramie, assuming that Governor Cumming would need an escort. On reaching the fort, Colonel Johnston ordered them forward, but they were now too far behind to join in time.

"The want of cavalry is severely felt," Alexander said, "and we are powerless on account of this deficiency to effect any chastisement of the marauding bands that are continually hovering about us." As he moved to flank Echo Canyon and threaten Utah settlements from the north, Alexander would find out just how little power his command possessed without cavalry. In the meantime, he advised that "troops should be sent from California and Oregon" and added, "the road from California to Salt Lake is passable all winter, and it is certainly so much earlier in the spring than that from the States."[42] Ominously, as he wrote his report, it began to snow.

41. Alexander to S. Cooper, 9 October 1857, in Buchanan, *Utah Expedition*, 31.
42. Ibid., 30–32.

Hams Fork had seen Indians, mountain men, and Gold Rush emigrants, but never anything like the parade on 11 October that moved slowly up the grassy valley. The line of infantry, artillery, animals, and wagons stretched for nine miles without a break. Captain Gove's company led the cavalcade, making cutoffs over ridges and sagebrush to shorten the route along the winding waterway. As they labored, it continued to snow all that day and night. Gove called it a "Godsend" because the wet grass was impossible for their enemies to burn.[43] But he would soon change his mind about which side the Lord was on when it came to the weather.

For a time, the Mormon scouts following Alexander's camp were uncertain whether the advance up Hams Fork was a serious incursion or a move to better grazing. As long as the army had stayed in camp on Hams Fork, as Captain Van Vliet agreed, no one had bothered the Utah Expedition's largest herd there, numbering about fourteen hundred head. But Alexander's possible attempt to bypass Echo Canyon freed Mormon forces from prior understandings. As the column began its northward march, a gap opened between it and the cattle herd. Major Lot Smith and Mormon gunmen Porter Rockwell and William A. Hickman struck the herd late in the afternoon on 12 October with a combined force of about eighty men.

Guarded only by a few frightened contractors' employees, the herd was an easy prize. The Mormon rustlers "struck in below theyer camp & took a heard of theyer cattle of a bout seven Hundred & 6 mules," wrote thirty-two-year-old blacksmith Newton Tuttle, a member of Smith's company.[44] "The troops were in sight all the time," General Wells told Brigham Young.[45] As the attackers broke into small groups to drive the animals to Blacks Fork and the Mormon camp, Rockwell stopped to talk with James Rupe, general superintendent for contractor Russell, Majors & Waddell. He told Rupe to inform Alexander that the federal intruders would all be killed if they did not release Hickman's two patriotically named brothers, Thomas Jefferson and George Washington, captured by the Fifth Infantry the day before.

The cattle raid was a hurtful blow against a hesitant adversary unable to respond, but not as consequential as Smith's destruction of the supply

---

43. Gove, *Utah Expedition*, 76.
44. Gardner, "A Territorial Militiaman," 309.
45. Wells to Young, 15 October 1857, BYC.

trains on Green River a week before. After allowing contractor employees to have a mule and a few oxen to pull their wagons to camp, and deducting some animals to fill empty stomachs, Rockwell and his men on 17 October triumphantly drove 624 cattle and four mules to Salt Lake Valley. Their raid raised to more than one thousand the number of animals stolen by Mormon rustlers in only a week. They would double this number in the days ahead.

Frustrated by the lack of a mounted force, Alexander on 15 October called for thirty volunteers from each of the infantry regiments to form what Wells scornfully titled the "jack-ass-cavalry." They rode out on mules that night under Captain Randolph Marcy to explore the road to Fort Bridger—and to corral Lot Smith and his raiders if the opportunity came up. Marcy had barely left camp when "a party of 55 Mormons came upon them suddenly from the rear, & our own party had scarcely time to form upon a hill side before the Mormons had halted & drawn up in a line two deep within about 150 yards," David A. Burr reported.[46]

The two forces, of about equal size, met the next day and squared off as if for battle in opposing lines about forty yards apart. Smith and Marcy met between the lines and exchanged banter. "What's your business here?" Marcy asked. "Watching you," Smith replied. "What's your business?" Smith later said he regretted his cheeky manner, for Marcy was "very gentlemanly during the whole of our interview."[47]

Neither man wanted to start a fight; they parted by mutual agreement, with each watching the other closely. But it did not end there. What followed was one of several close encounters between the U.S. Army and the Nauvoo Legion that threatened bloodshed, and transformation of the campaign from a farce into a national tragedy.

Like many incidents involving Mormons and outsiders, there are two versions of what happened. According to Gove, Alexander had given Marcy "positive orders" not to fire unless the other side opened hostilities, but Smith reported that "the enemy dismounted and opened their fire upon him, firing 25 or 30 shots, wounding one man's hat, and

46. Ibid.; David A. Burr, Journal, 16 October 1857, Burr Papers, Cornell University Library.

47. Wells, "Narrative of Lot Smith."

grazing a horse's leg."[48] Newton Tuttle said, "We all Made our retreat over the Hills when we were a going down a bluff they came up on us & shot at us, one ball hit Mark Halls Hat & one Hit a horse on the Leg."[49]

After the confrontation, Burr heard that Smith's troops "had not gone far, before they commenced shaking their blankets, yelling loud curses and shouts of defiance at our party, whose animals were however so weak that pursuit was useless." Jim Baker, "an old mountaineer" and Marcy's chief scout, led seven men to the top of a hill overlooking Smith's party. "The Mormons no sooner saw them than one of them fired. Whereupon our men returned the fire, wounding one & putting them all to flight, they no doubt supposing that Captain Marcy's whole party were upon them." Baker chased the raiders for more than a mile before his mules gave out, finding scattered packs of provisions that Smith's men had "dropped in their hasty flight."[50]

Whether Marcy's company fired these shots or they came from mountaineers or other troops from the main camp is not certain. What is apparent is that Smith felt that Marcy had deceived him. If it failed to impress Smith and his mountain-hardened company, the federal "jack-ass" brigade could claim one success before it got back to camp. Mormon major Joseph Taylor and his adjutant, William Stowell, were looking for Lot Smith's company, but blundered into Marcy's motley outfit instead and found themselves prisoners. It was not the first time the luckless major had been involved in a case of mistaken identity. On 4 October, Wells had sent him across country with fifty men to Soda Springs to scout the trail along Bear River. If he spied the enemy coming that way, Wells said, Taylor was to "Stampede their animals and set fire to the trains."[51] But a second scouting party from northern Utah spotted Taylor's men in the trees along Bear Lake on what is now the Utah-Idaho border and mistook them for American troops, setting off a short-lived alarm that the federals were marching north to flank Echo Canyon.

Stumbling into Marcy's camp was bad enough, but Taylor made another mistake: he forgot to burn his orders. Found on his person, they

48. Gove, *Utah Expedition*, 78; and Wells to Young, 18 October 1857, BYC.
49. Gardner, "A Territorial Militiaman," 310.
50. David A. Burr, Journal, 16 October 1857.
51. Wells to Joseph Taylor, 4 October 1857, in Buchanan, *Utah Expedition*, 56–57.

later became evidence of treason against him, Stowell, and other Utah leaders. When Wells wrote them, he sent a copy to Brigham Young.[52] On 21 November, Young got a second copy with a letter, addressed to him as the "Ex-Gov. of Utah Terr.," signed "Governor of this Territory." It said that acts of violence had been committed and government property destroyed, indicating that the territory was "in a state of rebellion." Taylor's orders had authorized "violent & treasonable acts," Alfred Cumming said, subjecting "their actors to the penalties accorded to traitors."[53]

Young himself had not only authorized such behavior, but also specified the proper penalty for treasonable acts against the Mormon side, and it was not limited to supply wagons. "I advise that no mountaineer be let to go at large whose operations are against us, or who are in favor of the enemy," he told Wells. "Bishop Callister has an undoubted right to cut off those whom he cant [sic] fellowship."[54]

Richard Yates was a mountaineer who sold his goods to emigrants from his shack on Green River. He had many Mormon friends, including the noted killer William A. Hickman, but Brigham Young was not one of them: Young resented Green River traders who stole emigrant business from Mormon ferry operators. At about this time, a rumor went around that Yates had sold ammunition to the U.S. Army and was serving as a federal spy. Nauvoo Legion lookout Charles Conover spotted him on the trail out of Fort Bridger and arrested him. He was taken back and held inside the ruins and rock wall.

On 15 October, Wells reported Yates's capture to Brigham Young. Three days later he told Young, "We send Yates on the road to the City, a prisoner in charge of Hickman."[55] It was a death sentence. At the mouth of Echo Canyon, Hickman stopped overnight with Colonel Nathaniel V. Jones, who said he had orders "when Yates came along to have him used up." That night, Jones and Nauvoo Legion adjutant general Hosea Stout appeared at Hickman's tent. They asked him whether Yates was asleep.

---

52. See Wells to Young, 5 October 1857, BYC.

53. Cumming to Young, 21 November 1857, in Hafen and Hafen, *Utah Expedition*, 296–97.

54. Young to Wells, Taylor, and Smith, 17 October 1857, BYC. Major Thomas Callister was bishop of the church's 17th Ward in Salt Lake City. The Isle of Man native commanded a company operating north of Fort Bridger.

55. Wells to Young, 18 October 1857, ibid.

The reply was yes, "upon which his brains were knocked out with an ax." While the camp slept, they dug a grave and dumped Yates's body into it with "the dirt well packed on it." Then they moved the campfire "onto the grave" to disguise the unmarked spot where the unfortunate trader lies today.[56]

Nor was that the end of it. Hickman later said that when he told Young that he had carried out his instructions, Young said, "that was right and a good thing." Hickman also handed over $900 taken from Yates's body, but asked to keep some of it to cover his costs. Young rebuked him, he said, and took it all to defray "expenses of the war."[57] Nauvoo Legion quartermaster general Lewis Robison finished the looting of Yates's assets. On 24 October, he and a party returned to Fort Bridger from Green River, where they had gathered the iron fittings from wagons burned by Lot Smith. On their way back, they visited Yates's place and stole "48 Horse[s] & colts, 36 pair of blankets &c."[58] Like the emigrants at Mountain Meadows, Yates was deceived, murdered, and robbed.

The critical point in the history of the nation's first civil war came over three days, 16–18 October, when visionary ideals would be weighed on the scales of reality. At widely separated places, decisions would be made on those days that would determine whether a homegrown frontier theocracy would come to an early end in a quixotic attempt to take a sovereign position that it was incapable of sustaining, or go on to become a major religion and a respected part of American society.

On 16 October, nearing Sublette's Cutoff under lowering skies, Alexander suffered another fit of indecision. Swallowing his pride, he went to Captain Gove's tent that day and asked his most outspoken critic what he should do—go on to enter Utah from the north or go back. Gove said that "to retreat would not only disgrace him but kill all the animals." When he got through, the Company I captain told his wife, Alexander said, "I'll swear I'll go on." The colonel spoke of it openly after he left his tent, and "everybody was very happy," the opinionated, if not insubordinate, officer said.[59]

---

56. Hickman and Beadle, *Brigham's Destroying Angel*, 122–26.
57. Ibid.
58. Gardner, "A Territorial Militiaman," 311.
59. Gove, *Utah Expedition*, 78–79.

The next day, anticipating that Alexander would ignore the course Van Vliet had imposed and do what Gove had proposed, Young ordered Wells to kill American soldiers. "If they undertake to swing round into Cache Valley or the Malad, let sleep depart from their eyes and slumber from the eyelids, both day and night, until they take their final sleep," he said. "Pick off their guards and sentries & fire into their camps by night, and pick off officers and as many men as possible by day."[60] The order applied if Alexander took Sublette's Cutoff to Bear River and headed north down this Great Basin river toward Soda Springs.

On 18 October, Wells told Young that he had carried out his instructions and ordered Nauvoo Legion forces on Bear River "to watch them closely but not molest them if they take the Fort Hall road but if they turn to the settlements to pitch into their pickets and other sentinels." For the first time, the armed forces of the theocratic, millennialistic religion were ordered to shed the blood of U.S. soldiers.[61]

Before the orders went out, Young on 16 October desperately tried to keep from crossing the line between bluff and bloodshed. He shot a barrage of words to stop Alexander before it was too late. Bombastic one moment and conciliatory the next, his words spoke of fear and an almost surreal concept of the confrontation and its causes. Writing as governor, Young "commanded" the colonel to "marshal your troops and leave this Territory." It could not help the officer "to wickedly waste treasures and blood" on the side of "a rebellion against the general government by its administrators," he roared. "It is now the kingdom of God and the kingdom of the devil." After making clear what side the colonel was on, he cordially invited him and the other officers to visit Salt Lake and see "the conditions and feelings of this people." Most would "revolt from all connexion with so ungodly, illegal, unconstitutional, and hellish a crusade against an innocent people," he said, "and if their blood is shed it shall rest upon the heads of their commanders."[62]

Young now dropped the facades, known as Utah Territory and the State of Deseret, and openly proclaimed the power that defied the authority of the United States to rule—"With us it is the kingdom

60. Young to Wells, Taylor, and Smith, 17 October 1857, BYC.
61. Wells to Young, 16 October 1857, ibid.
62. Young to Alexander, 16 October 1857, in Buchanan, *Utah Expedition*, 50–54.

of God or nothing."[63] His words made "our hearts to leap for joy," said Wells.[64]

The order with which Colonel Johnston finally took active command of the Utah Expedition on 16 October was a godsend indeed. Johnston informed Colonel Alexander he would concentrate his troops "with the view of wintering in an eligible spot," meaning Fort Bridger, which also meant that there would be no blood spilled as they fought to get into Salt Lake Valley that fall.[65] To the intense disgust of Captain Gove, Alexander was already marching back down Hams Fork before the order arrived.

Thus on 16–18 October, it was not Brigham Young who saved God's Kingdom in the Great Basin and helped to prepare the future of the Latter-day Saint church: it was Albert Sidney Johnston, commander of the U.S. Army's Utah Expedition, scornfully referred to in Utah ever since as "Johnson's army." He ordered Alexander to move by Sublette's road to Fontenelle Creek, where he would join him with all the forces in his rear. Since the Green River tributary was not the best site for the planned junction, the location would soon be changed to the mouth of Hams Fork. In the meantime, Johnston told Alexander "to treat as enemies all who oppose your march, molest your teams, appear in arms on your route, or in any manner annoy you."[66]

As he waited at South Pass for Lieutenant Smith to bring up the last elements of his command, the energetic colonel in typical style issued orders covering all aspects of his duties. He asked W. M. F. Magraw, the superintendent of the interrupted Pacific Wagon Road project, to provide mules and wagons for army supplies. He also said he would allow Magraw's employees to enlist in the army for three months. These requests were courteously stated but carried the ring of direct commands.

Aware of his dragoon commander's prideful nature, Johnston took a different tone in his order to Lieutenant Colonel Philip St. George Cooke. On 5 October, he had given Cooke permission to winter at Fort

63. Ibid.
64. Wells to Young, 17 October 1857, BYC.
65. Johnston to Alexander, 16 October 1857, in Buchanan, *Utah Expedition*, 40.
66. Ibid.

Laramie on the North Platte River. Now he first informed him that the army would winter on Henrys Fork of Green River, where he hoped "to see you and your command."[67] The opposition the army had encountered and "injuries committed to our trains, cause the absence of cavalry to be very much lamented," he went on, "while the mounted forces which hang upon our own skirts promise occupation and distinction to your command." The colonel would be "pleased to hear of your advance, and promises you a warm welcome on your arrival."[68] As intended, his carefully chosen words moved one of the army's finest frontier field officers to an immediate do-or-die effort.

Soon after he received the colonel's dispatch, a bugler sounded "the general" at Fort Laramie. Cooke then went before the officers assembled in front of the mounted regiment and read Johnston's order, announcing "hostilities in front, the great want of cavalry, and the strong hope of the colonel to see us with him." Cooke voiced his trust that the Second Dragoons would make "every exertion to meet the kindly-announced expectations of the commander of the army."[69] His progress would be little affected by the duty to see to the comfort of the civilians with the command, including Governor and Mrs. Cumming.

No special care was needed by Garland Hurt, the hardy U.S. Indian agent who traveled stretches of the 1776 Escalante Trail and later Outlaw Trail after his escape from the Spanish Fork Indian farm to meet Johnston's forces on the Sweetwater River. On 24 October, he described conditions in Utah and likely gave Cumming and Jacob Forney, the new superintendent of Utah Indian affairs, the first account of the massacre at Mountain Meadows. On 4 December, he submitted the first written report on the atrocity.[70]

Meanwhile, Lieutenant William D. Smith joined Johnston's command at South Pass on 26 October with two dragoon companies, a Tenth Infan-

---

67. Henrys Fork of Green River, site of the first mountain man rendezvous in 1825, rises in the mountains of northwestern Utah and flows north into southern Wyoming before entering today's Flaming Gorge Reservoir on the Wyoming-Utah border. Its valley was a favorite wintering ground for early traders and trappers.

68. Johnston to Cooke, 18 October 1857, in Buchanan, *Utah Expedition*, 68–69.

69. "Report of Philip St. George Cooke," 21 November 1857, ibid., 92–100; also published as Gardner, "March of 2d Dragoons," 43–59.

70. For these Hurt reports, see Buchanan, *Utah Expedition*, 199–205, 205–208.

try detachment, and a company of volunteers from Magraw's Wagon Road Survey—a total of three hundred men, not counting the final supply trains. With no other troops in his rear, Johnston on 27 October marched west from South Pass over the Oregon Trail as Alexander moved south down Hams Fork. The converging columns became one on 3 November at the junction of Hams Fork and Blacks Fork.

With the exception of Cooke's six dragoon companies, the commands met on 3 November at what is now Granger, Wyoming, where the Utah Expedition became united for the first time. In the meantime, Johnston's failure to march into Salt Lake Valley that fall had decided the destiny of six "gentlemen of good address" who had arrived in northern Utah four days after the colonel began his delayed advance from South Pass. Their fate, as told in the next chapter, reveals the absence of federal law in the territory and the absolute power Brigham Young exercised during this period over anyone who entered his Mormon domain.

In reporting his arrival at Hams Fork, Johnston said that the Mormons had shown "a matured and settled design" to occupy the territory outside the authority of the United States. "They have with premeditation, placed themselves in rebellion against the Union," he said, to establish a form of government "utterly repugnant to our institutions." As they had openly defied the federal government, "I have ordered that wherever they are met in arms, that they be treated as enemies."[71]

For the army that marched from Hams Fork on 6 November, the thirty miles to Fort Bridger would be their hardest on the trail from Fort Leavenworth. Well closed up, the expedition would occupy as many as twenty-five miles of the Oregon Trail along Blacks Fork, but from the start its men would not march in any formation. As if in answer to Mormon prayers, a mighty cold front swept over the high plain from the north, sending gale-force winds, plunging temperatures, and blowing snow that tore closed formations to shreds. The animals had no corn, "and the grass, what little there is, is under the snow," Gove said. After traveling more than a thousand miles, they were "as poor as can be, hundreds dropping down in the harness for want of strength to stand up." For men and animals, the march became a struggle for survival. "Never

---

71. Johnston to McDowell, 5 November 1857, ibid., 46, 47.

was men more exposed or had a harder tour of duty," the officer said, not excluding Napoleon's retreat from Moscow forty-five years before.[72]

Also on 6 November, Andrew Love and five companions from the Nauvoo Legion Company in Nephi, Utah, studied Johnston's column as it labored up Blacks Fork above Church Butte, a distinctive trail landform. "We being on horse back & sen[t] to watch had a fair view of the enemy on the move & were close to Them." Some two hours after dark, as they rode to Fort Bridger, they encountered the fort's picket guard and touched off "a regular stampede" of Mormon companies belonging to Major Warren S. Snow, Captain William Maxwell, and Captain Ephraim Hanks, who mistook them for U.S. cavalry and fled in every direction but east, making "a clean sweep to within about 3 miles of Bridger & there a halt was called untill the Scattering came in, (The Slow & The weak)," the Nephi men laughed.[73]

Joining the rout was the Nauvoo Legion's lieutenant general, Daniel H. Wells. At his camp five miles above Fort Bridger, he was "awoken by our picket guard, with the information that an advance Guard of the enemy composed of dragoons, was advancing upon Ft Bridger, and then within a few miles, and on the gallop," he reported next day from his new camp at Soda Springs on the Mormon Trail, some fifteen miles west of the fort. "By close hard running our Scouts got out of their way," he went on. "We broke up our camp about 5 miles above Ft Bridger, and bringing with us all the wagons, moved at 1/2 past 2 A.M. and striking across to the old pioneer trail moved up here." He added, "The old huts that were still standing at Bridger were burned last night."[74] There Andrew Love and his comrades from Nephi "warmed at the fires" that night as their leader fled.[75]

At Soda Springs, General Wells on 7 November held a war council with his top officers, including Majors Warren Snow and John D. T. McAllister and Captain Ephraim Hanks, where it was "our conclusion not to shoot them till they pass Bridger to come this way," he told Young.[76] In keeping with Young's orders, Wells drew the line on shed-

72. Gove, *Utah Expedition*, 92.
73. Love, Journal, 6 and 7 November 1857, Authors' Collection.
74. Wells, Charles C. Rich, and George D. Grant to Young, 7 November 1857, BYC.
75. Love, Journal, 7 November 1857.
76. Wells, Rich, and Grant to Young, 7 November 1857, BYC.

ding blood at Fort Bridger, as he had done earlier at Soda Springs in the north. Nauvoo Legion officers were told to watch the federal forces, but not trouble them unless they "demonstrated their intentions of pushing on to Salt Lake by moving west of the fort." If that should happen, "Pitch into them in every possible way," he ordered. They were to "make the first attack as soon as the army passed the fort."[77]

Before this Rubicon was crossed, news of the great Fort Bridger stampede sped all the way to Great Salt Lake. "An express ar[r]ived during the night," Apostle Wilford Woodruff related, "saying that the Cavalry was advanceing upon Bridger under a gallop and the picket guard had to run their Horses to get out of the way."[78] Nor were reports of the U.S. cavalry charge at Fort Bridger the only false alarms that kept the Mormon defenders on edge. As Johnston pushed his advance in the teeth of a blizzard, the rumor spread that the undaunted cavalry soldier intended to drive straight forward into Salt Lake Valley, despite hell and deep snow. It provoked a reaction almost as panicked as the one that lifted General Wells out of bed and chased him fifteen miles west from Fort Bridger.

More troops were rushed into the mountains to strengthen the Echo Canyon defenses, where the blood of Mormon and American soldiers alike might shortly be shed in battle. On 9 November, Woodruff reported that the city had been "alive with soldiers since mid night preparing to go into the mountains to meet with our enemies." It snowed hard the next day, when "1,300 men [were] ordered into the mountains in addition to those already there." Troops from Davis County passed Young's office, he said, and continued their march toward the mountains as some two thousand others had done before. "Many went with wet feet, poor shoes & straw hats on, without tents or fire at night, as they could not reach timber untill next day," he added. "Yet it shoes [shows] the willingness the saints have to maintain the king of God & defend themselves against our Enemies."[79]

Among the men going into the mountains was thirty-year-old John Pulsipher, who knew the route because he had lived with his wife at Fort Supply as an Indian missionary before Young had ordered the

---

77. Wells, Grant, and Rich to Young, 15 November 1857, ibid.
78. Kenney, *Wilford Woodruff's Journal*, 9 November 1857.
79. Ibid., 9 and 10 November 1857.

station burned. "Upwards of 2,000 men were on the move to stop the invading army," the New York native said. The long column climbing the mountains made him think of "Bonapart's army crossing the Alps in winter."[80] On the third day out, he struggled up the mountain through snow up to his armpits to cut wood, but it would not burn. It was a clear, bitterly cold night, and no one slept. Some walked up and down to save body heat. On his blankets spread in the snow, Pulsipher could hardly keep from freezing. On 14 November, his unit reached the Weber River, where he worked on fortifications and dug rifle pits near present-day Echo. Three days later, his outfit moved up to the mouth of Echo Canyon, where it brought to some sixteen hundred the number of men working on defenses there under Colonel Nathaniel V. Jones.

The suffering on both sides was all part of a divine plan, Wells had said, to force U.S. troops to meet Mormon terms "to leave the Territory or give up their arms."[81] He underestimated the U.S. Army's officers and men to whom the notion never occurred. To set the example, Johnston "footed it" like everyone else, and did not permit officers to "receive more than the soldier."[82] On the Sweetwater River, Cooke displayed the same attitude he spoke of in Johnston. His men suffered bitter cold— twelve degrees or more below zero—and "the air still filled with driven snow." The starving mules "cried piteously," he said, and more than fifty of them died in one night. But this was a "time for action," he said. "No murmurs, not a complaint was heard, and certainly none saw in their commander's face a doubt or clouds."[83]

William A. Carter, a civilian sutler who went with Cooke's dragoons, was deeply touched by the suffering of the animals. On 9 November, the wind along the Sweetwater River blew all night, "sweeping the snow in our direction," he wrote. "The piteous cries of the famished mules was heart rending." When he awoke in the morning, "the storm was still raging and the air dark with snow, mules were strewn about dead and some in the last agonies of death." Later, he described the trail along Blacks Fork in the wake of Johnston's passage as "one vast slaughter yard; from

80. Pulsipher, Diary, 10 November 1857, in Hafen and Hafen, *Utah Expedition*, 206.
81. Wells to Young, 13 October 1857, BYC.
82. Johnston, *Life of Gen. Albert Sidney Johnston*, 215.
83. Cooke, "Report," in Buchanan, *Utah Expedition*, 92–99.\

10 to 15 mules and horses could be seen in a heap. It would break the most uncaring heart," he said, "to see the noble Dragoon horses falling dead beneath their riders worn out by fatigue and hunger."[84] With nothing to eat on the ground and no corn in the wagons, animals died by the hundreds every day.

On 18 November, as Pulsipher labored on Mormon defenses, Colonel Johnston reached Fort Bridger at 8 P.M. It had taken twelve days to travel thirty miles from Hams Fork to the shelter of Bridger's trading post on Blacks Fork and had cost the lives of some three thousand cattle, horses, and mules left dead on the trail, mainly from starvation. The very next day, Cooke and his Second Dragoon companies reported for duty after a march from Fort Laramie that had tested their courage and endurance. The horse soldiers were finally up, but many were on foot. Their drive to render cavalry support had cost the lives of 134 horses—half the number they had started with. Most died of starvation, Cooke said, for "the earth has a no more lifeless, treeless, grassless desert" than the ground his dragoons had crossed. "It contains scarcely a wolf to glut itself on the hundreds of dead and frozen animals which for thirty miles nearly block the road; with abandoned and shattered property, they mark, perhaps, beyond example in history, the steps of an advancing army with the horrors of a disastrous retreat."[85]

True it was that Colonel Johnston had never taken a backward step since leaving Fort Leavenworth two months before. But it had required all of his energy, leadership, and resourcefulness to preserve his army, concentrate its scattered parts, and gain Bridger's protected trading post. Nor could he advance into the Mormon stronghold as Young had feared. "The army under my command took the last possible step forward at Bridger in the condition of the animals then alive," he said.[86] The Army of Utah, twenty-five hundred strong on paper, had lost few men to illness on the march but many to desertion, and most of its units had started from the Missouri at less than full strength. By the time they concentrated at Fort Bridger, federal forces probably numbered fewer

84. Carter, Diary, 1857, Wyoming Archives. Carter later became probate judge of Green River County.

85. Cooke, "Report," in Buchanan, *Utah Expedition*, 99.

86. Johnston, *Life of Gen. Albert Sidney Johnston*, 214.

than sixteen hundred regular troops, about one-fifth of the number then available for frontier duty.

Johnston was not given to exaggeration, and his grim admission spelled the success of the Mormon strategy. "The only feasible plan for them at present appears to be to winter themselves at Bridger," General Wells told Brigham Young on 16 November. But if the army tried to advance past that point, he went on, "we purpose pitching into them."[87] With the worst apparently over, Young now felt safe enough to boast. "If they did they could at once be surrounded with an overwhelming force and be used up or compelled to surrender," he replied.[88]

As historian William P. MacKinnon discovered, the consequences of the drama playing out in Utah Territory reached far beyond the Great Basin. During the fall of 1857, rumors had the Mormons fleeing to Mexico, Central America, the Hawaiian Islands, or the Dutch East Indies. A year later, President Buchanan sought congressional sanction to establish a military protectorate over northern Sonora and Chihuahua. Americans had long had their eyes on "the valuable mines of the country" south of the recent Gadsden Purchase: now "the probability of Brigham Young leading his followers from Salt Lake to the Mexican Province of Sonora" would close those lands to American interests. Once the Mormons were gone, *The New York Times* observed, the United States "would no more buy them back into our jurisdiction than it would purchase Delhi [from] the hands of the Sepoys."[89]

Better-informed observers suggested the Mormons had their eyes on Vancouver Island or Alaska, then under the control of the Hudson's Bay Company and the Russian-American Company. In the wake of Lot Smith's raid, Washington was alive with speculation about Brigham Young's plans. The British ambassador warned his foreign secretary that the Mormons might "break up from Utah and force their way across Oregon and Washington Territories to Her Majesty's possessions." He recommended alerting the Hudson's Bay Company to the threat so "that they may give directions to their agents adapted to such a contingency."

87. Wells to Young, 16 November 1857, BYC.

88. Young to Wells, Rich, and Grant, 18 November 1857, ibid.

89. "From Washington: Probability of the Mormons Occupying Sonora," *New York Times,* 25 November 1857, 2/5.

The next spring, England created a province, British Columbia, "as a bulwark against an unlikely but feared Mormon onslaught."[90]

With barely two hundred soldiers to police all of Alaska, the Russian-American Company's grip on the region was faltering. At the White House in November, Russia's minister to Washington, Edward de Stoeckl, asked the president if "the Mormons would resort to us as conquerors or as peaceful colonists." Buchanan declined to answer but said, "as for us, we shall be very happy to be rid of them." The ambassador thought the rumor was premature, but if it proved true Russia would have to choose between "providing an armed resistance or of giving up part of our territory." When the foreign minister informed the tsar of these developments, Alexander II wrote, "This supports the idea of settling henceforth the question of our American possessions" on Stoeckl's dispatch. By year's end the foreign ministry told Stoeckl to indicate to the U.S. government that Russia was open to the possibility of selling its territories in North America. Ten years later, the United States purchased Alaska for $7.2 million. The Utah War, as MacKinnon concluded, "was neither the reason for this sale, nor even its catalyst, but it was a factor."[91]

90. MacKinnon, *At Sword's Point,* 1:439–41.
91. Ibid., 1:442–43.

CHAPTER 10

Deleterious Ingredients
Of Murder, Salt, and Supply

Should any in your command be suspicious that the salt now forwarded
contains any deleterious ingredients other than those combined in
its natural deposition on the shore of Great Salt Lake, Mr. Woodard
or Mr. Earl . . . will freely partake of it to dispel any groundless
suspicions, or your doctors may be able to test it to your satisfaction.

—Brigham Young, 26 November 1857

Six impressive strangers from California rode up to Fort Box Elder, now
Brigham City in northern Utah, on 31 October. They expected to meet
the Utah Expedition in Salt Lake Valley and benefit from the stationing
of some twenty-five hundred men there. But Colonel Albert S. Johnston
was still marching west to join the Army of Utah at Hams Fork, where
he would collect his scattered troops and had made a decision to winter
outside the Mormon stronghold. The riders from California had landed
in a place outside federal law and torn by fanaticism, war fever, and paranoia. Brigham Young still ruled the rebellious territory, not his replacement as governor, Alfred Cumming.

At the northern Utah outpost, Nauvoo Legion major Samuel Smith
arrested and disarmed the half-dozen men, known as the Aiken party.
Mormon troops escorted them to Great Salt Lake, where they were confined under guard and interrogated for nineteen days, all done secretly, or
so Mormon authorities thought. Their fate might still be one of the West's
unsolved mysteries if their colorful outfits had not so impressed the many
who saw them and if the newspapers in California had not taken so lively
an interest in the vast Mormon territory on their eastern border.

In January 1858, the Placerville *Argus* broke the story when it reported the murder of "American gentlemen, well armed and equipped" in Utah. Major William Ormsby had sold them supplies at Genoa, now in western Nevada, and described them as being "gentlemen of good address," possessing a considerable amount of money and "excellent riding and pack animals."[1] Their leader, John Achard (or Eichard), and brothers Thomas and John Aiken, after whom the party was named, were from Los Angeles. Andrew Jackson "Honesty" Jones and John Chapman hailed from the Sierra Nevada mining town of Mariposa. Horace Bucklin, known as "Buck," joined the party at the Humboldt Sink, near today's Lovelock, Nevada.[2]

As Colonel Johnston settled in for the winter at Fort Bridger, on 20 November five of the men rode south from Salt Lake. "Buck" was no longer with them. At his personal request, Young had allowed him to stay in Salt Lake.[3] Chapman won permission to winter at Lehi, twenty-five miles south of Salt Lake. The remaining four were permitted to go back to California by the southern trail to Los Angeles, or so they were told. They would not go alone. Accompanying them, ostensibly to convoy them through hostile Indians, was a bodyguard of four men under the feared Mormon gunman Porter Rockwell. As Chapman left the group at Lehi, one of his former companions turned to him and said, "Goodbye, John. If you come this way and see our bones bleaching on the plains, bury them."[4]

The selective judgments rendered on the six men after nearly three weeks of close questioning were a blatant exhibition of the power of life and death that Young exercised over the people of the territory and anyone who entered it. On 21 November, as Achard, the brothers Aiken, and Jones resumed their fateful journey south, the lawful governor of Utah demonstrated his own impotence. Alfred Cumming announced that he was organizing a territorial government on the ashes of Fort

---

1. "Alleged Murder of Five American Citizens in Utah," Placerville *Argus*, reprinted in the *San Francisco Daily Evening Bulletin*, 18 January 1858, 2.

2. Bucks Lake, Bucks Valley, and Bucks Lake Wilderness Area in today's Plumas County, California, are all named for Bucklin.

3. Bucklin to Young, November 1857, BYC.

4. Thomas Singleton, "Collett Murder Case," *Daily Tribune* (Salt Lake City), 10 October 1878, 2.

Bridger, then in Utah Territory. Under his authority "as commander-in-chief of the militia," he ordered all armed bodies to disband.[5] Snickers and scorn greeted his proclamation in Salt Lake.

The legal governor's pronouncement gave little hope to the four doomed men, if they heard it at all, as they rode south on the same trail followed a few weeks earlier by the Baker-Fancher party to their destiny at Mountain Meadows. Twenty-seven-year-old Homer Brown announced their arrival at Nephi, eighty-five miles south of Salt Lake, on 24 November, and revealed the reason why their travels were almost at an end. "One of the men had a letter of recommendation from a commander of the U.S. Station in Callifornia [sic] to Col. Johnson stating that the bearer was a man that could be trusted and was capable of performing any scheme that he might undertake," he wrote. "This letter fell into Brighams hands, and thus he found out who they were."[6] Mormon interrogators had taken the letter as evidence that they were spies.

Brown was one of the four men Bishop Jacob G. Bigler sent that night to camp at the Sevier River crossing, some twenty-five miles south of the settlement on Salt Creek, and pretend to be a party of hunters. When the remaining Aiken party members and their escort overtook them the next day, all the men at the crossing decided to camp together for protection against the Indians. The alleged spies were now outnumbered eight to four.

As the group sat around the fire that night, the four escort members attacked Achard, the Aikens, and Jones from behind with iron bars. Two were killed at once; the other two, badly hurt, made it into the river and escaped. Separately they struggled back to Nephi, where the settlement medical practitioner cut a bullet from one man's shoulder and rendered first aid. On 28 November they boarded a buggy, allegedly for transportation to further medical treatment at Salt Lake. But at Willow Creek, a short distance north of the settlement, Sylvanus Collett and the three other escort members, Rockwell, John S. Lott, and John R. Murdock, waited to finish the job. They cut them down with shotguns and dumped their weighted bodies into the nearby Deep Spring.

5. Cumming, "To the People of Utah Territory," in Buchanan, *Utah Expedition*, 75, 76.
6. Homer Brown, Journal, 24 November, 1857, LDS Archives.

Soon after, William A. Hickman added Horace Bucklin to his long list of victims when Young allegedly told him to "use up" the fifth and sixth members of the Aiken party. The notorious executioner waylaid both on the lower road north of Salt Lake City as they tried to escape. "The man, Buck, got a shot through the head," Hickman later confessed, "and was put across the fence in a ditch."[7] John Chapman, the party's lone survivor, jumped from the wagon and "kept going" until he got back to California, where he was known in Lassen County as "Big John." Described as a powerful man, "always looking for trouble," he met the fate Young had pronounced when Albert A. Smith (not a Mormon) shot him to death in 1860 over a woman. But his story of how he fled from Utah confirms Hickman's account.[8]

Meanwhile, as Rockwell and his fellow assassins beat the sagebrush along the Sevier River on 26 November, looking for the two wounded Aiken party members who had survived their deadly attack the night before, a bizarre episode opened a hundred miles to the north in Salt Lake. That day Young welcomed a Native leader of Delaware lineage who may have been even shrewder than the Mormon chief. Ben Simons pretended that he was a friend of both sides in the war and played each against the other to the benefit of his mixed band of Bannocks, Shoshones, and Utes. After partaking of Johnston's hospitality for two days, Simons had come to report to Young on conditions in the federal post, now named Camp Scott after the nation's top general. He told him that "they wanted salt vary much," Wilford Woodruff noted.[9]

The shortage of salt was indeed acute. None had been issued to the command since early October. Even before reaching Fort Bridger, Johnston on 13 November had ordered Major William Hoffman at Fort Laramie to push ahead thirty pack mule loads. "There is no salt with this army," he said.[10] There was one, however, who had enough to last for six months, but was not about to share any. Captain Jesse Gove, who liked

7. Hickman and Beadle, *Brigham's Destroying Angel*, 129. See also Baskin, *Reminiscences*, 150–51.

8. For the most recent findings on the Aiken Party, see Bigler, "Aiken Party Executions," 457–76. Asa Merrill Fairfield, *Fairfield's Pioneer History of Lassen County California* (San Francisco: Published for the Author by H. S. Crocker Co., 1916).

9. Kenney, *Wilford Woodruff's Journal*, 26 November 1857, 5:125.

10. Johnston to Hoffman, 13 November 1857, in Buchanan, *Utah Expedition*, 87.

to tell his wife that he was always ready, boasted, "You know I am *smart* sometimes."[11] Not as clever were the other sufferers at the U.S. Army camp. "What will you pay to the price of salt!" Elizabeth Cumming, the new governor's wife, wrote her sister-in-law. "The traders paid five dollars a quart—& retail it at six—& not much to be had at that price."[12]

If there was one thing Brigham Young had plenty of, it was salt. The day he got this word, he decided to rub some of it into the hurts he had inflicted on his enemies at Fort Bridger. Four days later, during a driving snowfall, two men from Salt Lake Valley arrived at Camp Scott with heavily loaded mules, bringing with them a letter to Colonel Johnston. "Being reliably informed that your command . . . are much in need of salt," Young wrote, "I have taken the liberty to at once forward you a load (some eight hundred pounds)." His epistle was a mocking reminder of the officer's failure to reach the place named for its abundance of this necessary ingredient.[13] To rub it in further, Young's letter included an embarrassing aside to Colonel Edmund B. Alexander. Noting that "among the mules that have come into our settlements is a small white one, belonging to you, and is a favorite of yours," he promised to take care of it in his own stables, where it would be ready "for your use upon your return to the east in the spring."[14]

The most noteworthy aspect of his message, however, was the guarantee Young placed on the commodity he had sent. "Should any in your command be suspicious that the salt now forwarded contains any deleterious ingredients other than those combined in its natural deposition on the shore of Great Salt Lake," he said, "Mr. Woodard or Mr. Earl, in charge of its transportation and delivery, or doubtless Mr. Livingston, Mr. Gerrish, Mr. Perry, or any other person in your camp that is acquainted with us, will freely partake of it to dispel any groundless suspicions, or your doctors may be able to test it to your satisfaction."[15]

11. Gove, *Utah Expedition*, 102.

12. A. R. Mortensen, ed., "The Governor's Lady: A Letter from Camp Scott, 1857," *Utah Historical Quarterly* 22, no. 2 (April 1954): 165–73.

13. Young to Johnston and Alexander, 26 November 1857, in Buchanan, *Utah Expedition*, 110, 111.

14. Ibid.

15. Ibid. Merchants Howard Livingston, William Gerrish, and C. A. Perry left Salt Lake during the Reformation and now were returning or acting as contractors to the army.

Young's bizarre assurance that the salt had not been tampered with had a familiar ring, echoing his note to Native leader Walkara during the so-called Walker War between Mormon settlers and Ute Indians in 1853. "I send you some tobacco for you to smoke in the Mountains when you get lonesome," Young had told the Ute war chief. He then added: "If you are afraid of the tobacco which I send you, you can let some of your prisoners try it first and then you will know that it is good."[16] During a time of renewed Ute hostility, Walker died suddenly on 28 January 1855, just one day after Mormon Indian missionary David Lewis delivered a note and presents from Young.

Nor was this the only indication that Utah settlers may have used poison against troublesome Natives. In 1857, their leaders made the charge that the doomed Fancher train had poisoned a spring and an ox at Corn Creek, inciting the Indians to attack them at Mountain Meadows. George A. Smith and John D. Lee may have gotten the idea from their own transgressions. During the 1850 Provo River fight with the Utes, Young told General Daniel H. Wells not to allow any sick prisoners, known to be hostile, to go free until they were completely cured. "Your Surgeon, Mr. Blake, is no doubt well furnished with medicine, and will be ready to prescribe that which will effect that most desirable of all objects, *perfect health*," he advised.[17] Nauvoo Legion captain William McBride was more explicit a year later. He caught up with Goshute rustlers only to discover that they had already killed the cattle. "We wish you without a moment's hesitation to send us about a pound of arsenic," he reported. "We want to give the Indians' well a flavor." To this, he added: "A little strickenine would be of fine service, and serve instead of salt for their too fresh meat."[18]

If Johnston had known of such cases, he might not have dismissed the threat that came with the gift of salt as lightly as he did. As it was, he said, in essence, the idea that it might be poisoned would not have occurred to him if Young had not mentioned it. He would not honor the transmittal letter with a written reply, he told its deliverers, and he voiced regret

16. Young to Capt Wacher [Ute chief Walkara], 25 July 1853, UTMR.
17. Young to Wells, 14 February 1850, UTMR. The villainous Dr. James Blake served as surgeon with the 1849–50 Stansbury Expedition to explore the Great Salt Lake.
18. McBride, Report, 24 June 1851, ibid.

that the Mormon chief had "insinuated the probability of its refusal on account of its deleterious property." No American would be guilty of so base an act, he said, and none would suspect it. Take the salt back, he told Young's agents, but not because he feared it might be poisoned. "I will not accept a present from an enemy of my government."[19]

Johnston's gifts as a combat officer were never fully tested before he fell of an untended wound at Shiloh Church in April 1862, while leading a Confederate army against U. S. Grant. But the administrative ability of this energetic officer and his concern for the interests of his men were exceptional. On the first day after he assumed command of the Utah Expedition, he estimated the cost to build comfortable quarters for his troops in Utah and applied for an appropriation to construct them. And one of his first actions on reaching Fort Bridger was to order the Utah Army's medical director, Surgeon Madison Mills, to complete as soon as possible medical facilities for each of the regiments and batteries and a general hospital for the command.

Johnston gave his immediate attention to shelter and medical care. At the same time, he took a long view when it came to his mission to support the enforcement of federal law in Utah. To survive winter in the mountains and be ready to advance in the spring, he placed a high priority on restoring the heavy losses that Mormon raiders and an early winter had inflicted on his army's food supplies. He undertook to do it from an isolated mountainous location with a determined enemy on one side and the Continental Divide and a thousand miles of snowbound trail to the Utah Army's main supply source on the other.

At South Pass, he had stopped the movement of merchant and sutler wagons to Salt Lake, or any other point occupied by Mormons, and forbade any dealings with them as long as they remained hostile toward the United States. On reaching Fort Bridger, he sent troops and mule teams to seize these trains in the name of the U.S. government, and return them from the junction of Hams Fork and Blacks Fork to his encampment. They would brighten the army's food supply outlook.

On their arrival, Captain Gove was not smart enough to escape the duty to preside over a detailed inventory of supplies for the coming twelve months, "a mountain of labor," he complained to his wife. It

19. Johnston, *Life of Gen. Albert Sidney Johnston*, 218, 219.

required listing even tent pegs in "some 800 heavy wagon loads, 6000 lbs. each," he groaned.[20] But it did not take that long. Captain John H. Dickerson, the quartermaster of the army, reported on 28 November that supplies for an estimated 2,400 persons, including civilian dependents and 320 volunteers, organized in four companies, "may be certain to last until others can be brought forward next year." Until then, coffee, soap, and sugar could be bought from merchants at the camp to make up for a shortage of these items, he said, failing to credit Mormon major Lot Smith for having imposed these deficits when he burned the army's supply wagons that fall on Green River.[21]

If food supplies appeared promising, the shortage of animals to move the army and its supply trains forward in the spring was critical. Nearly six hundred mules had died since the army left Fort Leavenworth, nearly all of them from starvation during the winter march from Hams Fork to Bridger's trading post on Blacks Fork. The surviving mules were "leg-weary and without life, and many of them must die during the winter," the quartermaster said. Half of the artillery horses were dead, he added, and two-thirds of the dragoons were dismounted. He figured that four hundred horses and a thousand mules would "be required for any movement that may be contemplated in the future."[22]

On short notice, such demand could be met in only two places, Dickerson said: Fort Leavenworth and New Mexico. To obtain the animals at the Missouri River army post would take thirty days longer and delay Johnston's move forward in the spring, he estimated. He recommended that they be acquired in New Mexico, which was "six hundred miles nearer us at the starting point." If it was not as far, however, his confidence that the most direct route to New Mexico was "entirely practicable at this season of the year" was dangerously misleading.[23] Depending on the weather, the longest winter route from Fort Bridger to the U.S. Army post at Fort Union, near Las Vegas, was often the safest and quickest. It skirted the Rocky Mountains on the north along the lines of present-day Interstate 80, U.S. 287, and Interstate 25. In 1857, the

20. Gove, *Utah Expedition*, 98, 99.
21. Buchanan, *Utah Expedition*, 104, 105.
22. Ibid., 101, 102.
23. John H. Dickerson to F. J. Porter, 24 November 1857, ibid., 102.

Cherokee Trail and the northern branch of the Santa Fe Trail followed the same course.

Johnston acted at once to carry out the quartermaster's recommendation. On the day he got this report, he ordered Fifth Infantry captain Randolph Marcy to lead a company by the most direct route to New Mexico to acquire horses and mules and deliver them to Camp Scott by late April. With only three days to get ready, the officer left on 27 November with forty enlisted volunteers, twenty-four packers, sixty-five mules, and enough food for thirty days.

Unhampered by wagons, Marcy took the most dangerous route. The veteran officer, who would later produce a widely read book on western travel, jeopardized the lives of his men and the success of his mission and marched in as unbending a line as possible in midwinter right into the heart of the Rocky Mountains.[24] Even now, his route is difficult to trace exactly because the party left no marks of its passing on the ground. Tim Goodale, Marcy's guide, said the route was open all winter, but Jim Bridger reportedly warned that they would never make it. If "Old Gabe" really did say that, the captain came close to proving him right.

From Camp Scott, Marcy later said, he went "directly across the Uinta Mountains," but he actually followed Henrys Fork to its confluence with Green River, which he crossed at a point that now lies beneath Flaming Gorge Reservoir.[25] He then skirted Green River for a distance and continued south over a tableland to the junction of the Colorado River, then the Grand River, and the Gunnison River at present-day Grand Junction, Colorado. At this point he crossed the Colorado River and followed the Gunnison River and its Uncompahgre River tributary to today's city of Gunnison, Colorado, also named for John W. Gunnison. Prior to then, the party in one stretch had labored ahead for two hundred miles through snow so deep that its members often made only three miles a day. Nearing the crest, they took turns crawling through the snow on all fours to break trail as they searched for 10,149-foot Cochetopa Pass over the Continental Divide.

24. Marcy, *Prairie Traveler*. For Marcy's account of this desperate journey, see his *Thirty Years of Army Life*, 224–63.

25. R. B. Marcy to J. McDowell, 23 January 1858, in Floyd, *Annual Report, 1858*, 41.

With their guides, including Goodale, hopelessly lost, Mexican mule trader Miguel Alona came forward to lead them over America's backbone on Gunnison's 1853 trail, or nearby North Pass. At the eastern base of the mountains, the party came to a dead stop, unable to advance without help. By this time, its members had used up their rations and were eating their starving mules. While the rest waited, Alona traveled ahead to get assistance from Fort Massachusetts, some sixty miles to the east, built in 1852 to protect settlers in San Luis Valley. With him went Madino Mariano, who had delivered Young's first letter to Colonel Alexander and spied on U.S. forces for General Wells.[26] Whatever their past allegiance, the two mule traders now led a relief column back from the San Luis Valley post to save the suffering party. On 23 January, a chastened Marcy reported his arrival at Taos, New Mexico, where he swore that he would never go the same way again in midwinter: "I shall take a different route in returning."[27]

The captain later described his fifty-six-day winter ordeal and the odds against survival that he had overcome at the cost of only Sergeant William Morton, "a most excellent soldier," who died of exposure and overeating after relief had arrived.[28] For this, he won commendation from the commanding general himself. Winfield Scott lauded his "unconquerable energy, patience and devotion to duty."[29] What Marcy did not admit, however, was that his ill-considered winter plunge into the Rocky Mountains not only had risked a vital mission and claimed the life of a top enlisted officer, but it might also have cost the lives of the whole party, including his own, if not for the good judgment and courage of a civilian mule trader. Nor did the captain confess that if he had chosen the longer but safer avenue to New Mexico, he would have gained Taos at least three weeks sooner. Instead, he took credit he did not deserve for his part in an undertaking that was foolhardy from the outset, while the real heroes, Alona and Mariano, received scant acclaim or reward for saving the company and its mission.

But if Marcy expected to lead a triumphant return, he would be disappointed. In January 1858, Johnston alerted army headquarters and

26. See chap. 9, p. 210.

27. Marcy to McDowell, 23 January 1858, in Floyd, *Annual Report, 1858*, 41.

28. Marcy to Floyd, 25 November 1858, ibid., 220–23.

29. General-in-Chief to Captain Marcy, 29 March 1858, ibid., 106–107.

General John Garland at Fort Union to news that three mounted companies of one hundred men each were being readied at Salt Lake to intercept Marcy at Green River on his return. At this report, Garland Hurt volunteered to act as the eyes of the Utah Army in the Uinta Basin on the route the Mormon force would have to take. The Indian agent and five young Ute warriors rode over the mountains to a spot near today's Vernal, Utah, where he had lived with the tribe during the winter after his escape, surviving for days "upon roots alone."[30]

On 17 March, Marcy left Fort Union, going north on the Cherokee Trail east of the Rocky Mountains with 179 men, 160 horses, and 800 mules. He got only as far as today's Colorado Springs, where orders came to stop. The report of Mormon plans to cut him off at Green River had prompted General Scott to send a Mounted Rifles battalion from Fort Union to escort the officer back. Marcy had pushed hard to reach Camp Scott by late April, but he now had to hold up for a month at Pike's Peak until reinforcements under Colonel William W. Loring came. The added protection was unneeded and hurtful. Loring outranked the officer and assumed command of the united force. So he upstaged Marcy and announced its arrival at Camp Scott on 11 June, "all well and in good condition," to army headquarters in Washington.[31]

Meanwhile, the swarms of hungry Natives and other unplanned visitors at Camp Scott soon revealed to Johnston that his quartermaster had underestimated the number of mouths he would have to feed that winter. He had ordered supply trains from Fort Laramie on the east to push over South Pass to Blacks Fork by earliest June, and he had sent Marcy to Fort Union on his mule mission. By December, he decided to send a party in the only direction still open to him—north over uncharted mountains to the Beaverhead region of what is now southwestern Montana, to purchase beef on the hoof.

It was Edward "Ned" Williamson, a twenty-nine-year-old Pennsylvanian, who probably came up with the proposal to buy cattle from wintering mountaineers on the upper Columbia and Missouri rivers. He had gained his knowledge of the region while serving on Isaac I. Stevens's 1853 Northern Railroad Survey and stayed on to become one of the

---

30. See Bigler, "Garland Hurt," 149–70.
31. Loring to S. Cooper, 12 June 1858, in Floyd, *Annual Report, 1858,* 112.

denizens of the north country. Williamson was serving as an interpreter for Frederick W. Lander, chief engineer of the Fort Kearney, South Pass, and Honey Lake Wagon Road, when the Mormon rebellion broke up the project and he volunteered his services to the Utah Expedition.

Williamson knew the north country; he knew the mountaineers who lived there; and he knew about their practice of buying worn-out cattle and horses from emigrants on the Oregon-California Trail during the summer, then driving them north to fatten them over the winter for trade or resale at high prices to overland travelers the following summer. He would serve as the guide.

Chosen to lead the party was a fearless adventurer from Virginia. Benjamin Franklin Ficklin had filled his thirty years with risky behavior. Expelled from the Virginia Military Institute for firing a cannon on the parade ground, he was reinstated for heroism during the Mexican War. At graduation, he had endeared himself to the members of the class of 1849 by marching around the hall with his diploma pinned to the tip of a bayonet. The resourceful southerner was directing a scouting party for Lander when the Mormon war disrupted the venture. He soon won the trust of Johnston and civilian officials through his service as both an express rider and acting U.S. marshal.

More to his liking was the hazardous assignment Johnston now called him to perform: leading a party of volunteers more than four hundred miles north in the middle of winter to contract for the purchase of cattle and horses. Ficklin left Camp Scott on 9 December with ten men, four mules, and enough supplies to last until he reached the camps of wintering mountain men on the Beaverhead River and its tributaries. He also took four gallons of whiskey, possibly to fight frostbite.

Otherwise, the Virginian's expedition was serving essentially the same purpose as Captain Marcy's, but for one crucial difference. While it went with the blessing of the U.S. Army, it was made up entirely of civilian volunteers and was not under direct army control. And it was led by a man who was imaginative and highly capable, but also impetuous and ungoverned by code or custom when it came to a duty as important as the one he had been called to carry out.

As Ficklin headed north, Mormons applied the espionage system that Young had created in Utah. In this the Nauvoo Legion had a major advantage over the American army, which had no effective intelligence capability. Conversely, as the Mormon kingdom scrambled to deploy the Nauvoo Legion against the U.S. Army, it faced a highly professional organization with long traditions and skilled officers with a lifetime of experience in transporting men and materiel over hundreds of miles. The Quartermaster's Department had spent decades keeping frontier forces "*fully equipped and prepared for distant service*," as one officer put it.[32] Nonetheless, the requirements of the army's largest operation since the War with Mexico placed enormous demands on the frontier's transportation system. Alexander Majors, one of the army's main freight contractors, told General Harney in June 1857 "that it would be impossible for them to transport all of the necessary supplies for the troops, to Utah, this year—their means of transportation being much too limited." Despite such misgivings, Russell, Majors & Waddell sent hundreds of ox-drawn wagons to the Army of Utah. Historian Norman F. Furniss estimated that sutlers and other merchants sent another 160 wagons.[33] This represented a ratio of one wagon for every five soldiers, based on the army's paper strength of twenty-five hundred men, but a ratio of almost three to one to support its actual total of fifteen hundred. Given the freight burned by Lot Smith and the eight hundred wagons that Captain Gove inventoried at Fort Bridger, it is clear that the army's quartermasters had done a remarkable job of securing transportation.

When it came to the vital supply issue, Mormon forces also held the advantages of interior lines of travel and shorter distances. At the same time, their location in the arid Great Basin, their theocratic system of government, and their communal barter economy presented a unique set of problems. Even the much-touted Mormon emigration system did not provide adequate supplies for its overland parties. The failure in 1856 to deliver the one wagon promised as support for each ten handcarts had led to the single largest loss of life in American trails history. Young's initial reaction to the supply predicament involved wishful thinking: "I calculate they [the army] shall furnish us with Guns, powder, and lead, beef, pork, and all that is necessary," he announced in mid-August. "I mean to

32. George Dashiell Bayard to his father, 15 April 1857, in Bayard, *Life of George Dashiell Bayard*, 116.

33. Furniss, *Mormon Conflict*, 121.

go to war at their expence, not on ours. If we are driven to it, they shall find us what we want."[34]

Rather than develop a practical supply system for the impending campaign, Mormon leaders simply shifted responsibility for feeding their armed forces to the soldiers themselves. When Levi Savage, Jr., mustered "with a portion of the brethren" at the Sugarhouse Ward Schoolhouse to organize "in a military capacity," Nauvoo Legion colonel Jesse P. Harmon "read an order from General Wells requiring the brethren to furnish themselves with food, clothing, guns and ammunition sufficient for a winter's campaign and to be ready to march in ten days."[35]

This scattershot policy continued even after the Mormons began sending hundreds of men into the mountains. During Lot Smith's successful raids, the same policy applied: "Furnish your men and as many others as you conveniently can with supplies of clothing and food from any of the trains when you have a chance," Wells ordered him in mid-October.[36] "Endeavor to furnish yourself with beef at the enemy's expense," Wells directed another commander.[37]

The orders that Legionnaire George Brown Bailey received in mid-September to muster on the Jordan River "for a three day's campaign [and] find my own provisions" reflected the hierarchy's next solution to the problem—delegate the responsibility downward.[38] This meant that military companies were outfitted and provisioned unevenly by their communities. "As far as practicable," Wells instructed Colonel William B. Pace at Provo, "each Ten [men should] be provided with a good wagon and four horses or mules, as wells as the necessary clothing &c for a winter campaign." He also directed Pace to preserve grain supplies "and report without delay any person in your district that disposes of one Kernal of grain to any Gentile merchant or temporary Sojourner, or suffers it to go to waste."[39]

---

34. Young, unpublished discourse, 16 August 1857, BYC.

35. Savage, Diary, 12 August 1857, 81, USHS.

36. Wells to Smith, 14 October 1857, in Hafen and Hafen, *Utah Expedition*, 231.

37. Wells, Orders to Thomas Callister, 14 October 1857, UTMR, 611.

38. Bailey, Journal, Authors' Collection. Young later tried to use the same tactics to finance his Standing Army of Israel. Bailey reported, "it was allotted to our ward to raise 35 men which cost the Ward $22013.00 dollars."

39. Wells to Pace, 1 August 1857, LDS Archives.

On 21 August 1857, John Pack, a veteran of Young's 1847 Pioneer Camp, learned firsthand how determined local authorities were to meet their obligations. Pack was stacking wheat in his field when six armed men "came to me and demanded of me a horse to go back on the Planes." They said Bishop John Stoker of Bountiful had authorized the action, but Pack "told them that Bishops did not send an armed force to execute their orders and I had no horse to spare." Captain John Allsop said, "Well then we shall take one" and marched his men over to Pack's wagon. Allsop ordered the boys driving the load of wheat "to standstill and said if you stir one step we will shoot you down in your tracks." When the smallest boy, age twelve, began moving, one of Allsop's men said, "Boy if you stir another foot I will blow you through." The captain unhitched the horse and led it away.[40]

The attempt to transfer the costs of an expensive military campaign to local communities ignored the impoverished state of Utah's economy. "The harvest is most abundant, there is sufficient grain in the Territory for several years consumption, and all things are prospering with this people," Young had assured missionaries in August 1857, but Utah's farmers were still reeling from a two-year drought.[41] As men reported for military duty, it fell to those left behind to harvest the crops. "Where there were not enough men for these tasks, women and children worked in the fields, at times to the detriment of their health," one historian observed.[42] In addition, the lack of hard cash limited the acquisition of arms and munitions, which were in desperately short supply. With the closure of the territory's borders, tax collections levied on passing emigrants dried up, as did the substantial fees that Mormon ferries collected at river crossings as far as five hundred miles to the east.

The top-heavy Nauvoo Legion had two officers, Albert Rockwood and Lewis Robison, assigned as commissary and quartermaster generals, but both men treated their status more as an honorary position than as a military assignment. As often happened in frontier Utah, the job of handling the actual supply and logistics problem fell to one of Utah's multitalented pioneers, in this case Colonel Jesse C. Little, who had already

40. Pack to Young, 22 August 1857, BYC.

41. Young to Silas Smith, H. P. Richards, and Edward Partridge, 4 August 1857, BYC.

42. Furniss, *Mormon Conflict*, 133.

acted as "a savior and a deliverer" for his people when he pressured President James K. Polk into authorizing the Mormon Battalion in 1846.[43] By late September, Little had established a "forwarding station" at Spring Creek, thirty-six miles east of the capital, where he tackled his duties with enthusiasm and confidence. "The men so far as I have seen them feel first rate & on hand to Carry out your orders & will," he assured Young. "I would suggest the Propriety of sending out some ammunition to this Post also some Shovels, spades & Picks to dig Entrenchments &c if necessary." Based on orders from Wells "to retain provissions Except for 5 Days," Little requisitioned all surplus rations from passing units and concentrated food supplies at his station to form a reserve. He offered to have packsaddles made at his shop in Salt Lake to transfer supplies to the front lines. "We are getting a good supply of Provissions which could be used by Troops Coming out & then the supply replenished," he reported.[44]

In a single day, Little and his men built a fifteen-foot-square log cabin, including the roof, and began accumulating kegs of powder, caps, lead, and whiskey. "The men that are with me are on Hand for annything that is required," he reported. "We are neither Homesick or Lonesome but on Hand to do your bidding." The post, now known as Camp Little, had no medical supplies, but necessity might require it to be used as "a retreat for the sick & disabled," he hinted. He recommended keeping some fast horses on hand to carry expresses to headquarters in Salt Lake. "We keep our Camp open & a Cup of Coffe for Expresses Night & Day," he reported.[45]

As the fall campaign came to a close, Young told General Wells that he had received a message from Little and Rockwood "touching supplies, and the requisitions will be promptly attended to." The same day, Wells informed Young that he had ordered Little to "take the supervision of the whole of the Commissary & Quarter Master Departments this side of the City" and had directed General Rockwood to fill Little's requisitions.[46] If he did, Daniel Burbank, the "Comasary" for Warren Snow's command from Sanpete Valley, failed to see them. He complained that

43. Journal History, 6 July 1846, LDS Archives.
44. Little, Reports to Young, 29 and 30 September 1857, BYC.
45. Ibid., 2 and 6 October 1857.
46. Young to Wells, 26 November 1857, and Wells to Young, 26 November 1857, BYC.

during the "Extreme Cold" of November, "we Nearly starved having Nothing to Eat ownley some poor oxen left By the Rode that could not travel Enny futher." Like the American soldiers at Fort Bridger, "we had to eat them Without salt," but unlike the army's wards, Burbank and his comrades had "to Eat sum of a Wolf. The Cold was Entense. No shelter of Enny Kind No Coats or But one Blanket to each man." During the entire fall campaign, his company "got five plugs of Tobacco in all sum coffey sum tea & sum shugar sum flower & a little Meete." More impressive was the list of what they lacked: "No Blankets No over shirts no socks or Mittens or gloves none of the dried fruits that President Young sent to that command. None of the heavy over shirts made By the different Wards. No Salt to salt our dying Beefe with."[47]

By mid-November, Wells had 1,353 men assembled in and around Echo Canyon. His officers reported that most of them had enough rations for between fifteen and thirty days.[48] But even this relatively small force created enormous demands on the territory's debilitated economy. After a hard march, Lewis Robison and Robert T. Burton reported that they had worn out their horses and had only "a verry small amount of supplys about 4 days rations of flour, & one beef which we drove along, say rations of Beef for to day and to morrow, and everything else out." Their animals were too weak to fetch supplies from Echo Canyon.[49] Other commanders were upbeat: "We are beginning to get things systematized," William H. Kimball reported, "so that the machinery can run with less grease."[50]

In truth, the "general lack of supplies" was even worse than Wells and his commander-in-chief had assumed. "I supposed that the Brethren had all Brot 30 days rations," Wells reported, but it turned out that his impoverished troops had less than half that on hand. Even worse, "the large amount of flour & beef of which I was advised as being on hand" at different supply stations "have been diverted to another direction," and now it appeared "that we are now just out all round." Wells ordered

47. Burbank, Journal, 9 November 1857, LDS Archives.

48. Taylor, Richards, and Jones, Report to Wells, 15 November 1857, BYC. Furniss estimated that in November, "more than 2,000 Saints manned the fortifications in Echo Canyon"; *Mormon Conflict*, 146.

49. Robison and Burton, Report to Wells, 10 November 1857, BYC.

50. Kimball, Report to Wells, 24 November 1857, ibid.

Generals George D. Grant and James Ferguson to look into the matter, but in the meantime he asked Young to "be kind enough to let the supplies from the com[m]issary Bro Rockwood come forward as he informs me he has quite an amount on hand. It would be well to send teams from the City with the first supplies as they will come quicker."[51]

Major John Sharp had almost "completed a comfortable forwarding station near the west foot of the Big Mountain" and had done "considerable work" on a cutoff up Killian Canyon intended to shorten the road from Emigration Canyon to the post. Young seemed pleased with the progress Little and Sharp were making, but in a letter commenting on the "wearisome watching of the wicked," he made it clear that he was growing tired of the expense of keeping an army in the field. The Legion's incessant demands on "the Commissary for boots, coats, blankets, &c." seemed never-ending, and its stomach appeared bottomless: "Over 3000 lb of flour has to be forwarded daily, with beef, grain and other articles in proportion," Young observed. He now "deemed it most advisable to recall for the present those who report themselves so destitute, which will give them an opportunity to assist in supplying their own wants."[52]

Having fulfilled its mission of keeping the army out of Deseret, the Nauvoo Legion was about to be called home. Both sides hunkered down to face the rigors of winter in the Rocky Mountains and dream of their eventual triumph when spring melted the snows blocking the gates of Zion.

51. Wells to Young, 21 November 1857, ibid.
52. Young to Wells, 26 November 1857, ibid.

U.S. Army wagons and artillery crossing the plains to Utah, as pictured in *Harper's Weekly*, 24 April 1858. The smoke in the background is from grassfires set by Mormon guerrillas. Library of Congress.

As a captain in the Nauvoo Legion, Lot Smith burned army freight wagons during the Utah War. He was later promoted to brigadier general before becoming a pioneer of Arizona, where he was killed in a dispute with a Navajo. Authors' collection.

This 1858 image from *Harper's Weekly* captures the striking physical appearance of the officer who commanded the Mormon Battalion during the War with Mexico. Historian Durwood Ball judges Cooke to be the finest frontier officer in the U.S. Army.

As a Nauvoo Legion officer and bishop of the northern Utah settlement of Box Elder, Samuel Smith arrested the Aiken party when they entered Utah Territory. From Esshom, *Pioneers and Prominent Men of Utah*, 215.

As bishop of the Juab Valley settlement of Nephi, Bigler provided an insider's view of the Mormon Reformation in his journal and later helped organize the murders of the Aiken party. From Esshom, *Pioneers and Prominent Men of Utah*, 302.

Mounted Rifleman Joseph Heger's pencil sketch of Nephi shows the Juab Valley settlement where the Aiken massacre was orchestrated in October 1857. In the background is Mount Nebo, the probable site of Castle Ballagarth. Courtesy Yale Collection of Western Americana, Beinecke Rare Book and Manuscript Library.

This wood engraving from *Harper's Weekly*, 30 January 1858, pictures one of the frontier army's finest officers, Colonel Albert Sidney Johnston, during one of his most challenging assignments. Courtesy Library of Congress Prints and Photographs Division.

This image from *Harper's Weekly*, 24 April 1858, "illustrates the night service of the scouts," who General Johnston said "had proved themselves hardy enough for any service."

This image from *Harper's Weekly*, 30 January 1858, shows officers' quarters at Camp Scott during the winter of 1857–58. Courtesy Library of Congress Prints and Photographs Division.

This engraving from *Harper's Weekly*, 24 April 1858, captures the order and discipline that prevailed during the Utah Expedition's torturous march to winter quarters at Fort Bridger. Courtesy Library of Congress Prints and Photographs Division.

On the march to Great Salt Lake City, Mounted Rifleman Joseph Heger sketched part of the army's extensive camp on the Mormon Trail at Yellow Creek on 19 June 1858. Courtesy Yale Collection of Western Americana, Beinecke Rare Book and Manuscript Library.

In what may be the earliest image of Camp Floyd, Mounted Rifleman Joseph Heger pictured a Native couple and a mountaineer overlooking the army post in Cedar Valley. Courtesy Yale Collection of Western Americana, Beinecke Rare Book and Manuscript Library.

In 1871, the LDS Church's *Deseret News* claimed that John Cradlebaugh "rendered himself particularly obnoxious" when he served as U.S. associate justice for Utah Territory from 1858 to 1860 and investigated the Parrish-Potter murders and the massacre at Mountain Meadows. Authors' collection.

After serving as one of the Pacific Wagon Road Survey's most talented scouts, B. F. Ficklin sought to purchase cattle for the U.S. Army at Fort Bridger from traders in the Northern Rockies. After making a fortune in the Civil War commanding Confederate blockade runners, Ficklin was said to have "the appearance of a refined pirate" by authorities who suspected him of involvement in the plot to assassinate President Abraham Lincoln. Courtesy Virginia Military Institute Archives.

CHAPTER 11

The Days of Your Kingdom Are Numbered

I trust that moderation will prevail in your councils & that you will
submit freely & willingly to the authority of the U.S. for that is your
duty so long as you remain within the limits of this country. It is
your duty to God, as well as to man. I advised this course when I was
in Salt Lake City last fall, because it was right & I advise it still.

—Captain Stewart Van Vliet, 25 April 1858

As the winter of 1857–58 came on, a festive spirit prevailed in Utah.
Forgotten were the trials and hardships of recent years—the grasshopper
invasion of 1855, the famine and handcart disaster the following year,
and the great Reformation of 1856–57. Like Gideon and his three hundred, the hosts of latter-day Israel had vanquished the haughty invader
and forced the army of the republic to struggle for survival in the mountains until spring allowed its humbled warriors to go home the same way
they had come. Brigham Young still ruled in Zion.

At this joyous season, T. B. H. Stenhouse reported, Mormon congregations enlivened Sunday worship by loudly singing almost endless new
verses to the popular melody "Camptown Races":

Old Sam has sent, I understand,
Du dah!
A Missouri ass to rule our land,
Du dah! Du dah day!
But if he comes, we'll have some fun,
Du dah!

To see him and his juries run,
Du dah! Du dah day!
Chorus: Then let us be on hand,
By Brigham Young to stand,
And if our enemies do appear,
We'll sweep them from the land.[1]

Young gathered his family to celebrate the holiday, but his mind was on the coming confrontation. "Ten years ago last July when we were down upon that Temple Block, and I think by sister Whitney's house I stated that if we were let alone for ten years we would not ask any odds of our enemies, and I think it was ten years precisely that we were let alone at that time," the Mormon leader recalled. He then spoke of his confidence about how the coming battles would go: "this army that have come to Utah, all that is necessary is for me to point my finger and tell them to stay there, and they will wilt and dry up, and be known no more."[2]

In Washington, the mood at the White House was one of frustration. Throughout the summer, a long-simmering financial crisis grew steadily worse, with the collapse of the price of railroad stocks and a drop in European orders for American agricultural products. Then, on 12 September, the side-wheel steamship *Central America* sank in a hurricane off North Carolina and took to the bottom more than $1,344,000 in gold bars and coin consigned by banks and financial institutions, plus estimated holdings of over $1,000,000 in gold held by passengers returning to the East Coast from California. Creditors demanded their money in gold, but the gold that New York banks had planned to give them was resting on the floor of the Atlantic. Largely overlooked in the financial panic was the fate of almost 600 passengers and crew, 435 of whom drowned when the three-masted "gold ship" went down. Few also related the disaster at sea to a conflict in the far-off western mountains. For President James Buchanan, however, the financial consequences of the tragedy produced an overdue awakening about how much he had underestimated the

1. Stenhouse, *Rocky Mountain Saints*, 372.
2. Young, Instructions, 25 December 1857, 3, BYC. Some seventy-four separate narratives document the 1847 Pioneer Company, but to our knowledge, none of them mention this comment.

Mormon problem and what it might cost to bring it under federal control. Three months after his inauguration, he had reacted impulsively to reports by federal officers of a rebellion by a western territory. In May 1857, he decided to replace Young as the governor of Utah and ordered a fifth of the U.S. Army to march a thousand miles to enforce the law and sustain his actions. He did all this without so much as a "by-your-leave" to Congress and without seeking the understanding of the American people. Nor did he pay heed to General Winfield Scott's advice that it was too late in the season to mount major military operations in the western wilderness. It had all looked so easy.

How the picture had changed by December. Brigham Young was firmly stuck to his seat as Utah governor and Indian affairs superintendent. The army the president had sent to escort Young's replacement and enforce federal law in the frontier theocracy was stuck in the snow and forced to take desperate measures to ensure its food stores until spring. As the new governor, Alfred Cumming, and other officials tried to form a territorial government amid the ruins of Bridger's trading post, Buchanan confronted the first of his two civil wars.

Yet if the president was having second thoughts about his too-hasty actions or was ready to admit defeat, he showed no sign of it on 8 December when he delivered his first annual message to Congress. Instead, he sounded more determined than ever to put down the uprising by Young and his followers. It was the first rebellion by an American territory, he reminded federal lawmakers, "and humanity itself requires that we should put it down in such a manner that it shall be the last." As a way to show "these deluded people" that "we are their friends," he called on Congress to authorize four new regiments and voiced trust that Congress would back such action, cost what it might, to restore "the sovereignty of the Constitution and laws over the Territory of Utah."[3]

The stakes were indeed high. Secretary of War John B. Floyd stressed that Mormon settlements "lie across the grand pathway which leads from our Atlantic States to the new and flourishing communities" on the Pacific. "They stand as a lion in the path," he warned, defying military and civil officers and "encouraging, if not inciting," the Indians to attack emigrant families on the overland trails. Travel, commerce, and

3. Buchanan, "Message of the President," 8 December 1857, 5, 6.

communication between the country's eastern and western halves "all depend upon the prompt, absolute, and thorough removal of a hostile power besetting this path," he said.[4] He asked for five additional regiments, raising by one the president's ante.

The "grand pathway" that Young and his followers stood across was the vital link joining America's East with its fast-growing West. The Lion of the Lord had seized an area of the American West that stretched from the Rocky Mountains of today's Colorado to the California line and closed its borders. He had cut the nation in half and expected to make it stand. But what he had done was intolerable, Floyd said.

At Salt Lake City, if the mood was celebratory, it was also more defiant and determined than ever. Appearing before the Utah Legislative Assembly on 15 December, Young dropped the often-coarse rhetoric he had voiced in recent months. In his own annual message, the self-proclaimed governor of a U.S. territory, who had spent just eleven days in a classroom, gave an erudite rendition of the limited role of a legislature in the new government he had established to replace the unconstitutional colonial system that Utah had suffered under since 1850. In one lofty sentence, he explained why a theocracy, in which the people understand what they are supposed to do and unanimously do it, was the ideal form of republican government.[5]

> The people, for the promotion of whose advancement in correct government you are now assembled in a legislative capacity, are so remote from the high wrought excitement and consequent entangling questions common to the populous marts of national and international commerce, are so little prone to deem mere property, rank, titles and office the highest prizes for human effort, and through enlightened choice are so invariably peaceful and law-abiding, that your duties partake but in a small degree of that varied, perplexing and intricate description so characteristic of the legislation of most if not all other communities.[6]

4. Floyd, *Annual Report, 1857,* 7, 8.

5. For Young's philosophy on theocracy as republicanism, see "Remarks," *Deseret News,* 23 September 1857, 228.

6. Young, "Governor's Message," 15 December 1857, *Deseret News,* 23 December 1857, 330–32.

Young characteristically went on to discuss schools, manufacturing, agriculture, and random topics before making his point: "Congress has not one particle more Constitutional power to legislate for and officer Americans in Territories than they have to legislate for and officer Americans in States." He stood as firmly on the ground he had taken in September as Buchanan did in his message to Congress. He did not question the government's authority to send its soldiers where it pleased, within constitutional bounds. But when it did so "clearly without the pale of those authorities and limitations, unconstitutionally to oppress the people," as he saw the situation, "it commits a treason against itself, which demands the resistance of all good men, or freedom will depart our Nation." Afterward, the response of legislators was consistent with the territory's election law, which ruled out the right to vote in secret. They unanimously approved resolutions concurring "in the sentiments and doctrine" advanced by Young and vowed to "resist any attempt on the part of the Administration to bring us into a state of vassalage."[7]

To put them in such a state seemed the purpose of Buchanan's demand for new regiments, as indicated by "the General-in-Chief himself." On 23 January, Scott notified Colonel Albert S. Johnston at Fort Bridger that he planned to set sail for the Pacific coast. The general would come "clothed with full powers for an effective diversion or co-operation in your favor from that quarter," he said.[8] As historian William P. MacKinnon has shown, Scott's plan demonstrated that the army took the Mormon rebellion seriously, but the idea to approach Utah from the west was not original. Edmund B. Alexander and Johnston both had urged the strategy.[9] And the rush among men in the mining camps along the Sierra Nevada that month to volunteer for military service in Utah showed that the concept had broad popular appeal in the West.[10]

The need for their service, as presented by Buchanan and Floyd, was honest and compelling, but Congress found it hard to believe that fewer than forty thousand religionists in a far-off territory would be so foolish as to try to prevent the thirty million citizens of the world's most

7. Utah Legislative Assembly, "Resolutions," 21 December 1857, ibid., 132.
8. George W. Lay to Johnston, 23 January 1858, in Floyd, *Annual Report, 1858*, 32, 33.
9. MacKinnon, "Buchanan's Thrust," 226–60; Buchanan, *Utah Expedition*, 32, 37, 38.
10. "More Volunteers for the Mormon War," *San Francisco Daily Evening Bulletin*, 5 January 1858, 2.

dynamic nation from heading west. Underestimating the intensity of Mormon conviction, some lawmakers reacted with skepticism. The mood of Congress also pointed up the president's shortcomings in the art of communication and his failure to enlist the legislators' support for the actions he had taken. In addition, the issue opened the divide between members from northern states, including California, and those from the south, who favored local autonomy.[11]

An empty treasury added to Congress's reluctance to fund more troops to fight a war in the Far West. As lawmakers dragged their collective feet, the representative from Quincy, Illinois, knew just how to solve the Mormon problem. Isaac Morris had practiced law in Carthage, where the Mormon prophet Joseph Smith was murdered, and had led a citizens' committee to negotiate and oversee the removal of Smith's followers from the state in 1845–46. Since the roots of the Mormon wars in Utah and Illinois were basically the same, he seemingly figured, why not apply the same solution? On 26 January, Morris introduced a resolution calling for the appointment of three commissioners to negotiate the purchase of Mormon possessions on the condition that the owners would peaceably remove "from without the limits and jurisdiction of the United States" by 1 June 1859.[12]

The resolution failed, but it did illustrate the difference in attitude at the time between former Mormon neighbors and those who did not live next door to them. More in line with the latter was the resolution adopted on 27 January asking Buchanan to tell Congress his reasons for sending a U.S. Army expedition to Utah in the first place and to inform members on "how far Brigham Young and his followers were in a state of rebellion or resistance to the Government of the United States."[13]

By now, General Scott knew that he would not get the volunteer regiments he wanted. On 4 February, he told Johnston it was no longer probable that he would come to the West Coast or that any advance toward Utah would be sent from that quarter. He knew that even if Congress authorized some new regiments, it would be too little and too late to make any difference in the outcome of the conflict. And so it proved.

11. Hafen and Hafen, *Utah Expedition*, 247–61.
12. "The Mormons," 26 January 1858, *Congressional Globe*, 29 January 1858, 427.
13. "The Utah Expedition," 27 January 1858, ibid., 439.

Two months later, Congress finally approved the addition of two new regiments of volunteers, each of 740 privates, to serve for eighteen months in "quelling disturbances in Utah."[14] Scott may not have been too disappointed, since he was too overweight to travel in comfort to the Pacific coast; and from his own experience in the Black Hawk and Mexican-American wars, he distrusted volunteers anyway.

Well before Congress made up its collective mind, the U.S. Army moved on its own to quell the Mormon revolt as soon as spring opened the trail. Errors in Washington had forced the army to suffer the humiliation of being outmaneuvered and made to look inept by territorial militiamen. Unlike Congress, Scott suffered no wishful thinking about Young's intention to establish, by force if necessary, either a sovereign state or a separate nation within the United States. If he could not move against the rebels from two sides at once, the army would advance with overpowering force via Echo Canyon from the east.

On 11 January, the commanding general, with the sanction of the War Department, ordered more than three thousand regular troops to march in the spring to reinforce the Army of Utah. They included three regiments, each of ten companies, the First Cavalry, Sixth Infantry, and Seventh Infantry, plus Cooke's last two Second Dragoons companies. Ominously for Mormon defenders in Echo Canyon, they also numbered two light companies, Second Artillery, to go with Captain John W. Phelps's light battery, Fourth Artillery, and Captain Jesse L. Reno's heavy battery at Fort Bridger. In addition, the reinforcements would number 850 recruits to bring the units already at Camp Scott up to standard strength. The Army of Utah, additions included, would total 251 officers and 5,335 men, nearly a third of the U.S. Army at the time.

The spring reinforcements would put Johnston at the head of the largest regular American army. At the same time, the command exposed him to replacement by an officer of higher rank and seniority. In the meantime, from their commanding officer to the average private, they were also the most motivated troops in the army. There could be no doubt that Scott shared Johnston's opinion, as expressed on 20 January. "Their threat to oppose the march of the troops in the spring will not

14. *Public Laws of the United States of America, Passed at the First Session of the Thirty-Fifth Congress*, chap. 13, 7 April 1858, 262–63.

have the slightest influence in delaying it," he stressed, "and if they desire to join issue, I believe it is for the interest of the government that they should have the opportunity."[15]

One who had little confidence that the Echo Canyon defenses would hold was Nauvoo Legion adjutant general James Ferguson. Not yet thirty, the fiery Irish emigrant was one of few officers in the territory with actual military experience, having served as Philip St. George Cooke's sergeant major during the War with Mexico. On 7 January, the young general reported to Governor Young on the militia's operations over the past year, just as Secretary Floyd had done to President Buchanan a month before. "The works in Echo are very good and reflect much skill upon the superintendences," he said. "Still, if the enemy come that way, the barricades are not sufficient," he went on. "They will want repairs and additions." He placed the number of efficient men available to meet an oncoming army at 6,000, with about 1,000 more unreported or not yet enrolled. Ferguson listed private arms on hand of 2,364 rifles, 1,159 muskets, 99 pistols, 295 revolvers, and 41 swords, plus 1,500 pounds of powder and 3,224 pounds of lead.[16]

Young now considered an alternative means of preventing the army from entering his domain, which showed his determination to take the lives of American soldiers if necessary. At Nauvoo, Uriah Brown, one of three non-Mormons on the ultra-secret Council of Fifty, claimed to have invented a revolutionary method to destroy an army or navy "with liquid fire." At the bidding of Young's older brother Phinehas, the eccentric arsonist came from Illinois to describe his proposal to lay pipes in Echo Canyon and incinerate unwelcome intruders "without injuring the operator." Brown could do the same to an unlimited number of ships in port, he said.[17] His device no doubt appealed to the Mormons' desires to send their enemies to a very hot place, but its implementation was beyond their capability.

15. Johnston to McDowell, 20 January 1858, in Floyd, *Annual Report, 1858*, 44, 45.

16. Ferguson, Report to Young, 7 January 1858, UTMR. This detailed fourteen-page report summarized all of the Nauvoo Legion's 1857 campaigns except one: the operation at Mountain Meadows.

17. MacKinnon, *At Sword's Point*, 1:45; Quinn, *Mormon Hierarchy: Origins*, 128; Hanson, *Quest for Empire*, 223.

If Young and his people could not render their enemy's armaments obsolete, they were without peer in another field of human conflict—a war of words. On 6 January, territorial lawmakers, with their usual unanimity, bombarded the president and Congress with a long resolution. "If it is true that the army menacing this Territory is at the instance of the president and by the authority of the Government," it said, "we request to be informed of the fact and why it is so."[18] The petition portrayed an unoffending people of a territory being attacked for asking their government for the rights of sovereignty afforded to states, a reference to the resolutions and memorial sent to Washington a year before that Interior Secretary Jacob Thompson had stamped a "declaration of war."[19]

The memorialists said that if justice had its way, many of their enemies would either be "pulling hemp by the neck, or learning a trade in the confines of a prison." They were relying on the hope "that a stern sense of justice yet remaining among the worthy sons of patriotic sires will stay the suicidal hand of crawling sycophants and corrupt rulers, and that American Liberty may not be immolated upon her own altars, nor strangled in the halls of her own citadel by those whose sworn duty is to be her protectors. Withdraw your troops, give us our CONSTITU-TIONAL RIGHTS, and we are at home," they cried.[20] In the spirit of John Hancock, every member of the Utah Legislative Assembly signed the document and considered it to fulfill God's purpose in inspiring the Constitution's framers to establish a land of religious freedom where His Kingdom could be restored and supersede its parent as it prevailed to universal dominion.

Behind the memorial marched a parade of resolutions from mass meetings in each settlement signed by local leaders on behalf of all the citizens. Typical was Payson's resolution in support of "Governor" Young's message as being "a document replete with sound Constitutional doctrine." It added, "We most cordially approve of the highly republican and eminently loyal course of our Legislative Assembly as manifested in their resolutions."[21] The settlement memorials, legislative resolution,

18. "Memorial," 6 January 1858, *Deseret News*, 13 January 1858, 356–57.

19. Bernhisel to Young, 17 December 1857, BYC.

20. Ibid.

21. Ibid.; "Resolutions by Mass Meetings," 1 January 1858, *Deseret News*, 13 January 1858, 357.

and governor's message amounted to an impressive display of popular support for independence. But the unanimous response also revealed the suppression of independent opinion in the theocratic territory.

In Washington, territorial delegate John M. Bernhisel met with the president and the secretary of war but found them unreceptive to his attempts "to procure an amiable adjustment" of the crisis. He did get a favorable reception from Senator Sam Houston of Texas, who sent him a letter he had received from Seth Blair, one of four Mormons whom President Fillmore had appointed to territorial offices in 1850. Before he arrived in Utah that year, Blair allegedly served in the Texas Rangers during Houston's second term as president of the Texas Republic. He may also have known the hero of San Jacinto in 1853–54 when Blair served as a missionary in Texas. Now a U.S. senator, Houston said that he would see the president and recommend a commission to settle the Utah conflict.[22]

On 16 January, Bernhisel again saw the president, who told him that "the people must submit to the laws," the position Buchanan had consistently stood on from the beginning. Utah's delegate protested that "the people denied having violated any law or resisted any authority," in response to which the president fired back, insisting that "all the officers had stated that they had been driven from there." He seemed determined that "the military shall force their way into the valley, though he says he does not wish any blood to be shed," the delegate told Brigham Young.[23]

Even so, it began to appear as if somebody's blood might get shed if the conflict ended the way the president wanted it to. At Camp Scott, the territory's new chief justice, Delana R. Eckels, the sole federal justice of the three appointed by Buchanan to arrive at Fort Bridger with the Utah Expedition, collected evidence and impaneled a motley grand jury. The Indiana magistrate's panel was hardly unbiased, and the captured Mormon major Joseph Taylor and his adjutant, William Stowell, were promptly indicted for treason.[24] But far more worrisome was the indictment of Brigham Young, Daniel Wells, Lot Smith, and others for the same offense.

22. Bernhisel to Young, 18 January 1858, BYC.
23. Ibid.
24. Taylor had escaped during Johnston's tortured winter march to Fort Bridger.

Fear of indictment for treason or for the massacre at Mountain Meadows no doubt sparked Young's search for new strategies and weapons that might prevent the advance of federal troops and appointees into Utah. The Nauvoo Legion faced a severe lack of both firearms and gunpowder. In October, Young proposed that bows and arrows be adopted as weapons. "It has been suggested to my mind," he pronounced, indicating that what followed came from above, "to select some two thousand of the right kind of men" and provide them with excellent rifles. In addition, he said, "let them be furnished themselves with good bows and plenty of arrows, and learn to be as adept in their use as in sharp shooting with the Rifle."[25] James Ferguson discussed the feasibility of the new weapons system in his report on the preparedness of the Legion in January 1858. "If Bows are to be introduced I have yet to see an improvement on the light and effective weapon used by the Indians," he said. He deemed the crossbow unsuitable because it would cost as much to produce as a rifle, but he considered "a good Indian Bow and quiver of arrows an unburthening and valuable addition to the arms of a mountain trooper."[26]

The potential addition of such a primitive weapon could have a strategic value as well. For months, Young had told Washington, despite all evidence to the contrary, that he alone had stopped the Indians from attacking passing emigrant trains in retaliation for atrocities against the Natives. Keep the soldiers away, he warned, or he would no longer hold the Indians in check but would turn them loose on overland travelers. By itself, the threat was hollow. Except for the Utahs, the Great Basin tribes were destitute, not warlike; the Shoshones under Chief Washakie were friendly to travelers; and the Utahs were angry with the Mormons, not the emigrants.

The new weapons strategy Young recommended, combined with these conditions, gave his proposal a menacing tone. He intended to organize "a standing army to be most—or all—of the time on duty in the field," to guard all of the approaches to the territory. For example, he would locate about one hundred men on the southern route to California, the Spanish Trail, now I-15; two hundred men on "the Mary's

25. Young to Wells, Taylor, and Smith, 17 October 1857, BYC.
26. Ferguson, Report to Young, 7 January 1858, UTMR.

[Humboldt] River route," the California Trail, now I-80; another hundred "north to watch the Oregonians" on the Oregon Trail, now I-84; with the remaining troops placed as a reserve to operate in concert or apart, depending on circumstances, to watch the different eastern routes. "2000 men of the right stripe can prevent all the armies of the world from coming here," Young figured.[27]

Under Mormon doctrine, the Lamanites were to join their cousins and fellow Children of Israel, the Mormons, and establish God's Kingdom in North America, by peaceful methods if possible, or by any means it might require if not. But the Natives had ignored sacrificial Mormon attempts to forge an alliance. Young may have thought that if the Indians would not join his followers, his followers would take the lead and fill the role projected for the Indians. Consistent with this interpretation were the reports by U.S. Army officers that Mormons disguised as Indians had led the massacre at Mountain Meadows and charges by emigrants that Mormons, not Indians, had attacked them at Stony Point on the California Trail along the Humboldt River.[28]

Seen in this light, Young's idea to station men "of the right stripe" in guerrilla-type units on the nation's western arteries of travel and communications, armed with bows and arrows and rifles, answerable only to him, bore menacing inferences. If this was what he had in mind, it showed his confidence that God's Kingdom would sustain its independence from the United States, but it was impractical otherwise. In any event, Nauvoo Legion officers seem to have put the original proposal to rest the same way Young's followers ended the plan to build the temple at Salt Lake of adobe: they simply ignored it. Yet out of the idea he initially proposed sprang an armed body quite different in shape and purpose from the one he had first envisioned. Unveiled in January 1858, the Standing Army of Israel was a full-time body of horsemen more closely resembling a Middle Eastern religious militia than anything seen in the military annals of the American republic. This innovation probably led to reports that Young was preparing a force to intercept Captain Randolph Marcy on the return leg of his journey to New Mexico to purchase horses and mules. But its real purpose was undoubtedly something larger.

27. Ibid.
28. See Barrett, "Stony Point."

In organization, the new military body looked like the Nauvoo Legion at Nauvoo, except that it was a full-time professional army, not a state militia as the western Illinois force claimed to be. Until recently, the elite force's existence has been shrouded in closely held LDS records. Its immediate object was to fend off military threats from outside Deseret's massive borders, and it apparently was intended to launch guerrilla raids that would disrupt the U.S. Army's line of communications and supply, which stretched over a thousand miles of Indian country from the Missouri River to Fort Bridger. Fast-moving Mormon horsemen had already demonstrated the vulnerability of the Army of Utah to such tactics. An even likelier purpose would have been to guard a staged move of Young's followers from the Great Basin to a more remote and productive new homeland in Bitterroot Valley and the upper Missouri River region. But in the largest sense, Brigham Young created the Standing Army to advance the Kingdom of God's right to sovereign rule and provide a professional military power directly under the control of the prophet, seer, and revelator.

Patterned after Israel's armies of old, the Standing Army of latter-day Israel was organized as a brigade of one thousand mounted riflemen, comprising two regiments of five hundred, each with five battalions of one hundred men, ten companies of fifty and fifty companies of ten. Latter-day Israel's professional new host would train and operate apart from the Nauvoo Legion, but both would be commanded by Lieutenant General Daniel H. Wells, which meant, in practice, Brigham Young. Including officers of the line and staff, the force came to about twelve hundred men.

Named to command the new brigade of riflemen was William H. Kimball, the son of First Counselor Heber C. Kimball, at the grade of brigadier general. Chosen as colonels of the new regiments were George D. Grant, a New Yorker, and the capable Virginian Andrew Cunningham. The ten battalion majors and twenty company captains included many of the territory's best military leaders and plainsmen. Majors were Brigham Young, Jr., Thomas Callister, Lot Smith, Reddick N. Allred, Marcellus Monroe, Howard Egan, Ephraim Hanks, Henson Walker, Madison Hamilton, and Warren S. Snow. Captains were Stephen Taylor, Charles Decker, Wilford Hudson, George Knowlton, Horton D. Haight, John D. Parker, Charles Layton, Joseph Grover, Erastus Bingham, Heber P. Kimball, Daniel McArthur, William Maxwell, Jacob Truman, William W.

Casper, John R. Murdock, Abraham Conover, Isaac Bullock, George P. Billings, and Samuel S. White.

No Legislative Assembly action was required to enroll one thousand enlisted men. Young simply approved a levy by decree on the northern Utah military districts created in 1857. Great Salt Lake and Tooele were assigned to raise 375 men; Davis, 150; Weber (Ogden) and Box Elder (Brigham City), 175; Lehi, Provo, Peteetneet (Payson), Juab (Nephi), and Sanpete, 300. In meeting their quotas, military leaders in each district were warned not to weaken the existing Nauvoo Legion companies.

Once again, the burden of financing the prophet's latest inspired war-making scheme landed squarely on the already impoverished Mormon people. Individual wards and settlements were instructed to equip soldiers from their jurisdictions and support the men's families. This was done by subscription, with individuals committing to outfit one soldier and care for his dependents, others one-half or one-fourth of a man, and some just giving what they could: a horse, a rifle, a revolver, or even "5 bushels of potatoes."[29] In their report to Brigham Young, the leaders of West Jordan Ward in Salt Lake Valley on 15 January described how this process was handled. They had "met with the Brethren of this Ward" to ascertain "what they are willing to do." At the session, they proposed "that every three thousand dollars worth of property should outfit, support, and sustain one man and his family," which unanimously carried, "with one exception (Daniel R. Allen), who has refused."[30]

The report listed thirty-six men who together pledged to support sixteen soldiers of "a Standing Army for one year." By far the most generous was the feared William A. Hickman, who promised to equip and care for the families of two soldiers. His generosity may have shown either that the work of cutting off wrongdoers was more rewarding than farming or that no one would dare challenge him if he failed to make good on his pledge. Most of the others shared the expense in the ratio of two providers for each soldier.

James G. Willie, who the previous fall had led the next-to-last handcart company to disaster and was now serving as bishop of Salt Lake's

29. List of donations toward fitting out Soldiers, LDS Archives.

30. Joseph Harker, John Bennion, M. Gee Harris, William A. Hickman, and Samuel Bennion to Young, 15 January 1858, UTMR.

Seventh Ward, described his ward's desperate financial condition and asked Young to spare his congregation from the latest military levy. "I feel to sympathize with you in your poverty, and feel to do all I can to relieve you from the burdens, requirements and circumstances which seem to weigh so heavily upon you," Young responded the same day. He offered Bishop Willie and his flock the following proposition: he would pay $25,000 for all "the houses, lands, improvements and personal property of the inhabitants of that ward." In addition, he would "relieve you from all trouble in fitting up men for the Army. I will do that in the bargain." He demanded an immediate answer. He felt "assured that you will be glad to close with so advantageous an offer. I am not burlesquing but [am] in earnest; and if satisfactory to you, wish to close the bargain forthwith."[31]

Making war is an expensive proposition, and in Utah's cash-starved barter economy, it appears to have posed an insolvable problem. The $200,000 spent during the previous year to finance the Brigham Young Express and Carrying Company had now literally gone up in smoke, compounding the difficulty of raising money to run the war. Economic historian Leonard Arrington observed that the money needed for the Standing Army "must have exceeded half a million dollars for outfitting alone." Young addressed the situation with his typical creativity: he simply printed money known as "Deseret script." As church president, he called a meeting on 19 January 1858 and organized the Deseret Currency Association, with himself as president and Wells as treasurer. "This association was charged with the introduction, management, and redemption of the Mormon currency," Arrington noted.[32]

In the 1850s, such privately issued currency was common and was sometimes derisively known as "shinplasters." The Deseret script was a shinplaster to beat all shinplasters. The territorial legislature had disorganized Green River County and attached it to Great Salt Lake County in December 1857, but the Deseret script was stamped with the seal of the Green River County Probate Court—perhaps, Arrington speculated, to reflect "the sly humor of the Mormon leaders which prompted

---

31. Young said he would "pay you down in good available property," but it seems likely he intended to pay most of the amount in Deseret script.

32. Arrington, "Mormon Finance," 221, 223.

them to circulate their currency bearing the seal of the one county of the territory which was occupied by Johnston's Army."[33]

The *Deseret News* printed the Currency Association's first notes on such thin paper that most were worn out by year's end—and no known examples survive. Between 19 February and 17 July 1858, a total of $78,598 was issued in a run of much handsomer engraved notes. To provide what Henry Ballard called "a safe foundation" for the currency, the LDS Church backed the paper money with "horned stock" and horses— and the authority of Brigham Young. Much of the money was ultimately returned to the church president "as tithing, donations, payment on indebtedness, and so on," Arrington concluded, observing, "Cast thy bread upon the waters and it shall return to thee."[34] Ultimately, the attractive new currency proved of no more value than the shinplasters it replaced. Since church members used the script to pay their tithing, the latest exercise in Mormon finance essentially paid for the Utah War by borrowing against future tithing receipts.

But the unwanted burden of financing yet another military force imposed on the citizens of Utah Territory would soon be lightened by the exploits of one man who would make the Standing Army of Israel nothing but a curiosity of history within two months. When he led ten men north from Fort Bridger on 9 December 1857, Benjamin F. Ficklin did not intend to bring the Utah War to an abrupt end. His mission was to contract with mountaineers on the upper Columbia and Missouri rivers for the delivery of five hundred head of cattle to Camp Scott by spring. For this, he carried written authority from Johnston and letters of introduction by Utah's new governor, Alfred Cumming, to John Owen, U.S. agent to the Flatheads and owner of Fort Owen in Bitterroot Valley, near present-day Stevensville, Montana, and Father Adrian Hoecken at St. Ignatius Mission, seventy miles or so north of Fort Owen. As the superintendent of

33. Ibid., 226.

34. Ibid., 231. "Running the printing press to finance a war is generally considered to be inflationary and fraught with danger," Arrington acknowledged, but he made a persuasive case that it provided a much-needed circulating medium in Utah Territory. Ibid., 219. Forger Mark Hoffman printed his own examples of the Deseret script and sold them as "white notes," Mormon currency expert H. Robert Campbell observed, a clever fraud made easy by the lack of any authentic examples of the first issues of the currency. Notes by Will Bagley from conversation with Campbell, 21 December 2007.

Indian affairs at St. Louis, Cumming had worked with both in 1855 when he took part in Isaac I. Stevens's great Indian Council at Fort Benton.

Ficklin's assignment to replace animals lost to Mormon rustlers was similar in many respects to Marcy's, but there were some notable differences. For one thing, his party was smaller and was made up solely of civilian volunteers. While it carried Johnston's written authority, it lacked direct U.S. Army oversight. Even more significant was the difference in character between the two men who headed the relief missions. Marcy was a thoughtful career officer, ever mindful of regulations, while Ficklin was a spontaneous innovator who rewrote the regulations as he went along. As the crew chief on the Pacific Wagon Road Survey, he had seen the ashes of the army supply wagons that Lot Smith had burned on the Green and Big Sandy rivers. He had watched hundreds of animals perish on the winter march from Hams Fork to Fort Bridger. He undoubtedly believed that he was involved in a war and considered his task vital to winning it.

As the Virginian later reported, his party backtracked the trail to Hams Fork and followed Alexander's march up that stream to bypass Mormon patrols on upper Bear River.[35] At Sublette's Cutoff, he headed west over the rim of the Great Basin to meet the Oregon Trail on Bear River. His party left the emigrant road at Soda Springs and headed due north, fighting heavy snow to cross the mountains and reach the Snake River ford near what is now Blackfoot, Idaho. He knew about but did not see the Mormon station on the Blackfoot River. From there he went north on the Flathead Trail, which connected Bitterroot Valley to Fort Hall on the line of today's I-15. He struggled over the Continental Divide at or near the Monida Pass in a perilous winter crossing.

On 4 January, Ficklin's party, less one frozen mule, reached Red Rock River, a Missouri River headwater, and continued north toward the valley of the Beaverhead, a favorite wintering ground of the mountaineers. At this point he was less than fifty miles east of Fort Limhi, the Mormon Indian mission on the opposite side of the Continental Divide via the Lewis and Clark Pass.[36] On reaching his destination, he later reported,

35. For Ficklin's later report of his movements, see Ficklin to F. J. Porter, 15 April 1858, in Floyd, *Annual Report, 1858*, 68–71; and Bigler, *Fort Limhi*, 242–58.

36. Now known as Lemhi Pass. "Lemhi" is a misspelling of the name of the Book of Mormon king and the namesake of Fort Limhi. The incorrect spelling is also used in Lemhi County, Lemhi River, and Lemhi Shoshones.

"I found all the evidences of the mountaineers having left recently, and hastily, and taken the trail in the direction of Flathead valley."[37] His decision to take whiskey instead of added food supplies now left the party in tight circumstances. Failing to find the mountaineers, he "had to kill a broken down horse to eat."[38]

But where were the men and animals he had expected to find? Ironically, they had hurriedly departed to safer havens, having heard a report originating at Fort Limhi that the Mormons planned to move north. Nor was this news confined to the upper Missouri. In Bitterroot Valley, mountaineer Frederick H. Burr said, "News has arrived that the mormons have sworn to kill, Old [Richard] Grant, Johny Grant, [John W.] Powell & myself that they are about to build a fort on Beaver Head, and will make a descent here in the spring." The rumor spread like wildfire and touched off a panic by many mountain men, who thus failed to measure up to their reputation for courage. Retired Hudson's Bay chief trader Richard Grant "broke his wagon" coming down the Hell Gate in his hurry to get away, Burr said. Earlier he had found John Owen at his fort in Bitterroot Valley busily "taking account of stock and making an inventory of all the property for fear in case of its destruction by the Mormons whom it is feared will make an inroad here as soon as the spring opens."[39] Even before the Mormon scare broke forth, the Flathead chiefs had told their agent, Richard Lansdale, that they "feared the Mormons were coming to occupy their lands in force."[40]

To the Mormons, the mountaineers were old enemies who had poisoned the Flathead chiefs against them and welcomed the U.S. Army to put Brigham Young's followers in their place. But these loners and misfits of civilized society, who lived in the wilderness by choice, were above all else survivors. And this was a bad time to ask them for help.

Continuing north, Ficklin on 10 January found brothers James and Granville Stuart, Robert Hereford, Jacob Meeks, John Saunders, and others camped on the Big Hole River. One of them was his fellow

---

37. Ficklin to Porter, 15 April 1858, in Floyd, *Annual Report, 1858*, 68–71.

38. Ibid.

39. Frederick H. Burr, Diary, 1, 5, and 14 January 1858, Beinecke Library. The Hell Gate is now known as the Clark Fork River.

40. Lansdale to Nesmith, 22 September 1857, 35th Cong., 1st sess., 1857–58, vol. 2, S. Ex. Doc. 11, serial 919, 663–69.

Virginian John W. Powell, who had a reputation for being selfish and out of control. He also bore a grievance against the Mormons at Fort Limhi. In a December dispute between tribal visitors to the fort, the Saints had unintentionally appeared to favor the Nez Percés, who captured Powell and asked the missionaries to hold him inside their stockade. They did so more to protect him than to take sides, but it angered the Bannocks, the tribe to which his wife belonged. Powell escaped, but he was a dangerous man to have as an enemy.

Since the mountain men with large herds had fled farther north, Ficklin had little choice but to follow. Leaving the rest of his party on the Big Hole, he and his guide, Ned Williamson, made two visits to Bitterroot Valley, where he met Burr, Powell's occasional partner. They benefited from Owen's legendary hospitality but could not persuade him to deliver cattle to Fort Bridger. The Fort Owen trader was instead preparing to move his herd to Walla Walla for safety. Father Hoecken welcomed Ficklin with open-handed generosity at St. Ignatius Mission, but Flathead Valley residents were not willing to risk Mormon ire and deliver cattle on contract.

Typical of their reaction to this opportunity was the attitude of the noted Montana pioneer John F. "Johnny" Grant. Better known for survivability than for courage, Richard Grant's son recalled that Ficklin "wanted me to take the cattle I was selling to him to Fort Bridger, at my own risk." This he flatly refused to do. Grant was not eager "to give the Mormons a chance to give him any trouble." He was "certain to regret it if I attempted to take cattle to the troops, so I lost the sale of those cattle."[41]

The mission-driven Ficklin had traveled hundreds of miles in the mountainous northern region. He had pleaded with John Owen and threatened Johnny Grant without success. In all of the high waters of the two great rivers, the Missouri and the Columbia, there was only one location where cattle in the number he was after could be found: the Mormon Indian mission. There more than 250 beef cattle and some 40 horses could be his for the taking. The missionaries had acquired most of these animals in trade with the western Shoshones and Bannocks, who

---

41. Meikle, *Very Close to Trouble*, 67.

in turn had stolen them from travelers on the Oregon Trail. What they gave in return for them is unknown. Indian reports from as far away as Walla Walla said they gave the Natives arms and ammunition, but there is little evidence to support such stories.

To the temptation was added the justification that the Mormons were making war on the United States. Their mounted companies had stolen thousands of U.S. Army cattle, horses, and mules, threatening the survival of American soldiers and their dependents and making it necessary for Ficklin himself to undertake his perilous journey. This was probably reason enough for him to seize the mission herds. A likely partner in such a venture would have been the reckless potential ally Powell, who wanted revenge for being held a captive at the fort the month before. Moreover, Powell's influence over the Bannocks, who were thirsting for vengeance themselves, gave him the manpower to mount such a raid. Whether the pair deliberately conspired to carry it out will never be known, but there can be little doubt that Ficklin's mission, purposely or not, lit the fuse that set off what happened next at Fort Limhi.

On 25 February 1858, Mormons reported that some 250 Bannocks and a few Sheepeater Shoshones had swept down on the little settlement on the east fork of Salmon River. In scattered fighting, they killed two missionaries and wounded five others and seized more than thirty horses and nearly three hundred cattle. Surprised at their mid-morning work, the Mormons put up little organized resistance and inflicted no known casualties on the attackers. The settlers charged that Powell rode with the raiders, painted and attired like a Bannock. Six weeks later, he and Ficklin arrived together at Fort Bridger.

The raid on Fort Limhi cut off sixty-nine white settlers—thirty-nine men, seventeen women, and thirteen children—and stranded them more than three hundred miles north of the nearest Mormon settlement, isolated and fearful, in a stockade built to accommodate barely a third of that number. But the frightened men, women, and children under siege in the fort, far from friends and families, were only the immediate consequence of the attack.

At a stroke, the raid on Fort Limhi wiped out any hope that the northern tribes, Bannocks, Shoshones, and Flatheads, would welcome their professed Israelite cousins to their country in the event the frontier theocracy failed to prevail in its conflict with the United States. Even less likely was that the Lamanite "remnant of Jacob" would join with the Mormons in a continuing struggle against the federal government. And so it came to pass that Brigham Young's vision of a new home for his people in the remote and defensible northern Rocky Mountain valleys suddenly went dark.

CHAPTER 12

Let the Consequences Fall
Buchanan's Ultimatum

> I offer now a free and full pardon to all who will submit
> themselves to the authority of the federal government. If
> you refuse to accept it, let the consequences fall on your own
> heads. But I conjure you to pause deliberately, and reflect
> well, before you reject this tender of peace and good will.
>
> —President James Buchanan, 6 April 1858

As night fell on the day of the attack on Fort Limhi, 25 February 1858, a self-anointed peacemaker reached Great Salt Lake in a desperate attempt to rescue the Mormons from the corner Brigham Young had worked them into. Thomas L. Kane, son of a Philadelphia judge, had virtually made a career out of saving Young from himself. An ardent defender of the oppressed, the thirty-five-year-old Pennsylvanian stood five feet six inches, weighed not much more than 135 pounds, and suffered from "bilious fever," which made him often sick and normally passionate and high-strung. He was also intensely centered in *self*, conscious of his upper-class standing, and quixotically brave.

Kane's journey of fifty-two days and some three thousand miles to reach the Mormon stronghold, by sea and by land, sick most of the way, via Panama, Los Angeles, and the Mojave Desert, was not the first time he had exercised his father's influence on behalf of a controversial religious minority. In 1846 the skillful political operative had conceived the strategy that won the approval of President James K. Polk to enlist five hundred Mormons during the Mexican War, which helped finance the faith's move west. To no avail, he had tried to reverse Young's initial request for a territorial form of government in 1849, and his recommendation led Millard Fillmore to appoint the Mormon prophet as Utah's first governor. The Whig president later had reason to question Kane's favorable endorsement.

For years Kane had waved his father's reputation like a magic wand on the Mormons' behalf. But after their public acknowledgment in 1852 that they practiced polygamy, he deliberately neglected his old friends and turned a blind eye to the events that precipitated their trouble with the federal government. John M. Bernhisel hinted at the reason for this change in attitude: "Of late years he has treated us very coldly; we think on account of our religion which we all very much regret."[1] Kane had long accepted and repeated Mormons' denials that they practiced polygamy, and when he learned the truth in December 1851, he rightly felt he had been deceived.

It is uncertain what restored his loyalty, but as the year drew to a close, he threw himself into rescuing the millennial movement with a zeal that rang of religious conversion. Kane saw the president in November, but Buchanan had shown no interest in his appeal, and he figured it was too late in the season anyway to impose himself on the Mormons. But when the president asked Congress to approve four new regiments, the self-imagined peacemaker suddenly saw the light. He arranged for an audience with Buchanan through a mutual friend, U.S. attorney James Van Dyke at Philadelphia, who accompanied him to Washington. The pair arrived on 26 December 1857.

Convinced the Mormon leaders were misinformed and mistakenly believed that the president was bent on exterminating them and their people, Kane told Buchanan he was determined to hurry to Great Salt Lake in midwinter and straighten out this misunderstanding before spring brought bloodshed. He also asked for written authorization to serve as the president's representative in arranging a peaceful resolution of the conflict.

Buchanan was not as naïve as the passionate Mormon defender who appealed to him on their behalf. He had heard from credible federal officers, who had fled from Utah out of fear for their safety, and read their reports. In his message to Congress that month, he had acknowledged

1. Van Dyke to Kane, 28 March 1859, Marriott Library.

that he had no right to interfere with the "religious opinions of the Mormons": his purpose was only to enforce federal law in Utah, as his constitutional duties required.[2] The president further reminded Kane that Captain Stewart Van Vliet had already given Young these assurances. For good reason, he believed that Young had deliberately rebelled against the authority of the United States and intended to adopt a sovereign position as either a state of the Union or an independent nation, even if it took bloodshed to do it.

Kane later claimed that the power Buchanan gave him "was the same as those of Messrs. Powell and McCullough [sic]," the commissioners whom the president later named. This was true only in the sense that Buchanan gave none of them the power to negotiate, but it was also misleading. The president empowered the commissioners to present his conditions for amnesty, authority that he never gave to Kane.[3] On the contrary, he told Kane that he would not, "in view of the hostile attitude [the Mormons] have assumed against the United States, send any agent to visit them on behalf of the government."[4] In the most kindly terms, he tried to dissuade him from making such a perilous journey. But Kane went anyway.

On 5 January, Kane sailed from New York for the Isthmus of Panama. Why he chose to travel incognito is not clear. It may have been that Bernhisel had warned that his life would be in danger: his people had become so hostile to the United States, "they would sacrifice you if they discovered your design in visiting them." According to Bernhisel, the feeling was especially strong in "the outer settlements."[5] This may have been the reason his Negro servant, who was allegedly emigrating to California, paid the fare for both in his own name, Osborne, and Kane thought it best not to correct the mistake.[6] His love of secrecy served his sense of being at the center of great events.

The seasick peacemaker debarked at San Francisco and went by another vessel to Los Angeles, where he took the all-season Spanish Trail

2. Buchanan, "Message of the President," 8 December 1857, 2589–86.

3. Poll, "Thomas L. Kane and the Utah War," 112.

4. Buchanan to Kane, 31 December 1857, 35th Cong., 2nd sess., 1858, H. Ex. Doc. 2, serial 998, 162–63.

5. Van Dyke to Kane, 28 March 1859, Marriott Library.

6. Poll, "Thomas L. Kane and the Utah War," 121.

to southern Utah. He had not gone far before former Mormons and other protesters, who feared that he opposed the United States, stopped him for three days at San Bernardino, the recently evacuated Mormon colony. But the letter he bore from Bernhisel won the help of faithful church members who were preparing to return to Utah in obedience to Young's order. Ebenezer Hanks gave him a carriage and a note of introduction to Apostle Amasa Lyman, a San Bernardino founder who was then returning from a scout to the Colorado River to check on a reported U.S. Army invasion from that direction. They met on the road, and the apostle escorted him the rest of the way to Great Salt Lake.

As they approached Cedar City, Lyman took care to avoid the Mountain Meadows killing ground, where human bones and hair, torn clothing, and other remains of more than a hundred victims, men, women, and children, lay scattered on the surface. Even so, Kane heard about the atrocity at the southern Utah city whose militia company had led the orgy of murder. He also heard that the Indians had murdered the emigrants because they had poisoned the spring at Corn Creek, the first of many falsehoods designed to cover up Mormon involvement. Later, Kanosh, the faithful Mormon chief at Corn Creek, dutifully repeated this canard, claiming he was not there at the time.[7]

At Cedar City, Kane on 17 February alerted Young of his coming in a note furtively signed "A. Osborne," trusting that Young would "recognize his handwriting."[8] As he neared his destination, he dropped "the name of his colored servant" and requested in his own name "an early hour for the interview which he has traveled so far to seek."[9] The invitation came that same day, 25 February, at his lodging in the William C. Staines home, now the Devereaux House, in Salt Lake City.

Worn out by his long journey, Kane found himself on the evening of his arrival "surrounded by a large circle of friends and advisers."[10] They included members of the Mormon hierarchy: the First Presidency, Young, Heber C. Kimball, and Daniel H. Wells; Apostles Orson Hyde, Wilford Woodruff, John Taylor, Amasa Lyman, and Charles C.

7. Bagley, *Blood of the Prophets*, 197–98.
8. Kane to Buchanan, 5 March 1858, ibid.
9. Kane to Young, undated, but probably 25 February 1858, ibid.
10. Kane to Buchanan, 5 March 1858, ibid.

Rich; and Albert Carrington. If they expected Kane to report that the president had acceded to their demand for sovereignty as a state, they would be disappointed.

Kane later told Buchanan what he had said to this group. It was in his power, he told them, to satisfy them about the attitude of the American people and the intention of the president toward them. He had come as a citizen, he said, "to bring them authentic information about events in Washington as they affect the Mormons of Utah."[11] If he had actually said this, he would have been following Buchanan's instructions. But that was not what Apostle Woodruff heard that night. Instead, as reported by Woodruff, Kane proclaimed, "I come as an ambassador from the Cheif [sic] Executive of our Nation." Buchanan's alleged envoy was "fully prepared and duly authorized to lay before you" the opinions of the American people and the president's feelings toward them.[12] After correcting their misconceptions, he wanted them to send aid and comfort as a sign of goodwill to the U.S. soldiers suffering in the mountains.

At his own request, Kane met with Young privately and afterward drafted, probably at Young's request, a summary of their talks as if recorded by the Mormon leader himself. In this amazing account, Kane expressed surprise that Young had received "no adequate explanation" of why the president had ordered the army to Utah nor even been told that he had been replaced. Kane called this "a grave omission" and "begged" Young to accept his assurance that the president intended no disrespect. These explanations "received my due consideration," Young allegedly replied. "Though tardy I accepted them as the personal apology of Mr. Buchanan."[13] Undoubtedly, the reason Young never signed this document is that he never said these things. And since Buchanan would never have apologized to Young, Kane no doubt asked the Mormon leader to keep it "strictly confidential" so the president would never see it.

For more than a week, Kane's efforts to convince Mormon leaders that Buchanan meant them no harm failed to win a show of their own

11. Ibid.

12. Kenney, *Wilford Woodruff's Journal*, 25 February 1857, 5:168–69.

13. This memo was published for the first time in Poll, "Thomas L. Kane and the Utah War," 123.

peaceful intentions through relief to snowbound American soldiers. On 5 March, he wrote two letters to the president. He mailed the first, a factual account of his journey to Salt Lake, directly to Buchanan in Washington, but he addressed the second to his brother, Robert, for personal delivery. He did this, he told Buchanan in that second letter, because he was afraid to trust his writing to the mail delivery at Salt Lake. He apparently thought that a letter to Buchanan might be opened and read, but one addressed to his brother would not be. And he meant the second for Buchanan's eyes only. In it, he revealed a disposition to color, if not deliberately misrepresent, the success of his self-appointed mission. With little progress to report, he told Buchanan that his coming had "prevented the effusion of blood, and contributed to strengthen the hands of those—and they are not few here—who seek to do good." From the beginning of this unhappy conflict, he said, Young's "commanding influence has been exercised, to assuage passion, to control imprudent zeal, and at all risks, either of his own person or that of others" to prevent bloodshed. In a stunning deceit, he said that Young's "commanding influence" had been "exercised in favor of our army."[14]

Colonel Kane had a remarkable ability to be blissfully unaware of— or simply to ignore—the most grotesque manifestations of the Mormon theocracy, such as the punishment for adultery, real or imagined, in a culture that practiced polygamy as a religious obligation. On the Saturday night following his arrival in Great Salt Lake City, "several persons disguised as Indians entered the house of Henry Jones, and dragged him out of bed with a whore and castrated him by a square & close amputation," Hosea Stout reported.[15] Kane may not have heard of this outrage during his visit, but it soon became notorious both in and out of Utah.

Kane's gullibility apparently extended to an issue of overriding importance. If he had only had the time, he told Buchanan, "I could have well employed it in examining into the entire question of the relations of the Mormons with the Indian tribes around them." Then, possibly referring to the massacre at Mountain Meadows, he added that he was "not satisfied with regard to more than one matter which has been the sub-

14. Kane to Buchanan, 5 March 1858, Marriott Library.
15. Brooks, *On the Mormon Frontier*, 2:652–53. The word "whore" applied to wives who had affairs outside their polygamous marriage.

ject of public discussion."[16] Yet Kane dutifully recorded the improbable accounts of the atrocity he heard at Cedar City and Corn Creek without a hint of skepticism. Up until the Civil War drove the mass murder from public attention, Kane was instrumental in helping to derail an effective investigation of the crime.[17] A note in Kane's papers reveals that two decades later, Young's son John W. Young sought advice on how to help his father avoid being indicted for the Mountain Meadows massacre.[18]

On 8 March, as Kane prepared to leave for Fort Bridger, he had no reason to take heart that his mission might succeed. From the day he arrived in Salt Lake, he had enjoyed the warmest hospitality that leaders could provide to a tested and valued friend. But there was no sign he had told Young anything the latter did not already know about Buchanan's intentions or convinced him to hold out an olive branch in the form of food for the army. Mormon leaders were as disdainful of this idea as General Albert S. Johnston would later be. "It turns out that Col Tho. Kane's message is an unofficial one," Apostle George A. Smith said. "He designs our good & is a warm friend, but he wants us to spare the lives of the poor soldiers camping about Bridger," Smith said, and snorted: "Bah!"[19]

Then, on the day of his planned departure, change came like a sudden winter blast from out of the north. Two worn-out and half-starved men arrived in Salt Lake after a four-hundred-mile midwinter ride on a desperate mission. On 28 February, Ezra J. Barnard and Baldwin H. Watts had slipped out of the Fort Limhi stockade after dark on the only two sound horses left at the mission. For the last forty-eight hours of their journey prior to reaching Utah's northernmost outpost at Barnard's Fort, they had no food and but one horse between them.

Stitched into the lining of Barnard's coat was the shocking news they delivered to Brigham Young on 8 March, just as Kane prepared to leave Salt Lake. "Indians . . . 150 or over made a break on our herd . . . fired on Fountain Welch . . . left him for dead . . . shot Andrew Quigley . . .

---

16. Ibid.

17. Bagley, *Blood of the Prophets*, 198, 243–44.

18. Whittaker, *Register to the Kane Collection*, 1:421.

19. Smith to William H. Dame, 3 February [March] 1858, BYU Library. Despite searches by the leading historians of the Utah War, the long letter Wilford Woodruff wrote to Kane on 4 March 1858 to explain why Mormon leaders had rejected his overtures has not been located.

beat him on the head with iron war picks . . . George McBride shot from his horse . . . through the heart & scalped . . . James Miller through the heart." Bannocks and Sheepeater Shoshones had attacked Fort Limhi on 25 February, mission president Thomas S. Smith reported. They had killed two missionaries, wounded five, and made off with nearly three hundred cattle and more than thirty horses. "The Indians are watching every move we make," he said, "and I don't consider it safe to leave the fort."[20]

For northern Utah settlements, the news was devastating. Most of the sixty-seven men, women, and children in danger in the far north hailed from settlements north of Salt Lake. For the Mormon theocracy's struggle for sovereignty, the consequences of the raid were far-reaching. The attackers had been led by the powerful Bannock chief Le Grand Coquin, "the Big Rogue," who had welcomed the missionaries less than three years before. The hostility of the Bannocks and other tribes eliminated an essential element of Young's plan to move north in the event that his followers failed to prevail in their struggle for independence. No longer could the Saints rely on the friendship, much less the active support, of the "remnant of Jacob" in the north.

The grim news overturned Young's entire war strategy, which had counted on the Lamanites' being "made *one nation* in this glorious land" and joining their fellow Children of Israel to overthrow the existing order. "The door has already been unlocked to the Lamanites in these mountains," Wilford Woodruff had announced during the heat of the Reformation. "They will begin to embrace the gospel and the records of their fathers, and their chiefs will be filled with the spirit of God, and they will rise up in their strength and a nation will be born in a day."[21] It was now clear that the door was still locked. The assault on Fort Limhi proved that the Yankee guesser, Brigham Young, had guessed wrong when he calculated that forty thousand Mormons and their Indian allies could defeat a nation of more than thirty million citizens.

Kane noticed a dramatic change in Young's attitude, he later told the president, but he still did not realize how much it would affect his mission. Toward evening on 8 March, the Mormon leader "spoke out for

20. Smith, Report to Young, 28 February 1858, BYC.
21. Woodruff, "Discourse," 22 February 1857, *Deseret News*, 4 March 1857, 411.

the first time on a matter which I had not touched upon," Kane reported. "He confessed to me that he had regarded the 'sending of that salt' in the light of an overture." Young had then asked, "Wasn't that to be taken as a waiver of my position expressed to Van Vliet?" Later, as Young walked with Kane to his lodging, he did not mention the Fort Limhi disaster but "bade me good night & Godspeed with an effusion that was deeply touching," Kane informed Buchanan.[22]

In his rooms, Kane had welcomed some old friends, he continued, and realized at once that something had caused a stir in the community. For the first time, he heard that news had arrived of a "massacre of the Saints at Salmon River." Kane figured it was "a small affair" since only two men had been killed, and he could not understand what all the excitement was about. But when "Brigham Young called upon me the next day [9 March] to see me off according to promise," he continued, "I thought his manner dry, and he alluded to the matter too tersely to please me."[23]

By that morning, Young had already launched a military expedition to rescue his followers on Salmon River. Even then, Major Benjamin F. Cummings was riding north with ten men to break through the Indian encampments, take word to Fort Limhi that help was coming, and deliver Young's order to abandon the Indian mission in Oregon and return home. Close behind came a mounted command of one hundred led by Andrew Cunningham, the newly appointed colonel of a regiment in the Standing Army of Israel. His company would be followed by a hundred more from Lehi and northern Utah on 9 March.[24] After seeing Kane off, Young that night swallowed his disappointment and dictated a letter to him.

Fearing that his mission had failed, Kane rode north for the army camp on Blacks Fork, escorted by Porter Rockwell and other bodyguards. As they passed through northern Utah settlements toward the winter trail east along the Weber River from Ogden, he heard "'Salmon river' here, 'Salmon river' there to such an extent" that he "questioned myself if his [Young's] views were perhaps affected somewhat by the

22. Kane to Buchanan, 15 March 1858, BYU Library.
23. Ibid.
24. For more on the rescue, see Bigler, *Fort Limhi*, 265–77.

popular excitement."[25] As Kane bedded down that night in Weber Canyon, some forty-five miles north of Salt Lake City, Young confirmed his premonition.

As he broke his Weber River camp on 10 March, Kane "with great gratification" saw two horsemen ride up. They were Young's oldest son, Joseph A. Young, and George Stringham, who had ridden all night to overtake him before he reached Fort Bridger. They dismounted from horses that had been "badly hurt by falls on the ice," and handed him Young's letter, which was addressed to him, not Colonel Johnston.[26] "We have just learned through the southern Indians, that the troops are very destitute of provisions," Young began. He went on to offer to send nearly two hundred head of cattle, "a portion of which are tolerable good beef." In addition, he promised to deliver fifteen or twenty thousand pounds of flour, "to which they are perfectly welcome, or pay for, just as they choose."[27] If Johnston rejected his offer, he asked Kane to communicate this "to those who attend you, that we may be saved from the trouble." From this time on, Kane threw off any pretense of being an impartial arbiter. He was now Young's agent, if not his mouthpiece.

With hope renewed, the peacemaker pressed on to Camp Scott, where Captain Jesse Gove reported his arrival on 12 March, "so much fatigued that he could not apparently speak."[28] Having regained his voice by the next day, Kane showed off his disdain for the army and its commander. He rode up to Johnston's tent "as if he wished to ride into it instead of stopping outside," Captain John W. Phelps said. The colonel was engaged and kept him briefly waiting, a delay his prideful visitor appeared to take as an insult. When Johnston came out, he found the way blocked by Kane's horse, "whose head was nearly in the opening," with its rider discourteously still aboard. Forced to look up from a crouching position, "his own head being near the horse's head," the six-foot-plus colonel asked the five-foot-six rider, "Who are you?" Kane said he was the bearer of dispatches. "I ask your permission to see Governor Cumming first, I'll see you afterwards." Phelps noted that he appeared to have a red sash

25. Kane to Buchanan, 15 March 1858.

26. Ibid.

27. Young to Kane, 9 March 1858, in Floyd, *Annual Report, 1858*, 87, 88.

28. Gove, *Utah Expedition*, 134.

on under his undercoat.[29] The insolent arrival was led "like an ass" to Cumming, Major Fitz John Porter said. It was all "Quite Theatrical."[30]

Theatrical it may have been, but it was not a performance calculated to win many friends in the Army of Utah, from Johnston on down to the newest recruit. "The soldiers are very much incensed against this man Kane," Gove said.[31] Kane used Buchanan's letter commending him "to the favorable regard of all officers of the United States" as he used his father's name to make himself an important player in national events. Without it, it is doubtful that Johnston, who was ordered to support civil authorities in enforcing the law, but not to bargain, would have given him any notice. But after their first meeting, relations between them would be formal and conducted in writing.

Meanwhile, if Kane thought that an offer of food would soften Johnston's heart, he soon learned otherwise. "President Young is not correctly informed," the officer wrote. "There has been no deficiency, nor is there any now." Moreover, he said, "We would neither ask nor receive from President Young and his confederates any supplies while they continue to be enemies of the government."[32] He asked Kane to convey his reply to Young, which Kane agreed to do, but only at Cumming's request, not Johnston's. First, he insisted that the colonel reconsider his decision and pointedly reserved the right to offer his opinion on Johnston's action at some future date if he did not. The officer was not intimidated by the veiled threat to blame him for any failure of his peace mission.

Colonel Johnston's refusal to become involved in unofficial negotiations ended the Pennsylvanian's peace mission, however well intended it may have been. He could do no more under the restrictions that President Buchanan had imposed. He needed more than his letter of recommendation to continue.

On 17 March, Kane rode out of Camp Scott to deliver Johnston's stiff but polite reply. At Muddy Creek, some twelve miles west of the army post, he gave a copy of the letter to his Mormon escort to relay to Young and asked them to meet him on 25 March at Quaken Aspen Grove,

29. Phelps, Diary, 13 March 1858, in Hafen and Hafen, *Utah Expedition*.
30. Porter, "An incident of Army Life," 13 March 1858.
31. Gove, *Utah Expedition*, 135.
32. Johnston to Kane, 15 March 1857, in Floyd, *Annual Report, 1858*, 88.

twenty-five miles west of the army camp, and convoy him back to Salt Lake. That day, Captain Gove heard shots fired over Fort Bridger, followed by the long "to arms" drum roll of the Fifth Infantry. A patrol was sent out, and one of his men shot at Kane "and just missed him." They brought him back, Gove told his wife, and "a more frightened individual I never saw." Kane said he fired the shots himself to find his way into camp.[33]

The day before Johnston's reply arrived, Mormon religious and military leaders met at Salt Lake to decide what to do if the officer should spurn their peace offering. They decided that American public opinion would turn against them if "we whip out and use up the few troops at Bridger." Rather than kill the American soldiers, it would be better to "burn up" and flee, they concluded, so "the folly and the meanness of the President will be the more apparent."[34] With time running out, nowhere to go, and the peril of a federal investigation of the atrocity at Mountain Meadows and other crimes hanging over them, something had to be done. They decided on an approach that had never failed.

The following evening, Porter Rockwell and the other Kane escort members returned from Muddy Creek with Johnston's rejection of Young's peace offering, plus nine army mules "with lassos" they had rustled. The apparent collapse of Kane's plan to settle the confrontation peacefully touched off the new strategy, a campaign to cast Buchanan as an evildoer or dumbbell and present themselves as innocent victims of his badness. Launched on short notice, it was a desperate move, implemented as circumstances demanded, which lacked the faith's usual planning and organization. But its purpose by then had been validated by more than a quarter-century of church history.

Young opened the bid for public sympathy on 21 March with a confused and contradictory dissertation, "A Series of Instructions and Remarks," before a Special Council of the faithful in the Salt Lake Tabernacle. Two months before, he had vowed "by the eternal Gods" that if the "Damnd Scoundrells" tried to take him, "he would send them to Hell across Lots," and if the army tried, he and his followers "would make millions of them Bite the dust."[35] In his 15 March letter to Kane,

---

33. Gove, *Utah Expedition*, 135.
34. Brooks, *On the Mormon Frontier*, 2:654–55.
35. Larson and Larson, *Diary of Charles Lowell Walker*, 16 January 1858, 1:14.

Johnston had said that "a mere act of obedience to the law" was all the Mormons had to do to end the conflict, but Young countered, "Our enemies are determined to blot us out of existence."[36]

The Mormon prophet blamed Buchanan for violating the principle of popular sovereignty, which held that "the people of each State, each Territory" had the right to regulate their own domestic affairs in their own way, "subject to no other limitation than that which the Constitution of the United States imposes upon them." As expressed by its main advocate, Senator Stephen A. Douglas, the doctrine was intended to resolve the dispute over slavery in new territories, not to apply to such issues as polygamy.[37] Young simply took this principle to its logical conclusion. If it applied to slavery, then it applied across the board.

The president's treachery had led to a fateful choice. "If we open the ball upon them by slaying the United States soldiery," Young said, "just so sure they would be fired with anger to lavishly expend their means to compass our destruction, and thousands, and millions if necessary, would furnish means, if the government was not able, and turn out and drive us from our homes, and kill us if they could."[38] There was a better way, symbolized by one word: "Sebastopol," which became the code word for the operation. It referred to the port on the Black Sea where, during the Crimean War, the Russians blew up their ships in 1855, abandoned and burned the city, and left the ruins to British and French forces. Sebastopol represented Young's plan to burn their settlements and leave rather than coexist, compromise, or surrender to the enemy.

Where would they go? The unspoken question was on every face. "To the deserts and mountains," Young said. "There is a desert region in this Territory larger than any of the Eastern States," he went on, "that no white man knows anything about." He referred to the still largely unexplored central Great Basin, "a desert country with long distances from water to water, with wide sandy and alkali places entirely destitute of vegetation," within which his followers lived on the eastern edge. He

36. Young, "A Series of Instructions and Remarks," 4, Marriott Library. For a summary of this extraordinary sermon, see Stott, *Search for Sanctuary*, 49–65, 80–81. Stott's pathbreaking work remains one of the best books on the Utah War and a model of honest scholarship.

37. Holzer, *Lincoln-Douglas Debates*, 238.

38. Young, "A Series of Instructions and Remarks, " 6, Marriott Library.

had already sent exploring parties from Provo and southern Utah to find the mysterious White Mountains, an undiscovered hideaway where as many as a half-million people could live "scattered about where there is good grass and water."[39]

Thus began the heralded "Move South," a staged exodus of thousands of people from northern Utah towns and settlements to the southern part of the territory. The mass evacuation would start in Salt Lake City with five hundred families who had "never been driven from their homes" before. The bishops from the various wards were to select the ones to go, making sure "to take the poorest and most helpless."[40] It was the likeness of Sebastopol, not the reality, that counted. As the chosen five hundred families went south to Provo, the next assembly point, an equal number from the northern towns would move into those empty homes until their own turn came to head south. From southern settlements would roll hundreds of wagons and teams to facilitate the move.

"Horses, oxen, and cows were harnessed or yoked to wagons and carts; and one family by the name of Syphus, was moving their effects on a handcart drawn by a pair of yearling steers," said Brigham Young's nephew John R. Young, who met the movement on his return from overseas. "Mothers and children walked along as merrily as if going to a corn husking; each family moving its little bunch of cows and flock of sheep." At times, the traffic was so heavy that his company was "compelled to drive our wagon for miles outside the beaten path."[41]

Despite such charming recollections, this staged refugee movement was hardly a unified, voluntary act of solidarity. "An order from Brigham was issued that every man, woman, and child north of Utah County must abandon their homes and remove into the southern part of the Territory, under the penalty of having their houses burned over their heads," dissenter Charles Derry recalled. "The understanding was, they must be burned *if the soldiers came in.*"[42] As one Utah historian put it, Young "threatened condign punishment on those who did not comply" with his orders.[43]

39. Ibid., 7, 11.
40. Brooks, *On the Mormon Frontier*, 2:655.
41. John R. Young, *Memoirs*, 113–14.
42. Derry, *Autobiography*, 45.
43. Neff, *History of Utah*, 502.

Federal authorities concluded that such threats had compelled as many as one-third of the people to make the move, and a *New York Times* reporter wrote in late May that a party of some 150 apostates had escaped to Fort Bridger. They claimed that "fully one-half the entire Mormon community would embrace the opportunity to flee from the moral and physical slavery in which they are held." Cumming had promised Utah citizens that he would guarantee their right to move as they pleased, but "by driving the doubtful men and women southward," the evacuation drastically reduced "the number of those who attempted to avail themselves of Gov. Cumming's protection to a very small figure." The paper told the pathetic story of a woman whose request for a passport to leave the territory "was answered with a mocking affirmative, while at the same moment her children were torn from her arms and sent 'South!'" The refugees at Bridger said that not one of them had escaped without enduring "all sorts of amazing extortions, such as being compelled to pay unjust debts, in some cases two or three times over. When all other devices of extortion had been exhausted, they were each compelled to pay a year's taxes in advance."[44]

The massive removal began on 1 April, and Young himself led the parade. By the sixth, the single dirt track leading to Provo was "lined with men, women and Children, teams and waggons all moving south," Wilford Woodruff wrote. Two days later, the worst snowstorm of the winter struck the evacuation and froze it in place. From the center of Salt Lake Valley, the road "was lined with people and teams to Provo for 50 miles. Many suffered and some Came near perishing," Woodruff reported. "Horses died by the wayside. Men unloaded their goods in the mud. Others took their team off and left their waggons sticking in the mud. Some teams gave out and whole families lay in the mud under their waggons over night." By early May, the traffic jam extended over one hundred miles from Provo to Box Elder.[45] As the forced removal dragged on into June, however, events were taking place elsewhere that would make the mass movement south a waste of the time, work, and resources of a people whose margin of survival was thin under the best of conditions.

44. James W. Simonton, "Important from Utah," 28 May 1858, *New York Times*, 24 June 1858, 1.

45. Kenney, *Wilford Woodruff's Journal*, 5:180–81, 186.

Young himself stayed in Provo only long enough to give orders for the construction of a fortified compound to house himself and his extended family. An apostate Mormon Indian agent said the prophet seemed "to be preparing for his own escape in an emergency, having kept a herd of some fifty or sixty superior mules, belonging to the church, in fine condition down in San Pete Valley," which were "designed for his own and his harem's flight" should the situation deteriorate.[46] Young returned to Salt Lake on 4 April to conduct an abbreviated general conference, where he once again denounced the "Cursed meaness [*sic*]" and the "wickedness corruption and abomination" of the United States and its "Disposition to Destroy us from the face of the Earth." No official version of this odd sermon ever appeared in print, but Charles L. Walker recorded his statement that "he felt righteously mad enough to go right out to the camp of our enemies and slay them." But Young's remarks then took a strange diversion. He "said he would have to hold back and let the wicked slay the wicked showed that if we spilt their blood their [there] was an atonement but if we let them kill themselves, they would go to Hell and stay there."[47] Perhaps under this bizarre reasoning, the Fancher and Aiken parties had not been brutally slaughtered. Instead, their blood had been "spilt upon the ground, that the smoke thereof might ascend to heaven as an offering for their sins; and the smoking incense would atone for their sins, whereas, if such is not the case, they will stick to them and remain upon them in the spirit world," as Young had once explained. This was not murder: it was salvation.[48]

At Fort Bridger, Kane found a veneer of authority to continue his peace mission in portly Alfred Cumming, Utah's new governor. It was no doubt the persistent Kane who suggested that Cumming visit Great Salt Lake City and requested Young's approval on 17 March when he delivered Johnston's rejection of provisions. Cumming, in turn, knew that he was crowding the outer limit of his authority on 22 March when he asked Kane to give up his intention of returning home and authorized him to keep his peace quest alive. While recognizing his responsibility to

46. "Letter from the Army of Utah," 1 June 1858, *San Francisco Daily Evening Bulletin*, 21 July 1858, 3.

47. Larson and Larson, *Diary of Charles Lowell Walker*, 4 April 1858, 1:28.

48. Young, "Discourse," 21 September 1856, *Deseret News*, 1 October 1856, 6:236.\

enforce unconditional submission to the authority of the United States, he justified this request to "prevent the unnecessary effusion of blood," expressing special concern for the women and children.[49]

With high hopes, Kane and his servant rode out on 25 March to meet Nauvoo Legion general William H. Kimball and other military leaders at Quaken Aspen Spring. He would not be disappointed. Six months before, Young had told Captain Van Vliet that if a new governor arrived in Salt Lake, he would put him in a carriage and send him packing. Now he sent word that Utah would welcome its new governor. But he made clear through General Kimball, son of Mormon leader Heber C. Kimball, that the Nauvoo Legion, acting as the Utah Militia, must escort the governor into the Mormon capital, not the U.S. Army.

Kane accepted this stipulation on Cumming's behalf, but the commander of U.S. forces at Fort Bridger did not applaud such acquiescence. The condition clashed with his own responsibility to conduct Cumming to Great Salt Lake City and safeguard federal officers in a territory in armed rebellion against the United States. It also violated his orders to conform to the governor's wishes in all cases where "your military judgment and prudence do not forbid."[50] Johnston was not taken in by the sudden change from the military arm of God's Kingdom to the militia of Utah Territory, but he could do little more than voice his concern. And the switch in banners from the Kingdom's flag to Old Glory under which Cumming would enter the Mormon stronghold did not signify an end to the struggle between the United States and its theocratic territory, only that it would continue in less dangerous spheres.

For his part, Kane was ecstatic. Centered only on his own role in the war, after returning to Fort Bridger the ardent peacemaker wrote on 28 March, "And now behold my first Sunday—the first time since I embraced this work, that I have heard the Order to Halt & Stand at Ease." He had done his utmost and successfully made arrangements "for *introducing Governor C. into the Valley.*" Having performed his role, the ardent peacemaker had the feeling that it was now safe to "leave the future to a less finite Power."[51] But one man with greater authority

---

49. Cumming to Kane, 22 March 1858, in Hafen and Hafen, *Utah Expedition*, 273, 74.
50. Buchanan, *Utah Expedition*, 7–9.
51. Kane, Diary, 28 March 1858, in Hafen and Hafen, *Utah Expedition*, 280.

than Kane, if not the Almighty, was about to upstage both him and Cumming.

As the pair prepared to head for Salt Lake, President Buchanan decided to give Young and his followers a last chance to avoid the consequences of their defiance. He appointed two commissioners to go to Utah and explain to its people "the views and purposes of the Government, and to endeavor to recall them to a sense of their duty and to submission to the laws." He did not authorize them to investigate past wrongs, real or imagined, or to negotiate. Instead, he told them to make a straightforward, take-it-or-leave-it deal based squarely on the position he had taken from the beginning. Buchanan's offer to Mormon leaders: Obey the law and get a pardon; refuse and the U.S. Army would impose it and they would face trial for treason and other crimes.[52]

Buchanan acted at the behest of Utah delegate John M. Bernhisel, Texas senator Sam Houston, and Congress, not Kane or Cumming. The true if unheralded instigator of his decision was thirty-seven-year-old Seth Blair, the former U.S. attorney for Utah Territory, who had served with Houston during the Texas Revolution and enjoyed a close relationship with him. On Houston's recommendation, President Fillmore in 1850 had named Blair as one of the four Mormons, including Young, he appointed to posts in Utah's new territorial government. In December 1857, Blair had written to Houston detailing Mormon grievances and appealing for his help. In response, Houston became the faith's champion in Congress. He blocked the president's request for new regiments and advised him instead to appoint a commission to settle the conflict.

To deliver his ultimatum, Buchanan named senator-elect and former Kentucky governor Lazarus W. Powell and the renowned Texas Ranger captain Ben McCulloch, a compatriot of Blair who had fought under Houston at the Battle of San Jacinto. Both men had been "bred up" in Dyer County, Tennessee, according to Blair, and both were among the volunteers from Tennessee who had joined Houston during the Texas Revolution.[53] McCulloch's appointment may have reflected Blair's Texas connections.

52. Cass to Cumming, 7 April 1858, ibid., 328.
53. Blair, Reminiscences and Journals, 1851–1868, LDS Archives.

On 6 April, Buchanan signed a proclamation in which he spelled out his reasons for sending troops to Utah. They included driving federal officials from the territory, unlawful violence, and "a strange system of terrorism" that prevented inhabitants from expressing a favorable opinion about the government or obeying its laws. Warning against any belief that his action was "a crusade against your religion," he said the Mormon rebellion was without just cause, reason, or excuse. "Human wisdom never devised a political system which bestowed more blessings or imposed lighter burdens than the government of the United States in its operation upon the Territories," he stated.[54]

At the same time, "to save the effusion of blood," he offered Utah inhabitants who submitted to the law a free pardon for the seditions and treasons they had committed but warned those who persisted in the rebellion to anticipate no further clemency. The one condition that Young most wanted, the withdrawal of U.S. troops, Buchanan refused to grant. Instead he declared that the U.S. soldiers already in Utah and those who would come in the future would not be withdrawn "until the inhabitants of that Territory shall manifest a proper sense of the duty which they owe to this government."[55]

The commissioners who bore this word were both highly qualified but enjoyed no authority to use their diplomatic skills in negotiations. Their sole purpose, Secretary of War John B. Floyd instructed, was to convince the people of Utah that it was in their interest "to submit promptly and peaceably to the Constitution and laws of the United States." They could repeat Buchanan's assurance that the army's movement had no relation to their religious beliefs. But they were not authorized to enter into any treaty or agreement. With his directive, Floyd included copies of the president's December letters to Kane. While Buchanan did not recognize Kane as a government agent, he said, "He may render you essential service in accomplishing the object of your mission," if they found him still in Utah.[56]

54. James Buchanan, "Proclamation," 6 April 1858, in Hafen and Hafen, *Utah Expedition*, 332–37.

55. Ibid.

56. Floyd to Powell and McCulloch, 12 April 1858, in Floyd, *Annual Report, 1858*, 160–62.

It would take more than seven weeks for the news of all these developments to reach Cumming and Kane. And in that time, the self-important pair of peacemakers would undermine the president's uncompromising position and rescue Young's followers from their leader's misjudgments.

On his way east from Los Angeles, merchant Albert Gilbert was surprised to find preparations under way at Salt Lake "for the expected arrival of Governor Cumming." At Echo Canyon, he met the governor and members of his military escort "who were paying him every attention in his power." Earlier in his journey, he had seen a less pleasant sight. At Mountain Meadows, the ground "was strewn with human skulls and bones of all sizes, whilst the place was covered in every direction with locks and tresses of women's hair." It caused "a cold shudder" to pass through his whole frame.[57]

On the day before Buchanan signed his proclamation, Kane and Cumming, each with a black servant, boarded a carriage at Camp Scott and began the mission that would restore Mormon confidence and lead to more than thirty years of ongoing struggle in the courts and Congress. Porter Rockwell and his mounted party met them just on the perimeter of the army post and escorted them to the Quaken Aspen Spring headwaters of the Colorado River. There they met their official military escort, Nauvoo Legion general William H. Kimball and thirty picked men in full uniform aboard magnificent horses, and received a formal salute in recognition of Cumming's station.

Although no one from Utah had yet met the new governor, the extravagant reception the Mormons staged for Cumming suggests that they had gained considerable insight into the Georgian's character from Thomas L. Kane. At the first night's stop at Yellow Creek, the governor said "he expected to get a miserable meal, but Gen. Kimball had made the most complete arrangements," which were overseen by David Candland, whom Cumming praised as "a superb cook."[58] After completing the "plentiful repast," the governor reviewed 150 Nauvoo Legionnaires: all along the trail, Mormon soldiers dutifully saluted the new governor. "At one point a mock attempt was made to arrest him,"

57. "Highly Important from Utah," New York Times, 24 May 1858.

58. Brigham Young Manuscript History, quoted in Journal History, 13 April 1858, LDS Archives.

historian H. H. Bancroft reported, but Colonel Kimball dutifully rescued his charge.[59]

When Kimball told Cumming that they would pass through Echo Canyon at night, the governor figured "it was with the object of concealing the barricades and other defenses." But he was "agreeably surprised." As they approached the highest bluffs at the canyon's mouth, they met a stunning light show as huge bonfires, "from the base to the summit" of the canyon's red rock walls, illuminated the massive corridor through the Wasatch Mountains to Salt Lake Valley. As Cumming understood, the dazzling avenue of light that illumined "the snow-covered mountains" was a spectacular welcome. It symbolized that the scenic gateway to Zion for thousands of Mormon emigrants was also open to him, if not to the U.S. Army.[60] This was pointed up by the military outposts along the trail, where guards smartly saluted Utah's new head of state. It was also carefully planned in advance, as was everything else that followed. Young had already instructed the Council of Twelve, "If Gov Cummings Comes into the City I do not want any man to go and see him without a permit."[61]

With the main entry to Great Salt Lake from the east still snowbound, the governor and his escort followed the Weber River route to approach the city from the north. Everywhere he met the "respectful attentions" due a federal officer. Yet he also found northern Utah settlements largely vacated by the move south. At Warm Springs, north of Salt Lake, municipal officials were lined up to honor him "with a formal and respectful attention," he wrote Colonel Johnston. Salt Lake mayor A. O. Smoot took a seat in Cumming's carriage and escorted him to his lodgings in the home of William Staines, where Kane had stayed on arriving in the city. As soon as he had recovered, Young paid him a "visit of ceremony" and offered to provide any facilities Cumming needed to do his job.[62]

With these promising omens, Cumming got some bad news, also carefully planned and timed for his arrival. William H. Hooper, acting Utah

59. Bancroft, *History of Utah*, 526.
60. Cumming to Cass, 2 May 1858, in Hafen and Hafen, *Utah Expedition*, 304–14.
61. Kenney, *Wilford Woodruff's Journal*, 15 April 1858, 5:305.
62. Cumming to Johnston, 15 April 1858, in Floyd, *Annual Report, 1858*, 72, 73.

secretary of state under an illegal appointment by Young, charged that Garland Hurt had incited the Uinta Valley Indians to join the "assault upon the Mormons in the spring." In a separate letter, Hooper accused Hurt of promoting unrest among the Utes at his Spanish Fork Indian farm and of leaving his duties without cause after Young had promised to provide Hurt with "a comfortable carriage and safe escort to the troops." Evidence now confirms Hurt's own account of his escape and makes it likely that Young's letter was backdated after Hurt had left.[63]

Cumming had known Hurt at Camp Scott and probably shared the high opinion of him held even by many Mormons, if not by Young. Congress in 1857 had separated the offices of governor and Indian superintendent in the territories, so he had no official connection with the agent. But he knew Hurt had volunteered to watch for a reported Mormon attempt to intercept Marcy at the Green River crossing on his way back from New Mexico. To do this, he had lived in Ute Indian camps, near present-day Vernal, Utah, and survived for two months mainly on a diet of roots.

Far more serious was the next allegation, also timed for Cumming's arrival. To obtain cattle for the army, the secretary pro tem charged that a party of "soldiers" from Fort Bridger had conspired with mountaineer John W. Powell to incite the Shoshone and Bannock raid on Fort Limhi that killed two missionaries, wounded five, and seized the settlement's cattle. In an inflammatory story on 14 April, the church-owned *Deseret News* reported that "soldiers from Col. Johnston's camp" had caused the raid and said it had verified rumors that "our enemies have offered the Indians $150 for every Mormon they delivered to them." The following day, Salmon River Mission president Thomas S. Smith added further incriminating details in a sworn affidavit before the Salt Lake County probate court.[64]

The accusations against Hurt were contrived on their face and could be easily refuted. But the charge that the U.S. Army had instigated the attack on Fort Limhi struck home. Johnston had authorized civilians, the

63. For Hurt's account of his escape, see Buchanan, *Utah Expedition*, 205–207. See also Johnson, Report to Wells, UTMR, which complements Hurt's story, discrediting both Hooper's letter and Young's backdated assurance of safety.

64. Hooper to Cumming, 13 April 1858, in Buchanan, *Utah Expedition*, 74, 75; "Another Murder by Indians," *Deseret News*, 14 April 1858, 35; Smith, Affidavit, 15 April 1858, BYC.

unpredictable Benjamin F. Ficklin and his party, to contract to purchase cattle without army supervision, and Cumming had given him letters of recommendation to John Owen in Bitterroot Valley and Father Adrian Hoecken at St. Ignatius Mission. They could not be readily dismissed.

As all of this was going on at Salt Lake, the one who had caused the stir was busily composing his report at Fort Bridger. Ficklin and Powell, the now-notorious mountaineer, had arrived there on 11 April, four days after Cumming left for Salt Lake. If they had provoked the attack that changed the course of Mormon history, they had little to show for it. Mountaineers with cattle in the mountainous northern region were too afraid of the Mormons to deliver them to Fort Bridger, while the giant Bannock chief who led the attack had shown them why Hudson's Bay trader Richard Grant had named him Le Grand Coquin. "The Big Rogue" decided to keep the animals for himself. Ficklin did deliver about thirty horses, probably from the mission.[65]

What happened after these charges landed at Camp Scott gave the appearance of a cover-up. The planned campaign to defeat Johnston and the U.S. Army on the field of public opinion, embarrass Cumming, and discredit Hurt and the new Utah superintendent of Indian affairs, Jacob Forney, met an equally well-orchestrated defense and counterattack.

Hurt indignantly denied the allegations and fired back. He charged the Mormons with tampering with the Indians and challenged Hooper's authority to pose as Utah secretary. Ficklin had prudently failed to mention the Fort Limhi raid in his report, written before he was accused, but he revealed in a sworn affidavit that he knew all about it. He said the Mormons had caused the attack by providing arms and ammunition to the Nez Percés, which angered the Bannocks. Powell admitted that he was on the scene, as Thomas S. Smith charged, but swore he had warned the mission about the attack and was not involved in it himself.

Powell claimed that after the Nez Percés' raid on their horses, six of the Bannocks "determined to revenge themselves upon the Mormons" and asked for his help. Powell insisted that he tried to discourage the assault and warned the warriors that they "were fools to go off only six in number to attack so large a number of Mormons; they would all be

65. John W. Powell is remembered in Montana today in the names of Mount Powell and Powell County.

killed. They, however, said they were not afraid; that Mormon bullets could not hit them; and that the Mormons were cowards, squaws, and afraid to fight, and so they started off." Powell said the warriors killed two Mormon teamsters, burned their wagons, and "then charged up onto the herd, which was guarded by a large party of Mormons, and sounded the war-whoop." The terrified Mormons fled to the fort, firing only one pistol shot, while the Indians "drove off the herd, numbering some 400 head of cattle and about 60 head of horses." Another mountaineer, the unfortunately named Craven Jackson, swore that the Bannocks had told him the Mormons brought the raid on themselves by supplying ammunition to the Nez Percés while denying it to the Bannocks.[66]

Johnston's investigation showed that "no act of hostility or annoyance has been committed on Salmon River or any other place by the Indians in consequence of instigations of any one connected with this army." He also singled out Hurt for having "faithfully discharged his duty as agent" and given only good advice to the Indians. The colonel sent copies of these affidavits and other documents to U.S. Army headquarters, including letters by Mormon enemies W. M. F. Magraw and James Bridger, who came to his defense.[67] That ended it. Except not quite.

The colonel also showed that he was no novice when it came to defending his honor on the field of public opinion. He was aware that certain members of his command acted as covert (or so they thought) correspondents for major eastern newspapers, sending them stories under aliases, and he knew most of them. The colonel saw to it that they received information about his inquiry that put him and the army in the best light and cleared those charged with wrongdoing.

More innocence was found at Salt Lake, where Cumming examined the records of the supreme and district courts and reported them "as being perfect and uninjured." This would no doubt be welcome "information to those who have entertained any impression to the contrary," he added, tongue in cheek. As he knew, this information would discredit

66. "Is It Peace or War?" *New York Times*, 12 June 1858.

67. For the sources referred to above, see in Floyd, *Annual Report, 1858*, 68–84; and "The Mormon and Indian Fight at Salmon River Settlement," 15 April 1858, *New-York Times*, 12 June 1858. For more on the cover-up and the probability that Ficklin touched off the attack, see Bigler, *Fort Limhi*, 239–58 and 300–11.

Judge George P. Stiles, who had been taken in by the choreographed pretense to burn the records, and undoubtedly would embarrass Buchanan and others who had taken Stiles's word for it.[68]

As one report observed, Alfred Cumming's trip from Camp Scott to Salt Lake had been "one grand ovation of loyalty and profession of respect for the person of the chief representative of the Government." Only later did Cumming discover "how the Mormon leaders had imposed upon him and amused themselves with his credulity, and he was ever afterwards unpleasantly reticent when the affair was mentioned."[69] What Cumming apparently never grasped was the depth of the contempt in which the Mormon leaders and even Thomas L. Kane held him. As for the "formal and respectful" greeting the new governor received at Warm Springs, Apostle George A. Smith said that city officials had gone out "to meet the animal, styled Gov. Cumming." On delivering his charge to Young, Kane "told him he had caught the fish, now you can cook him as you have a mind to." Smith's first impression was that Cumming was a "toper"—a drunk—but on closer examination, he concluded that the governor was "a moderate drinker and a hearty eater," who Smith thought "had more chops than brains." As historian Norman F. Furniss concluded, "in spite of the surface appearance of good will, the Mormons looked at Cumming as only another Gentile come to destroy their religious and political freedom."[70]

On 24 April, Cumming received reports that a number of inhabitants who wanted to get away had been "unlawfully restrained of their liberty" and were afraid to leave Utah. He at once postponed a planned visit to Utah County and took "the most energetic measures to ascertain the truth or falsehood of the statements." What the new governor did not know was that Young had already ordered that if Cumming came into the city, he did "not want any man to go and see him without a permit." Cumming requested that a notice be read in his presence before the Sunday gathering the next day in the Salt Lake Temple. In it, he assumed "the protection of all such persons, if any there be," and

68. Cumming to Cass, 2 May 1858, in Floyd, *Annual Report, 1858*, 91–97.

69. Stenhouse, *Rocky Mountain Saints*, 389–90.

70. Journal History, 12 and 13 April 1858, LDS Archives; and Furniss, *Mormon Conflict*, 184–85.

requested that they communicate to him their names and places of residence, "under seal."[71]

Young did better than that. Before a full house of as many as four thousand believers, he introduced Cumming as the governor of Utah Territory and invited him to make the announcement himself and address the congregation. The governor took the stand and told the gathered faithful he had come to uphold the national sovereignty that he had sworn "to exact an unconditional submission on their parts to the dictates of the law."[72] Assuming that church women disliked polygamy, Cumming appealed "to the Women as he called them to back him up [and] said that he depended on them for support and many such strange things."[73] The congregation listened respectfully for about thirty-five minutes until Cumming asked if anyone had a comment or question.

Suddenly, "the wildest uproar ensued." Powerful speakers harangued Cumming on Mormon grievances, past and present, "exhibiting more frenzy than I had expected to witness among a people, who habitually exercise great self control," he told Secretary of State Lewis Cass. To loud cheers, Gilbert Clements shouted the objections they had to his being "our Gov while backed up by armed force." It was a perfect bedlam, one spectator said. "Send home your troops," the Irishman cried. Cumming replied that "he would not hang as a rag on our garments against our will," another said, but the governor was shouted down and hissed. Voices called out, "Send your soldiers back." Apostle John Taylor reportedly said, "We never intend to be yoked up with Gentiles again; no, never, world without end, for their dominion is sealed."[74] It all seemed spontaneous.

With Kane looking on, Cumming received the verbal baptism that never failed to intimidate the uninitiated. A similar reaction from a Mormon congregation had frightened Utah's first chief justice, Perry E. Brocchus, out of the territory in 1851. Like the earlier eruption, what

71. Kenney, *Wilford Woodruff's Journal*, 5:305; Cumming to Cass, 2 May 1858, in Hafen and Hafen, *Utah Expedition*, 304–14.

72. Ibid.

73. Brooks, *On the Mormon Frontier*, 2:658.

74. Cumming to Cass, 2 May 1858, in Floyd, *Annual Report*; Brooks, *On the Mormon Frontier*, 657–58; Gove, *Utah Expedition*, 289–91.

happened was deliberately planned and orchestrated, but appeared voluntary and impulsive.

Cumming later described the near-riot as an "occasion of intense interest," but it was much more than that. Not a brave man to start with, the overweight bureaucrat was unnerved by the experience. He had seen where the true power lay and realized how impotent and dangerous his position was. His verbal baptism had been a career-changing experience. Never again would he adopt a posture of authority in the territory. From that day forward, to the profound disgust of other federal officers, he was governor in name only and served the interests of the Mormon theocracy as decided by Brigham Young. And in return, it was Young who protected him and his wife, not the U.S. Army.

"He had his weaknesses and was full of them," Young later said of his hapless successor, who "understood that if he did not do right, and step forward and protect the innocent, all I had to do was to crook my little finger. He knew a host could be marshaled in a night that would have swept them out of existence." He told Cumming, "Toe the line, and mark by the law, and do right or I shall crook my little finger, and you know what will come then."[75] Perhaps this was simply more bluster, but events revealed that Brigham Young was determined to protect the guilty, not the innocent.

Cumming claimed that only fifty-six men, thirty-three women, and seventy-one children accepted his offer of "protection and assistance in proceeding to the States," and most were English converts who wanted to "leave the congregation from a desire to improve their circumstances."[76] Confirming this reason was the condition of the party that arrived at Fort Bridger in mid-May "in almost a state of nudity," Captain Gove said. None of its twenty-nine members had shoes, he noted, but "they were all clothed in a day after their arrival" by kindhearted soldiers who gave them "at least $200 in clothes and money." Their condition only made the men of his command more eager to avenge their suffering and "relieve those who may desire it from abiding bondage and poverty," the captain said. Another party of about 150 arrived several days later in

75. Van Wagoner, *Complete Discourses of Brigham Young*, 7 July 1861, 5:1882.
76. Hafen and Hafen, *Utah Expedition*, 307–308.

better condition, the captain added: "they came with teams, with good supplies of eggs and the like."[77]

One of the first party, Samuel Ramsden, an English survivor of the 1856 handcart disaster, possibly put his finger on why so few women took advantage of the opportunity Cumming offered to escape from Utah. He said that one of Milo Andrus's many wives had questioned the righteousness of the marriage dogma and planned to leave. Andrus found out and asked Young what to do, whereupon Young reportedly replied that "the only way to save the sister's soul was to cut her throat." She fell on her knees and begged for her life, he said, but Andrus took her by her hair and "while she was thus on her knees cut her throat from ear to ear, and held her with that grasp until her body ceased quivering." True or not, the widely circulated story of the early doctrine of blood atonement was believable to those who heard it and surely discouraged all but the bravest women from taking Cumming's promise of protection.[78]

Members of another party that month said that thousands did not want to go south but were compelled to. Women were "forced from their husbands and driven from the city at the point of the bayonet," some said. A Mr. Yancy from Tennessee said that his wife was taken from him against his will and "marched off south while Governor Cumming was in Salt Lake City," Gove wrote.[79] On 16 May, Cumming reached Camp Scott with several wagons filled with men and women. Some of them said that Young laughed his successor to scorn and declared the new governor "unfit to take care of even himself, let alone the people of a territory," according to Captain Albert Tracy. Another column of dissenters entered the army post ten days later. "Wagons, carts, oxen, ponies, people and all—a sad and poverty stricken lot—the whole of them," Tracy said.[80]

Peter K. Dotson, Utah's new federal marshal, cast further doubt on the credibility of Cumming's promise of protection for those who wanted to leave Utah. Joseph Convis, a non-Mormon Frenchman whom Dotson had met during an early stay in Salt Lake, told the marshal that

77. Gove, *Utah Expedition*, 283–84.

78. Ibid. As noted, the doctrine of blood atonement was intended to save sinners, not punish them. It is no longer believed or practiced in the LDS Church.

79. Ibid., 284–85.

80. Alter and Dwyer, "Utah War Journal," 16, 24, and 26 May 1858, 12–13.

"after the arrival of Governor Cumming in Salt Lake City, he tried at two different times to obtain an interview with him, but was prevented from approaching the house by a guard placed around it for this purpose, in charge of Howard Egan." Convis said he was only one of a "great many of the people" who had been prevented from seeing Cumming "unless they obtained the permission of Brigham Young."[81]

More welcome than Zion's disillusioned or even supply trains that spring was the express rider who arrived at Fort Bridger on 12 May with good news for Colonel Albert Sidney Johnston. For his judicious and effective leadership of U.S. forces under difficult and challenging conditions, the president had approved his brevet promotion to brigadier general. Tempering this deserved recognition, however, was disappointing news. When the strengthened Utah Army fought its way through Echo Canyon that spring, as expected, Johnston would serve under a new commander, one more senior and battle-tested than he—General William S. Harney, the original commander of the Utah Army. Among his exploits, Harney had won distinction in commanding the lead brigade of infantry and dragoons at the Battle of Cerro Gordo in 1847.

Johnston did not protest this move, but after he had established a new post west of Utah Lake, some thirty-six miles from both Great Salt Lake and Provo, he would request approval to rejoin his regiment or go on a four-month furlough with approval to extend it. The dignified officer had had "no relaxation from duty, not for a day, for more than nine years," he said.[82] By then, Young had accepted President Buchanan's conditions to receive a pardon, and the change in command had been canceled.

In the meantime, the new governor began his delayed trip to Utah County, where Young and other leaders had gone as an example to others to follow the mass flight from northern Utah settlements. On 6 May, he met a former Salmon River Indian missionary at Spanish Fork. Milton Hammond had abandoned the colony at Fort Limhi that spring and was now moving his family in the rain from their home in Ogden with barely one yoke of oxen and an overloaded wagon. Alfred Cumming

81. Dotson to Eckels, 27 April 1858, *New-York Times*, 11 June 1858, 1.
82. Johnston to Irvin McDowell, 8 July 1858, in Floyd, *Annual Report, 1858*, 123.

had not made a favorable impression on the sturdy New Yorker, who thought "he resembles a whiskey barrel."[83]

Hammond moved on to Willow Spring, north of Nephi, where he found a herder's shack and a mud corral near the spot where Porter Rockwell and companions had shot to death two Aiken party members the previous November. There he planted some grain and constructed a crude shelter "by digging into the bank south of the spring and covering it with brush." Nearly four weeks later, electrifying news arrived. "The general government has sent an investigating committee to examine into the Utah difficulty," Hammond said. They had met with Brigham Young and "come to his terms." Consequently, he went on, the Mormons, "being directed by our Heavenly Father," had gained the victory "over the greatest nation (according to their own statements) on earth."[84]

Contrary to Hammond's joyful appraisal, President Buchanan had not dispatched the commissioners to investigate, negotiate, or review past grievances, real and imagined. He sent them to present the conditions to obtain a pardon for treason in a last-ditch attempt to avoid bloodshed. Moreover, Brigham Young's unqualified acceptance of them would not signify a victory over the greatest nation on earth. It marked instead the beginning of the end for Young's vision to establish the Kingdom of God as a sovereign state in the American West, to initiate Christ's return to universal rule within the lifespan of believers of that day.

83. Hammond, *Journal Kept by Milton D. Hammond*, 6 May 1858, USHS.
84. Ibid., 15 June 1858.

CHAPTER 13

The Fall of Sebastopol

We are firmly impressed with the belief that the presence of
the army here, and the large additional force that had been
ordered to this Territory, were the chief inducements that
caused the Mormons to abandon the idea of resisting the
authority of the United States. A less decisive policy would
probably have resulted in a long, bloody, and expensive war.

—Lazarus W. Powell and Ben McCulloch, 3 July 1858

Captain Jesse Gove was on outpost duty when he heard "the sweet and harmonious strains" of the regimental band "through the stillness of the night," to honor important visitors at Fort Bridger. Captain Albert Tracy also listened as the Tenth Infantry musicians serenaded "these worthies" with the song his wife, Sarah, sang so beautifully—"When the Swallows Homeward Fly." As both men knew, the distinguished visitors were the commissioners whom President Buchanan had sent to give Brigham Young a last chance to avoid bloodshed.[1]

Lazarus W. Powell of Kentucky and the celebrated Texas Ranger Ben McCulloch arrived at Camp Scott on 29 May, completing their trip from Fort Leavenworth in thirty-five days. If they failed to move at the expected speed of thirty-five miles a day, they at least traveled in a style befitting representatives of the president and seldom enjoyed by overland emigrants. They covered the one thousand miles in five new ambulances with sleeping accommodations, purchased for their comfort in St. Louis, each drawn by four mules. Their party numbered a

---

1. Gove, *Utah Expedition*, 170; Alter and Dwyer, "Utah War Journal," 29 May 1858.

sergeant and five dragoons, five armed teamsters, a wagon master, and a guide to keep them on the road already made plain by untold thousands of wagons.

At Fort Bridger, the commissioners met Alfred Cumming, who had left Great Salt Lake with Thomas Kane on 12 May and arrived there three days later, escorted by Howard Egan and several other Mormon plainsmen. The new governor had remained to meet Buchanan's emissaries, while Kane continued to Philadelphia, accompanied by his Mormon lifeguards.

Coming off outpost duty, Captain Gove, the secret (or so he thought) *New York Herald* reporter, washed up and hurried to General Albert S. Johnston's tent to call on the commissioners. He described former Kentucky governor Powell as "a large portly man, and a fine gentleman in his appearance." The Texan, McCulloch, made a stronger impression. He is "a substantial plain spoken man, and as true as steel," Gove said. Both were "fully converted to the policy of the army and are on our side." The side he referred to did not include Cumming, who seemed to believe that the commissioners undercut his own importance, a feeling probably shared by Kane as well.[2] If so, the governor may have had good cause to fear that their work might reveal he had already made concessions that went beyond the president's policy and exceeded his own authority.

In meetings at Camp Scott, Cumming advocated Young's interest to keep the army away and make his capitulation appear to his people as a Mormon victory. Ten days before the commissioners arrived, Young, who often saw great portents in his night visions, had a strange dream, which George A. Smith dutifully recorded the next day. In it, Governor Cumming came to the Lion of the Lord and "appeared exceedingly friendly, and said to Prest. Young we must be united, we must act on concert; and commenced undressing himself to go to bed with him."[3] Acting more like a fox than a lion, Young had used a clever combination of flattery and intimidation to win over the pliable Georgian, who figuratively climbed into bed with his powerful rival for power and oblig-

2. Gove, *Utah Expedition*, 170.

3. Historian's Office Journal, 20 May 1858, Historical Department, Journals 1844–1990, CR 100 1, LDS Archives, cited in Quinn, *Same-Sex Dynamics*, 87.

ingly spent the rest of his term as Utah's symbolic executive diligently serving Mormon interests.

Cumming tried to persuade the commissioners and Johnston that there was no need for U.S. troops to enter Salt Lake Valley. Mormon military forces had been disbanded, he argued, except for a few men under his own control. But the commissioners knew better and reported to Washington that Mormon leaders had misinformed the governor. Moreover, they believed that the presence of the U.S. Army and the additional forces ordered to Utah would be the chief inducement for its people "to submit quietly and peaceably to the civil authorities," if they did so at all.[4]

To a question probably put to him by the governor, Johnston said that he could not fix the date he would advance because it depended on the arrival of supplies, animals, and reinforcements from Fort Leavenworth and New Mexico. But he should be "well prepared to execute the orders of the government between the 15th and 20th instant," he said, which meant in about two to three weeks.[5] At the same time, the general made clear, conditions he could not foresee would govern when he marched, not whether Mormon leaders took Buchanan's offer. Under the orders he had been given, he would enter Mormon settlements peacefully or, if not, shoot his way in. During the Camp Scott meetings, to which Gove had some access, Cumming was "highly indignant" at the feelings of the commissioners toward "his people."[6]

Commissioners Powell and McCulloch left Camp Scott on 2 June for Salt Lake Valley, escorted by their original party of six soldiers and civilian teamsters, plus the adventurous Benjamin F. Ficklin of Fort Limhi notoriety, who always succeeded in placing himself where the action was. They had expected Cumming to accompany them, but after they pulled out, he withdrew from the party and went back. He and his wife, Elizabeth, left the next day with their furniture; Jacob Forney, the superintendent of Indian affairs; and David A. Burr, the son of Surveyor General David H. Burr. If the few Mormon soldiers Cumming imagined to be under his orders escorted him into the city, that might

4. Powell and McCulloch to Floyd, 1 June 1858, in Floyd, *Annual Report, 1858,* 165–67.
5. Johnston to Irvin McDowell, 4 June 1858, ibid.
6. Gove, *Utah Expedition,* 157–58, 170.

explain why he refused to permit James Simonton, the *New York Times* correspondent, to accompany him. It also displayed his newfound allegiance, consistent with the peace-at-any-price policy he would cling to over the next three years.

On 7 June, the commissioners reached Great Salt Lake and sent word of their coming and their mission to Young, who was then at Provo. On Tuesday evening, Young sent three representatives with word that "the people of the Territory" wanted the meeting to take place. On that same day, Sixth Infantry major William Hoffman reached Fort Bridger from Fort Leavenworth earlier than expected, with supplies, mules, and reinforcements. At Great Salt Lake, Young's spokesmen notified the commissioners on Wednesday that he and his top leaders would be in the city Thursday evening, ready to meet with them the next morning, 11 June. Also on Friday, Colonel William W. Loring and Captain Randolph Marcy arrived at Fort Bridger with some nine hundred mules and additional reinforcements from New Mexico, also days ahead of schedule.

Sooner than he had predicted, the newly breveted brigadier general had the men, supplies, and animals he needed. For seven months, Johnston and some fifteen hundred men and their civilian dependents had been stuck in the snow at Bridger's trading post, preparing for the time they would make their adversaries suffer for so many days of short rations and cold nights on guard duty. "It will be a happy change to us all," rejoiced Captain Gove, but not everyone was as glad as he to say goodbye to his mountain home.[7] "It has been for us all the home we had for the time," observed Captain Tracy. "To view the long area of chimney stacks, roof-poles, and other relics and debris of a deserted camp, there rises in us a feeling really akin to sadness."[8]

On 13 June 1858, the Utah Expedition began its long-overdue advance to Salt Lake Valley, marching in three divisions over three consecutive days. Leading the parade were Cooke's Second Dragoons and Captain Barnard Bee's volunteer battalion. Waite's Fifth Infantry, Reno's heavy battery, and a company of the Seventh Infantry followed the horse soldiers the next day. Last to leave, on 15 June, were Colonel Loring's Fort Union battalion and Edmund B. Alexander's Tenth Infantry, ordered to

7. Ibid., 170.
8. Alter and Dwyer, "Utah War Journal," 15 June 1858.

push the supply trains along ahead of them and pick up stragglers. But not for long would Gove's regiment be relegated to the rear. It would be "placed in the van when we get to rough cañon country," Gove bragged, "since it is the best light troop in the army."[9] Reporter Simonton agreed: the Tenth Infantry was "the finest I have ever seen in the service," he said, "manifesting a perfection in military evolutions rarely attained and not to be surpassed."[10]

At Bear River, near present-day Evanston, Wyoming, Johnston paused on 16 June to concentrate his command and re-form it into an order of battle in case he ran into Mormon resistance in Echo Canyon. True to Gove's prediction, Tenth Infantry lieutenant colonel Charles F. Smith, one of the force's most aggressive officers, would lead the advance guard with one company from his regiment and two of the Second Dragoons. In a reversed order, the full Tenth Infantry regiment, Phelps's light battery, the Fifth Infantry, Loring's battalion, Bee's volunteers, and the Second Dragoons, acting as rear guard, would follow him. The battle-ready lineup would stand until the command entered Salt Lake Valley, Johnston ordered.

As his men prepared to fight, Johnston received news on 14 June that deprived one of the nation's most motivated armies of an opportunity to do so. Commissioners Powell and McCulloch sent word that Mormon leaders had accepted Buchanan's terms "and would make no resistance to the army of the United States in its march to the valley," or anywhere else. "Cheerfully" they had agreed to obey federal laws and allow civil officers to discharge their duties in the territory.[11] The unexpected capitulation gave little satisfaction to many in the army, who wanted to punish Young's followers for the embarrassment and discomfort they had imposed on the command. But it would be welcome news to most of those who had been uprooted from their homes and forced to move south.

To ease their fears and encourage the displaced Mormons to return home, the commissioners suggested that Johnston issue a proclamation stating that the army would respect their rights and property. The general assumed they would know that already, but he did so anyway. With

---

9. Gove, *Utah Expedition*, 310.

10. James W. Simonton, "Important from Utah," *New York Times*, 30 June 1858.

11. Powell and McCulloch to Johnston, in Floyd, *Annual Report, 1858*, 119, 120.

"great satisfaction," he assured Utah inhabitants that his command would molest no one in his rights or person. The U.S. Army, "always faithful to the obligations of duty," would be as ready "to assist and protect them as it was to oppose them" when it was believed they were resisting the laws of their country, he declared.[12] Cumming that same day got his own proclamation out, in which, in the name of President Buchanan, he pardoned all those who were willing to yield to the laws and authority of the United States "for all treasons and seditions heretofore committed" and urged people to go back home.

There was one person Cumming could never be conciliatory toward when it came to an imagined offense against his sense of self-importance. He had told Brigham Young that Johnston had pledged not to advance until he heard from the commissioners or from Cumming himself. Young told him afterward that he had learned that Johnston intended to march on 15 June without waiting for such word. The general would never do such a thing, Cumming said he replied. Later, he learned that Johnston did indeed intend to march sooner than he had planned. The general had violated his pledge, Cumming charged, and he demanded an explanation so that he would not be accused of duplicity.[13]

Stiffly Johnston dismissed the allegation. He had never meant to give his words the binding force of a promise that might conflict with military necessity, he said. Nor did he imagine at the time that either the commissioners or Cumming believed that he had. The president's instructions to the commissioners made it clear that the army should occupy Utah Territory, he went on. His own orders allowed him no discretion to wait, "unless reasons should be offered for so doing which should appear to me sufficiently cogent."[14] Johnston might have said that his pledge not to move until Cumming or the commissioners sent word would have encouraged Young to delay his advance, if not stall it indefinitely. It is also probable that Johnston's advance from Camp Scott to Bear River, which did not violate a promise not to march to the valley, was a deliberate action taken to produce the desired result—Mormon capitulation.

12. Johnston, "To the people of Utah," ibid., 121.
13. Cumming to Johnston, ibid., 114–15.
14. Johnston to Cumming, 19 June 1858, ibid., 116–17.

Young continued his war by proxy against Johnston and the army soon after, when his advocate, Governor Cumming, protested the army's occupancy of a location near Great Salt Lake or other populated site even before it occurred. He warned that if Johnston acted in opposition to his "solemn protest," it would lead to catastrophic consequences, "such as cannot be approved by our government."[15] Cumming's veiled threat had the ring of one that Kane had leveled against Johnston in the event that he should refuse to accept Young's offer of supplies. His orders, the general briefly replied, required him only to select suitable sites for posts that were healthy and provided good water, plenty of wood, and grass. It was not essential that a site be located near a city or settlement, he told Cumming, "nor would it be desirable to those in command."[16]

Johnston then revealed that he was no neophyte in dealing with self-important bureaucrats. Cumming had already shown that he preferred to have Mormon soldiers escort him rather than American troops. The general now invited him to make his loyalty public. He understood, he said, that the commissioners planned to meet him "between the two mountains."[17] This attractive spot, a few miles east of Great Salt Lake, now known as Mountain Dell, would be the army's final stop before it entered the city. Courteously Johnston invited the governor to join him and offer his suggestions on suitable places to camp in the valley. If Cumming accepted, he would enter the city with the army the next day and publicly identify with the president's position and the military force sent to impose it. If not, he would display his sympathy for the Mormon cause.

To their credit, the commissioners gave the army commander no similar problems. At the outset, they told Mormon leaders that they had no power to order the army, and in reports to Washington, they pointed up the value of Johnston's cooperation and support. Their first session with Young and his two counselors, Heber C. Kimball and Daniel H. Wells, was held late on 10 June after members of the church's First Presidency returned to the territorial capital from Utah Valley. The next morning, Buchanan's emissaries again met with the top leaders plus members of the Quorum of Twelve in the Council House at Great Salt Lake.

15. Cumming to Johnston, ibid., 115–16.
16. Johnston to Cumming, 19 June 1858, ibid., 116, 117.
17. Ibid., 116–17.\

Powell delivered Buchanan's message to those assembled. The president had sent the commissioners to induce the people of Utah "to submit quietly and peaceably to the authority of the United States," he said. They had no power to negotiate or enter into any compact or agreement. The president was determined to see that the authority of the United States was upheld and the laws of the nation were executed in the territory. To achieve this, Buchanan would send the Army of the United States to the valley of Great Salt Lake "in such numbers, at such times, and to such places in the valley or other parts of the Territory" as he considered necessary. Moreover, such military posts would be established in Utah as required to protect the emigration to and from the Pacific, to prevent Indian depredations, and to act as a *posse comitatus* if it became necessary. The president had ordered the army to enforce execution of the law and protect civil officials in the performance of their respective offices, Powell continued. If the inhabitants peacefully received the government's appointed officers and allowed them to do their jobs without interference, there would be no need for the army to enforce civil obedience. But if they resisted in any way the execution of "the laws of the United States within the Territory," he went on, "the president would employ the entire military power of the nation to enforce unconditional obedience to the Constitution and laws of the United States." The president asked nothing of them but to do their duty as good citizens, and his emissaries trusted that their mission would restore peace, quiet, and order in the territory.[18]

Prior to the commissioners' arrival, Young still clung to his visionary ideas and seemingly refused to accept what had happened since 1858 began. Even after he recognized Cumming as his successor, he acted as if he were still the legitimate governor of the territory. The Georgian was eager to win the people's favor, Young told John M. Bernhisel on 6 May, but they had not accepted him, as if they had any choice in the matter. If other federal officials followed, "they would have to chase up people to get any subjects," he said, and if the U.S. Army arrived, "it would find only blackened desolation." But he could see one way for Washington to get out of all the trouble that Buchanan had gotten it into.[19]

18. Ibid., 168–72.
19. Young to Bernhisel, 6 May 1858, BYC.

"Let the government admit us as a state in the union," he proposed to Bernhisel. "They cannot expect us to receive their officers much less their standing Army to enforce them upon us." Pretending that he was still the head of state, without Governor Cumming's knowledge Young ordered Utah's congressional delegate to submit the territory's petition for statehood, which had been withdrawn back in 1856. If it was approved, self-rule would place the theocracy in a strong position when the rest of the nation went to pieces, the Mormon leader said. The country could not endure in its present form, he prophesied, but was "liable to perish in an hour."[20] It went without saying that Young's solution would allow him under the theocracy's election system to serve as governor of the sovereign state or nation for life.

Now, as Young faced Buchanan's ultimatum, the Lion of the Lord backed squarely down. In meetings with the commissioners on 11 and 12 June, he grudgingly accepted the president's pardon while denying all the accusations against him, except for burning the army's supply trains and rustling its cattle. "The burning of a few U.S. wagons is but a small item," he blustered.[21] Young and the other Mormon leaders once again railed against the territory's former officials and rehearsed the well-known litany of old injuries and injustices that had been done them. But they promised the commissioners they would mount no resistance to officers of the United States, civil or military, who were exercising their duties in Utah.

While Young was "averse to the army coming to the valley of Salt Lake," the two presidential emissaries were pleased to report that the "people of this Territory had agreed to submit peaceably to the authority of the government."[22] The attitude of Mormon leaders, as expressed by Wilford Woodruff, hardly harmonized with this optimistic appraisal or held much hope for peace. Buchanan had "got into a bad scrape and wished to get out of it the best way he Could," the apostle said. The president wanted peace "because he is in the wrong & has met with a strong resistance by a strong high minded people in these mountains

---

20. Ibid.

21. Nibley, *Brigham Young*, 338.

22. Ibid. Quotes in the above paragraphs are from Powell and McCulloch to Floyd, 26 June 1858, in Floyd, *Annual Report, 1858*, 168–72.

which he did not expe[c]t," he wrote. "The Lord has herd our prayers and the President of the United States has been brought to a point whare he has been obliged to ask for peace."[23]

As Woodruff promised, the struggle between a theocracy and a republic would soon be renewed in less dangerous arenas. In the meantime, the president's emissaries headed south to encourage people to return to their homes north of the capital. Already, Nauvoo Legionnaire Henry Ballard said, "A great many was Apostatizing Daily from us."[24] The commissioners later reported that "discontented" Mormons in Provo said that they would have stayed home "had they not been threatened with forcible ejection. We were also told that at least one-third of the persons who had removed from their homes were compelled to do so." Their trip to Utah Valley convinced them that Mormon leaders had concentrated their followers "in order to exercise more immediate control over them, and thus prevent their secession from the church." Powell and McCulloch believed that once the people learned the military was in Utah to protect them, "all true, loyal, and patriotic citizens will rejoice that a portion of the army is in their midst." If a force large enough to protect the people were to be stationed in the territory, Young would never again be able to exercise such complete control over American citizens. They added, "The presence of the army here, and the large additional force that had been ordered to this Territory, were the chief inducements that caused the Mormons to abandon the idea of resisting the authority of the United States."[25]

The commissioners accurately estimated the territory's population at forty to fifty thousand, roughly half the number Young had claimed to justify his 1856 statehood bid, half of them foreign-born. Utah could not field an army of more than seven thousand men, they reported. Of this number, about one thousand were "fine horsemen, accustomed to the use of fire-arms."[26] The rest were industrious, hard-working citizens who would not make efficient soldiers without training in a regular army, they told Secretary of War John B. Floyd, who would find such information useful in the event of renewed hostilities.

23. Kenney, *Wilford Woodruff's* Journal, 5:195.
24. Ballard, Private Journal, 10 June 1858, USHS.
25. Powell and McCulloch to Floyd, 3 July 1858, in Floyd, *Annual Report, 1858*, 172–74.
26. Ibid., 173.

The large crowds that Powell and McCulloch addressed in Utah Valley seemed glad to know that peace had been restored, but Young and the other leaders were pointedly silent, and the harmony that seemed to prevail was little more than what historian Norman F. Furniss referred to as an armed truce.[27] Hosea Stout on 16 June saw the emissaries whom Buchanan had sent "to make peace on any terms which would save him from disgrace and his party from ruin." Powell's speech was "a miserable effort to eulogize Utah and Uncle Sam both and altogether was very shallow," he said, "& not much liked."[28] As his words foretold, U.S. troops would not find the road lined with cheering throngs waving American flags when they entered the Chief Stake of Zion. Instead, even nature rained on the army's parade.

At the Bear River crossing, a cold downpour welcomed the command with "one of the most disagreeable days I ever experienced," Gove said.[29] On 19 June, the army renewed its advance, following the 1846 Donner Trail from Bear River to the Needles, unusual spikes of stone on Yellow Creek, where it again met the Mormon Trail and camped. The next day the army passed Cache Cave, a hollow dome of rock on the hillside, where early mountaineers had stored furs and supplies, emigrants had inscribed their names, and General Wells had made his headquarters the fall before.

Here the column entered the twenty-three-mile corridor through the Wasatch Mountains that Captain Stewart Van Vliet had warned about. How many times the marchers forded Echo Creek was difficult to remember, Captain Tracy said, but the channel seemed to be a series of loops that undulated like a snake. That evening, the officer scrambled up the north wall of the canyon to sketch the army camped far below. As he looked down, the Tenth Infantry band struck up a tune, and he found out why the massive defile was called Echo Canyon. "The echoes among the rocks surpassed anything I ever heard, and are very sweet."[30]

Like a great snake itself, on 21 June the army wound its way through the red rock passage until it met abandoned Mormon fortifications within

27. Powell and McCulloch to Floyd, 12 June 1858, ibid., 171; Furniss, *Mormon Conflict*, 211.

28. Brooks, *On the Mormon Frontier*, 2:660.

29. Gove, *Utah Expedition*, 175.

30. Alter and Dwyer, "Utah War Journal," 20 June 1858.

three miles of the canyon mouth. With critical eyes, the professional soldiers, many of them veterans of the War with Mexico, studied Mormon defensive works in "the great bug bear Echo Canyon." Almost to a man, the officers pronounced the crude system of breastworks, ditches, and dam, as well as piles of rocks to roll down on unsuspecting invaders, unsuited to stop regular troops with artillery. Captain Gove made a detailed study of the flimsy fortifications and said they "could have been turned easily by 500 troops."[31]

To Captain Tracy, the designers of the fortifications appeared to believe that, "being regulars, we were necessarily to move in solid and compact bodies to whatever point was most convenient to them to resist us." Nor did they seem to realize that artillery would knock down the "corrals" of rocks "they had erected by the shelves and gulches and along the ridges of the cliffs," long before U.S. infantry could be brought under fire. The officers' inspection of the defenses "did but satisfy us the more thoroughly as to the opportunity we had lost," Tracy lamented. If the Tenth Infantry's second officer, Lieutenant Colonel C. F. Smith, a no-nonsense combat officer, had been in command, "we should undoubtedly have pushed on in the autumn," the captain concluded. It was an unspoken indictment of Colonel Alexander's leadership, or lack thereof.[32]

At the canyon mouth, the army passed abandoned habitations of Mormon soldiers, crude huts thatched with sage or straw, and camped on the Weber River, opposite the formations called Witch Rocks. On 23 June, the long column crossed the river near what is now Henefer and marched toward "the last grand range between ourselves and Salt Lake Valley." Following in the footsteps of thousands of pioneers over the prior decade, the marchers the next day reached the base of 7,420-foot Big Mountain, near Mormon Flat, which stood guard over the entry to Zion.

The four-mile climb to the divide was "long and toilsome," Tracy said, but the view from the top "was little less than magnificent": it reminded him of the vista from Mexico's Popocatepetl chain. The drop from the other side, however, was what emigrants usually referred to as "a jumping off place." To the delight of the infantrymen, a heavy

31. Gove, *Utah Expedition*, 176, 335–37.
32. Alter and Dwyer, "Utah War Journal," 21 June 1858.

dragoon wagon rolled out of control, taking with it the horse soldiers who were holding on to ropes trying to slow its descent, and crashed at the bottom, "a wreck and a ruin—tongue, wheels, mess chests, camp-kettles and all." There were no casualties, but the clouds of dust "well nigh brought us to suffocation."[33]

The expedition camped that night in Mountain Dell, which now lies beneath the Little Dell Reservoir, and made ready for its entry, long delayed for one side and long dreaded by the other, into the Mormon Sebastopol, Great Salt Lake City. Here General Johnston gave orders that any man, officer or enlisted, who left his place for any reason whatever as they passed through the city would be arrested at once. As he had probably anticipated, Governor Cumming did not arrive to join the army's entry.

Bugles sounded in the predawn darkness on 26 June to awaken the camp earlier than usual. At five A.M., more than two thousand soldiers of the United States began their march over Little Mountain and down the winding but gentle descent of Emigration Canyon to the territorial capital. Near the canyon's mouth, the columns halted to dress their lines and hear officers repeat Johnston's order to maintain the strictest discipline on penalty of instant arrest. As the troops passed the last bend of the canyon and arrived on a broad bench, suddenly the city "lay at our feet," Captain Tracy said. "We are surprised and refreshed with its general appearance of neatness and order."[34]

In columns of companies, with flags proudly flapping in the breeze, Smith led the color guard and the Tenth Infantry into the Mormon metropolis. They met "a spectacle not common" when U.S. soldiers paraded through an American city. Instead of the usual crowd "to gaze at or hang upon the heels of troops, no single living soul" was seen, Tracy said, except a few rough and sinister-looking men with "clubs in their hands, and pistols ready hanging from their belts," prepared to burn the city if the troops tried to occupy it. The rich strains of the band were wasted on "echoing, empty streets and tenements."[35]

The line of soldiers stretched for at least ten miles, correspondent James Simonton reported, and when the head of the column arrived at

33. Ibid., 25 June 1858.
34. Ibid., 26 June 1858.
35. Ibid.

their camp west of the Jordan River, about three miles south of what is today North Temple Street, he could look from the general's tent and see "the glistening bayonets, and the snowy wagon covers of the rear, still defiling from the mountains." The U.S. soldiers demonstrated "the most perfect decorum," he said, and manifested not the least symptom of their feelings "towards the people who had kept them freezing on Green River, during a long and comfortless winter."[36]

Their resentment burst forth the next day when Nauvoo Legion major Seth Blair, the designer of the Echo Canyon defenses, and a Mormon delegation visited Johnston and other army officers. According to one of the uninvited guests, Blair brazenly "instructed" the general that the army's needs would be best met in Cache Valley, some eighty miles north of the capital. Taking this unsolicited advice as an effort to negotiate the army's withdrawal from the territory, C. F. Smith exploded. The combative colonel told Blair that "as far as the army was concerned, it 'would like to see every damned Mormon hung by the neck.'" If Smith had known that more than two thousand cattle had frozen to death in the distant northern valley during the winter of 1855–56, he might have been even more indignant. Blair had spoken on behalf of Young and reported back the same day on how the army had received his proposal.[37]

For good reason, Young wanted the U.S. Army either withdrawn from the territory or moved as far away as possible from his own sphere of authority. The army gave federal officials the power to enforce an investigation of the murders at Mountain Meadows and other crimes and ensure the punishment of those who had committed or ordered them. The confrontation also displayed the anger just below the disciplined surface of virtually all the members of Johnston's command, officers and enlisted, toward the Mormon leader and his followers. But if Young had few friends in the army, he enjoyed a steadfast ally in the new governor, who publicly displayed his loyalty by declining to accept Johnston's invitation to enter the city with him.

Ben McCulloch was made of sterner stuff. The Texas Ranger captain not only accompanied the general, but also went with him on 29 June to

36. James W. Simonton, "Latest News from Mormondom," *San Francisco Daily Evening Bulletin*, 22 July 1858, 2.
37. Journal History, 27 June 1858, LDS Archives.

search for a location to establish a new post with access to water, wood, and grass. The company included a board of officers, Indian agent Garland Hurt, U.S. marshal Peter K. Dotson, David A. Burr, and other civilian officials, escorted by Captain William De Saussure's company, First U.S. Cavalry. The rest of the army moved to the southwest corner of Salt Lake Valley in search of better grass for their animals. Over the next week, the general and party inspected Tooele, Rush, Skull, and Cedar valleys, all south and west of Great Salt Lake.

McCulloch returned to the capital on 3 July. There a messenger gave him a sealed envelope from Young, "purporting to contain remarks made by me." It did not say where or when they had been made, but McCulloch figured it was during the 11 and 12 June meetings with Young and the other Mormon leaders because Young had promised the commissioners a copy of what was said. The straight-shooting Texan fired both barrels. "With a few slight exceptions," he said, "there is not a sentence correct." His own remarks were few, yet most were not mentioned in the report, he said. Moreover, he was as much surprised at how long it had taken to receive the alleged transcription "as he was at its incorrectness." McCulloch sent his reply addressed simply to "Ex Gov Brigham Young."[38]

Forewarned, McCulloch and Powell wrote an accurate account that same day of what had transpired to head off a fraudulent report of the Salt Lake meetings. In it the pair rehearsed much of what they had already reported to Washington, but this time they sent it to Young and asked him to certify its accuracy in writing. At the sessions, they had made it clear they had no authority to negotiate or investigate wrongdoings alleged by William W. Drummond and others. Their sole purpose was to induce Mormon leaders to submit peaceably to the authority of the United States. They further stressed that the president would send the U.S. Army to Salt Lake Valley, or anywhere else he considered necessary, to enforce the law and protect civil officials. They also stated that they had no authority to order the army to do anything, but Johnston had told them he would not march to the valley of Great Salt Lake until he heard from the commissioners.[39]

38. McCulloch to "Ex Gov Brigham Young," 3 July 1858, BYC.

39. Powell and McCulloch to Floyd, 24 August 1858, in Floyd, *Annual Report, 1858*, 175–77.

Young had confessed to burning the army's supply wagons and driving off its cattle, for which he accepted the president's pardon, but he denied all the other charges and claimed that his followers were "ardently attached to the Constitution of the United States," the commissioners wrote. It was agreed that "the officers, civil and military, of the United States should peaceably and without resistance enter the Territory of Utah, and discharge, unmolested, *all of their official duties*." Upon receipt of their account, Young grudgingly found it "a correct synoptical statement of what was said in said conference; the above is correct as far as I can recollect at present." On 24 August, the two men delivered their concise report, "which is certified by ex-Governor Brigham Young, as correct," to Secretary of War Floyd in Washington.[40]

Meanwhile, on 3 July, the army began its march from Salt Lake Valley to the site Johnston had chosen to establish a camp. Twice the soldiers crossed the Jordan River, which flowed north from Utah Lake to enter Great Salt Lake. First they forded to the east bank, where they shared the only road at the river narrows between the Salt Lake and Utah valleys with throngs of Mormons returning to Salt Lake Valley from their "Move South" as the army moved out. Returning to the Jordan River's west bank at Lehi, the column marched south along the shore of Utah Lake to a point opposite Provo.

There for two days the soldiers watched the town across the lake while its inhabitants eyed them from the other side. "No wonder the Mormons grin to see us marching out again today," Captain Tracy said on 9 July. "Your Mormon is of practical turn and by no means endorses the habit of beating about, to the loss of valuable time." The command that day at last moved to their final camping place, a scenic location "threaded by a small stream, and hemmed in at rear by bold elevations sprung with cedar and some pine." It gave "a beautiful view of Utah Lake, with the towns of Lehi, Battle Creek, and Provo on the opposite bank," and a spectacular uplift of the Wasatch Mountains in the background.[41]

General Johnston named his new post Camp Floyd after the secretary of war. The location at what is now Fairfield supplied the needs of his

40. Ibid. Italics in the original.
41. Alter and Dwyer, "Utah War Journal," 9 July 1858.

army for grass, fresh water, and wood, but it was less than ideal in relation to his mission to support officials appointed to enforce federal law.[42] The site was nearly forty miles from Great Salt Lake City, too far to render rapid support to the governor or other federal officials. The Echo Canyon corridor through the Wasatch Mountains, which had blocked his entry to Salt Lake Valley, now governed his line of supply and reinforcement from Fort Leavenworth. The northern approach to the California Trail ran through Jordan Narrows and Salt Lake Valley and around the north shore of Great Salt Lake, some two hundred miles out of the way, while the southern route from Camp Floyd passed through a string of fortified settlements for more than two hundred miles before meeting the Spanish Trail near Cedar City.

On 8 July, Johnston reported that his new post held "a commanding position," but his first actions made it clear he knew better. Keenly aware of the location's shortcomings in relation to his duties, he acted to open a new communication line to Fort Leavenworth that bypassed the Hastings-Mormon Trail from Fort Bridger and flanked Echo Canyon. He further planned to open a more direct route to northern California that would cut off the long swing around the north end of Great Salt Lake and follow the Humboldt River on the line of present-day I-80 to Donner Pass. Instead, the new road would run due west from Camp Floyd to pass Great Salt Lake on the south, meet the California Trail near Genoa, and cross the Sierra Nevada by Carson Pass.

At the general's request, Captain James H. Simpson of the U.S. Army's Corps of Topographical Engineers arrived at Camp Floyd on 20 August to serve as the Utah Army's chief engineer in mapping the wagon roads of the region. The West Point graduate first surveyed a road up the Timpanogos River, now Provo River and Canyon, to today's Midway. It then followed Silver Creek and the Weber River to today's Coalville. From there it ran up White Clay Creek, today's Chalk Creek, to the south of Echo Canyon and stretches of the Mormon Trail. During the military standoff the year before, Nauvoo Legion general Hiram B. Clawson had inspected this route to see if it might provide a way for the U.S. Army to flank Mormon defenses in Echo Canyon. He decided that

---

42. Johnston to McDowell, 8 July 1858, in Floyd, *Annual Report, 1858,* 122, 123.

without extensive roadwork, it would not. Simpson thought otherwise. The route he surveyed was "far superior to the old one," he reported on 3 September from Fort Bridger.[43]

That fall the topographical engineer carried out preliminary explorations to check on the feasibility of the larger undertaking that General Johnston had in mind. Over the winter, he and the general drew up and submitted to the War Department a proposal to carry out the first reported exploration of a virtually unknown region of the United States and open a new wagon road to California. In keeping with the U.S. Army's role in western exploration, travel, and settlement, the secretary of war promptly approved it.

In one of the most beneficial results of the Utah War, Simpson on 2 May 1859 led a full expedition from Camp Floyd to survey the vast region between the post and the Carson River, at the foot of the Sierra Nevada, for a more direct route to California. The historic undertaking would be the first recorded exploration of this section of the Great Basin of North America, a huge area of arid desert valleys and mountain ranges from which no water flows to any ocean. His sixty-four-member company included an artist, a geologist, a wheelwright, a blacksmith, teamsters, twelve six-mule wagons, scientific apparatus, and an escort of twenty soldiers.[44]

Over the next three months, Simpson's party traveled more than eleven hundred miles and opened a new route that slashed more than two hundred miles from the distance to California. Within a year, lean young men on swift horses were riding across the basin's lonely stretches to deliver the mail from Missouri to Sacramento in only ten days. After the Pony Express came the Pacific telegraph, the Overland Stage, the Lincoln Highway, and today's U.S. 50, now known as "the loneliest highway in America."[45]

Meanwhile, as the army labored to construct a new post in Cedar Valley, on 18 July 1858 Thomas L. Kane neared Philadelphia an "ill man," as usual, and released his bodyguard, Howard Egan, to take word of his

43. Simpson to Johnston, 3 September 1858, ibid., 145–46, 149–52.

44. Simpson, *Report of Explorations*.

45. For a detailed description of Simpson's routes and evaluation of this exploration on travel, see Petersen, *Route for the Overland Stage*.

return home to Young. He congratulated his friend's wisdom in accepting Buchanan's pardon. Since returning to the States, Kane had been struck by Washington's "frightful" unanimity in supporting the president. They were ready to "*vote supplies* in any amount" to the "miscreants in Utah," a reference to the U.S. Army. In a convoluted review of events, Kane said that Young's enemies had supported the president in sending the commissioners and issuing the pardon because they thought those actions would come too late: the subsequent conflict would unite the nation, and win their "holy war."[46]

Even so, Kane saw that a reaction had set in. There was no better proof of it, he said, than a contest to see who would get the credit for the pacification of Utah—Johnston or the peace commissioners. He thought the army, "having the greatest number of hired liars at command, will win (until the truth is told at last)" when Kane himself would be recognized as the peacemaker who had prevented bloodshed and saved Buchanan from his own mistakes.[47]

Even as he described the nation's deep and enduring resentment of the rebellion in Utah Territory, Kane shared Young's delusion that the conflict would somehow have a happy ending. He advised the deposed governor "to devote all your energies to the task of securing the recognition of Utah as a State." He assured him that the late war would end for good with the withdrawal of American armed forces from the Great Basin. "Get them out quietly," he said, and send him "a few sound facts and arguments [to] spread before the nation." Kane gave Young his word: "you have seen your last soldier marched across the plains—you have heard your last forever of all such wickedness and folly."[48]

Kane proved a false prophet on two counts. Except for eighteen months at the start of the Civil War, U.S. troops would be stationed in Utah from that time on. And only after a successor to Brigham Young had put an end to both polygamy and his vision of a theocratic Kingdom of God as an earthly state did one of the first places to be settled west of the Missouri River become, nearly forty years later, one of the last to enter the Union.

46. Kane to Young, 18 July 1858, BYC.
47. Ibid.
48. Ibid.

CHAPTER 14

One-Eyed Justice

You are the tools, the dupes, the instruments of a tyrannical Church despotism. The heads of your Church order and direct you. You are taught to obey their orders and commit these horrid murders. Deprived of your liberty, you have lost your manhood, and become the willing instruments of bad men. I say to you it will be my earnest effort while with you, to knock off your ecclesiastical shackles and set you free.

—Utah District judge John Cradlebaugh, 12 April 1859

The gangling lawyer who appeared on 3 November 1858 at the tavern in Mountain Dell, a few miles east of Salt Lake City, had the look of an ox driver to Ephraim Hanks, the Mormon innkeeper. He was very roughly dressed and had "but one eye," Hanks later told Brigham Young, "and that was a very good one." The unpretentious stranger obligingly turned his carriage over to a woman who wanted "to go to Zion" and proceeded on foot. When Hanks later met the newcomer on the road, he was riding into the city perched on a load of wood. He wanted no "airs" or special treatment, he said. "I have come here to do my duty."[1]

When it came to looks, John Cradlebaugh, the latest judge of Utah Territory's Second District, would not have turned many heads: his sole surviving portrait shows that he was as homely as another Midwestern lawyer, Abraham Lincoln. Nor did the thirty-nine-year-old widower from Circleville, Ohio, come in search of celebrity. Appointed in May, he had not endured the winter in the snow at Fort Bridger as had Judge

1. Journal History, 4 November 1858, LDS Archives.

Delana R. Eckels. At first, Cradlebaugh figured that the ordeal had frozen his colleague into a prejudicial attitude toward the Mormons. But the self-effacing justice's very good eye soon saw things differently. And when it spotted unpunished crimes not covered by the president's pardon, he set off a stampede of settlement leaders that shook the foundations of Zion.

The great Cradlebaugh scare began on 12 December 1858, when Alvira Parrish from Springville came before the Second District Court and swore that on 14 March 1857, eight men from her town had murdered her husband, William R. Parrish, and their son Beason. In an apparent act of blood atonement, William Parrish had been shot and disemboweled, and his throat had been cut. The judge issued a warrant for the arrest of the murderers and gave it to U.S. marshal Peter K. Dotson. The marshal in turn swore that he could not take them into custody without "a sufficient military posse," and Cradlebaugh approved his affidavit and sent it to Cumming.

It all seemed properly done, but in requesting the governor to requisition troops, Dotson and Cradlebaugh made a serious blunder. As the pair should have known, General Albert S. Johnston's orders did not limit the authority to request soldiers to act as a *posse comitatus* to the governor. Instead, they made it clear that if "the governor, the judges, or marshals of the Territory find it necessary directly to summon a part of your troops" in performance of their duties, Johnston should at once obey.[2] By going through Cumming, they set a precedent they would come to regret.

Six months before, Young had stated in writing that he understood and accepted Buchanan's conditions for a pardon, including that "officers, civil and military, of the United States should peaceably and without resistance enter the Territory of Utah, and discharge, unmolested, *all of their duties*."[3] This did not mean that he cared to see many of them return. "I cannot be responsible for the safety of certain Government appointees, such as Dr. Garland Hurt, H. F. Morrell, C. L. Craig, and, perhaps, others," he informed Governor Cumming.[4] What happened

2. George W. Lay to William S. Harney, 29 June 1857, in Buchanan, *Utah Expedition*, 7–9.

3. Lazarus W. Powell and Ben McCulloch to John B. Floyd, 24 August 1858, in Floyd, *Annual Report, 1858*,175–77.

4. Young to Cumming, 8 May 1858, BYC.

next showed that he had made his promise in bad faith, never intending to respect it or to give up any of the power he exercised over his theocratic domain. Moreover, the experience taught Mormon leaders that purposeful obstruction could make it virtually impossible for federal officials, civil and military, to perform their duties. For the next twenty years, obstruction of justice became their favorite legal tactic.

On the day he received Dotson's affidavit, Cumming sent it to Johnston and asked him to furnish the troops the lawman needed to perform his duty. But soon after, the governor suddenly changed his mind and rescinded the requisition. He gave no reason, but he had earlier expressed his fear that if troops were camped near populated places, it could lead to a collision with local inhabitants. If that happened, Young's hand would also be in it, for spontaneous protests and uprisings were hardly everyday occurrences in God's Kingdom.

Young's meddling did not stop there. Utah lawmakers, who did nothing unless he said so, quickly redrew the territory's judicial districts to relocate Cradlebaugh's court to Carson Valley, near what is now Reno, Nevada. Located five hundred miles west of Great Salt Lake City, on the east flank of the Sierra Nevada, it was inhabited by a small number of prospectors, backslidden Mormons, Indians, and entrepreneurs of various kinds. Such opposition, however, just made the plain-looking judge who wanted no airs or special treatment more dedicated to his duty, as he perceived it with his single but very clear eye. In so doing, he suffered none of the fears over provoking renewed hostilities that made Cumming a compliant instrument in the hands of Mormon leaders. The judge first noted that the governor had no more authority to call for troops than he did. He also saw that the new law that banished him to a distant bench would not take effect until 1 May, which gave him three months to pursue wrongdoers. The stouthearted judge took immediate action to make the most of the time and power he possessed.

Cradlebaugh told General Johnston that he would open court on 8 March at Provo to try six or eight prisoners in the Camp Floyd guardhouse as well as order the arrest of a band of thieves over the week ahead. Certain that he could not bring such offenders to trial without military aid, he asked the general to detail a "sufficient force" to perform this service. As instructed, Johnston ordered Tenth Infantry captain Henry Heth and his company to deliver the prisoners to Provo and stand by to receive and hold any persons indicted by the grand jury in the Second District Court.

To avoid trouble, Heth hoped to locate his camp outside the city limits. Since the population of Provo was less than four thousand, he innocently thought he could do so and still be within supporting distance of the judge's district court. He was soon disabused of this naïve notion, for the city limits were miles from the center of town on all sides. To the north and south, they extended some six miles to share the borders of neighboring towns. On the east, the city's border ran along the foot of the mountain, while a half-dozen miles or so on the west, the boundary followed the shore of Utah Lake. To establish a camp outside the city limits, Heth would have to locate in another town, on the steep side of the mountain, or in the fresh waters of the lake. He meant well, but he had run into a legal impediment created to obstruct the federal survey and sale of public lands and prevent outsiders from acquiring property divinely reserved for Young's followers.

President Buchanan had protested such practices in the 1857 proclamation that set forth his reasons to order an army to Utah, and he held out a pardon in return for obedience to federal law. "The land you live upon was purchased by the United States and paid for out of their treasury," he said. "The proprietary right and title to it is in them, and not in you."[5] Perhaps so, but as the territory's federal officials discovered, presidential decrees enjoyed little standing in a land run by decrees from on high. Happily, the town marshal had no objection to renting the soldiers the corral next to the seminary where Cradlebaugh held court. Heth named this convenient location Camp Ridgley and put up tents to protect witnesses and incarcerate prisoners.

As Heth set up camp, the judge impaneled a Mormon grand jury. Under territorial law, grand jurors were selected by the clerks of the county probate courts. Since territorial law had given Mormon probate courts exclusive legal jurisdiction, it was hardly surprising that grand juror Wilber J. Earl, the Springville police captain, had been involved in one of the murders under investigation.[6] Cradlebaugh quickly grasped

5. Buchanan, "A Proclamation," 35th Cong., 2nd sess., 1858, vol. 1, H. Ex. Doc. 2, serial 997, 69–72.

6. Earl attended the meetings that planned the Parrish murders in March 1857. For his involvement, see Aird, "'You Nasty Apostates,'" 178–90. Cradlebaugh dismissed Earl from the grand jury.

that the jury had been chosen beforehand to block trials for "crime after crime" he had learned about in his district. For this reason, he began his instructions to the grand jury with a lecture on the unconstitutionality of the territorial laws that vested probate courts with the powers Congress had given the three district courts, including original criminal and civil jurisdiction.[7]

In his instructions, Cradlebaugh reviewed some of these crimes and said that the perpetrators had escaped prosecution for years. "The reason why, I cannot tell," he said. They included the massacre of "a whole train" at Mountain Meadows; the slayings of William and Beason Parrish as they tried to escape from Utah, and of Gardner G. "Duff" Potter at Springville; the murder of Henry Forbes, who was on his way east from California; the Henry Jones murder at Pond Town; as well as the theft of property connected with these crimes.[8] Many others had gone unpunished in the judicial district, Cradlebaugh said. Typically, he vowed to do his duty, but questioned whether the grand jurors would do theirs and bring those guilty to trial.

Eyeing the first day's action in the judge's court was one of the men who had set up the murder of Californians Thomas and John Aiken, Andrew Jackson Jones, and John Achard in November 1857. Jacob G. Bigler, a Mormon bishop at Nephi, afterward rushed to Salt Lake to report on the proceedings to church historian Apostle George A. Smith, his brother-in-law, who had delivered orders to the southern Utah militia prior to the mass murder of the Fancher train at Mountain Meadows. Cradlebaugh "said he had the Testimony to prove it was done by white men [and] said it was the most outrageous massacre ever known," Bigler said. Among other crimes, the judge referred "to the murder of Potter & Parrishes, & said that was done by the sanction of authority."[9]

Bigler's report set the opposition wheels in motion. For three days, peace had prevailed in the corral where Heth's company was camped, and in the court where jurors had passively listened to testimony. But soon after Bigler delivered his report to Salt Lake, a messenger handed Cradlebaugh a memorial from Mayor Benjamin Bullock and the City Council protest-

7. "A Crisis in the Affairs of Utah Territory," *San Francisco Daily Evening Bulletin*, 12 April 1859, 3.

8. Ibid.

9. Jacob G. Bigler, Report, 12 March 1859, in W. W. Woodruff, Historian's Private Journal, LDS Archives.

ing the location of soldiers in the city, which they said was intimidating the people of Provo and making it difficult for the police to keep peace between citizens and soldiers. With tongue in cheek, they "respectfully" asked Cradlebaugh to move the troops beyond the city limits.

The judge's response was polite but pointed. He challenged city officials to show when, where, and in what way the troops had ever annoyed or interfered with any citizen. "A more quiet, orderly set of men I never saw," he said. Angered by the mayor's charge of intimidation, he shot back, "Good American citizens have no cause to fear American troops."[10] As if to contradict Cradlebaugh's opinion, a turf conflict broke out not far to the west that showed how much both sides were spoiling for a fight.

In fall 1858, the army gave Mormon luminary Daniel Spencer permission to graze his herd in the north end of Rush Valley, south of what is now Tooele. In March it notified him that it needed the range and gave him six weeks to move his animals. The quartermaster did not know that Spencer in the meantime had built a cabin on the site, where his caretaker, George Reeder, reportedly sold valley tan, a local Mormon whiskey, and quartered horse thieves.[11] On hearing this, the army told Spencer to move at once, but Reeder would not go. Colonel C. F. Smith then ordered Lieutenant Louis H. Marshall to shut down the tavern and remove its occupants, which he did. About this time, Spencer's nephew, nineteen-year-old Howard Spencer, and Alfred Clift arrived. On their refusal to leave, Marshall ordered First Sergeant Ralph Pike to move them, using force if necessary. As usual during this period, there are two versions of what happened next.[12]

According to Clift, "the man that seemed to Command the soldiers rode up to [Howard Spencer] on hors[e] back & took the gun by the brich [breech] & struck him over the Head with all his might." Spencer "straitened himself out as he fell," he said, "dead to all appearances."[13] More likely was Pike's account. He reported that upon Spencer's refusal to go, he had ordered two of his men to remove the resistant man to the guard tent. Spencer said no two men could take him. He then seized a

---

10. "A Crisis in the Affairs of Utah Territory."
11. F. J. Porter to Spencer, 23 May 1859, in Floyd, *Annual Report, 1859*, 180–82.
12. Marshall to Johnston, 25 March 1859, ibid., 157–58.
13. Kenney, *Wilford Woodruff's Journal*, 23 March 1859, 5:313.

pitchfork and "attempted to strike me with the pitchfork," Pike said. "I then knocked him down with my rifle." While the army cleared him, a Salt Lake City grand jury indicted the sergeant on a charge of assault with attempt to kill. Later, as Pike walked down Main Street after pleading not guilty a voice came from behind: "Is that you, Pike?" As he turned, Spencer shot him in the side at almost pointblank range. Pike cried out, "My God! I'm shot." He died three days later. When his body was returned to the post, an avenue of soldiers reached a quarter of a mile from camp out to the cemetery and, forming about the grave, filled the whole cemetery ground to present a square parallel with the sides.[14]

The grand jury at Great Salt Lake indicted Spencer, who resided in the city, but nothing ever came of it. Perhaps the reason had to do with the blessing that Brigham Young had given him two years after he killed the sergeant. "President Young set him apart to kill every poor devil that should seek to take his life and gave him permission when he came across a poor mobocrat to use him up."[15]

Young and Howard Spencer were not alone in resenting the U.S. Army in 1859. Six days after Cradlebaugh opened his court and four days after Bigler's report of the judge's grand jury instructions reached Great Salt Lake, Alfred Cumming arrived in Provo to find out why the U.S. troops were stationed in the Utah Valley town and what the crusading judge was doing to disturb the peace.

Cradlebaugh now demonstrated what Cumming and Mayor Bullock had to fear when the U.S. Army was empowered and ready to enforce the law. Based on testimony he had heard, he handed the U.S. marshal warrants for the arrest of a dozen or so men in Provo and Springville, including Bullock himself, who was implicated in the Parrish-Potter murders. The mayor was released for lack of evidence less than a day later, but the lesson was not lost on him and other local leaders.

In reporting these developments, Captain Heth told General Johnston that he and Cradlebaugh had consulted on how to keep the prisoners in custody in the event the judge moved his court from Provo to Camp

14. Alter and Dwyer, "Utah War Journal," 17 August 1859, 73. For more comprehensive looks at this episode, see Schindler, "Is That You, Pike?" in *In Another Time*, 100–102, first published in the *Salt Lake Tribune*; and Sadler, "Spencer-Pike Affair," 79–93.

15. Historian's Office Journal, 12 May 1861, LDS Archives, cited in Bagley, *Blood of the Prophets*, 246.

Floyd. At present, Heth was confident that his company could hold the seminary building in the city if anyone made an attempt to free the men awaiting trial. But if Cradlebaugh decided to close his court in Provo, as he apparently planned, he would do so on short notice, and Heth feared that his company would be too small to fight off a determined attempt to rescue any prisoners on the open road to the army post.

Heth did not request support, but the potentially explosive conditions he described moved Johnston to strengthen his position. He ordered Brevet Major Gabriel R. Paul of the Seventh Infantry to lead an impressive force of about eight hundred men to the settlement on Battle Creek, now Pleasant Grove, more than halfway from Camp Floyd to Provo, and to be "ready to act at a moment's notice." His duty was to guard the prisoners as they were moved to the army post. "On no pretence whatever, will you make an attack upon any body of citizens, except in sheer self-defense," Johnston instructed. He had selected Paul for this delicate duty because of the "prudence and judgment" that typified his career.[16]

The size and makeup of the force showed that its purpose was to discourage any trouble but to be fully prepared to handle any armed resistance. In number, it was more than a dozen times larger than Heth's company in the city. It was also a balanced small army that included three additional Tenth Infantry companies; four Seventh Infantry companies; a section of Phelps's Battery, Fourth Artillery; and a squadron of the Second Dragoons. On 21 March, Battle Creek inhabitants greeted Paul with exorbitant prices for fuel, forage, and campground rent, so he marched his men over the bench to the Provo River, opposite the mouth of the canyon. There he put them in an even more threatening position, some four miles from the city.

Johnston's show of force produced the results he intended. At Provo, Heth applauded the "very great change" that had suddenly occurred in the public attitude "since the news that eight companies had been ordered to take post near this place."[17] But not everyone welcomed the general's action. Thousands crowded Mormon churches in Salt Lake City to sign memorials calling for the troops to withdraw. And at Provo, Governor

16. Johnston to Cradlebaugh and Paul, 19 March 1859, in Floyd, *Annual Report, 1859*, 147–49.

17. Heth to F. J. Porter 21 March 1859, ibid., 153.

Cumming after six days finally got around to registering his disapproval to Johnston at finding troops "in and around" the schoolhouse where Cradlebaugh was holding court. He was especially offended that Heth had not considered it essential "to report to me officially, though I have been six days in this village."[18] He had further heard, no doubt from Mormon sources, that Major Paul and seven or eight hundred additional soldiers were on the way.

"After careful observation," Cumming announced that he was satisfied that the presence of a military force in the vicinity was unnecessary. He accordingly asked the general to order Heth's detachment to locate outside the city wall and to tell Paul to assume a position that would not place the inhabitants under "the influence of a military encampment in this vicinity."[19] His "careful observation" obviously did not include a visit to the judge's court or any interviews with witnesses. Otherwise he would have known what Cradlebaugh later told President Buchanan: "Witnesses under the obvious influence of fear, have burst into tears in open court on account of being compelled to testify to the horrid crimes of which they had knowledge," he said. They had been "threatened and intimidated," and many were in imminent peril of their lives without military protection.[20]

Johnston's reply was courteous but unequivocal. He reviewed the actions he had taken and why he considered them to be necessary. He rejected the notion that the movement could be construed as intimidation in a locality "whose police force greatly outnumbered the force sent among them." He "respectfully" told the governor that it would have been improper for Heth to report to him, since doing so would acknowledge military supremacy on his part, "which did not exist." The general finally made it clear that he was under "no obligation whatever to conform to your suggestions with regard to the military disposition of the troops of this department."[21]

Johnston's stiff reply spurred Cumming to go on the offensive in the war he waged with the pen against his fellow federal officers, judicial

18. Cumming to Johnston, 20 March 1859, ibid., 149–50.

19. Ibid.

20. Cradlebaugh and Charles E. Sinclair to Buchanan, 7 April 1859, 36th Cong., 1st sess., 1860, S. Ex. Doc. 32, serial 1031, 5–7.

21. Johnston to Cumming, 22 March 1859, in Floyd, *Annual Report, 1859*, 151–52.

and military. On 25 March, he told Secretary of State Lewis Cass that Cradlebaugh's dedication to investigating past crimes and punishing the guilty was "as much the result of *hatred* of Mormons as such, as, of a love for justice," a gratuitous accusation that he said would "lead to much bloodshed." To back up his attack, he enclosed a copy of Johnston's letter and recommended that requisitions for troops be made only with the governor's approval. In his zeal to keep the peace and appease Brigham Young, the governor even failed to mention the horrendous and unresolved massacre at Mountain Meadows.[22]

Two days later, the Georgian's pen produced a public statement that was even more remarkable for its duplicity and intent to mislead. Under the title "By Alfred Cumming, Governor of Utah Territory, A PROCLAMATION," he denounced the stationing of American troops near Cradlebaugh's court, as if it had not been requested by the judge himself, and the movement of Major Paul's force, also failing to state that it was done at the request of the U.S. marshal with Cradlebaugh's endorsement. He purposely made it appear that Johnston had taken these actions arbitrarily, "not only to terrify the inhabitants and disturb the peace of the Territory, but also to subvert the ends of justice by causing the intimidation of witnesses and jurors."[23]

President Buchanan had sent Cumming to enforce the law in a rebellious territory with an army to back him up. Now the governor was acting as Young's obedient servant in defeating the very purpose he had been sent to fulfill. His pronouncement, however, did gain him the public affection he craved. On reading it, Samuel Pitchforth said at Nephi on 1 April, "I feel to say God bless Gov C."[24]

By then, Judge Cradlebaugh had rebuked the grand jury and dismissed it. For two weeks, jurors had heard witnesses describe "hellish crimes" in their area, "done by authority," he said. They "had all the testimony before you in the Parrish case," he said, "and for some cause you refuse to do anything." The fearless judge minced no words: "The court feels that it has discharged its duty; it has furnished you with every facility for

22. Cumming to Cass, 25 March 1859, ibid.

23. Cumming, "A Proclamation," 27 March 1859, *Kirk Anderson's Valley Tan*, 5 April 1859, 2.

24. Pitchforth, Diary, 1 April 1857, BYU Library.

discharging yours," he said. Still they made no report. "To continue you longer in service would be wrong," he said. "The public interest would neither be promoted or benefited by it."[25]

The refusal of Mormon jurors to carry out their responsibility, however, did not deter the judge from doing his duty. On 24 March, he endorsed a request by Marshal Dotson for two hundred soldiers to arrest a dozen or so "criminals" in Provo and Springville who had "fled or secreted themselves." As authorized, General Johnston that same day ordered Major Paul to meet the request. The next day, Captain Albert Tracy detailed a Tenth Infantry company under Lieutenant John Forney to join the Seventh Infantry company of Captain Henry Little and a squadron of dragoons in making an arrest for the Parrish-Potter murders. Their quarry: Aaron Johnson, the fifty-three-year-old bishop of Springville, husband of nine wives, and brigadier general for the Nauvoo Legion the southern Utah Valley district.

The U.S. Army *posse comitatus* under the veteran Captain Little broke camp soon after midnight the next day and headed a few miles south to the nearby town, with infantrymen breaking step to keep their rhythmic tramp from being detected. Before dawn, they circled the bishop's house and moved in to capture the alleged offender. But when they broke into "Johnson's harem," Captain Tracy said, they met a verbal volley from some of the bishop's wives, who scolded them fiercely from a bed in the corner and called them "unmentionable names." The dragoons counterattacked with a war dance "after the manner of the plains" around a pot standing in the center of the room. "But the bird had flown."[26]

Bishop Johnson was not alone in flying to the mountains. The arrest of Provo mayor Benjamin Bullock a week before had touched off a regular stampede of settlement leaders to nearby hills and canyons. The Springville head and others from Utah Valley hid out in Hobble Creek Canyon and other locations that were given secret code names. The largest gathering of wanted leaders was at the "old castle," variously called Ballagarth, Valle Guard, and Castle Valle Guard, high on the mountain northeast of Nephi with an unobstructed view to the north and south. There men who had been involved in the atrocity at Mountain Meadows

25. "Discharge of the Grand Jury," *Kirk Anderson's Valley Tan*, 29 March 1859, 2.
26. Alter and Dwyer, "Utah War Journal," 2 April 1859, 64.

came from as far away as Cedar City, more than 150 miles to the south, to join their brethren from Nephi and Sanpete Valley.

On the day troops failed to nab Johnson, Bishop Bigler took off for a supposed "camp meeting in the quiet city of Freedomsburg," Samuel Pitchforth said at Nephi. One of the few who kept a journal during this time, the Englishman left a terse record of the panic that shook the territory in the wake of Cradlebaugh's crusade. James Picton returned from Payson to report that "they were after Bishop [George] Hancock of Payson but he had gone out." Soon after, he reported a rumor that troops planned to swoop down on his town on Salt Creek and arrest Israel Hoyt and others for the Aiken Party murders. "But he and Bro P[icton] has gone out this night to join their bretheren at Ballagarth Castle." On 5 April, Pitchforth wrote that "a person" had come in from Sanpete with word that Manti bishop Warren Snow wanted to join the others at Ballagarth. "A pilot went to show him over the marshey land to the old ruined castle," he said.[27] In a planned operation, Nauvoo Legion troops watched roads and crossings for troop movements and guarded the men hiding out in the mountains.

Fearing that the judge would close his court, six witnesses who had testified on the assurance of military protection pleaded for the troops to remain in Provo. In an affidavit before district judge Charles E. Sinclair, they swore that their local communities had threatened them not to divulge information about crimes of which they had knowledge. They moreover believed that the threats would have been carried out if General Johnston had not sent troops to protect them. "We believe our lives to be in danger henceforward without military protection from United States troops," they said.[28] They sent copies to Johnston and Cradlebaugh.

The affiants' case was desperate, but the judge had no choice. The U.S. soldiers could stay only so long as he held court at Provo. At best, his court could remain open until the end of April, when he would be banished five hundred miles to the west to Carson Valley under a territorial law signed by Cumming. He was determined to make the most of the few days left to him to investigate and bring to justice the men who had committed mass murder at Mountain Meadows. He knew they were not Indians.

27. Pitchforth, Diary, 4–6 April 1859, BYU Library.
28. "Second Judicial District Court," *Kirk Anderson's Valley Tan*, 5 April 1859, 3.

With time running out, the judge decided to close his court on 2 April and move it for the rest of the month to Camp Floyd. Captain Heth sent word to Paul, and early on 4 April the major's force left camp on the Timpanogos River, and after a four-mile march entered the town. "Taking seven columns of platoons, we pass down the principal street," Captain Tracy said, "halting at length, opposite to the Court buildings, and receiving, under strong guard, our charge." Nearly a thousand U.S. soldiers then moved in regular order of infantry, artillery, and dragoons that stretched out across the bench on their march back to their Cedar Valley post.[29]

As they passed American Fork, "the drums and fifes of the old-fashioned 7th [Infantry] struck up, and guidons were loosed to the breeze." The inhabitants, lined up along the road, greeted the display with the usual welcome they reserved at this time for American soldiers. "There were cat-calls, groans and whistles, and one ambitious party went so far as to maneuver at our flanks after the fashion of artillery," Tracy said. Several boys "kicked, and pranced and whinnied, and came into battery in a style quite ferocious." After each imaginary firing, "an old splint broom was thrust into the beer-barrel by an assistant and the piece sponged." Near the center of the parade, six-foot-four Alexander F. MacDonald, one of the prisoners, towered over the rest as he strode along with "an air of martyr-like defiance."[30]

If the tall Scotsman wanted to become a martyr, the officers and men at Camp Floyd, who turned out in "extraordinary numbers" to watch the return of Paul's men with the Mormon prisoners, seemed eager to accommodate him. "The excitement surpassed anything I had observed before," Tracy said, "and it is by no means improbable, that, without the strict discipline in which they were held, they would have seized, and lynched the Mormon Prisoners on the spot." Cradlebaugh, on the other hand, was accorded that evening the compliment of innumerable calls "of gratulation by officers from all sides, together with serenades by the bands of the 7th and 10th regiments."[31]

With U.S. Army support, Johnston and the judge put their heads together and came up with a way to carry out a purpose of primary

29. Alter and Dwyer, "Utah War Journal," 4 April 1859.
30. Ibid.
31. Ibid., 5 April 1859.

importance to both—to investigate the reports of the murders at Mountain Meadows. On 17 April, Johnston ordered Second Dragoons captain Reuben Campbell to lead an expedition of one dragoon company and two companies of infantry to the Santa Clara River to meet the paymaster, Major Henry Prince, who had been sent from southern California with the army payroll, and Brevet Major James H. Carleton's First Dragoons, assigned to investigate reported Indian depredations. Two days later, Johnston instructed Campbell to escort Judge Cradlebaugh to the region and hold any prisoners the U.S. marshal might authorize.

At Corn Creek, Campbell's command met Jacob Forney, Utah's Indian affairs superintendent, heading north to Great Salt Lake with sixteen children of massacre victims. He had recovered them, but only at a price. Those who had sheltered the children in southern Utah, including some who had helped to slaughter their parents, billed the United States more than $7,000 for taking care of them, but Forney considered less than half this amount worthy of reimbursement. At the Corn Creek home of the Pahvant Indians, William Rogers decided to return as deputy marshal to southern Utah with Campbell's force to search for two rumored children reported by Chief Kanosh. Cradlebaugh gave Rogers warrants for the arrest of massacre principals John D. Lee, Isaac C. Haight, and John M. Higbee.

As Campbell's command continued south, a Mormon messenger rode ahead to warn the three men that two hundred troops were coming to arrest them. Lee promptly headed into the nearby mountains, where he could hide out and watch what happened below at the same time. Joined by William Stewart and other massacre participants from Cedar City, Haight and Higbee fooled Cradlebaugh by heading in the opposite direction. Traveling at night, they bypassed the Camp Floyd expedition and rode to Nephi, where they hid in the tithing office until a pilot led them to the growing collection of wanted leaders at Castle Ballagarth in the mountains.

On 5 May, Campbell's force reached the Mountain Meadows killing field and beheld a shocking sight: "human skulls, bones, and hair, scattered about, and scraps of clothing of men women and children," he said. These were the remains of the emigrants from Arkansas, who had been met there "by the *Mormons* (assisted by such of the wretched Indians of the neighborhood as they could force or persuade to join them)," he reported, adding, "The Mormons had their faces painted so as to disguise themselves as Indians." He went on to tell how "the horrid affair was finished by an act of treachery." After the Arkansans surrendered, their assailants disarmed them and then marched them "about a mile and a half from the spring, where they, their wives, and their children, with the exception of some infants were ruthlessly killed." The surviving children "never have been with the Indians."[32]

Campbell and the soldiers from Camp Floyd marched to the Santa Clara River on 8 May, where they met Major Carleton and his First Dragoons company from Fort Tejón, near Los Angeles, a week later. The two professional soldiers agreed on what they had seen on the ground. Carleton wrote: "There is not the shadow of a doubt that the emigrants were butchered by the Mormons themselves, assisted doubtless by the Indians."[33] And Campbell expressed the opinion of both officers when he said the Southern Paiutes were "a miserable set of root-diggers, and nothing is to be apprehended from them but by the smallest and most careless party."[34]

Meanwhile, Cradlebaugh and Marshal Rogers went from the massacre site to Cedar City, a distance of some thirty-five miles, to hold an "examining court" to hear crime witnesses. While they were there, a number of horrified Mormons promised to provide the judge with "an abundance of evidence in regard to the matter, so soon as they were assured of military protection." Moreover, he said, some of the persons who were actually involved in the crime "came to see him in the night," vowing "to become witnesses" when protection was at hand.[35] Based on testimony filed before him in the southwestern Utah town, Cradlebaugh issued warrants for the arrest of nearly forty men for the unprecedented atrocity.

But Cradlebaugh's crusade to punish crimes during the 1856–58 Reformation and Utah War would come to a sudden and unexpected end. Campbell gave him the disheartening news. He had been called back to Camp Floyd, following Johnston's receipt of new orders from Washington.

32. Campbell to F. J. Porter, 6 July 1859, in Buchanan, *Presidential Message Communicating Correspondence, Etc., on Massacre at Mountain Meadows*, 14–16.

33. Carleton, *Special Report of the Mountain Meadows Massacre*.

34. Campbell to Porter, 6 July 1859, in Buchanan, *Presidential Message Communicating Correspondence, Etc., on Massacre at Mountain Meadows*, 16.

35. Cradlebaugh, *Utah and the Mormons*, 20.

Since peace had returned to the territory, President Buchanan, ignoring reports about the massacre and other crimes, had decided that the judicial administration of the laws would require no help from the army. It would now require "written application of the governor" for him to provide troops to assist in enforcing the laws.[36]

Cradlebaugh knew what that meant. Without military protection and with no hope of getting it, he had no choice but to return with Campbell's force to Camp Floyd and get ready to leave for Carson Valley. As they approached Nephi, they once again passed men they had been looking for in Cedar City, going back home. On the judge's arrival, he found a formal reprimand from U.S. Attorney General Jeremiah Black, addressed to him and Judge Sinclair, who had assisted him at Provo, for trying to do more than "hear patiently the cases brought before them." On behalf of Buchanan, Black told them that Cumming alone could requisition troops, that there had been no reason to station them at Provo, and that they should not have remained there "against his remonstrance."[37] The territory's great Cradlebaugh scare was over.

By once again playing on Cumming's zeal to keep peace at any price, Young, a shrewd judge of men, was able to regain total control of Utah's judicial system and render the U.S. Army as impotent as if it had never arrived in Utah. It would not be the last time he would make the self-important governor perform as his puppet. No sooner had Buchanan stripped the judges of the power to use troops than suddenly Young faced familiar charges. From the church's earliest days, its neighbors and unhappy dissenters had accused its leaders of engaging in the production of counterfeit money, both coins and printed bills. It appeared that the church repeatedly resorted to the printing press or coin stamp to cover its chronic financial shortfalls. In 1837, its leaders created a bank in Ohio and had currency printed before gaining state approval for its incorporation. When the state rejected the application, Joseph Smith changed the bank's name on the already printed bills from "The Kirtland Safety Society Bank" to "The Kirtland Safety Society Anti-Banking Co." and flooded the area with the illegitimate currency. The prophet took off one

36. John B. Floyd to Johnston, 6 May 1859, in Buchanan, *Presidential Message Communicating Correspondence, Etc., on Massacre at Mountain Meadows*, 9.

37. Black to Cradlebaugh and Sinclair, 17 May 1859, ibid., 2–4.

night for Zion in Missouri, just before the sheriff came with an arrest warrant for bank fraud.

Under Brigham Young, reports of counterfeiting followed the LDS Church as relentlessly as the allegations that its members practiced polygamy. Young repeatedly denied that Mormons had anything to do with the practice, but in January 1846 he conceded that a "set of bogus-makers" were working in Nauvoo, "determined to counterfeit coin here by wagon loads and make it pass upon the community as land office money."[38] A month later, Young and other leaders fled Nauvoo after the federal circuit court of appeals in Illinois indicted them for counterfeiting U.S. coin: *Niles' National Register* reported that the indictment alleged that Joseph Smith "used to work with his own hands at manufacturing those counterfeits."[39]

A number of similar episodes reveal that the only thing new about the Deseret Currency Association that Young created in January 1858 to finance the Utah War was the name he gave it. Twenty-five-year-old David McKenzie, who had learned his trade as an apprentice in Edinburgh, Scotland, engraved copper plates for the currency in the tithing office virtually under the Mormon leader's nose. McKenzie's plates made such attractive currency that he and others decided to put his art to profitable use in a scheme to pass hundreds of thousand of dollars' worth of bogus U.S. Treasury drafts throughout the United States. "It was one of the boldest, as well as one of the most dangerous attempts at forgery ever perpetrated," a *New York Times* correspondent said. The plotters planned to send an agent "to California with *half a million dollars in checks*, there to put them into circulation. If the scheme had not been nipped in the bud, the public would probably have been swindled out of a million of dollars."[40] But as the *Times* reported, General Johnston got wind of it.

When McKenzie's fellow conspirator Myron Brewer, a Mormon Concert Band member who had spent early 1858 manufacturing bows and arrows for the Nauvoo Legion, sold a counterfeit quartermaster's check for $365 to a man at Camp Floyd who had been assigned to buy it, he found himself under arrest.[41] Marshal Dotson seized McKenzie the next

38. Smith, *History of the Church*, 6:502, 7:525, 574, 609

39. "The Mormons," *Niles' National Register*, 3 January 1846, 288.

40. "The Great Forgery Case," *New York Times*, 10 August 1859, 4.

41. Brewer to William H. Kimball, 5 February 1858, Weber State University.

day. The discovery of the plates and paper intended for Deseret currency on Young's premises appeared to implicate the Mormon leader, but the governor refused to approve the use of U.S. troops to arrest him. "You can't touch Brigham Young while I live, by —!" Cumming swore.[42]

Young once again proved himself immune from indictment, let alone arrest, despite the conviction among non-Mormons in Utah that he was deeply involved in the latest counterfeiting operation. "Now recollect, this engraving and printing was done in a Church building, the tything office, within the enclosure of Brigham Young's palace and Harems:— that is, within a few steps of his residence;—that Brigham saw every day all the inmates of these houses, and has a particularly *sharp* eye to the tything rooms," wrote Camp Floyd quartermaster Colonel G. H. Crosman from what he called "the Mormon Siberia." Crosman noted that the engraving took more than a month, and Brigham Young had "such a perfect system of espionage" in Utah that nothing escaped his knowledge.[43]

Rumors about the army's intentions grew increasingly wild during April 1859, and fears mounted about the skeletons that Judge Cradlebaugh's trip to Mountain Meadows would inevitably uncover, eventually reaching hysterical levels. General Daniel H. Wells once again rallied the Nauvoo Legion to defend the Mormon prophet. Wells thought he had seen "gentlemen in stripes" surveying the heights above Young's estate for "artillery encampments"; Governor Cumming assured him that they were engineers trying to determine the city's longitude. Wells told Cumming that the army intended to batter down the walls around the Lion House, seize Young, and take him to Camp Floyd. Young said the army did not "want any thing of him only to lynch him." Spies watching Camp Floyd had alerted Wells that two regiments had left on a forced march to the north on Sunday, 17 April. Without so much as a by-your-leave from the governor, Wells called out the Legion, and "*by two o'clock on Monday morning, five thousand men were under arms.*" To the *New York Herald*'s Mormon correspondent, "the shedding of blood seems inevitable."[44]

But the alleged plot was all a fantasy: there were no orders to march on Salt Lake. For all the overheated tales of evil federal conspiracies told

42. Stenhouse, *Rocky Mountain Saints*, 411.
43. Crosman to W. A. Gordon, 5 October 1859, Bancroft Library.
44. Roberts, *Comprehensive History of the Church*, 508–509, 514–15.

in Mormon annals, the entire affair was based on nothing more than rumors, paranoia, and the now-common tendency of some Mormon leaders to flee "when no man persueth."[45] The episode did, however, demonstrate once again who controlled the levers of power in Utah Territory.

The scheme's alleged mastermind, former Mormon stalwart Myron Brewer, turned state's evidence during a preliminary hearing at Camp Floyd.[46] David McKenzie testified that he "had consulted Brigham Young, who frowned upon this enterprise, and disapproved": despite the prophet's condemnation, he was still "determined to go on with it."[47] McKenzie's trial took place at Nephi on 26 August 1859. He pleaded not guilty but mounted no defense. Claiming that it lacked the space to print it, the *Deseret News* assured its readers that the evidence showed conclusively "that Wallace, Brewer and others were principals in the counterfeiting transaction" and had employed McKenzie only as an engraver. Judge Eckels fined the engraver $50 and sentenced him to two years' hard labor in the territorial penitentiary.[48]

Brewer came to a bad end when he was gunned down on Salt Lake's main street in what the *Deseret News* called a "wholesale shooting affair."[49] Killed with him on the night of 17 May 1860 was a gambler named Robert K. "Joaquin" Johnston, "a handsome scoundrel, and princely in his attire," who had threatened to shoot a Mormon editor the previous day.[50] The police rushed to the scene, "but the slayers had fled," and "as yet no trace of the actors has been discovered," the *News* reported. "Who performed the bold deed will not probably be known very soon," the paper predicted accurately, for Brewer's murder remains a mystery to this day. It was obvious that both "renegadoes" had been blown apart with shotguns, the weapon of choice of Salt Lake's Mormon police force.[51] The coroner's jury found that they had killed each other, no mean feat since both were armed only with revolvers.

45. Prov. 28:1.
46. "The Forgery Case," *Deseret News*, 20 August 1859, 156.
47. Crosman to Gordon, 5 October 1859, Bancroft Library.
48. "First Judicial District Court," *Deseret News*, 7 September 1859, 213.
49. "Wholesale Shooting Affair," *Deseret News*, 23 May 1860, 92.
50. Stenhouse, *Rocky Mountain Saints*, 418.
51. "Wholesale Shooting Affair."

Utah's first senator, Frank Cannon, who later called the counterfeiting charge against Young "both malignant and absurd," put his finger on the right moral of the story. "The point worth noting in this episode is the completeness with which Brigham controlled the official head of the territory. Little more than a year had passed since Cumming was cooling his heels in a mountain camp, waiting for federal troops to disperse the rebellious Nauvoo Legion, and seat him in the governor's chair," he observed. "Now, from that very chair, he was calling on these same rebels to resist the troops who had brought him to the city. The federal governor had become a mere cog in Brigham's political machine. American history holds few, if any, more striking instances of the triumph of personal ascendancy over official power."[52]

Cumming's appeasement had become predictable, but it cost him the respect of other federal officials and the acceptance and adulation he craved from "his people," who held him in contempt and simply ignored him. When the noted British explorer Sir Richard Burton visited Great Salt Lake in 1860, he interviewed Cumming and afterward told how by "firmness, prudence, and reconciliation" he had restored "order and obedience throughout the territory."[53] But the governor in title knew better.

Cradlebaugh was made of sterner stuff. For him, the words "give up" did not appear in Blackstone's commentaries on the law, and he found ready allies in Carson Valley, where historian Sally Zanjani called him the nearest thing to a hero to appear on the Sierra Nevada's eastern slope.[54] If Washington ignored the murders at Mountain Meadows, the rugged collection of miners, prospectors, and Mormon dissenters on the territory's western periphery took an interest in it born of self-preservation. They knew who had committed the killings and applauded Cradlebaugh's fight to bring the guilty to justice. When he arrived at Genoa, they greeted him with booming cannons and a joyful demonstration.

Not only did the judge from Ohio bring law and order to a rough-and-ready citizenry, he also became a leader in the campaign to throw off Mormon rule from five hundred miles to the east. In July 1859, western Utah delegates convened at Genoa and approved a constitution for a

52. Cannon and Knapp, *Brigham Young and His Mormon Empire*, 313.
53. Burton, *City of the Saints*, 216.
54. Zanjani, *Devils Will Reign*, 122.

territory named Nevada.[55] In a memorial to Congress, they listed eleven grievances against "the Mormons of eastern Utah," including that their emissaries had "poisoned the minds of the Indians against us, forced us frequently to open war with them."[56] California lawmakers called on their state's congressional delegation "to use their best exertions" to win approval of the measure.[57]

Influenced by the 1857–58 Mormon war and Young's shutdown of overland travel and communications, Congress in March 1861 created Nevada Territory, the first in a series of actions to shrink God's Kingdom to a governable size. The new territory ran from the California line to near what is now Carlin, Nevada, and reduced the area ruled by Young by some seventy-three thousand square miles. Elected Nevada's first delegate to Congress was John Cradlebaugh himself, who promptly sponsored the 1862 measure that took another bite out of Utah Territory from the original eastern line to a point near present-day Wells.

Nor was that the end of Cradlebaugh's counterattack. Before resigning his seat to recruit an Ohio regiment during the Civil War, he dealt a heavy blow to the latest Mormon bid for sovereignty through statehood. He described what he had seen at Mountain Meadows and scored Congress for its failure to act. Its members often asked, "Why do not the courts act?" More than fifteen federal judges who had served in Utah had repeatedly told Congress that the territory's legislation had been purposely designed "to prevent the administration of the laws; that the Church authorities are determined that the law shall not be enforced in the federal courts," Cradlebaugh told U.S. House members. "The grand and trial jurors are Mormons, who are taught that the Mormon Church laws are the higher laws, and should prevail," he said.[58] Not for another twelve years would Congress pass the Poland Act and finally strip Utah's probate courts of the powers that Mormon lawmakers had so liberally bestowed.

The brave judge suffered a hard fate. Leading his regiment in the first charge at Vicksburg in 1863, Colonel Cradlebaugh was struck in

55. Nevada takes its name from the mountains on its western border, the Sierra Nevada, which means "snow-capped mountain range."

56. *History of Nevada*, 63.

57. *Resolution of the Legislature of California in Favor of the Establishment of a New Territory in Western Utah*, 36th Cong., 1st sess., 1860, S. Misc. Doc. 17, serial 1038, 15.

58. Cradlebaugh, *Utah and the Mormons*, 22.

the mouth by a minie ball that knocked out many of his teeth and blew away parts of his lip, palate, and tongue before emerging from his neck just below the earlobe. He eventually recovered and returned to Nevada, but his wound made it impossible to practice law. Mormon hatred of the judge endured: in 1871, the *Deseret News* rejoiced that he was "seemingly in a pitiable plight: 'destitute and helpless' from his wounds, it would have been a more enviable fate if he had died at Vicksburg, but doubtless Providence had other views in store with regard to him. When in authority here he acted like a miserable poltroon and trickster; and he is now reaping his reward."[59] Cradlebaugh died in 1872 at Eureka of pneumonia. As a respected war hero, his remains were later moved for final burial in Circleville, Ohio.

Meanwhile, since Young controlled the judicial system, for more than a decade there would be no investigation of or punishment for what may have been the worst atrocity in the nation's history, which the church today admits was committed by its southern Utah officials. The Mountain Meadows massacre "came close to being the only recorded instance of a perfect crime of mass murder," historian Dale L. Walker observed. "The only white witnesses were the perpetrators and they were not talking, nor were the Indians, who, for a long time, were accused as the sole culprits."[60] And with the U.S. Army's mission to enforce the law eliminated by President Buchanan's appeasement policy, there was little need to keep a brevet brigadier general and the nation's largest concentration of troops in Utah just to escort the mail carriers and chase raiding Shoshones and Bannocks.

Aware that he was no longer needed, General Johnston notified Washington in February 1860 that he would turn over his command to Lieutenant Colonel Charles F. Smith and leave by the southern route for the capital. He was too proud to admit that the bureaucrat's pen was mightier than his sword, and too self-disciplined to express how much he disliked dealing with Cumming, but such feelings no doubt affected his decision. He was not the only soldier to leave that year: 1860 saw a cut in the number of troops stationed at Camp Floyd from nearly twenty-five hundred to about a fifth that many. Among them was Smith, who turned

59. "Poor Old Cradlebaugh," *Deseret News*, 1 March 1871, 47:4.
60. Walker, *Legends and Lies*, 223.

the command over to Lieutenant Colonel Philip St. George Cooke of the Second Dragoons.

Not far behind was Johnston's chief adversary. Young allowed Alfred Cumming to imagine that he was governor, but the Georgian eventually came to know that he had been played for a fool. As he saw the soldiers he had betrayed, yet relied on for protection, leave the territory, the governor figured in 1861 that it was a good time to request a leave of absence. Asked how his successor would get along, he said, "Get along? Well enough, if he will do nothing. There is nothing to do. Alfred Cumming is governor of the Territory, but Brigham Young is governor *of the people*."[61]

As the officers and men left to take their stand with Dixie or the Union in the coming Civil War, Colonel Cooke renamed the post Fort Crittenden in honor of John J. Crittenden, the pro-Union U.S. senator from Kentucky. Former secretary of war John B. Floyd cast his destiny with the Confederate States of America, as did Johnston. To Cooke also went the task of auctioning off to the highest bidders the remaining supplies and surplus equipment for a few pennies on the dollar. Nearly half of the approximately $100,000 he took in came from Young. But in a final vote of no confidence in the former governor's loyalty, the army ordered Cooke to destroy all of the ammunition.

Before the last of the troops departed Utah, save only a sergeant's guard left to watch over Fort Bridger, Cooke wrecked the post's surplus firearms and detonated its powder magazine. With his typical flair for the theatrical, he presented the old Camp Floyd flagstaff to Young. The gift could be seen as an appropriate symbol for the end of the Utah War or as the loser's gracious acknowledgment of defeat. Whether Cooke intended to vest it with such imagery is not known.

Young surely seemed to take it both ways. With the army on its way out and Confederate guns in Charleston Harbor announcing the start of the Civil War, he felt safe enough in May 1861 to make his first journey to Mountain Meadows. There he ordered the destruction of the monument and cross that Carleton's company had erected over the bones of the innocent dead. Soon after, he sat down to a fine meal with his adopted son, John D. Lee, and afterward explained why it had been necessary to kill so many men, women, and children. "Pres. Young Said that the company that was used up at the Mountain Meadowes were the Fathers, Mothe[rs], Bros., Sisters & connections of those that Muerders the Prophets, they merittd their fate, & the only thing that ever troubled him was the lives of the Women & children, but that under the circumstances [it] could not be avoided," Lee reported.[62]

Even as Young viewed the atrocity site, the consequences of his misjudgment would affect Utah's people for years to come. For the American Union would not be like "water that is spilt upon the ground that cannot be gathered," as he prophesied on returning from the southern Utah killing field.[63] Nor would the bones of the slain forever cry in vain for justice.

Led by the new Republican Party, Congress in 1862 passed the Morrill Act outlawing polygamy in the territories. The new law imposed a fine of up to $500 and a maximum of five years in prison for anyone found guilty of bigamy. It also annulled the Utah law that had incorporated the Church of Jesus Christ of Latter-day Saints and empowered the church to perform and regulate marriages. In addition, it voided all territorial laws related to polygamy and disallowed any corporation for religious or charitable purposes to own property valued at more than $50,000. Young stamped the law unconstitutional, and his people ignored or laughed at it. But the fingers of Senator Justin S. Morrill from Vermont, who wrote the act, would be like those that wrote on the wall to the king of Babylon: "God hath numbered thy kingdom."[64]

As that fateful year drew to a close, Young's reward for declaring independence and closing the overland trails across an area of western America almost as large as Texas arrived in the form of an Irish Catholic Mexican War veteran who would threaten Young's claim as Utah's most influential early leader. Colonel P. Edward Connor led his Third California Volunteers regiment to Utah over James H. Simpson's central route to keep the lines of travel and communication open across the nation. Abraham Lincoln already knew much about the militant religious move-

---

62. Robert Glass Cleland and Juanita Brooks, eds., *A Mormon Chronicle: The Diaries of John D. Lee, 1848–1876* (San Marino, Calif.: Huntington Library, 1955), vol. 2, 314, 30 May 1861.

63. Kenney, *Wilford Woodruff's Journal*, 6:92, 93.

64. For the Morrill Act's references to polygamy, see Hardy, *Doing the Works of Abraham*, 241–42.

ment from personal experience in Illinois, where he had served as a state lawmaker during the Nauvoo period. As president, he could not tolerate a repeat performance by Young, who had virtually cut the nation in half, east to west, in 1857.

Connor took a more direct approach to his duty than had Johnston. He marched his regiment and its mounted component, 750 strong, straight up today's Main Street, then East Temple or Whiskey Street, with color guard in front and flags snapping in the wind. Spectators filled every street corner, window, and door, "but not a cheer nor a jeer" went up as they passed, the *San Francisco Daily Evening Bulletin* reported. "There were none of those manifestations of loyalty that any other city in a loyal territory would have made."[65] The Irish firebrand marched his men up to the bench above what is now the University of Utah, where he surveyed a four-mile-square mile post and named it in honor of Stephen A. Douglas, who had died the year before. His guns on the high ground, trained on the Chief Stake of Zion below, announced that the time was not yet for God's Kingdom to prevail over the American republic. Not for the rest of the nineteenth century would there be a time when U.S. troops were not stationed in Utah.

Perhaps the most hurtful of the consequences that flowed from Brigham Young's attempt to force Mormon independence was that Utah would remain outside the American Union of states until 1896. Thus one of the first places settled west of the Missouri River would become one of the last to fulfill Young's dream of sovereignty through statehood, long after the Civil War had forged a divided nation of autonomous states into the United States of America.

65. "From Our Special Correspondent," *San Francisco Daily Evening Bulletin*, 1 November 1862, 1–3.

Epilogue

The Mormon rebellion is one of those episodes that neither begin nor end with a major event that occurred on a specific day, such as the Confederates' firing on Fort Sumter on 12 April 1861 or Lee's surrender on 9 April 1865 at Appomattox Court House. Defining when America's first civil war ended is a completely arbitrary process. So when did it end?

Jane Richards, the polygamous wife of a prominent apostle, sat comfortably atop the hierarchy of the so-called "big bugs" who ruled the Great Basin during the Mormons' first decade in the Far West. Afterward, she came to regard the 1850s as a Paradise Lost. In her opinion, the U.S. Army played the serpent. For her the war and paradise ended when the army marched through Great Salt Lake City in 1858 and "demoralized the settlement," she told Matilda Bancroft in 1880. "It has never been the same since."[1]

She was right: after the U.S. Army took up its Great Basin station, the Mormons' mountain Zion would never again be the isolated bastion of theocracy it had been when Brigham Young controlled a vast region in his multiple roles as prophet, seer, and revelator, Indian affairs superintendent, and territorial governor. The assertion and presence of federal power changed many aspects of life in Utah Territory. Perhaps most important, it gave the untold number of people in the territory who were disgusted with the bloody excesses of Mormon theology and theocracy at least minimal protection.

Gauging the level of Young's popular support in the territory is difficult, but Utah Territory was hardly the monolithically unified society that its virtually unanimous elections might suggest. The highest Mormon authorities admitted the difficulty they had in retaining the people's loyalty. "How many of the brethren that are brought here by

1. Richards, Reminis[c]ences, 40, 43, LDS Archives.

the Perpetual Emigrating Fund from England and other countries will keep the faith, and stay with the people of God, and do right?" Jedediah M. Grant asked shortly after ascending to the church's First Presidency. "I am afraid not more than half."[2]

No matter how many stuck with him, certain it was that Brigham Young did not end his war with the United States when he accepted President Buchanan's offer of a full and free pardon for "seditions and treasons" and a vow to assist federal officers "in the performance of their duties."[3] His loyalty, first, last, and always, was to God's Kingdom, the theocratic system Joseph Smith had envisioned as a prerequisite of Christ's return in the latter days, which were then at hand. To take the president's offer in good faith would require Young to confess the primacy of man-made law over divine decree. It would also violate his belief that the U.S. Constitution was inspired by God to prepare a land of religious freedom where His kingdom would be established as an earthly entity that would supersede all other earthly realms within Young's lifetime.

The price was too high, and the Mormon leader would not pay it. Instead, at heavy cost to his people, he used his power over them to frustrate Buchanan's reconciliation and exploit the appeasement of Governor Alfred Cumming and the weakness of his successors to continue in his war with the American republic for the rest of his remaining twenty years of life. But in the end, Buchanan's decision to order troops to Utah, often called his blunder, proved decisive and beneficial for both Mormons and the American republic. Making the outcome inevitable were Young's own blunders, which arose from millennial convictions, a lack of formal education, and a compulsion to manage not only every aspect of his people's lives but even heaven itself.

Among the greatest of these came in 1856, when Congress refused to consider Deseret's bid for self-government through statehood. At this rebuff, Young foolishly threw down the gauntlet to the United States and declared Deseret's independence. To qualify for divine intervention, he launched a great revival that year to cleanse latter-day Israel and present before the Almighty a sanctified people. The Reformation saw the purging of apostates, Gentile merchants, federal judges, and other

2. Grant, "Discourse," 2 April 1854, in *Journal of Discourses*, 2:148.
3. Buchanan, "Proclamation," 6 April 1858, in Hafen and Hafen, *Utah Expedition*, 336.

unclean elements from the body of Israel. But it also introduced the fearful doctrine of blood atonement, a blunder that produced what historian Charles Kelly called "holy murder."

If Young meant to give heaven no choice but to intervene, his rejection of manmade laws left a new president, sworn to uphold them, with little choice but to replace him and send the U.S. Army to restore federal law in the insubordinate territory. Shortly after this news came, Young made an even bigger mistake. He ordered his Nauvoo Legion, posing as the Utah Militia, to repel the so-called "invasion" and sealed the borders of Utah Territory. These foolhardy acts not only placed the lives of his own people and American soldiers at risk, they also halted all travel "into or through or from" an area of the American West second only in size to Texas, which cut the nation almost in half on the eve of the Civil War.

The confrontation that Young provoked with the federal government also undermined the loyalty of many of his own people, especially those outside Utah. More than half of the population of the Mormon settlement of San Bernardino refused to heed his call to return to Utah. By early 1861, said Walter Murray Gibson, the place had become "a pestersome nest of apostates."[4] The ratio was apparently higher in the region that would soon become the state of Nevada. "As near as I could learn about two thirds of the old settlers of Carson Valey are apostate, and a great many in Calafornia, some say 1/4 or 1/3 of the whole," missionary Phineas Cook reported in 1860. "They say I am sent out as a spy to hunt up the dissenters."[5]

The guns that fired on Fort Sumter in April 1861 revived Young's spirits, for they reflected his belief that the struggle between the North and South was a fulfillment of prophecy and God's punishment of the guilty nation for persecuting the Saints and murdering His prophets. Under this scenario, the North and South would destroy each other, and the Kingdom of God would rise on the ashes.

Even so, when President Lincoln directly authorized him to raise, arm, and equip a company of cavalry for ninety days to guard the overland trail near Independence Rock, Young took the application as the

4. Gibson to Young, 9 January 1861, BYC.
5. Cook to Young, 8 June 1860, ibid.

president's recognition of Deseret's legitimacy and his own role as governor. He had a fully equipped company ready to ride in just two days. When events again proved him wrong, he rejected a request to extend their service by three months. Except for this instance, Utah Territory, alone among the states and territories, refused to participate in the Civil War. As a consequence, an armed force of about seven thousand men, known as the Nauvoo Legion, stood on the sidelines while volunteers from Ohio, California, and the newly created Nevada Territory kept open the Union's northern routes of travel and communications.

With little help from Utah, the United States emerged from the Civil War stronger than before, not as "water that is spilt upon the ground," as Young had predicted.[6] National attention now turned to the theocratic system that safeguarded polygamy and allowed church control of the judiciary. In 1874, Young's power over all aspects of life in Utah suffered two crippling blows. Congress that year passed the Poland Act, which stripped the church-controlled probate courts of the civil and criminal powers bestowed by Utah lawmakers. At the same time, the U.S. Supreme Court ruled that the territorial law that had granted such jurisdiction was invalid in the first place.

Both actions revealed the hand of Robert N. Baskin, a lawyer who had decided to practice in Utah. In 1866, the Harvard-educated Ohioan had seen one of his first clients, Dr. John King Robinson, another young outsider, murdered for trying to acquire property in Salt Lake City for a hospital. As he beheld Robinson's bloody body, Baskin declared his own war on Utah's theocratic rule. He would be heard from again.

In the meantime, passage of the Poland Act led to a number of sensational courtroom battles as U.S. prosecutors became more aggressive in bringing to trial known perpetrators of unpunished crimes, some from the Utah War era. By far the most sensational of these was the trial of John D. Lee for his role at Mountain Meadows. The end of the Utah War in 1858 introduced decades of cover-up, obfuscation, appeasement, bribery, and bureaucratic bungling concerning the massacre. Fearing an uprising, Governor Cumming and Utah Indian superintendent Jacob Forney tried to placate Mormon leaders. Cumming stopped an attempted investigation by John Cradlebaugh, a courageous district

6. Kenney, *Wilford Woodruff's Journal*, 6:92, 93.

judge. It seemed that everyone west of the Missouri River knew the truth except federal officials in Utah. California newspapers had it right as soon as the first reports reached the West Coast.

But the atrocity was too enormous to cover up. After the Civil War, pressure grew from the outside and from within the church as well for an investigation and punishment of the crime. So it came to pass that one man was chosen to pay the price for many. If he was the most likely candidate, however, he was not willingly sacrificed.

The LDS Church belatedly excommunicated Lee in 1870 and sent him off to run the ferry at a remote crossing on the Colorado River, now known as Lee's Ferry, a short distance downstream from today's Glen Canyon Dam. A year later, the guilt-ridden former bishop at Cedar City, Philip Klingensmith, appeared before the district court in Pioche, Nevada, and broke the oath of silence. His dispassionate and terrifying affidavit described in chilling detail how the "militia of the Territory of Utah" carried out "orders from headquarters to kill all of said company of emigrants except the little children." Lee had later told him he reported fully to the commander-in-chief, Klingensmith swore. "Brigham Young was at that time the commander-in-chief of the militia of the Territory of Utah; and further deponent saith not."[7]

Still, nothing happened, and for good reason. The only man who could open the way to an investigation and punishment chose instead to block it unless he controlled the outcome. Young had such power under the legal system that Mormon lawmakers had created after the 1850 creation of Utah Territory. A premillennial theocracy used democratic processes to short-circuit the court system enacted by Congress and rewire it under Young. The result was an exclusive judiciary for people who lived under a higher law, but one that offered little or no consistent equal protection to outsiders. Six months after the passage of the Poland Act, a federal marshal arrested John D. Lee and others for the mass murders.

The two trials of Lee, in 1875 and 1876 in Beaver, Utah, are unique in the annals of American jurisprudence as examples of jury tampering, first to exonerate the defendant, then to convict him for the same crime. As ordered in advance, Mormon jurors voted all one way in the first trial and all the other in the second. The first panel numbered eight

7. Ibid., 239, 240, 242.

active Mormons, one inactive Mormon, and three non-Saints. No faithful Mormon stepped forward to testify, but Klingensmith bravely took the stand, and sufficient other evidence came out to convict Lee. Even so, as most observers figured, the panel deadlocked nine to three. Only the non-Mormons voted to convict.

At the hung jury, a wave of indignation swept across the country, alarming Mormon leaders. Something had to be done to shut the book on the atrocity. At the same time, a new U.S. attorney was under pressure to gain a conviction and was ready to make a deal. The prosecutor agreed not to implicate Brigham Young, which meant the church, or anyone other than Lee. In return, Young laid his adopted son on the altar. He provided witnesses to convict him and even guaranteed a unanimous verdict. To make it look good, as well as work, the prosecutor impaneled only Mormon jurors. As scripted, the all-Mormon jury took less than four hours to find their former friend and brother guilty, twelve to zero. It was all neatly done.

In passing sentence, district judge Jacob Boreman pointed to the culpability of others in the crime. "The men who actually participated in the deed are not the only guilty parties," he said to Lee. "Altho the evidence shows plainly that you were a willing participant in the massacre, yet both trials taken together show that others, and some high in authority, inaugurated and decided upon the wholesale slaughter of the emigrants."[8]

On Wednesday, 21 March 1877, John D. Lee began his last journey. Federal authorities had selected the spot in hope "of obtaining any revelations from the condemned man touching his accomplices," the *New York Herald*'s man on the spot reported. However, the U.S. attorney who had prosecuted Lee discovered that "it is useless to expect any information from the prisoner as was expected and as he indirectly promised."[9]

A whole body of myths has grown up around the argument that neither Lee nor any other participant ever implicated Young, but Lee gave "the facts of my talk with George A. Smith" in Santa Clara Canyon in two confessions. In the one he gave to his attorney, Lee warned Smith that unless the emigrants had a pass from Young, they would "cer-

8. Bancroft, *History of Utah*, 568–69.

9. E. N. Fuller, "John D. Lee. Preparations for His Execution at Beaver City, Utah," *New York Herald*, 21 March 1877.

tainly never get safely through this country." Smith "laughed heartily." Lee wrote that he had always believed that Smith's mission to southern Utah was "to prepare the people for the work of exterminating Captain Fancher's train of emigrants, and I now believe that he was sent for that purpose by the direct command of Brigham Young."[10]

In his last words, Lee said that he had done everything in his power to save the emigrants; now he was being "sacrificed in a cowardly, dastardly manner," but he was not afraid to die. "Let them shoot the balls through my heart," he asked. "Don't let them mangle my body."[11] At the command "Fire!" five shots rang as one, and Lee fell back dead in his coffin. True to his words, the old man never flinched.

Meanwhile, for the people of Utah, the Poland Act soon produced an even greater shock than revelations from the Lee trials. On 6 January 1879, the U.S. Supreme Court reversed Young's own repeated rulings that the 1862 Morrill Act was unconstitutional and unanimously affirmed Vermont senator Justin S. Morrill's act outlawing polygamy in the territories. At a stroke, thousands of wives, and a smaller number of husbands, found their marriages illegal and their children illegitimate under federal law. The unanimous decision confirmed the conviction of George Reynolds, Young's private secretary, who thereby gained the distinction of becoming "the first among the polygamous martyrs." Reynolds did not agree to cooperate with prosecutors to create a test case, but like virtually all polygamists, he expected the High Court to strike down Morrill's intolerable law. The obedient scribe came to pay for ignoring the law, along with hundreds who later followed him to prison.

The High Court's ruling came some twenty months after Young died in severe pain at his Salt Lake City home of an affliction diagnosed as

10. Lee, *Mormonism Unveiled*, 221, 224–25. Young's defenders claim that William Bishop, Lee's attorney and editor, inserted this direct charge, but Bishop convincingly denied it. U.S. Attorney Sumner Howard, who prosecuted Lee, claimed he "had proof that whatever orders or directions were given by Brigham Young were verbal and communicated through George A. Smith." To refute accusations that he had suppressed vital portions of Lee's confession to accommodate Young, Howard said he had always believed that any written communications linking senior Mormon leaders to the crime had "long since been taken care of by Brigham Young." See "Howard's Defence," *New York Herald*, 9 May 1877, 4.

11. "'Justice at Last!' Execution of John D. Lee," *Supplement—Frank Leslie's Illustrated Newspaper*, 14 April 1877, 109–12.

"cholera morbus," or perhaps appendicitis. Some twelve thousand persons overflowed the buildings on Temple Square as Apostle George Q. Cannon eulogized the fallen leader as "the brain, the eye, the ear, the mouth and hand for the entire people of the Church." From the shape of the seats that the mourners sat on to the creation of territorial government, he said, "Nothing was too small for his mind, nothing was too large."[12]

The death of Brigham Young brought to a close a thirty-year struggle to establish the primacy of God's Kingdom over the United States and all earthly realms as a condition of the return of Joseph Smith with Jesus Christ. Divine Providence thus saved him from the pain of seeing the U.S. Supreme Court overrule him and uphold the constitutionality of the Morrill Anti-Bigamy Act. Nor would he live to see the revealed marriage doctrine, which his second counselor, Jedediah M. Grant, in 1856 had called "the cable of the Church of Christ," used as the means to destroy the original theocratic form of the American faith itself.

Over the next thirteen years, Baskin and other non-Mormon leaders wielded the marriage doctrine like a wrecking ball to destroy the theocratic structure Young had constructed. While angry preachers and journalists called for the army to launch a war against the Mormons, Baskin chose to deploy a more powerful weapon: American law. One after another, the blows fell in new federal legislation he wrote or promoted, laws that stiffened penalties for polygamy, denied civil rights to any who practiced or professed to believe in it, imposed dictatorial power over elections, and abridged other property and citizenship rights. The government sent more than a thousand men to jail for practicing polygamy in what its critics characterized as a "judicial crusade," but Baskin's long campaign had only one objective: to compel the Latter-day Saints and their theocratic prophets to obey the law. Unable to stop it, Young's successors went underground to hide from federal marshals and wait for the Lord, powerless to give Him the earthly support Young had mobilized in 1857.

The aging church president, Wilford Woodruff, sought divine advice in 1889 and was told to "be faithful until I come." When the Lord failed to arrive as anticipated, Woodruff found himself "under the necessity

---

12. Roberts, *Comprehensive History of the Church*, 5:517–18.

of acting for the Temporal Salvation of the Church."[13] The "official Declaration" he issued on 24 September 1890 was no forthright "Thus saith the Lord." Addressed "To whom it may concern," Woodruff's "Manifesto," as it is known today, declared his intention to submit to the federal laws forbidding plural marriage and to influence church members to do likewise. They did so unanimously at their semi-annual conference less than three weeks later, when many no doubt whispered "amen" as they raised their right hands.

Whether Woodruff really intended to accept the primacy of man-made law over divine decree and end polygamy may be arguable. What is certain is that Young would never have agreed to either proposition. If the fourth church president was out of tune with his strong-minded predecessor, his declaration clearly reflected the feelings of its members on both counts. Polygamy was no more popular with women of the church then than it would be if it were reintroduced today. And obedience to law enacted by representatives of the people is now a vital element of Mormon faith.

Today the Utah War of 1857–58 is largely forgotten and even less understood. So when did it end? In a larger sense, it ended on 29 August 1877, with the death of Brigham Young. It was always his war. He waged it from the day in June 1844 that a mob broke into the Carthage Jail in Illinois and murdered Joseph Smith, and he never accepted the steady decline in authority he experienced after 1857 as the federal government systematically stripped him of political office, private military power, and his iron grip on Utah's judicial system.

Instead he went to his death believing that he would lead his people back to Missouri and live to see Smith return with Jesus Christ. If he should die anywhere in the mountains, Young instructed in his will, he wished to be buried on his own property overlooking Salt Lake Valley at about 140 East First Avenue, where his grave can be seen today. "But if I should live to go back with the Church in Jackson County," the Zion of Mormonism and the location of its still unbuilt New Jerusalem, "I wish to be buried there," he said.[14]

13. Kenney, *Wilford Woodruff's Journal*, 9:69, 112–14.
14. Leonard J. Arrington, *Brigham Young: American Moses* (Urbana: University of Illinois Press, 1986), 399, 400.

Four hundred years after the death of Jacob's eleventh son, Moses and the children of Israel honored Joseph's dying words. During the exodus from Egypt, they carried his bones to the land God promised to Abraham. There they buried them at Shechem in the portion of ground Jacob had bought.

Perhaps someday Brigham Young will get his wish.

Selected Bibliography

ARCHIVAL SOURCES

Authors' Collection

Bailey, George Brown. Journal of George Brown and Elizabeth Young Bailey. Copy in authors' possession.

Hicks, George Armstrong. "Family Record and History of Geo. A. Hicks Containing the Principle Events of a Life among the Poor of Utah & the 'Saints' Generally." Manuscript copy from the estate of J. Will Lewis of Salt Lake City, Utah. In possession of Will Bagley.

Love, Andrew. Journal. David L. Bigler transcription.

Smith, Azariah. Journal. Copy in possession of David L. Bigler.

Bancroft Library. University of California, Berkeley.

Crosman, George Hampton. Letter to W. A. Gordon. 5 October 1859. Letters to W. A. Gordon, Camp Floyd, Utah Territory: ALS, 1860. BANC MSS 68/49 p.

Downes, Clara E. "Journal across the Plains: Kept by Miss Clara E. Downes and most humbly dedicated to her sister, Miss Elisabeth M. Downes, 7 May to 15 August 1860." MSS 84/ 161 c.

Beinecke Rare Book and Manuscript Library, Yale University. New Haven, Conn. [Beinecke Library]

Burr, Frederick H. Diary. Western Americana Collection. WA MSS S-1748.

Dorsey, Thomas. Journals and Letters, 1854–1861. UNCAT MSS 1110.

Ellerbeck, Thomas W. Report to James Ferguson. 14 January 1858. Nauvoo Legion Papers, 1853–1864. WA MSS S-1012 N226.

Livingston, LaRhett L. Letter to James G. Livingston. 16 September 1854. WA MSS S-1852.

Young, Brigham. Letters to William H. Hooper, 1859–1861. WA MSS 535.

———. Letter to David Rogers. 5 December 1844. WA MSS S-13 Y84.

Brigham Young Collection. Church History Library and Archives, Church of Jesus Christ of Latter-day Saints. Salt Lake City, Utah. MS 1234. [BYC]

The core collection of original manuscripts of Brigham Young's papers is found at the Church History Library and Archives in Salt Lake City. LDS Church historian Leonard J. Arrington hired Edyth Romney to create typescripts of virtually every letter in this collection, and most of them can be found in his papers at Logan, Utah, in Utah State University's Leonard J. Arrington Historical Archives as LJAHA COLL 1. Copies of Young's correspondence, including many items cited in this work, can also be found in archives from Connecticut to California. The Marriott Library at the University of Utah has eight microfilms in its Brigham Young collection, MS 566 Brigham Young Papers, 1857–1877. The Utah State Historical Society has a small but useful collection of Young items in its Brigham Young Papers, 1857–1877, MSS B 93. The Beinecke Rare Book and Manuscript Library at Yale University also has a number of significant Brigham Young letters, as does the Huntington Library.

Appleby, William I. Letter to Brigham Young. 13 April 1857.

Bernhisel, John M. Letters to Brigham Young. 18 March and 17 July 1856; 2 April, 17 October, and 17 December 1857; 18 January 1858.

———. Summary of Interview with President Buchanan. Spring 1858.

Bucklin, Horace. Letter to Brigham Young. November 1857.

Callister, Thomas. Report to Daniel H. Wells. 5 October 1857.

Cook, Phineas. Letter to Brigham Young. 8 June 1860.

Cummings, James W., and Robert T. Burton. Report to Daniel H. Wells. 27 September 1857.

Gibson, Walter Murray. Letter to Brigham Young. 9 January 1861.

Huntington, Dimick B. Letter to George A. Smith. 1 September 1856.

Hurt, Garland. Letter to Brigham Young. 6 July 1855.

———. "Remarks." As reported by J. V. Long and revised in Hurt's own handwriting. 4 July 1855.

Kane, Thomas L. Letter to Brigham Young. 18 July 1858.

Kimball, William H. Report to Daniel H. Wells. 24 November 1857.

Lander, Frederick W. Letter to Brigham Young. 23 September 1858.

Little, Jesse C. Reports to Brigham Young. 29 and 30 September, 2 and 6 October 1857.

Martenas, M. S. "Statement." 6 July 1853. Box 58, Folder 14.

McCulloch, Ben. Letter to "Ex Gov Brigham Young." 3 July 1858.

Pack, John. Letter to Brigham Young. 22 August 1857.

Richards, Samuel W., and Bryant Stringham. Report to Brigham Young. 18 August 1857.

Robison, Lewis, and Robert T. Burton. Report to Daniel H. Wells. 10 November 1857.

Smith, Thomas S. Affidavit. 15 April 1858.

———. Letter to Brigham Young. 30 June 1856.

———. Report to Brigham Young. 28 February 1858.

Taylor, John. Letters to Brigham Young. 12 and 18 July 1858.

Taylor, John, F. D. Richards, and Nathaniel V. Jones. Report to Daniel H. Wells. 15 November 1857.

Wells, Daniel H. Letters to Brigham Young. 29 and 30 September 1857; 2, 5, 13, 15, 17, and 18 October 1857; 16, 21, and 26 November 1857.

Wells, Daniel H., George D. Grant, and Charles C. Rich. Letter to Brigham Young. 15 November 1857.

Wells, Daniel H., Charles C. Rich, and George D. Grant. Letter to Brigham Young. 7 November 1857.

Wells, Daniel H., John Taylor, and George A. Smith. Letter to Brigham Young. 2 October 1852.

Young, Brigham. Instructions by President Brigham Young. 25 December 1857.

———. Letters to John M. Bernhisel. 1 April, 17 July, 30 August, 4 November, and 10 December 1856; 6 May 1858.

———. Letter to Lewis Brunson and Isaac C. Haight. 2 August 1857.

———. Letter to Alfred Cumming. 8 May 1858.

————. Letter to Andrew Cunningham. 4 August 1857.

————. Letter to Thomas L. Kane. 14 April 1856.

————. Letter to Peter Maughn. 4 August 1857.

————. Letter to C. P. Merrill. 28 September 1857.

————. Letter to James K. Polk. 9 August 1846.

————. Letter to George A. Smith, John M. Bernhisel, and John Taylor. 30 August 1856.

————. Letter to Silas Smith, H. P. Richards, and Edward Partridge. 4 August 1857.

————. Letter to John Taylor. 10 April 1856.

————. Letter to John Taylor and George A. Smith. 3 January 1857.

————. Letter to Daniel H. Wells. 26 November 1857.

————. Letter to Daniel H. Wells, Charles C. Rich, and George D. Grant. 18 November 1857.

————. Letters to Daniel H. Wells, John Taylor, and George A. Smith. 7, 9, and 17 October 1857.

————. Unpublished discourse. 16 August 1857.

California State Library. Sacramento.

Bloom, Henry Sterling. Gold Rush Letters and Bloom Family Miscellany, 1850–1867. Manuscript Box 2315. *See also* Burroughs.

Burroughs, Burt E., ed. "Tales of the Pioneers of the Kankakee, Taken from the Diary of Henry S. Bloom." Typewritten transcription of articles from the *Kankakee Daily Republic*, Kankakee, Ill. CALIF qB B65.

Church History Library and Archives, Church of Jesus Christ of Latter-day Saints.
Salt Lake City, Utah. [LDS Archives]

Bagley, John. Record Book. 1894. P M270.1 B146B.

Blair, Seth Millington. Reminiscences and Journals, 1851–1868. John Bond transcription. MS 1710, Fd. 1.

Brown, Homer. Journal. Transcribed by Keith Franklin Larson. Film #MS 2181 1.

Burbank, Daniel Mark. Journal. *See also* "Life Story of Daniel Mark Burbank," FHC microfilm #0000608.

Collected Statements on Mountain Meadows. MS 2674.

Huntington, Dimick B. Journal. MS 1419 2.

Journal History of the Church of Jesus Christ of Latter-day Saints, 1830–1972. 1,200 vols. Compiled by the Church Historian's Office from diaries, letters, newspapers, sermons, etc.

The Latter-day Saints' Millennial Star. LDS periodical. British Mission, 1840–1970.

A List of donations toward fitting out Soldiers for the Army of Israel, 1st Ward, Ogden City, Weber County. l February 1858. MS 9310.

McLean, Eleanor J. McComb. "Account of the Death of Parley P. Pratt." Ca. 1857. MS 525 1.

Richards, Jane Snyder. Reminis[c]ences of Mrs. F. D. Richards, San Francisco, 1880. The original is in the H. H. Bancroft Collection at the Bancroft Library, University of California, Berkeley.

Smith, Azariah. Journal.

Utah Stake Minutes. General Meetings, 1855–1860. Typescript. MS 2737.

Wells, Daniel H. Letter to William B. Pace. 1 August 1857. William B. Pace Letters, 1857–1866. MS 4664.

Woodruff, W. W. Historian's Private Journal.

Cornell University Library. Ithaca, N.Y.

Burr, David A. Papers. Collection 1333.

Duke University Library. Durham, N.C.

Cumming, Alfred. Papers, 1792–1889. 2nd 93:C Box 1 (Manuscripts).

Hudson's Bay Company Archives, Archives of Manitoba. Winnipeg.

Simpson, George. Incoming Correspondence. R3C 1T5.

Huntington Library. San Marino, Calif.

Kane, Thomas L. Diary. FAC 515.
Martineau, James H. "My Life." Diary of James Henry Martineau. Photocopies circa 1850–2004 (bulk circa 1850–circa 1921). MSS FAC 1499. Robert Briggs transcription.

Harold B. Lee Library, Special Collections. Brigham Young University,
Provo, Utah. [BYU Library]

Bigler, Jacob G. Letter to John Pyper, David Webb, and counselors. 23 December 1856. Record of the Nephi Mass Quorum of Seventies, 1857–1858. MSS Sc 3244.
Brown, Lorenzo. Journal of Lorenzo Brown, 1823–1900. Americana Collection. 1130 HBLL/BX 8670.1 .B8142.
Burr, David A. "Map of a Survey of the Indian Reservation on Spanish Fork Cr." Rare Maps Collection. 1130 HBLL/G 4342 .S6 1856 .B8.
Cummings, Benjamin Franklin. Biography and Journals of Benjamin Franklin Cummings, Pioneer of Utah, 1847. Americana Collection. 1130 HBLL/BX 8670.1 .C912.
Dame, William Horne. Patriarchal Blessing. 1854. William Horne Dame Papers, 1846–1884. Vault Manuscript Collection. 1130 HBLL/Vault MSS 55.
Hamblin, Jacob. Daybook, August–September 1857. Amer M270.1 H17.
Kane, Thomas L. Letter to James Buchanan. 15 March 1858. Thomas L. Kane Collection. Vault Manuscript Collection. 1130 HBLL/Vault MSS 792.
Pitchforth, Samuel. Diary of Samuel Pitchforth, 1857–1868. Americana Collection. 1130 HBLL/BX 8670.1 .P68d.
Pulsipher, John. Diary. Typescript. Americana Collection. 1130 HBLL/BX 8670.1 .P968. Utah War account reprinted in Hafen and Hafen, *The Utah Expedition*, 198–219.
Smith, George A., to William H. Dame. 3 February [March] 1858. William Horne Dame Papers, 1846–1884. Vault Manuscript Collection. 1130 HBLL/Vault MSS 55.
Terry, James Parshall. Autobiography, 1880–1905. Manuscript Collection. 1130 HBLL/MSS SC 1698.

Library of Congress, Manuscripts Division. Washington, D.C.

Porter, Fitz-John. "An incident of Army Life among the Mormons during the Utah troubles of 1859 to 1860," including extracts from diary. Undated. Fitz-John Porter Papers. Articles, 1861–1862. Box 53, Reel 25.

J. Willard Marriott Library, Special Collections, University of Utah.
Salt Lake City. [Marriott Library]

Hanks, Ebenezer. Letter to Amasa Lyman. 6 February 1858. Richard Douglas Poll Papers. MS 0674.

Kane, Thomas L. Letter to Brigham Young. Undated, but probably 25 February 1858. Richard Douglas Poll Papers. MS 0674.

Taylor, John. Letters from Brigham Young. Raymond Taylor Typescripts, John Taylor Family Papers. UU_MS 0050.

Van Dyke, James. Letter to James Buchanan. 5 March 1858. Richard Douglas Poll Papers. MS 0674.

———. Letter to Thomas L. Kane. 28 March 1859. Richard Douglas Poll Papers. MS 0674.

Young, Brigham. "A Series of Instructions and Remarks by Brigham Young, at a Special Council, Tabernacle, March 21, 1858." Printed pamphlet. Frederick Kesler Papers. MS 49. Box 4, Folder 24.

Young, Joseph A. Journal of a Mission to the Eastern States, 1864. MSS 233.

National Archives and Records Administration. Washington, D.C.

Harney, William S. Letter to J. Thomas. U.S. War Department, Department of the West, Letters Sent, 1857–61. RG 338.

Hoffman, William H. Letter to Samuel Cooper. 27 May 1856. Fort Laramie Letter Book, Fort Laramie, Wyoming, Letters Sent, 1855. Pt. V, Entry 2, Vol. 1 of 14. RG 393.

Indian Depredation Claim 8479. *Malinda Thurston v. United States and Ute Indians.* RG 123.

New York Public Library, Manuscripts and Archives Division. New York, N.Y.

Phelps, John Wolcott. Diary. John Wolcott Phelps Papers, 1833–1884. Series III: Diaries, 1838–1871. Diary entries from 14 June 1857 to 20 September 1857 reprinted in Hafen and Hafen, *The Utah Expedition,* 89–138.

Gerald R. Sherratt Library. Southern Utah University, Cedar City.

Cedar Stake Journal, Notes copied from. Caroline Parry Woolley Collection. MS 34. Box 17, Folder 14.

Wells, Daniel H. Letter to William H. Dame. 13 August 1857. William R. Palmer Collection. Ph.1.

University of Arizona Library, Special Collections. Tucson.

Smith, Lot. Papers. AZ 186. Folder 3.

Utah State Archives and Records Service. Salt Lake City.

Hurt, Garland. Letter to Brigham Young. 15 September 1855. Governor Young Letterbook, 1853–1857. Series 13844.

Memorials and Resolutions, General Assembly, Utah Territory. 1856–57. Series 3148. Reel 2, Box 1.

Young, Brigham. Letters to Garland Hurt and George Armstrong. 11 and 12 February 1856. Governor Young Letterbook, 1853–1857. Series 13844.

Utah State Historical Society. Salt Lake City. [USHS]

Ames, Ira. Journal and Record of the Life and Family of Ira Ames. MSS A 5199.

Ballard, Henry. Private Journal. MS A 18.

Borrowman, John. Patriarchal Blessing. 1846. Journal. Vol. 1, item 4. Joel E. Ricks Collection of Transcriptions [from diaries and journals of pioneers who settled in Cache Valley (Utah)]. Microfilm. MIC A 341.

Hammond, Milton D. *A Journal Kept by Milton D. Hammond with a Short Sketch of My Life, 1856–1858.* PAM 2068.

Harney, William S. Letter to Brigham Young. 28 July 1857. U.S. War Department, Army of Utah, Letters Sent, 1857–61, National Archives microfilm.

Hurt, Garland. Letter to Alfred Cumming. 17 December 1857. Territorial Papers: Utah Series, 1853–1873, National Archives.

———. Letter to John M. Elliott. 1 October 1856. Letters Received by the Office of Indian Affairs, 1824–81, Utah Superintendency, National Archives.

———. Letter to George W. Manypenny. 30 March 1857.

———. Letters to Brigham Young. March and 31 December 1855. Letters Received by the Office of Indian Affairs, 1824–81, Utah Superintendency, National Archives.

King, Hannah Tapfield. Diary. MSS A 1883.

Kinney, John F. Letter to U.S. Attorney General Jeremiah Black. Undated. Records Relating to Appointment of Federal Judges, Attorneys, and Marshals for Utah Territory and State, 1853–1901. MIC 1, A-527.

———. Letter to Caleb Cushing. 1 April 1855. Ibid.

Savage, Levi, Jr. Diary. Levi Savage Papers, 1852–1902. MSS B 122.

Steptoe, Edward J. Letters to Samuel Cooper. 26 March and 15 April 1855. Selected Letters from Col. E. J. Steptoe, 1854–55, U.S. War Department, Office of the Adjutant General, National Archives.

Wells, Daniel H. Letter to David Evans. 13 August 1857. David Evans Papers, 1845–1883. MIC A 1136.

Young, Brigham. Papers, 1857–1877. MSS B 93.

Utah Territorial Militia Records, 1849–1877. Utah State Archives and Records Service, Salt Lake City, Series 2210. [UTMR]

Ferguson, James. General Orders No. 3. 18 September 1857. Doc. 591.

———. Report to Brigham Young. 7 January 1858.

Floyd, John R. Letter to Brigham Young. 11 May 1857.

Harker, Joseph, John Bennion, M. Gee Harris, William A. Hickman, and Samuel Bennion. Letter to Brigham Young. 15 January 1858.

Johnson, Aaron. Report of Genl. A. Johnson to Lt. Genl. D. H. Wells in regard to the flight of Dr. Garland Hurt, U.S. Indian Agent. October 1857.

McBride, William. Report. 24 June 1851.

Monroe, Marcellus. "Report of a Party of Observation." September 1857.

Wells, Daniel H. Orders to Thomas Callister. 14 October 1857.

———. Orders to George D. Grant. 31 January 1850.

———. Report to Brigham Young. 13–14 February 1850.

Young, Brigham. Letter to Capt Wacher [Ute chief Walkara]. 25 July 1853. Doc. 289, reel 5.

———. Letter to Daniel H. Wells. 14 February 1850.

Weber State University, Archives and Special Collections. Ogden, Utah.

Brewer, Myron, to Gen. Wm. H. Kimball. 5 February 1858. Donald R. Moorman Collection, Box 21, Folder 1-6. WA 86 5.

Wyoming Archives. Cheyenne.

Carter, Judge W. A. Diary, 1857. Judge W. A. Carter Papers. B-864 thru H63-41/70 and H72-42, MA6240, 72-22-131 (H229).

PUBLISHED SOURCES

Acts, Resolutions and Memorials, Passed at the Several Annual Sessions of the Legislative Assembly of the Territory of Utah, from 1851 to 1870 Inclusive. Salt Lake City: G. Q. Cannon, 1872.

Aird, Polly. *Mormon Convert, Mormon Defector: A Scottish Immigrant in the American West, 1848–1861.* Norman, Okla.: Arthur H. Clark Co., 2009.

———. "'You Nasty Apostates, Clear Out': Reasons for Disaffection in the Late 1850s." *Journal of Mormon History* 30, no. 2 (Fall 2004): 129–207.

Alexander, Thomas G. *Utah, the Right Place: The Official Centennial History.* Salt Lake City: Gibbs Smith, 1995. 2nd rev. ed., 2003.

Alter, J. Cecil, and Robert J. Dwyer, eds. "The Utah War Journal of Albert Tracy." *Utah Historical Quarterly* 13 (January, April, July, October 1945): 1–128.

Angel, Myron. *History of Nevada: With Illustrations and Biographical Sketches of Its Prominent Men and Pioneers.* Oakland, Calif.: Thompson & West, 1881.

Arrington, Leonard J. *Great Basin Kingdom: An Economic History of the Latter-day Saints.* Cambridge, Mass.: Harvard University Press, 1958. Reprint, Salt Lake City: University of Utah Press, 1993.

———. "Mormon Finance and the Utah War." *Utah Historical Quarterly* 20 (July 1952): 219–37.

Backus, Anna Jean. *Mountain Meadows Witness: The Life of Bishop Philip Klingensmith.* Spokane, Wash.: Arthur H. Clark Co., 1995.

Bagley, Will. *Blood of the Prophets: Brigham Young and the Massacre at Mountain Meadows.* Norman: University of Oklahoma Press, 2002.

———. "A Great Wall Once Circled Salt Lake City." *Salt Lake Tribune,* 25 November 2001, B1.

———. "'One Long Funeral March': A Revisionist's View of the Mormon Handcart Disasters." *Journal of Mormon History* 35, no. 1 (Winter 2009): 50–115.

———, ed. *The Pioneer Camp of the Saints: The 1846 and 1847 Mormon Trail Journals of Thomas Bullock.* Spokane, Wash.: Arthur H. Clark Co., 1997.

———. *Stones, Clubs, and Gun Barrels: Two Lost Accounts of the Mountain Meadows Massacre.* Norman, Okla.: Arthur H. Clark Co., 2008.

Ball, Durwood. *Army Regulars on the Western Frontier, 1848–1861.* Norman: University of Oklahoma Press, 2001.

Bancroft, Hubert Howe. *History of Utah, 1540–1886.* San Francisco: History Co., 1889.

Barney, Ronald O., ed. *The Mormon Vanguard Brigade of 1847: Norton Jacob's Record.* Logan: Utah State University Press, 2005.

Barrett, Chuck. "Stony Point: Nevada's Bloody Landmark on the California Trail." *Overland Journal* 25 (Spring 2007): 3–23.

Baskin, R. N. *Reminiscences of Early Utah.* Salt Lake City: R. N. Baskin, 1914. Reprint, Salt Lake City: Signature Books, 2006.

Bayard, Samuel J. *The Life of George Dashiell Bayard, Late Captain, U.S.A., and Brigadier-General of Volunteers, Killed in the Battle of Fredericksburg, Dec., 1862.* New York: G. P. Putnam's Sons, 1874.

Bigler, David L. "The Aiken Party Executions and the Utah War, 1857–1858." *Western Historical Quarterly* 38 (Winter 2007): 457–76.

———. *Fort Limhi: The Mormon Adventure in Oregon Territory, 1855–1858.* Spokane, Wash.: Arthur H. Clark Co., 2003.

———. "Garland Hurt, the American Friend of the Utahs." *Utah Historical Quarterly* 62 (Spring 1994): 149–70.

————, ed. *The Gold Discovery Journal of Azariah Smith*. Salt Lake City: University of Utah Press, 1990.

————, ed. *A Winter with the Mormons: The 1852 Letters of Jotham Goodell*. Salt Lake City: Tanner Trust Fund, University of Utah Library, 2001.

Bigler, David L., and Will Bagley, eds. *Army of Israel: Mormon Battalion Narratives*. Spokane, Wash.: Arthur H. Clark Co., 2000.

————, eds. *Innocent Blood: Essential Narratives of the Mountain Meadows Massacre*. Norman, Okla.: Arthur H. Clark Co., 2008.

Boorstin, Daniel J. *The Americans: The National Experience*. New York: Random House, 1965.

Brooks, Juanita. "Indian Relations on the Mormon Frontier." *Utah Historical Quarterly* 12, nos. 1–2 (January–April 1944): 1–48.

————, ed. *Journal of the Southern Indian Mission: Diary of Thomas D. Brown*. Logan: Utah State University Press, 1964.

————. *The Mountain Meadows Massacre*. Stanford, Calif.: Stanford University Press, 1950. Reprint, Norman: University of Oklahoma Press, 1991.

————, ed. *On the Mormon Frontier: The Diary of Hosea Stout*. 2 vols. Salt Lake City: University of Utah Press, 1964.

Brough, Franklin Keith. *Freely I Gave: The Life of Jacob G. Bigler*. Wichita, Kans.: Grit Printing Co., 1958.

Brown, John. *Autobiography of Pioneer John Brown, 1820–1896*. Arranged and published by his son, John Zimmerman Brown. Salt Lake City: Press of Stevens & Wallis, 1941.

Buchanan, James. Inaugural Address. 4 March 1857. American Presidency Project, University of California, Santa Barbara. http://www.presidency.ucsb.edu/sou.php.

————. "Message of the President." 8 December 1857. *Congressional Globe*, 35th Cong., 1st sess., 1857–58, Appendix, 1–7.

————. *Message of the President, Transmitting Copies of Correspondence on Affairs in Territory of Utah*. 36th Cong., 1st sess., 1859–60, vol. 12, H. Ex. Doc. 78, serial 1056.

————. *Presidential Message Communicating Correspondence, Etc., on Massacre at Mountain Meadows, and Other Massacres in Utah Territory*. 36th Cong., 1st sess., 1860, vol. 11, S. Ex. Doc. 42, serial 1033.

————. *The Utah Expedition: Message Transmitting Reports from the Secretaries of War, of the Interior, and of the Attorney General, Relative to the Military Expedition Ordered into the Territory of Utah*. 35th Cong., 1st sess., 1857–58, H. Ex. Doc. 71, serial 956.

Burr, David H. *Annual Report of Surveyor General of Utah*. 34th Cong., 3rd sess., 1856, vol. 1, pt. 1, H. Ex. Doc. 1, serial 893, 542–49.

Burton, Richard F. *The City of the Saints; and, Across the Rocky Mountains*. New York: Harper & Brothers, 1862.

Call, Asa. "The Mormons." *Sacramento Daily Union* 1, no. 88 (28 June 1851): 2.

Cannon, Frank J., and George L. Knapp. *Brigham Young and His Mormon Empire*. New York: Fleming H. Revell Co., 1913.

Carleton, James H. *Special Report of the Mountain Meadows Massacre*. 57th Cong., 1st sess., 1902, H. Doc. 605, serial 4377.

Carter, D. Robert. "Fish and the Famine of 1855–56." *Journal of Mormon History* 27, no. 2 (Fall 2001): 92–124.

————. *Founding Fort Utah: Provo's Native Inhabitants, Early Explorers, and First Year of Settlement*. Provo, Utah: Provo City Corp., 2003.

Chandless, William. *A Visit to Salt Lake: Being a Journey across the Plains, and a Residence in the Mormon Settlements at Utah.* London: Smith, Elder, and Co., 1857. Reprint, New York: AMS Press, 1971.

A Compilation of the Messages and Papers of the Presidents. New York: Bureau of National Literature, 1897.

Cooley, Everett, ed. *Diary of Brigham Young, 1857.* Salt Lake City: Tanner Trust Fund, University of Utah Library, 1980.

Cradlebaugh, John. *Utah and the Mormons: Speech of Hon. John Cradlebaugh of Nevada, on the Admission of Utah as a State. Delivered in the House of Representatives, February 7, 1863.* Washington, D.C.: L. Towers & Co., 1863.

Crampton, C. Gregory, and Steven K. Madsen. *In Search of the Spanish Trail: Santa Fe to Los Angeles, 1829–1848.* Salt Lake City: Gibbs Smith, 1994.

Crawley, Peter L. *The Essential Parley P. Pratt.* Salt Lake City: Signature Books, 1990.

Derry, Charles. *Autobiography of Elder Charles Derry: "The Apostle of Purity."* Independence, Mo.: Price Publishing Co., 1997.

Doctrine and Covenants of the Church of Jesus Christ of Latter-day Saints. Salt Lake City: LDS Church, 1970.

Dorius, Carl C. N. "Autobiography." In Earl N. Dorius and Ruth C. Rasmussen, *The Dorius Heritage,* 86–88. Salt Lake City: E. N. Dorius, 1979.

Du Bois, John Van Deusen. *Campaigns in the West, 1856–1861: The Journal and Letters of Colonel John Van Deusen Du Bois; with Pencil Sketches of Joseph Heger.* Edited by George P. Hammond. Tucson, Ariz.: Pioneers Historical Society, 1949. Reprint, with a new foreword by Durwood Ball, Tucson: Arizona Historical Society, 2003.

Ekins, Roger Robin, ed. *Defending Zion: George Q. Cannon and the California Newspaper Wars of 1856–1857.* Spokane, Wash.: Arthur H. Clark Co., 2002.

Esshom, Frank. *Pioneers and Prominent Men of Utah.* Salt Lake City: Utah Pioneers Book Publishing Co., 1913.

Farmer, Jared. *On Zion's Mount: Mormons, Indians, and the American Landscape.* Cambridge, Mass.: Harvard University Press, 2008.

Floyd, John B. *Annual Report of the Secretary of War, 1857.* 35th Cong., 1st sess., 1857–58, S. Ex. Doc. 11, serial 920.

———. *Annual Report of the Secretary of War, 1858.* 35th Cong., 2nd sess., 1858, vol. 2, S. Ex. Doc. 1, serial 975.

———. *Annual Report of the Secretary of War, 1859.* 36th Cong., 1st sess., 1859, vol. 2, S. Ex. Doc. 2, serial 1024.

———. *Annual Report of the Secretary of War, 1860.* 36th Cong., 2nd sess., 1860, vol. 2, S. Ex. Doc. 1, serial 1079.

Ford, Thomas. *A History of Illinois: From Its Commencement as a State in 1818 to 1847.* Chicago: S. C. Griggs & Co., 1854. Reprint, Lakeside Classics Edition, ed. Milo Milton Quaife, 2 vols., Chicago: Lakeside Press, 1945.

Freeman, Douglas Southall. *Lee's Lieutenants: A Study in Command.* 3 vols. New York: Charles Scribner's Sons, 1942–44.

Furniss, Norman F. *The Mormon Conflict, 1850–1859.* New Haven: Yale University Press, 1960.

Gardner, Hamilton. "March of 2d Dragoons." *Annals of Wyoming* 27 (April 1855): 43–60.

———, ed. "A Territorial Militiaman in the Utah War Journal of Newton Tuttle." *Utah Historical Quarterly* 22 (Fall 1954): 297–320.

Godfrey, Kenneth W. "Crime and Punishment in Mormon Nauvoo, 1839–1846." *Brigham Young University Studies* 32, no. 1 (Winter 1992): 195–227.

Gottfredson, Peter. *History of Indian Depredations in Utah.* Salt Lake City: Skelton Publishing, 1919.

Gove, Jesse. *The Utah Expedition, 1857–1858: Letters of Capt. Jesse A. Gove, 10th Inf., U.S.A., of Concord, N.H., to Mrs. Gove, and Special Correspondence of the New York Herald.* Edited by Otis G. Hammond. Concord: New Hampshire Historical Society, 1928.

Gowans, Fred R., and Eugene E. Campbell. *Fort Supply: Brigham Young's Green River Experiment.* Provo, Utah: Brigham Young University Publications, 1976.

Gunnison, John W. *The Mormons; or, Latter-day Saints, in the Valley of the Great Salt Lake: A History of their rise and progress, peculiar doctrines, present condition and prospects, derived from personal observation during a residence among them.* Philadelphia: Lippincott, Grambo & Co., 1852.

Hafen, Ann W., and LeRoy R. Hafen, eds. *Handcarts to Zion: The Story of a Unique Western Migration, 1856–1860.* Glendale, Calif.: Arthur H. Clark Co., 1960.

———. *The Utah Expedition, 1857–1858: A Documentary Account of the United States Military Movement under Colonel Albert Sidney Johnston and the Resistance by Brigham Young and the Mormon Nauvoo Legion.* Glendale, Calif.: Arthur H. Clark Co., 1958.

Hallwas, John E., and Roger D. Launius. *Cultures in Conflict: A Documentary History of the Mormon War in Illinois.* Logan: Utah State University Press, 1995.

Hanson, Klaus J. *Quest for Empire: The Political Kingdom of God and the Council of Fifty in Mormon History.* East Lansing: Michigan State University Press, 1967.

Hardy, B. Carmon, ed. *Doing the Works of Abraham: Mormon Polygamy, Its Origin, Practice, and Demise.* Norman, Okla.: Arthur H. Clark Co., 2007.

Hickman, William A., and John H. Beadle. *Brigham's Destroying Angel: Being the Life, Confession, and Startling Disclosures of the Notorious Bill Hickman, the Danite Chief of Utah.* New York: George A. Crofutt & Co., 1872. Reprint, Salt Lake City: Shepard Publishing Co., 1904.

Holzer, Harold, ed. *The Lincoln-Douglas Debates: The First Complete, Unexpurgated Text.* New York: HarperCollins, 1993.

Jensen, Richard L. "Without Purse or Scrip? Financing Latter-day Saint Missionary Work in Europe in the Nineteenth Century." *Journal of Mormon History* 12 (1985): 3–14.

Johnson, Clark V., ed. *Mormon Redress Petitions: Documents of the 1833–1838 Missouri Conflict.* Provo, Utah: Bookcraft, 1992.

Johnston, William Preston. *The Life of Gen. Albert Sidney Johnston: Embracing His Services in the Armies of the United States, the Republic of Texas, and the Confederate States.* New York: D. Appleton and Co., 1878.

Journal of Discourses. 26 vols. London: Latter-day Saints Book Depot, 1854–86.

Kenney, Scott G., ed. *Wilford Woodruff's Journal.* 10 vols. Midvale, Utah: Signature Books, 1983.

Landon, Michael N. "A Continuous Line of Stock and Wagons: A Reappraisal of the 1857 Overland Emigration." Paper presented at the Oregon-California Trail Association Convention, 21 August 2009.

Langworthy, Franklin. *Scenery of the Plains, Mountains and Mines; or, A Diary kept upon the Overland Route to California, by way of the Great Salt Lake.* Ogdensburgh, N.Y.: J. S. Sprague, Bookseller; Hitchcock & Tillotson, Printers, 1855.

Larson, Andrew Karl, and Katherine Miles Larson, eds. *Diary of Charles Lowell Walker.* 2 vols. Logan: Utah State University Press, 1980.

Larson, Gustive O. "Land Contest in Early Utah." *Utah Historical Quarterly* 29 (Fall 1961): 309–25.

Lee, John D. *Mormonism Unveiled; or, The Life and Confessions of the Late Mormon Bishop, John D. Lee*. Edited by William Bishop. St. Louis: Bryan, Brand & Co., 1877.

LeSueur, Stephen C. *The 1838 Mormon War in Missouri*. Columbia: University of Missouri Press, 1987.

MacKinnon, William P., ed. *At Sword's Point, Part 1: A Documentary History of the Utah War*. Norman, Okla.: Arthur H. Clark Co., 2008.

———. "The Buchanan Spoils System and the Utah Expedition: Careers of W. M. F. Magraw and John M. Hockaday." *Utah Historical Quarterly* 31 (Spring 1963): 127–50.

———. "Buchanan's Thrust from the Pacific: The Utah War's Ill-Fated Second Front." *Journal of Mormon History* 34 (Fall 2008): 226–60.

———. "Epilogue to the Utah War: Impact and Legacy." *Journal of Mormon History* 29 (Fall 2003): 186–248.

———. "'Lonely Bones': Leadership and Utah War Violence." *Journal of Mormon History* 33 (Spring 2007): 121–78.

Madsen, Brigham D. *The Essential B. H. Roberts*. Salt Lake City: Signature Books, 1999.

———, ed. *Exploring the Great Salt Lake: The Stansbury Expedition of 1849–50*. Salt Lake City: University of Utah Press, 1989.

Marcy, Randolph B. *The Prairie Traveler: A Handbook for Overland Expeditions, with Maps, Illustrations, and Itineraries of the Principal Routes between the Mississippi and the Pacific*. New York: Harper & Brothers, 1866.

———. *Thirty Years of Army Life on the Border*. New York: Harper & Brothers, 1866.

McCall, Ansel James. *The Great California Trail in 1849*. Bath, N.Y.: Steuben Courier, 1882.

McCullough, David. "Knowing History and Knowing Who We Are." *Imprimis* 23, no. 4 (April 2005): 1–7.

Meikle, Lyndel. *Very Close to Trouble: The Johnny Grant Memoir*. Pullman: Washington State University Press, 1996.

Miller, David Henry. "The Impact of the Gunnison Massacre on Mormon-Federal Relations: Colonel Edward Jenner Steptoe's Command in Utah Territory, 1854–1855." M.A. thesis, University of Utah, 1968.

Moorman, Donald, and Gene A. Sessions. *Camp Floyd and the Mormons: The Utah War*. Salt Lake City: University of Utah Press, 1992.

Morgan, Dale L. *Shoshonean Peoples and the Overland Trails: Frontiers of the Utah Superintendency of Indian Affairs*. Edited and introduced by Richard L. Saunders, with an essay by Gregory E. Smoak. Logan: Utah State University Press, 2007.

———. *The State of Deseret*. Logan: Utah State University Press with the Utah State Historical Society, 1987.

Morgan, Dale L., et al. *Provo: Pioneer Mormon City*. Portland, Ore.: Binfords & Mort, 1942.

Neff, Andrew Love. *History of Utah, 1847 to 1869*. Salt Lake City: Deseret News Press, 1940.

Nibley, Preston. *Brigham Young: The Man and His Work*. Salt Lake City: Deseret Book Co., 1936.

Owens, Kenneth N., ed. *Gold Rush Saints: California Mormons and the Great Rush for Riches*. Spokane, Wash.: Arthur H. Clark Co., 2004.

Parshall, Ardis E. "'Pursue, Retake & Punish': The 1857 Santa Clara Ambush." *Utah Historical Quarterly* 73 (Winter 2005): 64–86.

Paul, Rodman W. *The California Gold Discovery: Sources, Documents, Accounts and Memoirs Relating to the Discovery of Gold at Sutter's Mill*. Georgetown, Calif.: Talisman Press, 1966.

Petersen, Jesse G. *A Route for the Overland Stage: James H. Simpson's 1859 Trail across the Great Basin*. Logan: Utah State University Press, 2008.

Peterson, John A. "Warren Stone Snow, a Man in Between: The Biography of a Mormon Defender." M.A. thesis, Brigham Young University, 1985.

Phillips, Paul C., ed. *Forty Years on the Frontier, as Seen in the Journals and Reminiscences of Granville Stuart, Gold Miner, Trader, Merchant, Rancher and Politician.* 2 vols. Cleveland: Arthur H. Clark Co., 1925. Reprint, as 2 vols. in one, Glendale, Calif.: Arthur H. Clark Co., 1967.

Poll, Richard D. "Thomas L. Kane and the Utah War." *Utah Historical Quarterly* 61 (Spring 1993): 112–35.

Powell, Allan Kent. *Utah History Encyclopedia.* Salt Lake City: University of Utah Press, 1994.

Pratt, Parley P. *Proclamation of the Twelve Apostles of the Church of Jesus Christ of Latter-day Saints to All the Kings of the World, to the President of the United States of America; to the Governors of the Several States, and to the Rulers and People of All Nations.* New York: Pratt and Brannan, 1845.

Quinn, D. Michael. *The Mormon Hierarchy: Extensions of Power.* Salt Lake City: Signature Books, 1997.

———. *The Mormon Hierarchy: Origins of Power.* Salt Lake City: Signature Books, 1994.

———. *Same-Sex Dynamics among Nineteenth-Century Americans: A Mormon Example.* Urbana: University of Illinois Press, 1996.

Reavis, L. U. *The Life and Military Services of Gen. William Selby Harney.* St. Louis: Bryan, Brand & Co., 1878.

Roberts, Brigham H. *A Comprehensive History of the Church of Jesus Christ of Latter-day Saints.* 6 vols. Salt Lake City: Deseret News Press, 1930.

Roberts, David. *Devil's Gate: Brigham Young and the Mormon Handcart Tragedy.* New York: Simon & Schuster, 2008.

Sadler, Richard W. "The Spencer-Pike Affair." *Utah Historical Quarterly* 76 (Winter 2008): 79–93.

Schindler, Harold. *In Another Time: Sketches of Utah History.* Logan: Utah State University Press, 1998.

———. *Orrin Porter Rockwell: Man of God, Son of Thunder.* Salt Lake City: University of Utah Press, 1966. 2nd ed., 1982.

Sessions, Gene A., ed. *Mormon Thunder: A Documentary History of Jedediah Morgan Grant.* Urbana: University of Illinois Press, 1982.

Simpson, James Hervey. *Report of Explorations across the Great Basin of the Territory of Utah for a Direct Wagon Route from Camp Floyd to Genoa, in Carson Valley.* Washington, D.C.: U.S. Government Printing Office, 1876.

Slater, Nelson. *Fruits of Mormonism; or, A Fair and Candid Statement of Facts Illustrative of Mormon Principles, Mormon Policy and Mormon Character, by More than Forty Eye-Witnesses.* Coloma, Calif., 1851.

Smith, Caleb B. *Accounts of Brigham Young, Superintendent of Indian Affairs in Utah Territory.* 37th Cong., 2nd sess., 1862, H. Ex. Doc. 29, serial 1128. Washington, D.C.: Government Printing Office, 1862.

Smith, George D., ed. *An Intimate Chronicle: The Journals of William Clayton.* Salt Lake City: Signature Books, 1991.

Smith, Joseph, Jr. *History of the Church.* 7 vols. Edited by Brigham H. Roberts. Salt Lake City: Deseret News Press, 1932.

Stansbury, Howard. *Exploration and Survey of the Valley of the Great Salt Lake of Utah, including a Reconnaissance of a New Route through the Rocky Mountains.* Philadelphia: Lippincott, Grambo & Co., 1853.

Stenhouse, T. B. H. *The Rocky Mountain Saints: A Full and Complete History of the Mormons, from the First Vision of Joseph Smith to the Last Courtship of Brigham Young.* New York: D. Appleton and Co., 1873.

Stott, Clifford L. *Search for Sanctuary: Brigham Young and the White Mountain Expedition.* Salt Lake City: University of Utah Press, 1984.

Taylor, Lillie Jane Orr. *Life History of Thomas Orr, Jr.: Pioneer Stories of California and Utah.* Shingle Springs, Calif.: Published by author, 1930.

Thomas, Sarah C., ed. *Elias Smith's Journal.* 3 vols. Salt Lake City: Sarah S. Castle Thomas, 1984.

Turley, Richard E., ed. *Selected Collections from the Archives of the Church of Jesus Christ of Latter-day Saints.* Provo, Utah: Brigham Young University Press, 2002.

Turley, Richard E., Jr., and Ronald W. Walker. "Mountain Meadows Massacre Documents." *Brigham Young University Studies* 47, no. 3 (2008): 5–183.

Unruh, John D., Jr. *The Plains Across: The Overland Emigrants and the Trans-Mississippi West, 1840–1860.* Urbana: University of Illinois Press, 1979.

Utley, Robert M. *Frontiersmen in Blue: The United States Army and the Indian, 1848–1865.* New York: Macmillan, 1967.

———. *The Indian Frontier of the American West, 1846–1890.* New York: Macmillan, 1973.

Van Wagoner, Richard, ed. *The Complete Discourses of Brigham Young.* 5 vols. Salt Lake City: Smith-Pettit Foundation, 2009.

Vaux. *See* Wells, Junius F.

Walker, Dale L. *Legends and Lies: Great Mysteries of the American West.* Foreword by John Jakes. New York: Forge, 1997.

Walker, Ronald W., Richard E. Turley, Jr., and Glen M. Leonard. *Massacre at Mountain Meadows: An American Tragedy.* New York: Oxford University Press, 2008.

Weller, John B. "Inaugural Address of Governor Weller." In *Journal of the Ninth Session of the Assembly of the State of California,* 71–77. Sacramento: John O'Meara, State Printer, 1858.

Wells, Junius F. "The Narrative of Lot Smith." *The Contributor* (Salt Lake City) 3 (1882): 271–74; 4 (1883): 27–29, 47–50, 167–69, 224–26.

West, Elliott. *The Contested Plains: Indians, Goldseekers, and the Rush to Colorado.* Lawrence: University Press of Kansas, 1998.

Whitney, Orson F. *History of Utah.* 4 vols. Salt Lake City: George Q. Cannon & Sons, 1892.

Whittaker, David J. *Register to the Thomas L. Kane and Elizabeth W. Kane Collection.* 2 vols. Provo, Utah: Brigham Young University, 2001.

Young, John R. *Memoirs of John R. Young, Utah Pioneer.* Salt Lake City: Deseret News, 1920.

Zanjani, Sally. *Devils Will Reign: How Nevada Began.* Reno: University of Nevada Press, 2006.

Index

Made in the USA
Coppell, TX
13 January 2025

44324311R00240